THE SCOTCH-IRISH

A Social History

THE SCOTCH-IRISH

A Social History

By

JAMES G. LEYBURN

Chapel Hill

THE UNIVERSITY OF NORTH CAROLINA PRESS

Foreword

THIS BOOK HAD ITS INCEPTION when one of my students, undertaking a study of the social adjustments made by the Scotch-Irish after their arrival in America, complained that he could find no general account of the people from the time they left Scotland. Many accounts of their life in this country contained introductory chapters, generally brief, on their residence in northern Ireland, but even these were largely concerned with political events, not with their familiar and characteristic culture. If one is to perceive the transformation of Ulster Scots into Americans, he must know something of their life and character and social institutions in Scotland and in the northern part of Ireland and then envisage the newcomers to America as they spread through the colonies.

The student's complaint was valid. Histories of Scotland rarely devote more than a paragraph to the departure of thousands of Lowland Scots to Ireland in the seventeenth century. Histories of Ireland usually treat the Plantation of Ulster as a political development aimed at the subjection of the Irish. Accounts of the Scotch-Irish in America range from careful monographs on local settlements to almost useless books of exaggerated praise or of sweeping criticism of a whole people. The Scotch-Irish have been written about as a "racial" group, as if their virtues and defects were inherent in their stock; they have been called the first typical American pioneers, the bulwark of the Revolution, the first radical element in American politics; occasionally, their contribution to a particular colony has been justly estimated.

Later immigrant groups have often fared well at the hands of social historians. It seems fitting that there should be a general work on the Scotch-Irish, showing the gradual development of Lowland Scots into Ulstermen and the modification of these Ulstermen and their institutions when they came, two hundred thousand strong, to the American colonies in the eighteenth century. It is the contention of this book that, after the Revolution, the Scotch-Irish were no longer a separate national stock but were Americans; thus, little attention is paid to immigrants of Scottish ancestry from Ulster after the colonies became the United States.

I was encouraged at the outset of my investigations by my friend Professor Wallace Notestein of Yale. Researches in Scotland, particularly at the National Library and the Public Records Office in Edinburgh, were indispensable; and I am especially grateful for the assistance of the noted Scottish historian, Annie I. Dunlop, of Kilmarnock, and for her patience in furthering my efforts. In Belfast the Irish Presbyterian Historical Society and its officials were cordial in their help. I am grateful also to Professor Mildred Campbell of Vassar, to Washington and Lee University for grants from the John M. Glenn Fund, and to the staff of the Library of Congress. I should like to thank the Ford Foundation for a grant extended through its program for assisting American university presses in the publication of works in the humanities and the social sciences. To all those who have encouraged and counseled me during the five years of work spent on the preparation of this book I express my gratitude.

James G. Leyburn

Washington and Lee University
September, 1961

Contents

Maps

Introduction

THE TERM "SCOTCH-IRISH" is an Americanism, generally unknown in Scotland and Ireland, and rarely used by British historians.* In American usage, it refers to people of Scottish descent who, having lived for a time in the north of Ireland, migrated in considerable numbers to the American colonies in the eighteenth century.

Millions of Americans have Scotch-Irish ancestors, for when this country gained its independence at least one out of every ten or fifteen Americans was Scotch-Irish. Already these recent newcomers had begun to intermarry with their neighbors, in a way that was to become characteristically American, with no particular concern about whether they were descended from Scots or Englishmen or any other national groups. The first Scotch-Irishmen went to the frontier regions of the colonies, especially in the back-country from Pennsylvania southward to Georgia. They were enthusiastic supporters of the American Revolution, and thus were soon thought of as Americans, not as Scotch-Irish; and so they regarded themselves. After the Revolution, when the United States expanded into the region of the Ohio Valley, the Scotch-Irish were among the vanguard of pioneers who crossed the Alleghenies. Beyond the mountains the intermingling of peoples proceeded apace, and by 1800 few families, except in certain Virginian and Pennsylvanian communities, were any longer wholly Scotch-Irish.

As this country matures, its people become increasingly in-

* The *Encyclopaedia Britannica* has no article on the Scotch-Irish, nor any reference in its index to the term. British historians speak of the migration of "Ulster Scots" to the American colonies. For an account of the origin and adoption of the term "Scotch-Irish," see Appendix I, page 327.

terested in their history. Colonial towns are rebuilt, houses are reconstructed and preserved with appropriate markers, battle-fields become national monuments, the writings of the Founding Fathers are published in definitive editions, historical documents and family records and letters are collected and examined. In this rediscovery of the past the Scotch-Irish have not fared so well as some other folk.

Often enough, they have been overpraised. Theodore Roosevelt, John Fiske, and Henry Cabot Lodge paid extravagant testimony to the virtues of the Scotch-Irish in colonial times and to their leadership in the winning of the West. Local historical societies have often listened to, and published, accounts of the sterling qualities of the Scotch-Irish that would make this people appear to be paragons, the true founders of everything that is best in the nation.* More often than not, the superior virtues and achievements of the Scotch-Irish were attributed to their race or their blood, as mystically inherent, not acquired.

There have, at the other extreme, been scholarly accounts of the Scotch-Irish within a single colony or a particular county.† By assiduous reading of many of these monographs one may, by his own industry, piece together the story of this element of the American population. Not since 1915, however, with Henry Jones Ford's *The Scotch-Irish in America,* has there been an attempt to recount the entire history of these people in this country or to estimate their distinctive contributions.‡

The full story of the Scotch-Irish is more than a summary of their immediate reasons for leaving Ireland and the details of their life in America. If the Scotch-Irish were a distinctive

* The Scotch-Irish Congress of 1889, for example, heard the claim that the Scotch-Irish contributed more to constitutional liberty in America than any other people. See the *Proceedings* of that Congress, I, 136.

† See, for example, the admirable volume of Professor Wayland F. Dunaway, *The Scotch-Irish of Colonial Pennsylvania* (Chapel Hill, 1944), or J. A. Waddell's *Annals of Augusta County, Virginia,* published in 1886 and long since out of print.

‡ Ford, as might be expected of a political scientist, goes into considerable detail about the political events in the background of the migration to the American colonies, with little attention to social influences. The last third of his book is devoted primarily to the establishment of Presbyterianism in America, the founding of Princeton (by Presbyterians, but not by the Scotch-Irish), and the role of the Scotch-Irish in the Revolutionary War. Another valuable work is Charles A. Hanna's *The Scotch-Irish*—more of a compendium of random detail than a history. Both this work and Ford's are now out of print.

people, it was because of their heritage and experiences. There are, indeed, three principal chapters in their story: their life in Scotland, when the essentials of their character and culture were being shaped; their removal to northern Ireland and the action of events of their residence in that region upon their outlook on life; and their successive migrations to America, the nature of their life as pioneers, and an estimate of their importance to their adopted country. In even the best monographs the first two of these chapters are presented in brief survey, as mere prologue. This present volume gives equal weight to each episode of Scotch-Irish history.

Lacking a general knowledge of the social background of the Scotch-Irish in their first two mother countries, descendants of this people have often come to inaccurate conclusions about their forebears. A person in search of his ancestors naturally likes to believe the best of them, and the best in terms of contemporary standards. Where genealogical facts are few, and these located in the remote past, reconstruction of family history is often more imaginative than correct. What American has a clear idea of Scottish history in the period before 1600, the moment when numbers of Scots were about to cross over into Ireland? The sojourn in the northern part of that island is equally obscure to most people who have Scotch-Irish ancestors.

George Pierson remarks that the colonizing process brought America a "decapitated society." He means that this country received as immigrants "no royalty, no aristocracy, no leisure class. Practically no bishops or judges or scientists or great statesmen made the journey. With insignificant exceptions the highest ranks, the highest professions, the men of the highest learning and the highest crafts and skills all stayed at home."* People who migrate are usually either dissatisfied at home or ambitious to improve their lot; but upper classes are already successful, and so have no reason to go to a wilderness to start afresh.

Plain as these facts are, people still look for distinguished ancestors. It seems not to be enough that one's family tree shows

---

* G. W. Pierson, "The Moving American," *Yale Review*, XLIV (autumn, 1954), 108.

decent, ambitious, God-fearing people; they must be wellborn. The search for aristocrats among the early Scotch-Irish will prove futile. These people were doubly a "decapitated society," for they had migrated twice. The move from Scotland to Ireland had been made by the optimistic poor; the move to America once more left behind most of those who had risen to prominence.

European society four centuries ago was clearly divided into social classes, an inheritance of the feudal age. One was born to his "proper station" as he was born a Scot or an Englishman: his social class was an unalterable fact of life. To move out of it, especially upwards, was conceivable in rare cases, but highly unlikely. The lowest class in the pyramid consisted of peasants —and it was from this class that practically all Scots whose descendants became Scotch-Irish came. To American ears the word "peasant" has an invidious sound, with connotations of dull conservatism, boorishness, and even stupidity. In European usage, however, it meant simply a tiller of the soil who, in the natural order of things lacked the privileges and responsibilities of the gentry and nobility. A peasant might indeed be dull and hidebound; but he might also be thrifty and ambitious, a real force in his community. There were as many kinds of peasants as there were of lords.

The Scots who went across the Channel to northern Ireland to participate in the "Plantation of Ulster" from 1610 onwards ran the gamut of character. They all went to look for a better life or to escape miserable conditions or for sheer excitement— and such motives indicate their ambition and initiative. Some proved to be shiftless men who would never manage to make good; but many had qualities that needed only opportunity to bring them to full flower. The records show that most of the migrants intended, if Ulster proved hospitable, to live there permanently. They took their families with them, and they soon began to make Ulster flourish. It was their descendants who, in the following century, in the same search for a still better life or for escape or for excitement, came as Scotch-Irish to the American colonies.

Scots who went to Ulster, then, were humble folk with ambition and with qualities of character that made them good pioneers. Even Presbyterian ministers who worked among them were usually of the humbler walks of Scottish life, for the Scottish Kirk offered no sinecures for younger sons of the gentry. To say that one is born into a peasant family is not to impugn a person's integrity or morality, his imagination or insight, his persistence or ingenuity. It was a Scottish poet of a later day who perceived that rank is but a tinsel show. The pioneers to Ulster, like their descendants who became pioneers to America, were proof of Burns's insight into what makes a man.

A modern myth sometimes misleads the Scotch-Irish descendant. It is a pleasant myth, deriving principally from the romantic view of Scotland that has spread since the novels of Sir Walter Scott. It conceives of historical Scotland as picturesque in landscape and of its people as adventurous, a bit wild and uncouth no doubt, but essentially romantic and chivalrous and charming.

The Scotland from which the exodus began in 1610 was one of the poorest and most backward of European countries. Poverty-stricken, generally lawless, still lingering in the Middle Ages in the seventeenth century (and even into the eighteenth), with agricultural methods hardly better than primitive, there was every reason why an ambitious Scot should look elsewhere for improvement of his condition. The story of the Scotch-Irish (as of Scotland itself) is one of progress from something near barbarism in 1600 to civilization, from ignorance to a passion for education, from backwardness in most fields to daring achievement, from static traditionalism to dynamic individualism—and all of this in the space of two centuries. Just as the uncouth Vikings became the civilized Scandinavians, the barbarian Achaeans the classical Greeks, the forlorn toilers of the Dark Ages the great French people, so did the Scots of their own later Middle Ages transform themselves into a nation whose philosophers, inventors, literary men, and manufacturers were the admiration of the world.*

Another misconception must be cleared away. Few ancestors of the Scotch-Irish had anything to do with clans, tartans, bagpipes, and the other charming extravagances that beguile the

---

* Even to have been a Scottish lord in 1600 would not, by present standards, have been cause for boasting. Many of the lords were unprincipled, lawless, and arrogant; few had wealth in anything but land; most of them were illiterate.

modern tourist in Scotland. To many Americans the word "clan" refers to a trait of the Scottish social order; if, then, one has Scottish ancestors, these must have been members of a clan. A genealogical search for clan ancestors on the part of Scotch-Irish descendants is likely to prove discouraging, unless one's forebears were not in the main stream of the migration to America.

Kilts, sporrans, and their accouterments derive almost entirely from the Highlands of Scotland, not from the Lowlands, whence came the Scots who went over to Ireland. The clan was the Celtic equivalent of a primitive tribe, and a good part of Scotland had at one time been Celtic. Around the twelfth century the Lowlands, however, began a slow progress toward civilization; and in the process, clan organization in this region became more and more shadowy, giving way to feudalism. By 1600 few clans remained in the Lowlands, although loyalty to one's feudal overlord remained characteristic, showing itself in violent feuds, raids, and other acts of lawlessness.

It is northwestern Scotland, the Highlands, that is the home of the clan and its kilts and tartans. This portion of Scotland was regarded, even (and sometimes especially) by Lowlanders, as late as 1745, as the home of wild tribesmen who kept the country in turmoil. Here Gaelic was still almost the only language; here, two centuries after the Reformation had made the Presbyterian Church the Kirk of Scotland, the people were filled with primitive superstition; and here the clan chieftain led his uncouth "redshanks" on raids that made life unsafe for everyone. Blackmail was an invention of the Highlanders; theft of cattle was a favorite pastime; to live near the borders of the Highlands was to be perpetually on guard.* It required stern measures after 1745 to

* The turning point in Highland affairs came in 1746, when the Highland supporters of the Pretender, Charles Stuart (Bonnie Prince Charlie) were defeated at Culloden. The British government took stern measures, for it was determined to bring the tribesmen into the influence of orderly and civilized government. The clan organization was now broken up, and the wearing of a tartan was forbidden; no longer could a chief dispense justice (and death) to his clansmen.

It is instructive to note how the modern age has made glamorous what was once a mark of bitter poverty and wildness. The word "kilt" is of Scandinavian origin, meaning "to tuck up." The kilt was little more than a breech-clout in origin; eventually it became a short, pleated petticoat, ill-adapted to the bleak weather of the Highlands, but economical in a poor country. Trews, or close-fitting trousers, were more comfortable if one could afford them. (These, too, have been revived in our antiquarian day.) No doubt the Highland chief on

civilize the wild men of the northwest—and the rapidity of that process once more indicates the speed with which men can change their institutions and culture.

A few Highlanders drifted over into Northern Ireland, for the Western Isles and portions of Argyll are very near to Ulster. Their Gaelic language and sometimes their Catholicism made them more welcome than Lowland Scots to the native Irish. King James, however, had specifically excluded Highlanders from his design for the Plantation of Ulster: he wanted to civilize Ireland by settlers with British ways, not to confirm Irishmen in their intransigence. Highlanders, therefore, have no real place in the ancestry of the Scotch-Irish.*

The present book is a social history of the Scotch-Irish. In this day of specialization, a social historian who undertakes to recount the life of people through three centuries and in three countries knowingly risks his scholarly head. Experts in Scottish, Irish, and American colonial history can only regard him as an unprofessional interloper, ignorant of the fine points within their special fields. Moreover, each area has its special thorns. Scottish history is full of old controversies that engender heat; indeed, as Wallace Notestein remarks, it is probable that Scots still enjoy their old quarrels. Irish history has been so turbulent that the interpretation of few of its events is agreed upon. American colonial historians have so meticulously cultivated each county garden that broad generalization is immediately protested by specialists who are aware of exceptions.

More than this, the social historian relies upon the findings of those who have done original research in special areas. The documents he cites are not often fresh discoveries; he cannot pass the test of having contributed something entirely new to histori-

---

occasion decked himself in full regalia, with kilt, brooch, sporran, dirk, and bonnet; but only the romantic imagination can conceive that in these earlier ages there were trim regiments of Highlanders in "uniform," marching behind the skirling pipes through the glens.

* It should be noted, however, that Highland Scots in numbers, after 1746, migrated directly to the American colonies, where many of them achieved high distinction. History offers little support for the thesis that the low cultural estate of one's ancestors has any important bearing upon later achievement and even brilliance. The best account of the Highlanders in America is Ian Charles Cargill Graham's *Colonists from Scotland* (Ithaca, 1956).

cal knowledge. He compounds his offense against historiography by discussing national character, mental and moral qualities, and temperament—all of them matters of debate and interpretation, not of precise documentation. If he alienates the academic historian by his generalization, he may equally offend those readers whose ancestors he shows to have been ordinary folk.

All of these risks seem worth taking, if the result is a clearer picture of the sweep of the life of a people who have earned a name for themselves.

Social history has at least three purposes: to recount the historical sequence of events that bore upon the development of a people; to make the daily life of the average man so vivid that the reader may sympathetically enter into his customs and habits; and to suggest the mental qualities, the character and emotional outlook, that made these people different from every other.

The starting point of the social history of the Scotch-Irish is in Scotland, long before the name "Scotch-Irish" was known. Many of the characteristics this people were to show had come into being by the slow process of life in an identifiable part of Scotland in which their qualities of mind, their attitudes, and their loyalties were being shaped by their way of life in the Lowlands and by the manner in which Scottish events impinged upon them. Scottish history in itself is endlessly absorbing, yet few Americans know its details. While most colleges in the United States have courses in English history, there are none in Scottish history. Events in Scotland are brought into a student's purview only as they are related to English affairs. One does not need a full survey of Scottish history from the time of the primitive Caledonians in order to understand the Scotch-Irish; yet the better Scotland's past is known, the more clearly the Scotch-Irish are understood.

Anthropologists have made us familiar with the concept of culture. The origins of national culture are generally obscure, for the moral ideas and customs of a people have been quietly growing by accretion through the centuries. A complete change of environment inevitably introduces new elements that must somehow be absorbed before men can feel at ease. The fundamental elements of the national culture—the Scottish Lowland, the considerably modified Ulster Presbyterian culture, and the notably different Scotch-Irish—went back ultimately to feudal Scotland.

A logical point for beginning the story is 1600, when King James, the Scottish Stuart king soon to become King of England as well, was about to make grants of land in northern Ireland to Scottish landlords and English merchants. These recipients of estates were to persuade tenants to migrate to the northern Irish province and take up farms. Those in Scotland who accepted the invitation became the ancestors of all the Scotch-Irish in America.

PART I: THE SCOT IN 1600

1

Poverty and Insecurity

SCOTLAND IS, BY AMERICAN STANDARDS, a small country. With its 30,405 square miles, it is approximately the size of Maine or of South Carolina. At least three-fifths of its territory comprises the Highlands of the north and west and the islands off the west coast; in these regions the soil is so scanty and the climate so difficult that farming is often impossible. In 1600 only about half a million people lived in the whole country, and only the capital, Edinburgh, had as many as ten thousand. All towns, and a majority of the population, were in the Lowlands, the territory south of the narrow waist of Scotland between Glasgow and Edinburgh, and the coastal strip north of Edinburgh. In the interior parts of the Lowlands are high hills and moors known as the Southern Uplands; but although some of its prominences rise more than twenty-five hundred feet, the south has no such proliferation of isolated valleys and inaccessible places as abound in the Highlands. Every royal burgh in old Scotland, like practically every modern city, was within ten miles of the sea.

In 1600 Scotland had never known orderly government or a rule by law instead of by men, nor had the country ever, for many years at a time, known peace. Life everywhere was insecure, not only because of recurrent wars with the English, but even more because of abominable economic methods, a niggardly soil, and constant cattle raiding and feuds.* No policemen kept order. Although there was a large measure of local justice,

* Scotland had its Wild West much earlier and much longer than did the United States. It is not much of an exaggeration to say that, if in America there was no law west of the Missouri, similarly in Britain there was no law north of the Tweed, except as one lord was powerful enough to keep peace on his own lands.

Scots had not yet learned general respect for property rights, nor had they been converted to admiration for principles of law and impersonal justice. Royal burghs and farm "touns" were mere villages with filthy mudholes for streets and foul shanties for the average inhabitant to live in.

Scotland was a poor country. Scots themselves had a wry saying that when the Devil showed all the countries of the world to our Lord, he kept his "mickle thoomb" upon Scotland.*[1] A later poet concluded that

> Had Cain been Scot, God had ne'er changed his doom,
> Not made him wander, but confined him home.[2]

The best of its farming land was in the eastern Lowlands, between the English border and Edinburgh; but this was the very region most open to constant English invasion and depredation. The southwestern Lowlands had a thin soil. Stony moors covered with heath and whin, long stretches of bog and moss in the lower districts, gravelly soil along the coast, and numerous burns and lochs, more plentiful then than now, made farming difficult under any circumstances, and especially for a people who had no knowledge of drainage and who used only the most primitive methods and implements.

The Lowland countryside in 1600 hardly resembled what it is now, for it was practically treeless. The region had once been covered with woods, but the continued waste of timber had made trees almost disappear everywhere except around the houses of a few lairds. A traveler might walk many miles (and he must either walk or pick his way on horseback over unkempt paths, since there were no roads nor any public conveyances) without even seeing a bush. To such an extent had the land been denuded in the south that Parliament passed several laws to encourage the planting of trees and to prevent mischievous persons from injuring young trees.† Despite such laws, little

---

* In the pages that follow, references to and citations from authorities, with no information of general interest to the reader, will be numbered and relegated to a special section, NOTES, at the end of the book.

† For example, if anyone did damage to a young tree, he was to be fined £10 for the first offense and £20 for the second; if he broke the law a third time he was to be put to death. (*Acts of the Parliament of Scotland*, II, 13) Surely this last punishment was never carried out; but it bespoke the earnestness

timber was grown, and consequently there was no wood for building and little for furniture; certainly there was none for shipbuilding, an enterprise Parliament would have liked to encourage.

Destruction of forests had led to the extermination of such wild animals as formerly inhabited the woods. The wild boar, once common, was scarcely seen after 1500, nor were wolves, formerly numerous and dangerous. For fuel the Lowlanders burned turf, stone peat, and coal.*

All over the Lowlands were marshes and small lochs which no longer exist. Arable areas were still further limited by the ignorance of the people about drainage. A serious drawback to decent farming was that there were no fences, hedges, or stone walls to separate farms, fields, or strips ("rigs," as the Scots called them). All fields lay open, and even the employment of shepherds could not keep animals from straying. When a farmer's cattle trampled the crops of another, and the second farmer retaliated, another element was added to the insecurity of life and another cause existed for ill-feeling between neighbors.

Scotland was noted in the eyes of foreigners as a barren land. Shakespeare compares it for nakedness to the palm of the hand.[3] The soil in the southwest was miserable. Sir William Brereton, an Englishman who traveled from Glasgow to the southern part of Ayrshire at the very moment many of the Scots were going

of parliamentary concern. Again, in 1504 it was "ordanit . . . that everilk lord and lard mak thame to have parkis with dere stankis, cunyngaris, dowcatis, orchartis, heggis and plant at the leist ane aker of wod quhare thair is na greit woddis nor forestis." (*Ibid.*, p. 251, c.19) An Act of James II (ruled 1437-60) decreed that "freeholders cause their tenants to plant woods, trees, and hedges, and sow broom in convenient places." (*Ibid.*, p. 14, c.80) This act was ratified in the fourth Parliament of James V (1535), with the added stipulation that "Every man having an hundred pound land of new extent whereon there is no wood, [shall] plant wood and make hedges and haining extending to three acres, and [require] their tenants to plant for every merk land a tree under the pain of ten pounds to be paid by every laird that fails." (*Ibid.*, c.10) An Act of James VI (*Ibid.*, p. 11, c.83) enacts "that wilful destroyers and cutters of growing trees be punished to death as thieves." See also, in 1541, Royal Rentals, *Exchequer Rolls of Scotland*, XVII, 719.

* The earliest mention of the working of coal, or "blackstones," is said to be in a charter of 1291. (Innes, *Sketches of Early Scottish History*, p. 235. See also Brown, *Early Travellers in Scotland*, p. 26.) John Major, writing in 1521, said that "heather or bog-myrtle grows in moors in greatest abundance, and for fuel is but little less serviceable than juniper." (*History of Greater Britain*, p. 51)

across to Ireland, said: "We passed through a barren and poor country, the most of it yielding neither corn [grain] nor grass; and that which yields corn is very poor, much punished with drought."[4]   Only the higher portions of land were chosen for tillage. The valleys and banks of rivers were too marshy and too much exposed to sudden inundation for farming by a people who had neither the knowledge nor the industry to build dams, sluice off excess water, or prevent floods.*

One of the chief reasons, and possibly the primary cause, for the continued backwardness of farming methods was the insecurity of life and property; and this in turn was a corollary of the addiction of the Scots to fighting and violence. Cause and effect are here intermingled. It is the lawlessness and violence of life in Scotland throughout the period from 1400 to 1600 that made the deepest impression on visitors from more stable countries and that justify one in speaking of the life of Lowland Scotland as barbarous.

Noblemen set the example, even by their determination to defend the rights of their underlings. They took the law, what there was of it, into their own hands. They constantly feuded with one another, and the lairds† followed the lead of their overlords by feuding with other lairds. When local quarrels were quiescent, there was the constant threat of war with England, or the frequent actuality of English raids across the Scottish border, where the dividing line of the Cheviot Hills and the Tweed River interposed no true barrier. Scottish farmers formed the armies. It was a rare farmer who was not a returned soldier, and an even rarer one who had not participated in a foray with arms; thus violence was confirmed as a way of life. "In a country where feudalism still prevailed and where there was little general

---

* In Scotland the laird seems to have taken little or no part in overseeing the farming methods of his tenants. Here was a great contrast to England of the time. Despite the primitiveness of English agriculture by our modern standards, one gains the impression of gradual and steady improvement of methods in late medieval times. The English farmer certainly knew how to drain his lands; security of tenure made him try to improve his lands and houses; and the surveillance of the squire was a bulwark against shoddy work and methods. (For comment on the state of farming in the Lowlands, see Mackenzie, *History of Galloway*, I, 229.)

† The laird is a landholder, a member of the gentry, not a nobleman. He corresponds generally to the English squire.

organization of justice, driving off cattle and sheep was almost one of the recognized sports of the time. You appealed to your feudal overlord to help you regain your stock; in that foray to regain what had been lost your lord and his fellow retainers were not unlikely to bring back more if possible than what had been driven away."[5]

In those unspacious times, when even few barons could read and write,[6] and before the church established by the Reformation had begun to promote education, when cities were few and roads were mere paths, people had little to occupy either the mind or the imagination. It is understandable that customs should have resembled more those of the time of Beowulf or of the tribes of central Europe during the Dark Ages than those of the present. When people are isolated, farming is monotonous and life is drab, with no visitors, no news, and little diversion. Fighting and raiding were not only traditional: they were an exciting relief from tedium.

The root of the trouble was political, for no king since the time of Robert the Bruce (d. 1329) had been able to keep the English out, or to rule over the whole country and so provide national law and order. Seven monarchs ruled between 1406 and 1625, and, of the seven, five had been infants or mere children upon their accession. Long regencies gave noblemen an opportunity for cabal, bickering, maneuver, and most of all for assertion of their independence from royal control. Scotland had no standing army, no regular taxation, no police force, and very few civil servants. Under such conditions every baron was a law unto himself.

Feudalism everywhere implied the right of noblemen to carry on their private quarrels. In this it corresponded with the clan tradition of much earlier times in Scotland.* Since barons lived in strong castles, the king was rarely powerful enough to subdue them to his rule, even if he could have persuaded other barons to fight on his side to establish a principle that would curb their own independence. Nor were the kings always wise and good

---

* Feudalism had been brought in by David I in the twelfth century, under the influence of the Normans living in England. Its principle of making a lord responsible for his own land and people so well accorded with clan organization that David had little trouble in introducing feudalism to Scotland.

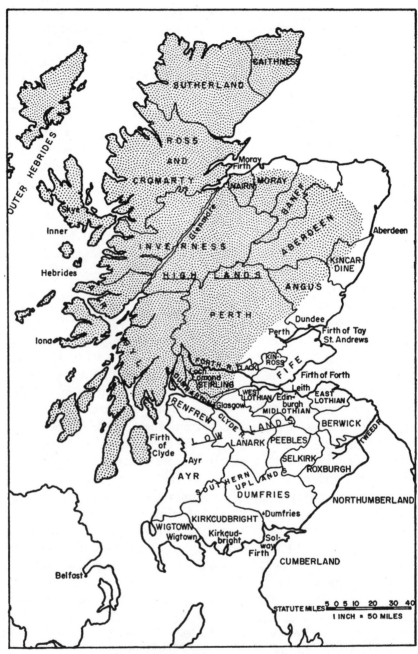

Scotland: Highlands and Lowlands

and constructive in their policies.   Noblemen regarded the king as merely another power, sometimes useful as an ally in their ambitious enterprises, but always to be made to realize that he was no better a man than they.   Few felt any personal loyalty to him or any dedication to the principle of unified central authority. The national government, if it can be called such, was rule by faction.

What can be said for the lords is that most of them felt deeply responsible for the life and goods of every dweller on their domains.   An unavenged injury to any person or thing, however indirectly connected with the lord, was at once a personal insult and a derogation from his authority.   If he could not defend those who looked to him for protection, the very reason for his existence was at an end.[7]   It must be said, too, that a lord's protection was really valuable to his people in the unpoliced land; without it the tenant would have been helpless.   But one man's security was another man's insecurity; one raid led to another in endless succession.   Parliament took constant note of the rapine, spoil, and lawlessness,[8] yet the very barons who composed the Parliament refused to apply the Acts to themselves and submit to restriction.

The other side of the picture is that the lords were often as unprincipled as they were rank individualists.   A modern historian calls them "as brutal tyrants as ever lived."[9]   Thomas Carlyle, himself a Scot, made the "swingeing generalization" about them that they were "a selfish, ferocious, unprincipled set of hyenas."[10]   The author of the anonymous *Complaynt of Scotlande* in the sixteenth century made Dame Scotia bitterly reproach her noblemen, saying: "Thou are the special cause of my reuyne, for thou and thy sect that professes you to be nobilis ande gentill men, there is nocht ane sperk of nobilnes nor gentrice among the maist part of you."[11]

Feuds were not only traditionally customary but in contemporary minds were justifiable.   Sicily's vendettas had their counterpart all over Scotland.   In the southwest, especially, these blood feuds were violent and unending.   Montgomery and Cunningham were the Montague and Capulet of Ayrshire, if the Kennedys and their opponents could not contest the designation.

Since the Crown was not strong enough to put down the rivals, it stood aside and let them fight it out.[12]   One historian names a list of families who "lived in a great measure by robbing and oppressing their neighbors. Occasionally, too, they would make predatory forays into England, and thereby endanger the peace existing between the two realms."[13]   The *Records* of the Privy Council are full of instances of assaults made by men of rank and property with deadly weapons. Despite Acts of Parliament prohibiting going about armed defensively or offensively, men still "set about their vengeful proceedings in steel bonnets, gauntlets, and plait sleeves, and with swords and pistolets."[14]   The traveler John Major attributes much of the violence to pride, for "among the Scots 'tis held to be a base man's part to die in his bed, but death in battle they think a noble thing."[15]

Emissaries from the king who tried to enforce the law were often handled summarily. Letters and summons were taken from officers and torn to tatters, and once an officer was made to eat and swallow the summons he bore. "Evildoers boasted, menaced, disobeyed, struck, and pursued the officers, and sometimes killed them outright." The officers themselves were peccant, sometimes taking bribes from the rich and powerful.[16]

The most constant crime, more likely than the feuds of noblemen and lairds to keep the farmers in a turmoil, was cattle stealing.* Theft of stock often led to assault, and assault to a general fight to the death. This private avenging of wrong, combined with the feuds, makes it seem that Scotland was in a constant state of undeclared civil war. Tenants of those lords who got the worst of any of the frequent broils suffered severely, and the lot of men living upon the land of a freeholder who was not strong enough to defend them must have been a hard one.†

* This achieved the dignity of a special term, "hership" or "herdship," which Hume (*Commentaries on the Laws of Scotland*, I, 126) defines as "the driving away of numbers of cattle, or other bestial, by the masterful force of armed people."

† The violence of the country can be seen from the types of law cases. John Hill Burton (in his preface to the *Register of the Privy Council*, II, xxiii) notes the prevalence of the arrangement of pacts of guarantee and suretyship for the preservation of the peace, and comments that they convey "the impression of a turbulent people, likely to suffer from each other's violent propensities." He refers to such actions as "spuilzie," whereby redress was sought for violent or wrongful taking away of movable property; "assythments" and "letters of slains,"

Added to all this, there were the constant wars between England and Scotland, generally fought on Lowland territory, and usually accompanied by the burning of crops and other property. Englishmen of Cumberland and Northumberland, the counties adjacent to the Lowlands, were not above making their own raids across the border. Between 1377 and 1550 "there was either tacit or open war between Scotland and England during fifty-two years;"[17] moreover, when there was not actual fighting, the truces were precarious. Life on the Border was notoriously unsafe. At least until the Reformation, travel was dangerous anywhere in Scotland unless one went accompanied by armed men.[18] "War continued to be the universal trade; and all who had not devoted themselves to the duties of religion considered it as the principal business of their lives; all other duties were secondary and incidental. Every chieftain's vassals held themselves in readiness, at the most unexpected summons, to rise in arms."[19]

When Scottish poets appear in the sixteenth century, in what for a moment promised to be the beginning of a Renaissance, they reveal the violence of the times and the hard lot of the man "whose hands cannot keep his head."[20] The curious point must be made, however, that the humble farmer, who suffered most, did not attribute his calamities to the noblemen and lairds. He seems to have regarded violent lawlessness as simply the way of the world. It is a notable fact that in Scotland, probably alone among all the countries of Europe, there was never anything approaching a general uprising against the lords. On the contrary, the sense of personal and reciprocal loyalty between barons and underlings, lairds and tenants, usually made the farmers devoted retainers. Feudal ties, like assaults on the peace, seemed to accord very well with the pugnacity and clannishness of the Scot's traditional ways. A farmer knew his woes, but he did not blame them on his superiors; and the migrations to Ireland were not protests against the overlords.

True, the farmers had their complaints, the chief one being

---

devices to prevent violent reprisals for wrongs already committed; and "law-burrows," or surety to prevent feuds and troubles. See *Register of the Privy Council*, VI (1599-1604), 609-660; *Acts of the Lords of the Council in Secret Causes*, I, lxix-lxx; and Grant, *Social and Economic Development*, p. 191.

the large fees they had to pay on the renewal of their leases.[21] Laws were enacted in 1546 and 1555 to assure orderly legal eviction, requiring the landlord to give fifty days' notice; yet evictions remained fairly common. Two acts of Parliament specifically enjoined that the plow-beasts of tenants were never to be destrained for debt, and the grievance of inconsiderate taking of teinds (tithes) was also legislated about.[22]

Occasionally, too, a tenant had to endure the injustices of an unprincipled laird. There is, for example, an account of a turbulent laird, Gordon of Avochy, who, attended by a motley crew, including the miller and cobbler, kept the surrounding country-folk in terror for over twenty years. His gang murdered and stole, and forced tenants to perform unpaid services for the laird. The height of his insolence consisted of tearing the wooden fittings out of their houses and forcing them to carry these themselves to his mansion-house. But such cases were clearly exceptional.[23]

The Borders between Scotland and England, which had always vied with the Highlands and the Western Islands in disorderliness, finally began to be brought under control during the very years of the first settlement of Scots in northern Ireland. When James VI of Scotland became James I of England, at the death of Queen Elizabeth in 1603, the two kingdoms had a common ruler. During the same week that the monarch was on his way to be crowned in London, a group of Armstrongs with their retainers made a raid into the English county of Cumberland, killing the inhabitants and then carrying off whatever booty they could. James sent against them an armed force with instructions to wipe out the Armstrongs. So many were put to death that other Borderers accepted the fact that James intended Border raids to cease.

Since it was always possible for a Lowlander who had committed a crime to flee to England, where he was beyond the reach of Scottish law, James decided upon a plan to eliminate this source of disturbance. He appointed a commission consisting of five Englishmen and five Scots to try criminals on the Borders. If a Scot fled to England, the English commissioners sent him back to Scotland to be tried; if an Englishman fled to

Scotland, he was returned to be tried by English judges. To make sure that no criminal would escape, a troop of twenty-five mounted police was stationed upon the Borders, and were commanded to slay anyone who resisted arrest. It was further ordered that no Borderer except a nobleman or gentleman should carry any weapon. Finally, James sent many of the "broken men" (those who had defied the law) abroad to serve as soldiers in the German wars.

The Borders had become so tamed and disciplined by 1610 that the Chancellor could assure the King that they had been purged "of all the chiefest malefactors, robbers and brigands," as completely as Hercules had cleansed the Augean stables, and that they were now "as lawful, as peaceable and quiet as any part of any civil kingdom in Christendom."[24] This was an exaggeration; but the Borders were at least now safe enough for trade to begin for the first time in four centuries between the neighboring countries.

James took other steps to promote institutional justice. In every Scottish county a Court was set up, to meet twice a year. To it anyone might repair. Having observed the benefit of justices of the peace in England, he ordered that in every Scottish county there should be justices to try all crimes that did not deserve death.

But if the English border now became quieter, there was still the age-long danger from the wild Highlanders. These barbarians, living in a truly desolate and niggardly region, derived a considerable part of their livelihood by their depredations on Lowland farms and towns. There was constant stealing, "reiving," lifting cows from the more civilized people to the south; and the Highlander prided himself on his prowess at these sports. Dr. Johnson in the eighteenth century noted that the dislike of Lowlander and Highlander for each other was mutual, usually compounded of contempt for a way of life entirely different from their own.[25]

2

Domestic Life of the Lowland Scot

SCOTLAND IN THE SEVENTEENTH CENTURY, like other countries of the Old World, had a clearly defined system of social classes. It had endured for hundreds of years, and was no more questioned than the stars in their courses. The lords at the top were the owners of extensive land, over which they ruled, in the chaos of Scottish feudalism, as monarchs. Below them came the gentry—at least in the Lowlands, for the Highlanders were still so wild and their lands so ill-suited to agriculture that there was no middle class of gentry.* The Lowland gentry included the burghers of some means in the towns known as royal burghs, and the lairds (or squires) in the countryside. The rest of the population, chiefly agricultural, consisted of tenants and sub-tenants and their workers.

People knew their place and kept it. The calm acceptance of social distinction and privilege is repugnant to American ideas; yet the world has known so much of it during five thousand years that it clearly has its social advantages for survival. One of these is the assurance of always having a superior to whom one may turn for defense, aid, and counsel; the ordinary person is freed from large responsibility and from having to take the consequences of wrong decision; and there is the real comfort of knowing who and what one is, without the anguish of competitive social climbing. Scotland had no John Ball to question the social order, nor had it any Peasants' Revolt, such as had occurred in

---

* It cannot be said that the Highlands had a clearly defined system of social classes; indeed, its absence was one reason they were regarded as uncivilized. The Highland clan resembled a large family, all of whose members bore the same name. The chief was not "upper class"; he was rather the leader who traditionally made the decisions and took responsibilities. As kinsman to all members of the clan, he rarely tried to lord it over them.

England in 1381. Whatever grievances and complaints may have arisen against individual landlords, the meager Scottish records before 1600 show little that might be called democratic stirrings.*

In actuality, there was a rough and practical sense of belonging that gave humanity to the class system in the Lowlands and kept it from becoming onerous. Sir Walter Scott explains it by saying, "Perhaps one ought to be actually a Scotchman to conceive how ardently, under all distinctions of rank and situation, they feel their mutual connexion with each other. . . . There are, I believe, more associations common to the inhabitants of a rude and wild than of a well-cultivated and fertile country; . . . the high and low are more interested in each other's welfare; the feelings of kindred and relationship are more widely extended; and, in a word, the bonds of patriotic affection . . . have more influence on men's feelings and actions."[1]

When King David I (d. 1153) introduced feudalism to Scotland he must have assumed that it would benefit his country on both the local and national levels; yet however much order thereafter existed within a lord's territories, feudalism induced chaos on the national level. It is the judgment of historians that nation-states could emerge only after feudalism had broken down, for the essence of the feudal system is local loyalty. Everywhere in Europe feudalism meant pluralism in society—and probably most of all in Scotland. Despite the common hatred of Lowlanders for the English, there was no general patriotism in Scotland of the sort that would build a nation; and Scotland was still feudal in 1600.

The ordering of a Scots feudal estate in the Lowlands of 1600 approximated some such scheme as the following, with many local variations:

* Ralph Linton (in *The Study of Man* [New York, 1936], chapter 8) makes a useful distinction between *ascribed* status, assigned individuals without reference to their innate abilities and differences, and *achieved* status, accorded a person because of his special qualities. A caste system like that of India is the extreme example of ascribed status, while American society, despite ascription of certain statuses by race and sex, lays emphasis on achieved status. Both kinds are a collection of rights and duties; these, known from birth in ascribed status, can be trained for until their performance becomes second nature. The status of a Lowland peasant in Scotland, thus, was ascribed.

A *nobleman*—the owner of extensive land holdings in one locality.

Free-holders—who eventually came to be called lairds, and so, as gentry, members of the small middle class in the country. The laird arranged and ordered the tenancies and the actual farming; thus it was to him that farmers felt their immediate personal loyalty.

Kindly tenants. This quaint term denoted those who received the same lands at each periodic re-allotment, because their ancestors of worth had resided on these farms for generations. Many of these were younger brothers and humble cousins to the *n*th degree of the laird. (Other Scottish names applied to them were "wadsetters" and "tacksmen." A wadset is a mortgage or pledge, and a tack is a lease.)

Joint tenants—the largest class. These men were too poor for a single family to provide the necessary implements and animals to cultivate a farm; thus the laird assigned the land to several men. Primitive methods made it necessary to use eight oxen to a plow; consequently the farm of the joint tenants was called a "plowgate." If the tenant could supply but a single ox, his holding was termed an "oxgate." A farm might thus have from two to eight joint tenants, depending upon how many were necessary to compose a plowgate.

Sub-tenants might be hired by the kindly or joint tenants to help with the work. These hirelings, variously known as cotters, laborers, and mailers (a "mailing" is a rented piece of land of small size), were granted small "tacks" or "steadings" for a home and garden in return for the work. The tasks of these hired handy men were closely supervised.[*2]

Those Scots who migrated to Ulster early in the seventeenth century were almost without exception tenants of one sort or

[*] In earlier days there had been serfs and bondsmen in Scotland, but they had gradually become free men, without any uprising and with no formal notice being taken of what was happening. This "great, peaceful, silent revolution," as Cosmo Innes calls it (*Scotch Legal Antiquities*, p. 159), was apparently proceeding throughout the fourteenth century, long before it happened elsewhere. (In England serfdom finally disappeared in 1536.) No historian has ever accounted adequately for the end of serfdom in Scotland, except to say that it fitted neither the agricultural economy on a poor soil nor the temperament of the people. The freedmen now simply became tenants, probably of the lower sort, or found some kind of life in the scattered burghs.

another. They owed to their lairds specific rents, paid in kind, and various services, such as work on the laird's estate (especially at harvest), cutting and carrying peat, or thatching his buildings; and, if the laird had a mill, the tenant must have his grain ground there, at a fee. To the nobleman, but not the laird, the tenant owed military service at his call.

For all the recognized social distinctions among the five classes on a feudal estate, daily life led to a great deal of social intercourse, carried on without haughtiness on the one hand or servility on the other. The practical democracy of the social system was best seen after the Reformation, when the laird's son sat on the school bench beside the tenant's son, while the laird himself served on the same Kirk Session with his underlings. Between tenants and their workers there was often actual intimacy of personal relationship. When the right to construct a separate cottage had not been granted, workers lived in the same house with the farmer's family, eating at the same table, sitting together by the fireside at night, while the women spun and the men shod their brogues. Sometimes two or three men and women lived with the farmer and his family. Nevertheless, in all these cases, and despite the intimacy, differences in rank were never for a moment forgotten or imposed upon.

Few social systems are so rigid that there is no possibility of rising to a higher class. Ambition is not so general a desire as many nowadays assume it; but if ambition struck a Lowland youth he might, if he could find the means, attend a university and prepare himself for a position in church or state. He might, by removing to a town, acquire enough income to become a burgher and so work his way into the class of gentry. He might even go abroad and make a fortune which, upon his return, would give him a status higher than that into which he had been born. These avenues of escape from one's inherited position were, however, few and arduous to travel.

The squalor and meanness of country life around 1600 can hardly be conceived by a person of the twentieth century.* A cluster of hovels housed the tenants and their helpers, and near-

* What is said here is as valid of 1700 as for 1600, for it was only in the eighteenth century that rural conditions began to improve in Scotland. See Graham, *Social Life of Scotland,* throughout.

by were whatever sheds and outhouses might have been built. A home was likely to be little more than a shanty, constructed of stones, banked with turf, without mortar, and with straw, heather, or moss stuffed in the holes to keep out the blasts.* The roof was of thatch or of turf. There were no chimneys, but only holes in the roof for the smoke to escape. The fire, usually in the middle of the house floor, often filled the whole hut with malodorous clouds, since the smoke-clotted roof gradually stopped the venthole. Cattle were tethered at night at one end of the room, while the family lay at the other on heather piled upon the floor. Light came from an opening at either gable; when the wind blew and winter came, these holes were stuffed with brackens or old rags to keep out the sleet and blast. Floors were of the earth itself, and mud from the farm-yard was tracked into the house to compound the filthiness. Since sanitary arrangements were wholly lacking and since animals slept in the same fetid room, vermin abounded. The people professed to like their small, filthy hovels because of their warmth.†

* Scots during the wars said, "If the English burn our houses, what consequence is it to us? We can rebuild them cheap enough, for we require only three days to do so." A traveler in 1702 reported that the houses were "low and feeble, their walls made of a few stones jumbled together without mortar to cement 'em, so ordered that it does not cost much more time to erect such a cottage than to pull it down." (Notestein, *The Scot in History,* p. 72)

† Testimony from three centuries shows the persistence of these domestic arrangements. Froissart in the fifteenth century tells how the country seems to be ruined after an English raid, but how the country-folk made light of it, declaring that they had driven their cattle into the hills, and that with six or eight stakes they would soon have new houses. (Brown, *Early Travellers in Scotland,* pp. 12-16)

Mackenzie, an antiquarian, says of the houses of the sixteenth century in the southwestern Lowlands that they were "formed of rude materials. . . . The walls of cottages were constructed of rude piles of [drift-]wood, with branches interwoven between them, and covered on both sides with a tenacious mixture of clay and straw. The roof consisted of heath and turf or straw and turf. Both the cottagers and the cattle inhabited the same dwelling, and entered at the same door." (*History of Galloway,* I, 232)

A report of 1670 says: "The houses of the commonalty are very mean, mud-wall and thatch, the best; but the poorer sort live in such miserable huts as never eye beheld. . . . In some parts, where turf is plentiful, they build up little cabbins [*sic*] thereof, with arched roofs of turf, without a stick of timber in it; when the house is dry enough to burn, it serves them for fuel, and they remove to another." (*Harleian Miscellany,* VI, 139)

Graham says of the eighteenth century: "The houses of the tenantry were very little better in most cases than those of their ploughmen and herds, from whom the farmer differed little in dress, manners, or rank. Even in Ayrshire,

Since the land was almost wholly treeless, wood was valuable. It was common practice for an outgoing tenant to remove from the farmhouse all the beams and timbers which he himself had put in; and consequently his successor came not to a home, but to a ruin consisting of four broken walls. He had virtually to rebuild the house—which he in turn dismantled when it was his turn to leave. In these dismal, ill-lighted shanties when night set in there was only the fitful light of the peat fire to illuminate the spinning and other chores that must be performed. "Ruffies," split roots of fir found in the peat moss, were lighted for special purposes, such as family worship.

Illness was frequent and epidemics recurrent. Skin diseases were prevalent in the dirty, dank homes. Infectious diseases were propagated readily, since the people had no notion of quarantine. In sick huts on the Sabbath day neighbors would gather to extend their sympathy, till the hovel was more foul than ever, the patient stifled by the heat, and the friends now probably carriers of the disease. Smallpox often ravaged a countryside. Not even this dread disease restrained visitors, who believed that everything was ordained of God and that no one could hasten or hinder a death. Rheumatism was a constant complaint, for the farm work had to be done in wet weather as in fair, and damp clothes were not changed inside the house. Malaria (ague, as it was called) beset the people, the mosquitoes breeding freely in the swamps, bogs, and morasses which were never drained. The Black Death, which had destroyed probably a third of the population in 1348, returned at intervals, the last

till long after the middle of the century, they were little removed from hovels with clay floors, open hearths, sometimes in the middle of the room, with walls seven feet high, yet three feet thick, built of stones and mud. Only the better class of farmers had two rooms, the house getting scanty light by two tiny windows, the upper part only glazed with two panes of bottle glass." (*Social Life of Scotland*, pp. 182-83)

One who has seen the eighteenth-century birthplace of Robert Burns in Alloway may, by a little use of the imagination, perceive what domestic arrangements must have been even in 1759. The Burns cottage is now neatly whitewashed and is kept trim; yet one sees that the whole family lived in one small room, with no privacy, and with the cattle adjacent. The mud of the farmyard was on one side and that of the village street on the other. Burns's poems to a louse and to a mouse suggest the prevalence of these vermin—and of others less mentionable.

outbreak of this virulent (bubonic) plague being reported in 1648.[3]

Agricultural methods were of an unbelievable primitiveness. The people were utterly ignorant of any improvement elsewhere that had come to agriculture since the Dark Ages, and their conservatism kept them from adopting the few suggestions for change made by Parliament.

The land of the farm was divided into infield and outfield. That nearest the house was the infield, or croft, and was the best land, to which all care was devoted. It was leased to the joint-tenants by lot, with one man's strips intermixed with another's, so that no person might have two contiguous strips or gain too much of the preferred land. The allotment was changed every few years.* The Scots name for the strip system is "run-rig" (a rig being simply a piece of land), and the rigs ran vertically down the slopes rather than across them. Since the bottomland was quite likely to be marshy and the people ignorant of drainage, most of the cultivation was done on the drier hillsides. The vertical strips contributed to the erosion of the already thin soil. The infield received all the manure of the farm, sometimes making the soil so rank that it was luxuriant chiefly in weeds. On this land there was a constant cultivation of the two staple crops, oats and barley.

A traveler of the sixteenth century makes a shrewd observation on the effects of the constant shifting of leases and the transferrence of rigs. Because of this, he says, men "do not dare to build good houses, though stone abound; neither do they plant trees or hedges for their orchards, nor do they dung the land; and this is no small loss and damage to the whole realm. If the landlords would let their land in perpetuity, they might have double or treble the profit that now comes to them—and for this reason: the country folk would then cultivate their land beyond all comparison better, would grow richer, and would build fair

* Ayala, a Spanish traveler of 1498, says the re-allotment occurred every three years; John Major, writing in 1521, says every five years. (Brown, *Early Travellers in Scotland*, p. 42; Brown, *Scotland before 1700*, p. 44) The outstanding historian of the feudal system, I. F. Grant (*Social and Economic Development*, p. 252) notes that the practice varied in different parts of the country and that the leases might also be for seven, nine, thirteen, fifteen, or even seventeen years, in addition to those granted for life to the kindly tenants.

dwellings that should be an ornament to the country; nor would those murders take place which follow the eviction of a holder."[4] His last remark refers to what others often noted: that if a landlord shifted the allotment in a manner a tenant thought unfair or if natural jealousy made a man resent seeing another acquire the benefit of his small improvements, a quarrel and even a murder might occur in those lawless times.

The outfield, some six times the size of the infield, was also in rigs, and the complete absence of fences or hedges to mark boundaries caused disputes. A portion of the outfield was planted in oats for three years in succession or until it produced only two or three seeds for each one sown; then it was allowed to lie fallow for the next three, four, or six years. During this period it acquired a thick growth of weeds, moss, and thistles on which the cattle, horses, and sheep fed. Thus it could be called pasture land of a sort, although the pasture was wretched in quality.

The grain sown was the poorest and least prolific kind, which had been long since abandoned in most countries of Europe. Grey oats, according to Graham,[5] "at its best only gave increase of three seeds for one;" and the variety of barley, called "bere," is the least nutritious of the barleys but was grown because it was believed to be the only sort that would flourish in Scottish soil. Parliament tried at least once to induce the farmers to vary the two staples by adding wheat: an Act of 1427[6] required that "each man tilling with a plough of eight oxen shall sow a firlot of wheat, half a firlot of peas, and xl beans, under the pain of x shillings to the baron of the land that he dwells in, as often as he be found guilty. And if the baron sows not the said corn in like manner in his demesnes he shall pay to the king xl shillings."* The qualities specified are small, and there is no evidence that the law was anywhere observed. Visitors to Scotland comment on the complete absence of wheaten bread.† The introduction

---

* A "firlot" is a dry measure equal to the fourth part of a "boll"—and a boll amounts to some six bushels. The firlot, therefore, is about a bushel and a half. No explanation is given of the requirement of "xl beans" in the Act; if it means literally only forty beans, even the Act itself is modest, and the results would have been trivial.

† An evidence that little wheat was raised, at least in the southwestern Lowlands, is that no records speak of it. Rents were always paid in kind, and church tithes were also collected in farm products; yet there is no record that

of beans and peas would have been a most important innovation, for they might have increased the fertility of the land and limited the wasteful practice of fallow.

There were no enclosures, no dykes or hedges between fields, or even between farms. When the cereals were growing and until the harvest was over, the cattle had either to be tethered or (more usually) put into the care of a cow-herd or shepherd, who took them out every morning to pick up what whins or weeds they could find and who chased them out of the unfenced fields of grain. As soon as the harvest was over, the cattle wandered all over the place, till the land became dirty and the ground was saturated with the water that stood in the holes made by their hoofs. Graham says that "the horses and oxen, being fed in winter on straw or boiled chaff, were so weak and emaciated that when yoked to the plough in spring they help-lessly fell into bogs and furrows; even although, to fit them more thoroughly for their work, they had been first copiously bled. . . . Cattle at the time of their return to the pasture, after the long confinement and starving of winter, were mere skeletons, and required to be lifted on their legs when put into the grass, where they could barely totter. This period and this annual operation, when all neighbours were summoned to carry and support the poor beasts, were known as the 'lifting.' "[7]

The farming instruments were as primitive as those of ancient Mesopotamia. Plows were, as they continued to be late in the eighteenth century, huge, clumsy affairs constructed almost whol-ly of wood. There was no iron in the country nor any blacksmith and worker in iron. The unwieldy plow, whose material cost only about eight shillings, could be made in a morning for a shilling. For all its size, it made only a shallow rut in the ground rather than a furrow, leaving the soil for the most part equally fast on both sides of it. The pieces of wood in the plow were held together by wooden pins; the only iron parts, a treasured inheritance in a family, were the coulter and the share.

Because they worked in rocky soil, it normally required eight,

---

the Bishop of Galloway, the Abbey of Dundrennan, the Abbey of Salseat, the priory of Whithern, or the Abbey of Crossregal (all important religious houses of the region) received any wheat. See Wallace, *The Nature and . . . State of Scotland*, p. 25.

and sometimes as many as twelve, oxen to draw the plows. The oxen were almost sure to be mismatched, so that their management required brute strength on the part of the men. Plowing could never be accomplished by a single person; on the contrary, a whole band participated. The strongest man held the plow, and must be able to bear the shock of collision with "sit-fast" stones; another led the team, walking backwards in order to stop the oxen from running into boulders; a third went in front with a triangular spade to "mend the land" and fill up the hollows; usually another, known as the "gad-man," was armed with a long pole sharply pointed, with which he goaded the lagging beasts. (The gad-man was especially valuable if he could whistle loudly and tunefully, to stimulate the oxen to their work.) With all this entourage, a plow scratched the surface of only half an acre a day.[8]

Harrows were still more primitive. Some of them were nothing more than a bundle of thorns; more generally they were constructed of wood, at a cost of seven pence. Until the Privy Council condemned the practice, the wooden harrows in some districts were dragged by the tails of the horses; and even when this practice ended it was still customary to fasten the thorn-harrows to the tails of the animals. Harness for the beasts consisted of collars and saddles made of straw, and of ropes made either of hair out of the horses' tails or of rushes from which the pith had been stripped.

The run-rig, or strip, system not only prevented any permanent improvements to the land; it caused incessant bickering about the operation of the farm. Even a small field might be divided among four to eight persons, whose cottages were clustered together in the farm "toun." No operation could begin without mutual help with oxen, horses, and men, and without agreement as to crops and time for labor. Each man was likely to have his obstinate opinion as to the day and hour of beginning work, and as to the time and method of plowing, sowing, and reaping. If one man dared cultivate a neglected bit of ground, the others denounced him for infringing on their right of grazing in the outfields.

A crop, once planted, received little or no care, so that it might easily degenerate into empty chaff and straw. The land, undrained and uncleaned, with no lime, and cultivated by such abominable implements and methods, could not always support the inhabitants of a district. Men renting from forty to a hundred acres sometimes had to buy meal for their families. When bad seasons came and the grey oats failed, people were in destitution and despair. They were then reduced to the straits of bleeding the half-starved cattle to mix the blood with a little meal, "a practice which in many quarters began in dire necessity and was continued as a matter of taste."[9]

In normal years, however, the people had enough food, monotonous though it certainly was. The high death rate, a result of disease, kept the population fairly stationary despite the fecundity of the Scots.* Oaten cakes or oatmeal, greens or "pot herbs" from the yard, and ale or beer were the steady diet, year in and year out. Near the seacoasts and lochs fish were added to the diet. Except in some of the truly favored regions, beef and mutton were rare (progressively so) unless a cow or sheep was found dead of starvation, old age, or disease. Milk could be used only sparingly, for the ill-fed cows gave only about two pints a day—and this was almost certain to turn sour by being kept in dirty containers. Pork was not eaten. Every farmer brewed ale and beer at home by turning a considerable quantity of his oats and barley into malt and mixing it with heather.[10]

After the grain had been reaped it was stored in stone sheds. To prepare it for consumption, it was parched in small quantities and ground between two stones, one of which was fitted with a handle which turned it. Mills and kilns were sometimes erected upon lands belonging to the king, the clergy, and some of the landowners. When they existed, the tenant was required to have his grain ground at them, and the price for this service was steep. The miller was often suspected of cheating, and tenants came to regard the milling requirement as one of their greatest burdens.

The dirtiness of the hovels in which the people lived was accepted not only casually as one of the inevitabilities of life; it was often positively preferred to cleanliness. No doubt the

* It is estimated that the average expectancy of life at this time was thirty-five years—as compared with the present expectancy in the United States of from sixty-eight to seventy-one years.

people were correct in believing that the accumulation of dirt kept the house warm. "Their old sluttish proverbs," as Scott called them,[11] taught that "the mair dirt the less hurt," and "the clartier the cosier" (clarty meaning foul with stickiness and mud). It was considered unlucky to wash the churns; a frog was put into the tubs to make the milk churn; the consistency of butter was thought to depend upon the number of hairs it contained.[12]

Tenants paid their rent by a proportion of the crop agreed upon when the land was re-allotted, but the tenant's wife must also take eggs and fowls regularly to the Big House. The landlord not only called on tenants for regular work on his farm lands but could also call them to help him, even at the busiest seasons. According to a bitter saying, all a man's produce went into three shares: "ane to saw [sow], ane to gnaw, and ane to pay the laird witha'."

The personal life of the farmers was as simple and niggardly as their agricultural methods were primitive. Houses had little furniture, for beds were bundles of straw and heather laid on the floor, and seats were generally flat boulders. Kitchen implements were rude and few. Some people had to be content to wear skins of animals for clothing, although the usual dress was plaid and bonnet. Wool was spun into yarn by the women and woven into coarse cloth, which was then colored by "dirty dyes." Portions of black and white wool in their natural state were also mixed and manufactured into cloth, and from this cloth garments were devised. Although flax grew in some places, linen was little used in country regions. The feet of the people generally remained bare, although rude shoes, made of untanned or ill-tanned hides, were sometimes worn.[13]

Towards the close of the sixteenth century, several parts of southwestern Scotland had become chiefly pastoral. Wool was sent from Galloway to the burgh of Dumfries to be made into broadcloth, for the manufacture of which this town obtained much celebrity. In the central parts of Galloway woolen stuffs then began to be manufactured on a small scale. This same southwestern district also became famous for its fleet and handsome breed of horses.[14]

The best indication of the barrenness of life can be gathered from a comment about travelers to the western region of the Lowlands. The author is describing the early eighteenth century, a hundred years after the migrations to Ireland had begun; by that time one might suppose conditions to have improved. Yet

The few Englishmen who journeyed to North Britain [that is, Scotland], from a spirit of adventurous curiosity or from stress of business, entered upon the expedition with the air of heroic courage with which a modern traveller sets forth to explore the wild region of a savage land. If the tourist entered Scotland by way of Berwick and the Lothians, he did not at first meet much to shock him by ugly contrast. If he entered by Dumfriesshire and the moors of Galloway, he was at once filled with dismay by the dismal change from his own country—the landscape a bleak and bare solitude, destitute of trees, abounding in heather and morass and barren hills; soil where cultivation was found only in dirty patches of crops, on ground surrounded by heather and bog; regions where the inhabitants spoke an uncouth dialect, were dressed in rags, lived in hovels, and fed on grain, with which he fed his horse; and when night fell, and he reached a town of dirty thatched huts, and gained refuge in a miserable abode that passed for an inn, only to get a bed he could not sleep in, and fare he could not eat, his disgust was inexpressible. After he had departed, and finally reached his English home in safety, he wrote down his adventures as a modern explorer pens his experiences in Darkest Africa; and then he uttered frankly to the world his vehement emotions. It is thus one English gentleman, escaping to his native soil, summed up his impressions of the North: "I passed to English ground, and hope I may never go to such a country again. I thank God I never saw such another."[15]

Natural vicissitudes added to the misery of life. Bad weather might cause the failure of crops and so lead to famine. No provision could be made for storing up grain to tide people over lean years, even if the thin soil had provided a surplus.* Another constant problem was saving the cattle over the winter months. Provision of winter fodder remained one of the most serious problems of Scottish agriculture until much later, for the country was very deficient in natural hay.

Another dire misery of Scotland was the constant appearance of plague. The bubonic plague first appeared, in the form of the

---

* Many Acts of Parliament dealt with famine and its consequences, chiefly by forbidding any export of food from the country. See, for example, Acts of 1449, 1455, 1526, 1540, 1551, 1567, 1578, 1581, 1587, and 1592.

Black Death, in England in 1348 and in Scotland two years later. In the northern realm it is estimated to have destroyed a third of the population. Once introduced, it returned frequently.* It hit the villages and burghs even worse than the farms, for there the houses were close together, the streets littered with offal, and rats considered to be scavengers. When the pest struck, there was little the people could do about it. Some of the burghs engaged, at a stiff price, "foul clengers"—that is, male and female cleaners, generally of the lowest stratum of society— to boil the clothes of the infected people, and to care for, and bury, those who had been isolated upon some "foul mure" outside the village.[16] But such methods did not do anything to get rid of the rats who carried the disease nor of the filth of the houses and outhouses upon which the vermin lived.

To immerse oneself in the details of life in the Scottish Lowlands during this period is to understand the designation given them by one writer, as "dark and drublie days."[17] Poor and barren soil ill-suited to agriculture; primitive methods; lack of education and of contact with people from other countries whose agricultural procedures were superior; superstition; constant raw weather which at any time might result in crop failure and famine; recurrence of plagues; and a steady round of wars, internal dissensions, theft of cattle, violence and lawlessness—these were the components of life in the humble annals of the poor farmer.

Life was not wholly drab. A peddler might appear in the neighborhood, his pack on his back or his goods carried in a small cart. He both bought and sold—which is to say that most of his dealings were achieved by barter. If the farmer needed goods he might attend the market day in the nearest burgh. The occasion of real festivity was the fair, held in the royal burghs. Establishment of these burghs had been another of the forward-looking measures of King David I (ruled 1124-53). Seeing that his kingdom needed trade, that trade depended upon peace, and that burghers might help secure peace, he conceived the burgh as a strong point that would be a center for trade; he gave it the

---

* There were outbreaks in 1362, 1380, 1411, 1430-32, 1439, 1456, and so on until 1648, when the plague finally disappeared.

monopoly of trade over a certain area.[18] By the end of the thirteenth century, thirty burghs, some of them little more than villages, had been founded in the Lowlands.*

To the burgh on fair-day the farmer was almost sure to come with his whole family. There he would dispose of his surplus goods and buy what he needed.[19] Quite aside from the business conducted at them, fairs were almost a necessity of medieval life: fun, the excitement of novelty, and the gaiety of a crowd afforded a relief from the isolation and loneliness of a farm where one sees only his fellow-tenants day after day. Farmers sold their wool, cattle, and horses; merchants displayed the wares of tinsmith, jeweler, shoemaker, cooper, brasier, turner, haberdasher, and in the later days, the china-merchant and French soap-seller.† Dillon gives a vivid account of the July Fair in the royal burgh of Ayr: "An atmosphere of chaotic gaiety mellowed the hard bargainings. Drambooths offered whisky galore; taverns tempted with foaming tankards and unending penny reels, sideshows, shooting galleries, swings, roundabouts, coconut shies, boxing booths and a motley of freaks, mountebanks and pickpockets, lured the pennies from the visiting lads and lasses who toured the stalls gaudy with balloons, cheap toys, and tawdry fairings."[20]

Goods to be exposed for sale were conveyed in carts of wicker work, in sledges, on the backs of horses, or on the shoulders of peddlers. The king's officers exacted duties from those who sold at fairs (each burgh had its Tolbooth, or place for collecting the royal toll), for the protection they received and for the privilege they enjoyed of gaining a profit from the king's subjects.[21]

Among the goods most commonly sold by the merchants were salt (since the people lived on salted meat five months of the

---

* In Ayrshire, the largest county of the southwest, there were four royal burghs: Prestwick, founded in 1165; Ayr (1203); Irvine (1214); and Newton-upon-Ayr (1306?). See Dunlop, *The Royal Burgh of Ayr*, p. 27. Mackie ("Notestein's *The Scot in History*," *Scot. Hist. Rev.*, XXVII, 100) says that "most of our Scottish villages were born" only during and after the industrial expansion of the eighteenth century; before that period there were only small burghs and farm touns.

† No soap was made in Scotland until 1619. (Chambers, *Domestic Annals of Scotland*, I, 507; Balfour, *Annales*, IV, 68) Buckle (*History of Civilization in England*, p. 642) says scornfully that, since even the higher classes "were alike filthy in their persons as in their houses, the demand for soap was too small to induce any one to attempt its manufacture."

year), iron for those who could afford it,* fish (especially in the days before the Reformation, when the Church required fast days), and furs (often worn even by farmers who lived most exposed to the weather). Beyond the reach of the humble folk were the spices, leather, and wine imported from abroad.†

Around 1550 economic conditions seemed to be improving. A French clergyman, after noting that the people had little money, remarked that they had plenty of provisions, which were as cheap in Scotland as in any other part of the world, thanks to the abundance of cattle and the grain crops.[22] Under James VI there was still further improvement. The most powerful king Scotland had known for centuries, James undertook to subdue the anarchy of the nobles, so that peace and order might prevail on the farm lands. It is probably correct to say with Brown[23] that as far as food was concerned the farmers of Scotland were, throughout this whole period, better off than the peasants of France. Their condition remained, however, perilously close to the margin of subsistence. An attractive opportunity to go elsewhere and improve their lot was incentive enough to make thousands desert Scotland for Ulster.

There is no indication that the nature of the people was depressed; on the contrary, they seem to have lived a robustly cheerful life. Local singers with their ballads were in the tradition of the Celt, and many communities had their harpists and pipe-players. The people were rich in folk tales. Dances drew neighbors together. Yule (Christmas), Pasch (Easter), and the various saints' days were observed with gaiety until the Reformation sternly repressed their celebration. May-games and other holiday amusements were enjoyed.‡[24]

---

* The Scots were unable to make even the arms they fought with and had to import their armor, spears, bows and arrows from Flanders; ordinary farming implements, such as cart wheels and wheelbarrows, were also imported from the Low Countries. See Pinkerton, *History of Scotland*, I, 163, 408; Macpherson, *Annals of Commerce*, I, 575.

† It is a mark of the economic backwardness of Scotland that no glass was manufactured in that country until the seventeenth century. Tanning of leather was not introduced until 1620, and the making of paper not until the middle of the eighteenth century. See Chambers, *Domestic Annals of Scotland*, I 506-7; II, 399; Balfour, *Annales*, IV, 68; Ray, *Itineraries*, 153; Andrew Brown, *History of Glasgow*, II, 265.

‡ We have more detailed accounts of diversions in the towns than in the rural areas. Brown (*Short History of Scotland*, pp. 347 ff.) describes the popular

Marriage among country-folk occurred at an early age. As soon as the boy was able to do a man's work and had proved his ability to bear arms, he was considered old enough to marry; and the girl might marry shortly after she became nubile. Even after the Reformation the age of marriage was often as early as fourteen for boys and twelve for girls.[25] At the wedding it was customary for neighbors to contribute not only to a feast but also to some of the essentials for setting up a household for the young couple. Weddings were occasions for rough festivity—a feast, dancing, and ribaldry. The Church after the Reformation did its best to change these wedding practices.[26]

One of the tasks the newly established Kirk set itself after 1561 was the reform of morals. It may be contended that the reform was too thoroughgoing and that it went beyond the bounds of morality to make the Scots dour and puritanical; yet there is ample evidence that the moral sense of the people had been feeble, quite aside from the common practices of cattle thefts and personal violence. Parliament in 1528 had attached severe penalties to the crime of rape, yet the courts often passed over the crime with light punishment. Bigamy and adultery were legislated against in 1551. The new Kirk, through its parish Sessions, constantly hammered at the people for their fornication, adultery, murder, conjuring, giving of drink "to destroy children," drunkenness, blasphemy, and other offenses against morality, in addition to its campaign for the observance of the Sabbath, which under the Catholic Church had been a holiday for games, sport, and dancing.[27] All classes of people were in the habit of swearing; one writer notes that Sir David Lyndsay uses fifty forms of swearing in his works.[28]

Feast of Fools, which occurred in December. A man was dressed to resemble a donkey, while others masqueraded as the Pope, bishops, priests, and monks, with their dresses turned inside out. "Then the donkey braying, and the others making every kind of strange noise, the whole procession proceeded to a church, and went through the service with the books turned upside down." This amusement obviously came to an abrupt end at the Reformation. A day of practical joking, known as Robin Hood's Day, often ended in riot and drunkenness; Queen Mary commanded the magistrates of Edinburgh to put an end to it, but it was given up only after many years.

Brown also says that people played golf, tennis (called *catchpully*), and football, though not as these games are now played. Most burghs had an annual horse race, with prizes given by the magistrates. Indoors, the burghers played cards, backgammon, and dice—before the Reformation.

Superstition was widespread, with a common belief in magic, sorcery, witchcraft, and necromancy, in ghosts, spirits, and demons.[29] As with other European countries, the belief in witchcraft was of long standing: there had been witches in Scotland at least since the days when the thwarted emissaries of Satan hurled Dumbarton Rock at the fleeing St. Patrick. After that many witches had been punished at the stake, usually for getting their witchcraft mixed up with their politics. However, it was witchcraft mixed up with religion that brought persecution to a climax after the Reformation. King James VI himself wrote a learned disquisition on the discovery and punishment of witches.[30]

No one in those days had any general conceptions regarding the processes of nature. "They saw the grass grow and their nolt feed, and thought no more of it. Any extraordinary event, as an eclipse of the sun or an earthquake, affected them as an immediate expression of a frowning Providence. The great diseases, such as pestilence, which arose in consequence of their uncleanly habits, the wide-spread famines from which they often suffered, appeared to them as divine chastisements; not perhaps for the sins of those who suffered—which would have been comparatively reasonable—but probably for the sins of a ruler who did not suffer at all."[31] Superstition was limited to no one class: if the bearded farmer believed that a few muttered words could take away or give back the milk of his cows, the archbishop of the Roman Church expected to be cured of a deadly ailment by a charm pronounced by an ignorant country woman.

Satan, the chief of the fallen spirits, was powerful, and a piece of every farm should be left untilled for his especial honor. (This piece was called the "Goodman's Croft.") New fires were kindled at Midsummer and on St. Peter's Eve. If a mother's milk failed, she might be suspected of adultery.[32] In the days before the Reformation people of course believed in the healing power of saints' shrines and in the efficacy of charms. Clergymen "could employ all the motives of fear and of hope, of terror and of consolation, which operate most powerfully on the human mind. They haunted the weak and the credulous; they besieged the beds of the sick and of the dying; they suffered few to go out of the world without leaving marks of their liberality to the

Church, and taught them to compound with the Almighty for their sins by bestowing riches upon those who called themselves his servants."[33]

The status of women was, quite simply, that of many primitive agricultural tribes. Women did most of the duties connected with the house and worked in the fields, not only alongside the men, but especially when men were away at war. On women "devolved almost all the duties both of the house and of the field; in short every task of mean and painful drudgery."[34] They had few legal rights. Marriage was a practical necessity. Chivalry was absent, politeness was regarded as an affectation, and abductions, both "under the impulse of passion and from motives of cupidity," were frequent.* [35]

When a farmer went, at the call of his lord, to war against England, his equipment was scanty. Only barons and knights could afford defensive armor; the ordinary "soldier" relied for defense upon his wooden shield, covered with the skin of an animal. His offensive weapons were a long pointed spear, sometimes a battle-axe, a small sword, and a knife. If he rode a horse, he guided the animal's head by a rope or thong; in his other hand he held his spear. An unshorn hide served him for a saddle, and he used no stirrups or spurs.[36] The account of the French chronicler Froissart, in the fourteenth century, probably applied for the next two centuries:

They bring no carriages [that is, wagons] with them . . . neither do they carry with them any provisions of bread or wine. . . . They have no occasion for pots or cauldrons, for they dress the flesh of their cattle in the skins, after they have taken them off, and, being sure to find plenty of them in the country which they invade, they

* Women were no cleaner in their habits than men nor any better in this matter in the upper classes than in the lower. As late as 1650 it was stated that "many of the women are so sluttish, that they do not wash their linen above once a month, nor their hands and faces above once a year." (Bulstrode White-locke, Memorials of the English Affairs [London, 1732], p. 468) Six or seven years after this, a traveler in Scotland says, "The linen they supplied us with, were it not to boast of, was little or nothing different from those female complexions that never washed their faces to retain their christendom." (Franck, Northern Memoirs, p. 94) In the eighteenth century a Scot writes that table and body linen were seldom shifted. (Sir Archibald Grant of Monymusk, Memoires, in Spalding Club Miscellany, II, 100) In some parts of Scotland until late in the eighteenth century, the people used, says Sinclair, "instead of soap, a substitute too disgusting to mention." (Statistical Account of Scotland, IX, 177)

carry none with them. Under the flap of his saddle, each man carries a broad plate of metal, behind the saddle a little bag of oatmeal. . . . They place this plate over the fire, mix with water their oatmeal, and when the plate is heated, they put a little of the paste upon it, and make a thin cake . . . which they eat, to warm their stomachs; it is therefore no wonder that they perform a longer day's march than other soldiers.[37]

Ready as any Scot was to assemble for a fight, no one expected to stay long. According to feudal theory, a man had to give forty days of service each year to his lord for war; actually, men were ready to go home after a week or two, and often did so, whether the war were finished or not. Scottish generals could not plan campaigns, but had to make sudden forays, burn and capture, and then move back again. Neither could they count much upon the surprise of their enemies: the summons to arms had to be widely given out, and the enemy could learn of the summons and where the army was to meet.

Many have speculated upon what the history of Scotland might have been had its borders with England consisted of Highlands, with their forests, glens, and wild clansmen. Instead of such barriers as these, the country's best farm lands lay open to the invaders from England. Lyndsay of the Mount speaks feelingly of the effect of war:

> Oppression did so loud his bugle blow
> That none durst ride but into fear of weir [war]
> Jok-upon-the-land that time did miss his mair.

Jock lost not only his mare but his cows and his sheep; his grain was burned and his fields were overrun. It was little wonder that farmers were careless in their work. To farm at all must have required long patience.[38]

Like other warriors of earlier times, Scots felt the raising of cattle more manly than the raising of crops. There is little indication of an actual love of the land itself or even of one particular plot of it that is dear above all others, nor is there evidence of any delight in the daily and seasonal round of work that makes peasants mere creatures of habit.

The farmer's relation to his overlord preserved his individuality; his raiding and fighting made him feel that his own strength and shrewdness mattered. When men take the law into their own hands they necessarily cultivate initiative and accept change. Humility is a characteristic of some peasants, but not of the Scot; the nearest approach to humility in Scotland was a man's loyalty to his lord or laird who had proved his quality as a man and had shown himself worthy of the loyalty.

Patient endurance is a virtue when present conditions are inevitable; but when an alternative is available, a man may escape. The plantation of Ulster was to provide such an escape after 1610, and one near at hand; its accessibility partly accounts for the migration that was to produce the Scotch-Irish of the next century. Before 1610, however, thousands of other Scots left home to go abroad, to the continent. Because of the distance to be traveled overseas, this exodus was one of young men only, without wives or families.

Sir Walter Scott speaks of "the national disposition to wandering and adventure," which, combined with the poverty of the land and the disinclination of the people to manufacture and trade, "conduced to lead the Scots abroad into the military service of countries which were at war with each other."[39] An English proverb put it more pithily, noting that in every port one might find a Scot, a rat, and a Newcastle grindstone. The Scottish Bishop Leslie remarked upon the tendency of younger sons of the gentry and farming class to seek their fortunes elsewhere. "So many of our countrymen have so good success among strange nations, some in the wars, some in professing of sciences, and some in merchandise." William Lithgow, visiting Poland in 1616, called it "Mother and Nurse for the youth and younglings of Scotland, who are yearly sent hither in great numbers, thirty thousand Scots families that live incorporate in her bowells." A modern German historian, Bruno Fuchs, has reckoned that "some 2,500 Scottish families sought their fortunes in East Prussia, West Prussia, and Pomerania between 1500 and 1700. There had been officers of the Scots Brigade in Dutch service for three hundred years."[40]

The Scots Guard was formed from the survivors of that Scottish army which had helped France to win back the rich plains of Gascony and Poitou from the English. The Scots Brigade did considerable fighting for the Dutch against the Spanish infantry of Parma and Spinola. "Often, too, in the chronicles of these centuries, one gets a peep at the Scottish emigrants who had sought their fortune in trade, at Middleburg or Campvere, at Amsterdam or Lubeck, or even among the Tartars in the far-off Baltic Sea. The emigrants who lived out the fighting and the toiling, and settled in these foreign lands, founded families, in whose names may still be traced some faint record of their Scottish origin."[41]

The opening to the Scot of Ulster lands in 1610 was his first opportunity near at hand to escape a drab and dreary life.

3

Scottish Social Institutions in 1600

THE MIDDLE AGES IN EUROPE began to give way to the modern era
when trade and industry increased, with the growth of a merchant
class living in cities where they could find active markets. One
thinks of Venice, Florence, Ghent, Bruges, Antwerp, Hamburg,
Paris, and London, as well as of dozens of smaller cities, all
flourishing during the fifteenth and sixteenth centuries as manufacture, wealth, money-lending, trade, specialization, guilds, and
commerce increased. Scotland in 1600, however, still had no
real city, even though for more than four hundred years it had
had a number of royal burghs—towns whose royal charters from
the king had been granted primarily for the purpose of stimulating trade. Some of these burghs were still in 1600 mere
villages of less than a thousand people; only Edinburgh, the
capital, was a considerable town.

There had been a period, during the thirteenth century, when,
with an expansion of commerce, it had seemed possible that
Scotland might progress with the rest of western Europe out of
the Middle Ages. Scots sold abroad their salmon, herring, and
other fish, hides and skins, wool, and coarse woolen cloth—not
impressive exports, but a fair beginning. They imported wood,
wine, spices, fruit, thread for nets, knives, cooking pots, wax, and
soap. But in 1292 began what some historians have called
Scotland's Four Hundred Years' War with England. During
this long period trade made little progress, and most of Scotland's
towns depended for their existence not upon commerce abroad,
but upon the agriculture of surrounding farms. Despite the
dignity of their designation as royal burghs, they were country

market towns, not mercantile cities. During the long period from Bruce to Knox, import and export trade was meager.

A gauge of the commercial backwardness of the country was the absence of guilds. These organizations of merchants had, on the Continent and in England, helped not only to increase the power of the king against the feudal nobility and thus assure a strong central government but had stimulated individual enterprise and the accumulation of wealth. Because they sought markets at a distance they wanted national peace, law and order, and good roads; their trade brought new ideas as well as goods into their cities. Scotland in 1600, however, was still relying upon the casual medieval institution of the local fair and upon the enterprise of the individual trader in small wares, with no guilds to serve as a dynamic force in the country. When King James planned his great Plantation in Ulster in 1610 he called upon the powerful merchant guilds of London for his English support; but in Scotland he could call only upon lords and lairds, for Scotland had no great merchants and no mercantile organizations.

Insecurity of life would have been enough to make impossible the development of industrial enterprise. Nowhere in the Lowlands was any town free from the danger of destruction by war with the English, while in the Highlands neither geographical conditions nor primitive life made towns conceivable. The consequence was that Scotland had no manufactures and only a minimum of trade abroad—this chiefly with the Lowlands and with her old ally, France. Practically all of the shipping was done from seaports along the east coast, nearest the continent—Edinburgh, Dundee, Perth, and St. Andrews.

Glasgow, now the metropolis of Scotland, had no trade at all until the fifteenth century, when its inhabitants began to cure salmon and export it.[1] The population of that royal burgh, called "the prettiest in Scotland," in 1600 was about fifteen hundred. The largest town in the country was Edinburgh, with some sixteen thousand people; this was followed by Perth, with an estimated nine thousand, and then Aberdeen, with only twenty-nine hundred. Such figures may be compared with continental cities. Already in the fourteenth century four cities had a population of more than one hundred thousand—Palermo, Venice, Florence, and Paris. London then had some fifty thousand, while Ghent, Bruges, Lubeck, and Hamburg numbered between twenty and forty thousand. Froissart, writing around 1400, said that Edinburgh was not so big as Valenciennes or Tournai, and that there were about four hundred houses. He spoke of Dunfermline, Kelso, Dunbar, and Dalkeith as villages. Even the larger Scottish towns of 1600 were still "a small huddle of thatched houses . . . set haphazardwise beside the natural haven or the castle or the great religious house that was its chief *raison d'être*."[2]

Insecurity of life also gave the population of towns a fluctuating and vagabond character, which prevented the formation of settled habits of industry and thus took away one reason men have for congregating together. Petty bargaining over farm products and exchange by barter are not conducive to the growth of a mercantile class of substantial burghers. If one's house is likely to be burned to the ground at any moment, there is small incentive to build a stately home and fill it with luxuries from abroad, even if one could afford these.

Few burghs elected their chief magistrate from among their own people. The usual course was to choose a neighboring peer as provost or bailie. This "right" then tended to become hereditary. Scotland early (1326) had her Parliament, but there was no popular representation, nor anything that corresponded to the House of Commons in England. Burgesses who were sent to Parliament were completely dependent upon the nobleman who dominated the town.[3]

In other countries of Europe the power of the nobility was curbed by an effective alliance between the king and the citizens of towns. By such an alliance the King's Peace was increasingly established throughout the land. Nationalism, it is true, was a late development. The French did not begin to feel themselves Frenchmen rather than Burgundians and Gascons until almost modern days. In England there were evidences of nationalism in the reign of Henry III (d. 1272), but it was Henry V (d. 1422) and his successful wars with France, and even more the defeat of the Spanish Armada in the late days of Elizabeth (1588), that made national patriotism a significant feature of English life. Scotland's kings, even if they had commanded the loyalty and enthusiasm of the people, had no strong mercantile class to press for peace, no allies to help them crush the power of the nobles.

It would be a mistake to imply that Scotland had no middle class: it was merely a small one. Whenever a king appeared, such as James IV (ruled 1488-1513), who brought peace for several years, encouraged shipbuilding, and stimulated commerce, there were townsmen who profited. During the Reformation and afterwards, they supported the Reform and eventually became a dominant element in Scottish life; but in 1600 they were still insignificant in numbers and influence.

As one ponders the history of Scotland, it seems that from the time of David I in the twelfth century to the wars of independence against England in the fourteenth, there were promises of true development of a Scottish constitution. Thereafter, however, such development came almost to a full stop. As F. W. Maitland puts it, "In the sixteenth century its barons still belonged to the twelfth, despite a thin veneer of French manners. Its institutions were rudimentary; its Parliaments were feudal assemblies. . . . Sometimes there was a little imitation of England and sometimes a little imitation of France, the King appearing as a more or less radical reformer. But the King died young, leaving an infant son, and his feudatories had no desire for reformation."[4]

It is true that the Scottish monarchy was a limited one, but the limitation (a strict one, indeed) was set by the power of headstrong noblemen, not by a representative body of the citizens of an organized community. The Scottish Parliament had but one Chamber, in which sat prelates, lords, and representatives (usually noblemen) of the burghs. An attempt to induce the lesser tenants-in-chief to choose representatives, after the pattern of the English knights of the shire, proved abortive. The work of Parliament was often delegated to a committee known as the Lords of the Articles, and Parliament merely confirmed foregone conclusions. On many occasions a faction of noblemen would hold a Parliament that excluded another faction. "When in 1560 an unusually full, free, and important Parliament was held for the reformation of religion, an elementary question concerning the right of the minor barons to sit and vote was still debatable, and for many years afterwards those who desire to see the true contribution of Scotland to the history of representative institutions will look, not to the blighted and stunted conclave of the three Estates with its titular Bishops and Abbots commendatory, but to the fresh and vigorous Assembly of the Presbyterian Church."[5]

The king was regarded by the powerful barons as one of themselves, and certainly due no more honor and privilege. He was expected to live on the income from his own estates, with no power of taxation, and consequently no means of rising above his lords. Since the country knew no regular taxes, there were no public moneys by which a far-sighted king might have maintained public order, stimulated industry, encouraged shipbuilding and commerce, or paid soldiers in a truly national army. In order to bring the "unhistoric land of the savages," the Highlanders, under control, and to make Scots of these "red-shanks," earlier kings had created feudal baronies in many parts of the northwest; but now these lords were among the most turbulent and arrogant in Scotland. As Maitland says, in reading Scottish history of the centuries just before 1600 "we think of the dark age: of Charles the Simple and Rolf the Pirate."[6]

Andrew Lang says that Scotland had little constitution before the seventeenth century, when English influences enter; this patriotic Scots historian wryly resents the way in which "England mixed itself up with our honest old plots and dirkings."[7] Other historians (Rait and Hannay, for example) argue that Scotland had a constitution. George Neilson even insists that Scotland had a common law, though what he notes is chiefly that the decisions of eighteenth-century lawyers showed a regard for precedent.[8] Surely no scholar looks to Scotland as one of the fountainheads of the concept of common law.

The end of the Middle Ages in Europe is generally marked as the beginning of the Renaissance. If Scotland was still medieval around 1600, as historians usually agree, the conclusion must be that she had missed her share in the Renaissance that had so stimulated the continent. This is not wholly true, although, as

Lang puts it, "slowly and obscurely the Renaissance came to Scotland."[9]

For one brief moment, beginning around 1460, it seemed that Scotland's star might gleam at least in the literary heavens. This is the period of the "Scottish Chaucerians," as they are called, because of the influence exerted upon them by the great English poet who had died in 1400. But Chaucer was of the Middle Ages, and the Scots he influenced wrote in the medieval tradition— Robert Henryson (1430-1506), author of a brilliant narrative poem full of vivid Scottish touches; William Dunbar (1460-1520), court poet writing in almost every medieval form; Gawin Douglas (1474-1522), allegorist and translator of the *Aeneid* in verse. In the early 1500's Scotland could more than hold its own with England in the number and quality of its men of literary talent. There were also, besides the Chaucerians, poets who broke with the medieval tradition: Sir David Lyndsay of the Mount (1490-1555), castigating the evils of his time in his *Satyre of the Thrie Estaitis*; the anonymous author of the *Complaynt of Scotlande*; Sir Richard Maitland of Lethington (1496-1586), collector of old Scottish poems and a dextrous versifier; and the unknown authors of some of the most haunting ballads of the world.[10] At the same time George Buchanan (1506-92) wrote a twenty-volume history of Scotland in Latin, said by a number of scholars to be superior to the work of Livy and Tacitus. His poems, likewise in Latin, were even more admired by his contemporaries, Scaliger maintaining that Buchanan's Latin verse was the finest in Europe.[11]

This flowering came chiefly during the reigns of James III and IV. The former (ruled 1460-88) came to the throne at the age of nine, and "happinit to be slain" twenty-eight years later. To the disgust of his virile noblemen, he surrounded himself with men of low birth because they shared his interest in art. The names of these men are recorded, but they mean little except to the antiquarian: Ireland, scholar and diplomatist; Rogers, a musician; Cochrane, "mason or stone-cutter," who may have been a sculptor. James IV (ruled 1488-1513) inherited his father's love of art and nascent science; "but this fault was forgiven him, as his manners were popular, his horsemanship good, and his bearing frank and free."[12]   But he was killed at Flodden Field, leaving an infant son whose long minority stopped any royal bounty to artists, marked as it was by tortuous intrigues and by the shift of many nobles to the English party, in opposition to James V's stand for the Auld Alliance with France and Catholicism.   By 1600 not even a literary figure can be named; the Reformation for the time being ended all interest in the arts.

Scotland had, nevertheless, three universities before the Reformation, with a fourth added by the Reformers.   The University of St. Andrews had been founded in 1411, that of Glasgow in 1451, and that of Aberdeen in 1494; the Presbyterians established the University of Edinburgh in 1583.   These institutions, however, seem to be more a mark of medievalism than of a renaissance, for they were little more during their early days than seminaries for the clergy.   The curriculum, patterned primarily upon that of the University of Paris, was centered upon theology and dialectic.[13]   There is no indication that any of the four institutions was touched by the new learning.   No notable name appears at any time among either faculty or student body.   By the time of James VI (1567-1625), the universities of both St. Andrews and Aberdeen were in equally low estate both as regards their incomes and their provision for instruction.[14]   Before the Reformation only the higher ranks of the Roman Catholic clergy were likely to have had a university education.   It would be difficult to specify any "intellectual classes" in Scotland before 1600.

Until the Reformation implanted a zeal for education in Scottish hearts, schools lower than the universities had been few. There were two kinds of schools to which the sons of the gentry might go: the "lecture-school" (relatively infrequent), where children were taught to read the vernacular; and the grammar schools, attached to cathedrals, houses of the Friars Preachers, and the monasteries, and in the burghs. In these grammar schools only Latin was taught.[15]   With comparatively few exceptions, all educational institutions of Scotland were under the control of the Church, both before and after the Reformation.

Boys went from the grammar schools to the university at an early age, often as young as fourteen or fifteen, having acquired the "essentials" (meaning an ability to read Latin). Before the Reform, their object in attending university was to secure a good job in Church or State. Some of them went on to Paris or Cologne—when they generally acquired a reputation for boastfulness.*[16] The number of educated men, however, being small and being channeled almost wholly into the church, left most of the people (certainly before the Reformation) illiterate. John Major in 1521 writes that "the gentry educate their children neither in letters nor in morals—no small calamity to the state. They ought to search out men learned in history, upright in character, and to them intrust the education of their children."[17] It is true that Parliament in 1496 passed an Act enjoining all barons and freeholders who were of substance to send their sons to school until they should have acquired "perfyt Latin;" but the intent of the measure seems to have been to make the sons familiar with legal terminology. Neither the illiterate barons nor the gentry seem to have followed the suggestion of the Parliament.[18]

One of the notable features of the Reformation was the ardor of the new Kirk for education. The Presbyterian Church desired that elementary schools be set up in every parish, with grammar schools in the larger towns, and it made a concerted effort to discover boys of ability in these schools, so that they might go on to the universities. The primary aim of this zeal was, quite understandably, the development of an educated clergy. Since the ministers of the Kirk became, and continued to be throughout the seventeenth century, among the dominant figures in Scottish life, and their career a respected one for young men with ambition, the country thereupon came to regard education as of the highest value. From this time forward Scotland was to take its place at the forefront in the enthusiasm for learning.

Money to carry out the Presbyterian scheme for schools in every parish was to come from the confiscated wealth of the

* Notestein (*The Scot in History,* p. 94) remarks that it had been a jest at the University of Paris that each Scot was by his own account a cousin of the king of Scots—which he may well have been, since kinship ramified. Notestein also suggests that, since the Scot abroad had little money and great confidence in himself, he "might easily have compensated for his want of cash by talking about his ancestry."

Roman Church. The nobles, however, had had their materialistic reasons for supporting the Reform, and a large part of the old Church's wealth went to the barons. It had probably been idealistic of Knox to suppose that the Kirk would automatically inherit the moneys of the former established Church. Lacking finances, the new Kirk had to turn to the burgh councils to supply the means to support the schools. A schoolmaster's salary was generally provided from the "common good"—the town's rents, customs dues, and fees. Many towns found it difficult to meet the obligation, and the whole Presbyterian program for education had to be considerably curtailed.

The new schools were like the old ones: they were grammar schools whose sole subject was likely to be Latin grammar and literature. All teaching was done in Latin—questions, answers, and explanations. The teaching day consisted of ten hours, except on Saturday, when there were only five. Even on Sunday, to judge from one example, there was no day of rest for the scholar. "Morning and afternoon the master walked to church with his pupils and sat beside them in the scholars' desks. The children were expected to take notes of the sermons and seem to have returned to the school to be examined on them by the master."[19]

In the matter of education Scotland was little different from England. The grammar school attended by Shakespeare in Stratford was also a Latin school whose pupils were forbidden even to talk to each other in their mother tongue on pain of being flogged. Such schools were a heritage from the Middle Ages, when the purpose had been to turn out "clerks" for church positions.* It seems curious, however, that the Scottish Presbyterians, particularly after the appearance of the Authorized Version of the Bible in 1611, the metrical Psalms, the Westminster Confession of Faith (1647), and the Shorter and Larger Catechisms, should have continued the tradition of forbidding any teaching of the mother tongue.

* "What the little boys of Renaissance England learned was Latin, more Latin, and still more Latin. About a decade after Shakespeare entered the class room a London teacher urged that English should also be taught in the schools, but no one paid any attention to so radical a suggestion." (Marchette Chute, *Shakespeare of London* [New York, 1949], p. 15)

The Renaissance indeed came slowly to Scotland. One might say that it arrived only in the eighteenth century. But when it came, it reached such a flowering that Edinburgh could call itself, with considerable justification, "the Athens of the North." The learning possessed by any of the Scottish emigrants to Ulster in the seventeenth century, however—even that of the ministers—was likely to be little more than the scholarship of a theologian.

Although Scotland had no truly national institutions of law, policy, and the administration of justice in 1600, local justice was generally fair—and, since the farmers and tenants were the ones who became ancestors of the Scotch-Irish, it is primarily local justice that concerns us. Complaints of venality and of the slowness of justice are found, as they are in most countries and most systems; by modern standards, the legal methods were clumsy; yet the lords and lairds seem to have shown commendable public spirit in giving fair trials to their tenants.[20]

The mischievous part of Scottish justice consisted in the assumptions of feudalism: that because the lord was responsible for the life and goods of every dweller on his domain, he should avenge—not simply protest before some higher tribunal—every trespass; and that the lord was not himself subject to any higher law than his own. To use the familiar phrases, feudal Scotland was a government of men, not of laws; and might made right, even though "might" was partly the well-founded sense of tradition. The armed power of great lords overshadowed that of the officers of the Crown, thus preventing the increase of centralized authority which, during the Tudor period in England, was bringing that country to a rule of law.

We are not concerned here with justice as it affected the upper classes. As it was meted out to tenants, everything depended upon the fairness of the nobleman. His sense of *noblesse oblige* and Scotland's tradition of reciprocal loyalty between chief and man would, in the majority of cases, assure a full hearing and an equitable judgment. There were two defects of such a system, however: the great lord might himself be the offender, so that even if a case were brought against him, he would hardly declare against himself; and an unscrupulous baron had plenty of opportunities for self-aggrandizement at the expense of his tenants.

There was something approximating a hierarchy of "courts" in the feudal system. Smaller cases were heard by the laird, while larger ones went to the lord. In this latter instance, the local lairds, the gentry, would serve upon the jury. One finds no instance of a judgment, so far as tenants were concerned, by one's peers, for it was not the Scottish custom for the tenant to serve on juries.

The chronic insecurity of life before 1600, like the age-old custom of settling disputes and injuries by one's own efforts, made for a tenuous concept of justice. Many years later, certain Scotch-Irish descendants of the Scottish tenants were to exhibit the same trait, on the American frontier, of taking the law into their own hands to right their wrongs.

4

Religion in Scotland

A. Before the Reformation

RELIGIOUS FERVOR IS NOT A CONSTANT. When it flames most brightly, it transforms not only individuals but history; yet among the same people it may die down into smoldering ashes that give no heat to personal life nor any energy to national life.

At the time of the migration to Ulster, Scotland (at least the Lowland part of that country, and especially the southwestern region of the Lowlands) was at fever heat with religious zeal. Because religion was a primary reason for a considerable part of the migration to Ulster, because it gave to the people of the North of Ireland a character they have never lost (one still considered a divisive force in Ireland), and because the fervor was still alive when the Ulster Scots came on to the American colonies, it is important to have a reasonably full understanding of religion in Scotland.

Its crucial moment was a mere two years, from 1559 to 1561. Before that period the Scots had shown only rarely any deep concern for religion; after it, however, and increasingly for more than a century, the Scots were so fervid in their religious intensity that few people in modern times have ever matched them.

Christianity began in Scotland in the sixth century when an Irish monk, St. Columba (521-597), made the small western island of Iona the seat of his mission work among the pagan Picts and Scots. A generation later, Aidan, a missionary from Iona, preached among the Angles who had settled in the southeast, between what is now Edinburgh and the English border. The real conversion of the Angles, who were to become a dominant strain in the Lowlands, resulted from the efforts of St.

Cuthbert (d. 687), bishop of Lindisfarne, who as a Scot knew well the people he was working with.*

Religion languished during the next centuries, which had to endure the raids of Norse Vikings, the wars between Scots, Britons, Angles, and Normans, and a lack of zealous churchmen; but it revived brightly in the reign of David I (1124-53). That king, determined to Anglicize his domain and give it stability, promoted the Church to further his policies. He organized new bishoprics and richly endowed them with lands, so that the prelates might enhance the royal position as territorial magnates; he founded a house of Austin Canons at Scone, the coronation place of Picts and Scots, and filled it with English monks; he planted English monasteries in many districts; and he suppressed the pious Culdees because they were associated with Gaelic speech and customs and because they followed the old rules of Iona rather than the Roman forms.

Now well established, the Roman Church in Scotland during the next four centuries began to display the characteristics often seen in institutions which are unchallenged in their monopoly. With no competitor to criticize or emulate and with the keys to heaven in its hands alone, the power of the Church increased while its service to the people declined. Its worldly might was evident in material form, for by 1560 it had amassed, through donations and wills, property estimated to consist of more than a third of all the land in the country and half of its wealth. In politics it was certainly a power to be reckoned with. That it sided consistently with the king irked those noblemen who challenged his prerogatives.

At its best—and the best seems to have been shown by the regular rather than the secular clergy—the Church lived up to its ideals. Eight houses of Dominicans, Friars Preachers, had been established since Alexander II in 1230 had brought in this great mendicant order. Among the others, Augustines, Carthusians, Grey Friars, Observantine Franciscans or Friars Minor, the Observants were the strictest of the orders. As mendicants,

* Cuthbert's name survives in many legends and in many places. The southwestern shire of Kirkcudbright, which provided many of the immigrants to Ulster, preserves his memory in its very name, which means "the church of Cuthbert."

they desired no property and had little land; they derived their livelihood from begging, donations, and work on their own gardens. Their care for the poor, especially the lepers and pest-ridden, was devoted, and many brothers died during years of plague.[1] The Church also maintained learning, even though it may not have increased it. It owned the only libraries in the country, ran the grammar schools, and established three universities for the training of churchmen.*

The falling off of the Church from its ideals, which even contemporary Catholics admitted, is understandable in the light of Scottish conditions of the time. So much of the country was thinly populated, with its villages so far apart, that it was difficult to build parish churches for them or supply them with priests. Perennial violence made the work of the Church difficult, for it discouraged those habits of peace and regularity in which religious habits may become a daily part of life. The influence of Rome, which might have checked laxity, was far away and rarely exerted. The king used the Church for his political ends and the noblemen regarded it as a refuge for their sons and kinsmen who were too feckless to become warriors or who merited a reward for service rendered.

On the fringe of Christendom as it was, Scotland had been untouched by many movements that agitated and disturbed other parts of medieval Europe—the Cathari, the Albigensians, the Waldensians. It had not shared in the new enthusiasms of the faith of St. Francis. At a time when saints were a common feature of the landscape, Scotland had produced no saints; when scholars like Aquinas, Albertus, and Abelard were flourishing abroad, no Scottish scholar appeared; in the wider councils of the Church no Scottish prelate made his mark.

By the middle of the sixteenth century the Roman Church in Scotland was in a lamentable state. It was a Catholic apologist, Hilaire Belloc, who affirmed that the corruption of the Church, which he characterized as very bad everywhere throughout Europe in the sixteenth century, was worst of all in Scotland.[2] The names of "dumb dogs" and "idle bellies" fixed upon the

* Mackenzie (*History of Galloway*, I, 240) speaks of them as the "only repositories of learning" in the country during the fourteenth century.

clergy were not unearned. Says Maitland: "Abuses which had been superficial and sporadic in England were widely spread and deeply rooted in the northern kingdom. In particular, the commendation of ecclesiastical benefices to laymen, to babies, had become a matter of course. The Lord James Stewart, the King's base-born son, who at the critical moment (1559) is Prior of St Andrews and sits in Parliament as a member of the spiritual Estate, is a typical figure. The corselet had 'clattered' beneath the Archbishop's cassock" as he took his seat. Maitland calls the clergy "numerous, laic, and lazy."[3]

Condemnation of clerical immorality was hardly more severe by the Protestants than by the Catholics themselves. In the slashing report of Cardinal Sermoneta to Pope Paul IV in 1556 he says that the nuns in Scotland "have come to such a pass of boldness that they utterly contemn the safeguards of chastity."[4] The Jesuit father Nicholas Floris of Gouda in 1562 says bitterly, "It is no wonder that with such shepherds, the wolves invade the flock of the Lord and ruin all."[5] Hector Boece (1527), John Major (1521), and Ninian Winzet (1564), all three faithful sons of the Church, had cried aloud at the venality, avarice, and luxurious living of the higher clergy. "But now for many years," wrote Major, "we have seen shepherds whose only care it is to find pasture for themselves, men neglectful of the duties of religion. . . . By open flattery do the worthless sons of our nobility get the governance of convents *in commendam* . . . , and they covet these ample revenues, not for the good help that they thence might render to their brethren, but solely for the high position that these places offer."[6] The records of the Church's own Provincial Council of 1549 confess that the root of the evils besetting the Church is the incompetence and vicious lives of the clergy.[7]

An Act of Parliament for "the reforming of kirks and kirkmen" in 1541 cites "the unhonestie and misreule of kirkmen baith in witt, knowlege and maneris."[8] As a result of these, "the kirk and kirkmen are lychtlyit [despised] and contempnit." Chaplains and chantry priests of the time were "uncouth, unlearned and troublesome . . . quarrelling among themselves," while altar priests were "generally illiterate, and many of them could only with difficulty stumble through the words of the mass."[9]

It is to the credit of a Provincial Council of the Church that in 1552 it sanctioned the publication of an admirable exposition of Catholic doctrine written by Archbishop Hamilton of Glasgow, who wished to reform the Church from within.[10] Yet the directions for its use provide the most striking attestation to the need of a vital religious reform. Rectors, vicars, and curates are warned not to read it in church unless they can do so without stumbling, as otherwise they might excite the jeers of their congregations; and they are exhorted to qualify themselves by daily practice to discharge this office in a manner that will tend to the edification of their flocks.*[11]

Clearly the Church as a whole had long since ceased to be the hard-working, unselfish Mother she had been in her youth. She had been grasping of lands, of heritages, of influence. Abbeys were flourishing while religion was at low ebb. Cathedrals and other establishments were rich, and prosperous churchmen walked among people who were poor, distressed, and burdened.[12]

It is unlikely that the Reformation in any country in Europe was wholly religious in its motivation. Religious protest was variously compounded with economic distress or ambition, political tension, local animosities, democratic stirrings, and even personal motives. Protestant movements before the middle of the sixteenth century had touched the people of Scotland only slightly. The country had had its touch of Lollardy, when the followers of John Wycliffe (1320-84) had pled for an open Bible and a more Christian daily life. A Lollard was tried for heresy and burnt at the stake in 1407, and a Bohemian follower of John Hus was also martyred; but no popular movement followed.†[13] Even Luther's teaching after 1517 affected a few bright young clergymen rather than the people. With the appearance of Knox, Wishart, Melville, and the other great Reforming preachers, however, the religious impetus for a great awakening was provided.

* The Church on the Continent had achieved what has been called a "medieval synthesis." The sorry state of clerical learning in Scotland made such a synthesis unthinkable in that kingdom.

† The Lollard executed was James Resby; the Czech was Paul Craw or Crawar, a skillful doctor.

Hazardous as generalizations may be, one is driven to conclude that the Reformation would not have come to Scotland when it did except for the noblemen; and further, that the Scottish Reformation actually began as a political movement with economic overtones. It appears that a few sincere Protestants, motivated by the highest interests of religion, indicated to the lords a direction in which they might go and that the low condition to which the Roman Church had fallen provided the fertile soil for Protestant seed. But the transformation of Reform into a movement that touched the people, winning their hearts, engaging their minds, and commanding their fervent loyalty, began to occur after the politicians had done their work.

Religious matters had already begun to take a political shape in the last years of the reign of James V (ruled 1513-42). That king, who had a great desire to improve the lot of the ordinary people of his dominion, was counseled by his uncle, Henry VIII of England, to follow his example and enrich his exchequer by seizure of Church property. James drew most of his support, however, from an alliance with the Church and so declined his uncle's advice; on the contrary, he drew closer than ever to his strong cardinal, Beaton. As James was dying after the battle of Solway, he received news of the birth of his heir, a daughter who was to become Mary Queen of Scots. During the tumultuous nineteen years of the regency that followed, adherents of "political Protestantism" began to make headway.

Foreign policy was at issue. Many lords now proposed that Scotland reverse her policy of two centuries, giving up the old alliance with Catholic France and becoming instead the ally of Protestant England. There was an element of stern realism in this proposal. It was true that every good Scot had cause for hating the ancient enemy to the south; but it was also true that Scotland, sharing the same island with England and once her peer, had now fallen far behind her in population, wealth, industry, trade, and power, with the distance almost certain to increase. To continue to fight England was to doom Scotland to endless defeat and conquest. Many felt, too, that France had often used the alliance to make Scots fight only for French interests. Peace and prosperity might come by friendship with

England; and since England had now become Protestant the issue upon which the alliance could best be shifted was Protestantism.*

Quite aside from the statesmanship of this reasoning, the example of Henry VIII had not been lost upon the Scottish barons. The Church of Rome was enormously wealthy by Scottish standards; if its vast properties were confiscated, the nobles would gain—not (as in England) the Crown, for the Scottish king supported the Church and gained in return its devoted loyalty. One can little doubt that self-interest converted many barons to the Protestant side and to the policy of an English alliance.

Economic motives already appear, and to these others were added. For the upper classes there were complaints against the protracted processes of Consistorial Courts and the frequent appeals to the Roman Curia, by which both their means and their patience were exhausted.[14] But such complaints were small in comparison to the economic sufferings of the poor. These were, in the main, borne patiently, as another of the inevitable facts of life. The Scottish historian Lang makes the remarkable statement that there is "no record of public feeling on the eve of the Reformation."[15] It required only a dramatic expression of their woes, however, and a suggestion that these need not be endured to arouse public sentiment. Humble folk had simply never before had an advocate. Their resentments, hitherto unexpressed, were enumerated in the First Book of Discipline of the Reformed Kirk: "the uppermost claith [cloth—i.e., bishops], the corpse-present, the clerk-maill, the Pasche offeringis, teynd aill, and all handelings up a land"—that is, requiring the best a man raised or produced, having to pay special fees for burials and weddings, the giving of tithes, and the like.[16]

On New Year's Day, 1559, a remarkable document was found placarded on the gates of every religious establishment in Scotland. Its author was unknown; its language clearly indicates that it was written by a scholar, but its complaint was that of the poor man. Known as the Beggars' Summons, it was a manifesto

---

* There was a definite setback to this political Protestantism during the five-year reign of Catholic Mary in England, from 1553-58; but it was renewed with energy when Elizabeth ascended the throne in 1558 and returned England to Protestantism.

of revolutionary spirit.   The opening words name those for whom and to whom it spoke: "The blind, crooked, lame, widows, orphans, and all other poor visited by the hand of God as may not work, to the flocks of all friars within this realm, we wish restitution of wrongs past, and reformation in times coming."   Then followed the complaints in detail.   The document ends with an inflammatory threat:

Wherefore, seeing our number is so great, so indigent, and so heavily oppressed by your false means that none taketh care of our misery, and that it is better to provide for these our impotent members which God hath given us, to oppose to you in plain controversy than to see you hereafter, as you have done before, steal from us our lodging, and ourselves in the mean time to perish, and die for want of the same; we have thought good, therefore, ere we enter into conflict with you to warn you in the name of the great God by this public writing affixed on your gates where ye now dwell that ye remove forth of our said hospitals, betwixt this and the feast of Whitsunday next, so that we the lawful proprietors thereof may enter thereto, and afterward enjoy the commodities of the Church which ye have heretofore wrongfully holden from us: certifying you if ye fail, we will at the said term, in whole number and with the help of God and assistance of his saints on earth, of whose ready support we doubt not, enter and take possession of our said patrimony, and eject you utterly forth of the same.   Let him, therefore, that before hath stolen, steal no more; but rather let him work with his hands that he may be helpful to the poor.[17]

At this crucial moment John Knox appeared upon the scene. This dour, passionate, devout, but remorseless Reformer was precisely the leader needed for the Protestant movement.   He was a man of the people who had fought Cardinal Beaton, suffered imprisonment for his faith, rowed as a galley slave for the French to whom he had been turned over, and become a friend and colleague of John Calvin's at Geneva.   To him the Roman Church was the instrument of the devil, while Reform was the will of God.   Rather small of stature and not strong in body, he had such courage that it was said of him that he never feared the face of man.   With his fiery eloquence, "he managed men's souls as he wished," according to a French Catholic.   An English Protestant said that Knox in one hour could by his voice put more life into his hearers "than five hundred trumpets blustering" in their ears. Narrow and bigoted and humorless he clearly was; but no one ever impugned his sincerity, however many of his other faults they named.

The tinder had been well laid at the moment of his arrival from exile in 1559. Catholic authorities had executed a number of "heretics," including a saintly old man; the Beggars' Summons and the zealous preaching of the Protestants were reaching the passions of the people; and the noblemen were ready to strike. The spark that lighted the tinder was an incident in the parish church at Perth. Knox had just finished a fiery sermon, and the priest was beginning the mass. The confusion of the scene obscures what happened precisely; probably the priest boxed the ears of a careless altar-boy. Whatever it was, a riot broke out. The people destroyed all the statues in the church and then went forth to carry their iconoclasm to other religious houses in the town. The queen-regent, deciding that an example must be made if the movement were not to spread, sent a French army to punish Perth. The Protestants responded by raising an army themselves and by inviting Elizabeth of England to come to their aid. The Catholic queen-regent, dying, was spared the humiliation of seeing the defeat of the French army and the triumph of the Protestants. The treaty of Leith, July 6, 1560, ended the struggle with the stipulation that the French army immediately leave the country. The religious-civil war had lasted only a year.

Parliament, meeting on July 10, 1560, put an end to the Church of Rome as the national church of Scotland. In a single day it passed three Acts, the first of which cast off the Pope, the second condemned all doctrines and practices contrary to those of the Protestants, and the third forbade the saying of Mass. Parliament now asked the Protestant ministers to draw up a Confession of Faith, a statement of the doctrines which members of the new Church were to believe. Next the ministers prepared the First Book of Discipline for the government of the Church, and the Presbyterian Church now became the established Kirk of Scotland.

Young Queen Mary, a fervent Catholic, returning to ascend her Scottish throne in 1561, had to face this triumphant Protestantism. The fight which ensued between Kirk and Crown was chiefly a fight between John Knox and Queen Mary. It is a story marked by pathos, with Knox bluntly upbraiding the Queen, and with Mary, for all her charm, losing supporters by her marriages, intrigues, and folly. With her flight to England in 1567 to win the support of her cousin Elizabeth (but to meet imprisonment and death instead), the Reformation in Scotland may be said to have been officially over, with Protestantism assured.

B. The Reform and After

The new Kirk saw to it that Scotland had a real Reformation. Rarely in Europe had the change from Catholicism to Protestantism been effected more peacefully than in Scotland. Whereas in England the Reform had been chiefly the work of the sovereign and the court party, in Scotland it immediately won the people to its *ideals*. It is this fact that underlies the claim of some that Scotland emerged within the span of a single generation from barbarism to civilization.

With only about six hundred ministers to lead it,[18] the Kirk started its work. During the next century it accomplished many things: it won first the awe, then the admiration, and finally the intense affection of the people; it instilled into the Scot a devotion to education; it set about the reform of morals, and succeeded so well in this effort that Scotland became puritanical; more than any other force in Scottish history, it welded into a nation (at least in the Lowlands) a bickering people; it introduced a measure of democracy in church government. But it also persecuted witches, carried the censorship of morals to the point of tyranny, preached intolerance, and (some say) made the cheerful Scot dour in temperament. The harshness of Scottish Protestantism was partly the result of the battles it had to fight during the seventeenth century and partly a consequence of the fact that the Scottish reform was not brightened, as it was in England, by a revival of letters.

Although its full triumph was to be postponed for at least a century, the Kirk was immediately popular with a majority of Lowlanders. Presbyterian ministers, in contrast to their predecessors, tried to lead exemplary lives, devoting their whole time to religious instruction of their parishioners and to pastoral duties. By modern standards they preached inordinately long sermons, to people who had seldom heard discourses from the pulpit but now seemed to hang on every word. One is almost persuaded that the latent intellects of the Scots had never before been stirred and that the preachers for the first time made humble folk feel their own dignity and worth. Like true ministers everywhere, they visited the sick, helped the poor, consoled the sorrowing, and became models of character. Such attention the people had never known, and they responded warmly to it.

Aside from the reform in religious belief and practice, the Kirk was intent upon two further fundamental reforms in Scottish life. It wanted to wipe out illiteracy among the people, especially in order that there might be an educated clergy and that the people might for themselves "search the Word." And it wanted to transform the morals of the people.

From all accounts, morals were in need of reform. Ministers became, as it were, prophets calling the people to repentance. The Session of the local kirk now haled before it offenders who had been guilty not only of fornication, drunkenness, and the more heinous sins, but also of swearing, breaking the Sabbath, "vain words," and "uncomely gestures."*[19] In Ayr, where strife among county families was sometimes waged by their respective servants in street brawls, the minister even rushed into the fray to separate the combatants.[20] The English traveler, William Lithgow, who visited the southwest in 1628, noted with astonishment that "Galloway is become more civil of late."[21] As the years passed and people became more accustomed to oversight of their morals by the church, it often happened that the Kirk Session acted as an omnipresent censor, as it did in New England and other puritan centers. Lowlanders, who before the Reformation had never given any indication of prudery or inordinate concern for the moral behavior of their neighbors, gradually became rigorous puritans. One may justifiably criticize the extent to which the censorship of personal morality went after

---

* "The punishment of branking, which was a customary one for scolds, slanderers, and other offenders of a secondary class, consisted in having the head enclosed in an iron frame, from which projected a kind of spike, so as to enter the mouth and prevent speech." (Chambers, *Domestic Annals of Scotland*, I, 47)

the Scottish Reformation; yet it is notable that the Scots for the first time in their history were beginning to learn discipline by society as well as self-discipline.[22]

Never since the days of Wallace and Bruce, and probably not even then, had the Scots had a rallying point for the development of national unity as a positive and continuing force. True, there had for centuries been the hostility to England, which reached fever heat at an invasion; yet this feeling did not prevent local animosities, feuds, and factionalism from reappearing as soon as the English threat had receded. Now, however, the Protestant faith constituted a positive force, steadily exerted through the years, daily evident in every parish. Moreover, the deliberations of the national Kirk brought men of all regions and classes together annually, so that they could perceive their common interests and likenesses; town and country, rich and poor, lord and tenant, east and west, met in the General Assembly to promote the welfare of all and met for an ideal that transcended personal and local self-interest.

The Kirk introduced the Scots to the principle of limited democracy. Members of the local parish had their self-governing Session, whose representatives attended the regional Presbytery, while representatives of the Presbytery went on to the national Assembly. Both laymen and ministers sat in all governing bodies and voted. There is no doubt that respect for the minister gave him a dominant voice in Session, Presbytery, and Assembly; nor can it be denied that a minister might, in many cases, practically name the members of the Session in his kirk. The fact remains that ministers, who came from all walks of life, even the humblest, now expressed themselves on national issues, and that laymen, many of them tenants, felt they had both a right and a duty to speak their minds. Authoritarian though the polity of the Kirk may have been, Calvinistic theology invested the individual with primary importance, and this importance could be realized because of the educational system the Kirk had developed.

Modern critics find much that is unlovely in the religion established by the Scottish reformers. It was Hebraic and Old Testament in its emphasis, stressing the thou-shalt-nots and the denunciation of sin. It was not a religion of kindness to one's fel-

lows or of gentle manners.   Scots, like their fellow-Calvinist
contemporaries of the seventeenth century, the Boers of South
Africa, regarded themselves as a chosen people, elect of God,
and their God was an awful Majesty, given to revenge upon His
enemies.   The Kirk of Scotland, its ministers and its members,
had little feeling for beauty, order, and dignified restraint, especially as compared with the Anglicans in England.   At the Reform, Knox had chosen no Middle Way, keeping the best of the
Roman liturgy and ceremonial; on the contrary, he led his people
into a complete break, casting off the music, the complex ritual,
the appeal to the senses, and the observance of all feast days.*
The Roman Church in Scotland had, in its heyday, lagged far
behind the Church on the continent in aesthetic development, so
that Scots had little tradition of the beautiful in religion, even if
they had chosen to want it.   The new Kirk was a made-to-order
structure, based on logic.   "It was not a growth.   It was a new
building, unweathered, unimproved by the slow accretions and
repairs of time."[23]

It is customary to blame this disdain of beauty, like the
rigorousness of personal discipline, upon Calvinism; yet the history of Scotland, as well as its natural environment, must be held
partly responsible.   Scots had had few chances to think of the
beautiful or to cultivate the fine arts; they had been poor, embroiled in constant fights among themselves and with England,
and occupied in a bitter struggle against hunger and cold.

One black mark against the new Kirk was its stimulation of
a prolonged persecution of witches.   The Scots were not alone in
this, for Puritans in England and America were doing the same
thing at the same time, and King James VI wrote a learned treatise on how to discover and punish witches.   Ministers felt that
they were simply following Scripture in their actions (the Old
Testament again—"thou shalt not suffer a witch to live"); but
they caused the death of many harmless old women, perpetuated
superstitious terror in the minds of the people, and made it pos-

* It might be suggested that this abandonment of Catholic liturgy, ritual,
and aesthetic stimulation was the Scottish equivalent of iconoclasm.   There was
little spoliation of religious statues, pictures, and great church edifices for two
simple reasons: few statues and pictures existed; and most of the historic religious
edifices in the country had long since been ruined by English wars and raids.

sible for the Kirk Session to intrude into the most private lives
of parishioners. Witchcraft was not abolished until 1727.[24]

It is hopeless to search the records of the Kirk for any signs
of a tolerant spirit in these early days. Scots, like every other
people in Western Europe, seemed unable to imagine the existence of one form of public worship unless all others were
prohibited. At its inception the Reformation had seemed to be
a call for liberty of mind and of worship; as it developed, the
newly established churches became as tyrannical as the ones
they had replaced. One mild point may be made: while a grim
example had been set during the Catholic ascendancy in putting
heretics to death, the Scottish Presbyterians merely imprisoned
and fined those who persisted in celebrating and attending
Mass.[25]

Whether the interest in religion, which in the seventeenth
century became passionate and all-consuming, had the effect of
opening the minds of the people or of substituting narrow-
mindedness for indifference, is debatable. The people clearly
had a new topic that gave itself to endless discussion and one
that called for the exercise of mental powers; yet the temper of
the times gave no spur to free inquiry. One might say, with
Buckle, that the Scots, "instead of cultivating the arts of life,
improving their minds, or adding to their wealth, passed the
greater part of their time in what were called religious exercises," so that the country made no real progress at all, either
material or intellectual.[26] Or he might say, with Mackintosh,
looking ahead, that the Reformation tended "to weaken the
claims and chains of authority, and thus give a new impetus
to those habits of mind so necessary to the branches of
scientific inquiry."[27] Mackintosh adds that "men began with
greater freedom and boldness to interrogate nature; the human
mind awoke from a long sleep, and with refreshed strength and
glowing energy entered on the course of modern scientific progress." It was not, however, until the eighteenth century, when
religious fervor began to subside, that any signs of this scientific
and speculative awakening appeared.

The insatiability of the Scot during the first century after
the Reform for sermons and religious discussion was altogether

remarkable. Sermons were so long and frequent that they absorbed almost all leisure, yet the people seemed never to weary of hearing them. Once a preacher was in the pulpit, apparently the only limit to his loquacity was his own strength.* Intense attention to his discourse was homage of a flattering sort; when it was given in almost every church, it cannot be surprising that ministers imperceptibly gained a tremendous authority in national life or that young men regarded the ministry as the profession of prestige.

Protestantism was exciting news to the Scots. For the first time in their history the people had been given something to think about, seriously and deeply. This great new idea had come to them from the Continent, and if the channels of communication with Europe had been wide open, instead of being confined to the impulse from Geneva, the Reformation in Scotland might have led forthwith to an awakening of scientific interest and an awareness of what was happening in the great worlds of philosophy, literature, and the arts. But Scotland had merely the one stimulus; the other channels remained closed. Besides this, the establishment of a national church prevented the "distraction" of Scottish minds by a variety of religious opinion, since the Kirk permitted no dissident sects. Seizing eagerly, therefore, upon the one absorbingly fascinating idea provided by Knox and his followers, the Scots for a century discussed it endlessly. It was still "news" to them in 1700.

The Lowlands had indeed undergone a reformation, one affecting both religion and character. The exodus of Scots to northern Ireland—the first step in the making of the Scotch-Irish—occurred at the very moment when religious zeal was at its peak. It was to have a powerful effect upon the people who became Scotch-Irish.

* The classicist, S. P. Bovie (*Satires and Epistles of Horace* [Chicago, 1960], p. 87) makes a telling pun upon the Greek story of the Calydonian boar: he says that the Scots minister, in his interminable sermons, can only be called the great Caledonian Bore.

5

The Mind and Character of the Lowlander

To UNDERSTAND THE MENTALITY and behavior of a people at three centuries' remove, one must try to eliminate from his mind all the salient ideas and opinions that have helped to shape the thinking of the modern Westerner. This almost impossible task requires not only the complete eradication of ways of thinking that have become a matter of course; it demands substituting for them another set of ideas that were equally matter of course to the men of the earlier age. Simply to name the powerful discoveries, inventions, and ideas that have changed men's minds since 1600—all of them unknown to the Scot of the time—is to glimpse life and the world as he saw them in his day.

Science in all of its modern variety and significance was completely absent from his mind. Skepticism, the demands of the laboratory method and of evidence that could be tested by anyone competent, induction, the attitude of Francis Bacon, and the revolution of Isaac Newton's work—all these were still in the future. The Scot knew none of the revolutionary discoveries about the age of the earth, the magnitude of the universe, the assumption that there are natural laws in all spheres, the theory of evolution. His faith in the literal truth of the Bible account of creation was entirely adequate for him. No higher criticism nor any study of comparative religions or of textual analysis had appeared to weaken his faith in the inerrancy of Scripture.

Democracy, in the sense of the right of universal suffrage and social equality, had not entered his mind. No one had suggested the idea of the relativism of cultures or the notion that customs abhorrent to him (such as polygamy) might be justifiable in circumstances different from his own. The doctrine of progress, or even the suggestion that progress is desirable, would have had short shrift from one who believed in stability and tradition, and preferred them. He did not believe in the separation of Church and State. If he completely rejected the claims of Unam Sanctam—that Bull of Boniface VIII which roundly proclaimed as a tenet necessary to salvation the dogma that all peoples of the earth were the subjects of the Pontiff—he completely accepted claims of Calvin that were equally dogmatic.

The technological discoveries that led to the Industrial Revolution and thence to the transformation of economic and social life had not been made. Scotland of 1600 was still a country of subsistence agriculture. The Scot may have been earthy and practical, but he was not yet materialistic in his outlook, as men of the nineteenth century increasingly became. He was more isolated from the rest of the Western World than the Englishman or than most Europeans; only the Irish, among his neighbors, were more cut off from the great world of events and ideas. He knew no scientific theory of disease, no modern medicine and surgery, no theories of the causes of psychological disturbances.

The catalogue of his mental limitations could, of course, be greatly extended. The point to make is that he shared most of them with his contemporaries in the world of 1600. If none of these "modern" ideas were known to him, what were his great convictions, the ideas accepted as matters of course at the time? Again a partial list will suffice: monarchy as the one approved form of government; the divine ordering of social classes; prestige inherent in birth; the rightness of separate spheres of activity for the two sexes; the reality of heaven and hell, with a single way of salvation; the wisdom of the familiar and traditional, whether one thought of folk cures, of moral standards, or of ways of work; the permanence of family ties (with no divorce) and the subordination of children in an almost patriarchal family; community opinion as the criterion for all moral judgments.

Possibly the word "community" best conveys the mentality of the Scot of 1600—not community in the sense of organized enterprises, but rather in the sense of a society in which people feel they belong together because they are of the same kind. They are kin, in that they cannot freely renounce membership and in that belonging to the community involves great emotional security. People do not decide to join such a community, as our contemporaries do: they are born into it and grow up into its "natural" relationships.*

It cannot be assumed that a desire for change is inherent in "human nature." Certain sociologists have posited as fundamental to all mankind a "desire for new experience,"[1] which would imply a constant drive toward change; but these same scholars name as a complementary trait the "desire for stability." The second seems throughout history to have predominated, certainly where social institutions are concerned; and the first is more evident in small matters, such as personal adornment and escaping from boredom, than in trying new social arrangements in society. Scots had never, at least before modern times, shown any noticeable inclination to transform their traditional way of life. It has been suggested that modern man is dominated by memory and hope. For the Scot of 1600, memory, in all its conservatism, was the safer emotion. Hope, as a freeing of creative energies, developed later.

After we have cleared away from our minds all congenial modern ways of thinking, it should be possible, by exploring what was written and said about him, to estimate the mind and character of the Lowlander of the seventeenth century. Presumptuous as it may be to make large generalizations about a whole people, these inferences are necessary if the ancestors of the Scotch-Irish are to appear as living men and women, not as impersonal immigrants who, in statistical tables, constitute merely an "ethnic group."†

* This is the idea of *Gemeinschaft* as analyzed by Ferdinand Tönnies in his perceptive work, *Gemeinschaft und Gesellschaft* (1st ed.; Leipzig, 1887). In contrast to the community of primitive and folk societies, the modern world, says Tönnies, is typified by the association, the *Gesellschaft*, whose major social bonds are voluntary ones, based upon the rational pursuit of self-interest.

† The study of national character has received a new impetus in recent years, with the importance of national morale, the emphasis on propaganda in international relations, and the psychological concept of basic, or representative personality. Ruth Benedict's *The Chrysanthemum and the Sword*, Margaret Mead's *Soviet Attitudes toward Authority*, and Alexander H. Leighton's *Human Relations in a Changing World* are examples of recent studies of national character.

National character cannot be attributed to "race" or to biological inheritance. What is distinctive in it is attitudes of mind, strongly-held custom, moral standards; and science has long since controverted the notion that these can be passed from one generation to another through biological inheritance. Popular opinion, however, still holds so strongly to the idea that "races" are what they are simply because the Latin, Oriental, or Jewish traits (if these exist) are "inherent" in the people, that it is worth refuting the idea again. The literature is full of comment about Celtic mysticism, excitability, and impracticality, as if Celtic children did not learn these traits from infancy because they are socially approved, but as if they were inborn in every Celt, transmitted to him through his genes. Since a large component of the Scottish stock was Celtic, such generalizations would seem, if true, to apply to most Scots.

Lowlanders who left Scotland for Ireland between 1610 and 1690 were biologically compounded of many ancestral strains. While the Gaelic Highlanders of that time were (as they are probably still) overwhelmingly Celtic in ancestry, this was not true of the Lowlanders. Even if the theory of "racial" inheritance of character were sound, the Lowlander had long since become a biological mixture, in which at least nine strains had met and mingled in different proportions. Three of the nine had been present in the Scotland of dim antiquity, before the Roman conquest: the aborigines of the Stone Ages, whoever they may have been; the Gaels, a Celtic people who overran the whole island of Britain from the continent around 500 B.C.; and the Britons, another Celtic folk of the same period, whose arrival pushed the Gaels northward into Scotland and westward into Wales. During the thousand years following the Roman occupation, four more elements were added to the Scottish mixture: the Roman itself—for, although Romans did not colonize the island, their soldiers can hardly have been celibate; the Teutonic Angles and Saxons, especially the former, who dominated the eastern Lowlands of Scotland for centuries; the Scots, a Celtic tribe which, by one of the ironies of history, invaded from Ireland the country that was eventually to bear their name (so that the Scotch-Irish were, in effect, returning to the home of some of their ancestors);

and Norse adventurers and pirates, who raided and harassed the countryside and sometimes remained to settle. The two final and much smaller components of the mixture were Normans, who pushed north after they had dealt with England (many of them were actually invited by King David of Scotland to settle in his country), and Flemish traders, a small contingent who mostly remained in the towns of the eastern Lowlands. In addition to these, a tenth element, Englishmen—themselves quite as diverse in ancestry as the Scots, though with more of the Teutonic than the Celtic strains—constantly came across the Border to add to the mixture.

Because the southern part of Scotland is, as its usual designation indicates, low land, with few natural barriers to hinder movement back and forth, intermingling of all of these strains would inevitably occur in the course of centuries.

One can hardly contest the predominance of the Celtic stock in the Lowlander's heritage, with the Teutonic Angles clearly the next element in order.* The question is whether the Celtic traits of personality, as these are commonly spoken of, are those of the Lowlanders. Countries in which Celtic stock predominates are Ireland, Wales, parts of France, and the Scottish Highlands. Even if there be any similarity among the national character of these people, their traits are hardly those of the Lowlander. The supposed emotionalism of the Celt ill consorts with the "dourness" of the southern Scot. Does the sentimentality attributed to the Irish, weeping over their lost leaders and "keening" publicly, or the wistfulness of the Highlander, singing the ghosts of the past while "the grey wind weeps," characterize the proverbially practical Frenchman or Lowland Scot? One finds it difficult to imagine an elder of the Kirk believing in the reality of leprechauns and other small folk. Is the Celt quick of wit, like the Irish, or deficient even in a sense of humor, as outsiders sometimes (wrongly) claim the Scots to be? Are the logicality and deductive philosophizing, of which both Lowlanders and Frenchmen boast, Celtic qualities?

Individual traits of personality are, of course, to some degree

* The schoolboy's comment, that the acute angles went north while the obtuse angles remained in the south, is probably apocryphal.

not yet determined by scientists, the result of biological inheritance, although one can hardly deny even here the enormous
influence of personal experience and the pressures of society
upon individual temperament.* For a whole people, however,
the influence of their daily life, their history, their environment,
and their attitudes (as these have developed over centuries of
living together) make their "national character." This way of
life, with all of its ideals, beliefs, ideas, and approved customs,
is inevitably passed on to each succeeding generation of children
—who, knowing no other, readily accept it and gradually modify
it with little conscious attempt at rebellion. Every individual
naturally brings his uniqueness to what his society's culture
teaches him; but it is one of the commonplaces of anthropology
and psychology that group approval and disapproval exert compelling influences upon the temperamental qualities of individuals.

We have now seen the outward influences that worked upon
the mind and spirit of the Scottish Lowlander—the comparative
isolation from the great world, the backward agricultural methods, the centuries of conflict with the English, the particularism
of a feudal system that undermined any tendency toward constitutional institutions, the niggardly soil, the meager life of the
mind. It now remains to explore the qualities of the Lowland
character as it was during the seventeenth century when many
Scots moved across to northern Ireland.

The most obvious characteristic must be given its Scottish
name, "dourness." This word, derived from the Latin *durus* and
the French *dur*, literally means hardness and durability, having
the qualities of iron. Men who survive centuries of living in a
hard environment, both physical and social, learn how to endure
the worst that life can send them. The Scot knew famine and
plague, thin soil, insecurity of life and property, raids, and ag-
gression. He early learned to fight back, to give blow for blow,
and then, when he had done his best, to endure. From the beginning of their history no one had ever called the Scots a

* Margaret Mead undertakes to prove that each society, having agreed upon
the "proper" temperament for males and for females, proceeds, through the
training of children, to require such traits of the members of each sex—and does
so with remarkable success everywhere. See her *Sex and Temperament.*

submissive people. Whether one thinks of the farmer rebuilding his crude home after its destruction by an English army, or of the resistance to the King's attempts to interfere with their religious convictions, the story is the same. They might bend, but they would not break. The national emblem is the thistle, and its motto, *Nemo me impune lacessit*—no one attacks me with impunity! It was not, as some suggest, Calvinism that made Scots hard: it was Scottish character that made Calvinism, already congenial to the national spirit, even more rock-ribbed than its Genevan counterpart. Dourness also has overtones of stubbornness—and even Scots are likely to admit this as a characteristic of the people.

This hardness combined with it a tendency toward violence which sometimes was not far removed from cruelty. The Scot had had ruthless enemies to fight, and the customs of his country had not taught him to gloss over his encounters with the lacquer of chivalry. The Middle Ages everywhere were hard times. Pity and sympathy were no more characteristic of its centuries than they had been during the civilization of classical Greece and Rome. The Scot fought his own battles because he had no one else to do it for him and because courage was the mark of a man. If he was cruel, his record is no worse than that of most of his contemporaries and is even better than some: he instituted no Inquisition, and testimony was not extracted by torture. In a rough age he was merely retaining a centuries-old trait of his ancestors which nothing in his present experience induced him to modify. On the contrary, the lawless condition of his country re-enforced the custom of violence and made occasional mercilessness appear to be practical good sense. If civilization curbs violence, then in the literal sense of the word, the Scots were not civilized, for the country had no real cities to teach urbanity, civility, and the values of peace. Its overgrown villages were scenes of constant brawls.

When a country lacks any kind of police and the rule of law, it is to be expected that the people, if they have any sense of pride (and the Scot had an abundance), will attempt to settle their own disputes and defend their own rights, by violence if necessary. In so doing, the Scot revealed another of his mental attitudes: that a man's "rights" are worth defending. This is to say that the Scot was quick to take offense, lest any man consider him a weakling. No peasant mentality persuaded him to bow his head to what he felt to be an infringement of his liberty; on the contrary, his lord's example and his own experience taught him that if he did not fight for his own rights he would lose them. Scottish ballads and folk tales, the tradition of William Wallace and the Bruce, and the absence of constraining national institutions encouraged him to react with physical vigor against any semblance of injustice. He wanted freedom—although he did not mean by this what the democrats of other nations might have meant, such as a right to vote, to participate in government, or to rise in the social order. The freedom he wanted was the right to live his life as a traditional Scot, with no man saying nay to the familiar rights.

His scale of values was not that of the saint, nor yet that of the pragmatist. In defense of his rights he was willing to give up everything else—home, family, and life itself. Often enough his courageous fights were not in causes that posterity would consider noble, such as struggles against tyranny or against repressions of freedom of speech; sometimes, indeed, the right being defended was nothing more than the freedom to engage in cattle raids. At other times, however, they were struggles to drive out the hated Southron (and return him tit for tat), to worship as he chose, to show his loyalty to his chief.

Among his values, then, was freedom as Scottish tradition interpreted the word. He would not tolerate subservience. One might ask whether the clear-cut social distinctions and the authority of the lord did not constitute the subservience of the average man. The Scot did not think so. The lord might share the same name; he fought endlessly for his men. The laird's exactions might be onerous, but he was a part of the scheme of things: he knew his people and was loyal to them. As noted, when schools were established, the laird sent his sons to sit under the local dominie, who might be "wee Jock's laddie" from the village. Recognizing established leadership was not subservience. Scots could stand hardship and pain like Spartans;

they could, and did, fight on their own when their leaders had
been killed; but

> Thralldom is much worse than death;
> For while a thrall his life may lead,
> It mars him, body and bones;
> And death annoys him but once.[2]

There was nothing automatic about the loyalty a Scot gave
to his chief. The Lowlander was "canny" long before modern
times, and the chief, himself a Scot, knew this and respected the
canniness as a virtue. Allegiance, as among most warriors, was
freely given because a man had proved himself worthy of it;
when he had shown his mettle, no display of loyalty was too
much. The Catholic clergy in the years before the Reformation
gained no such loyal support; their successors, the Presbyterian
ministers, did—and this was the Scot's judgment on the respective
worth of the two.

Independence of mind about many matters had long been a
characteristic, although it had not by 1600 become intense individualism. It was stimulated by the new Calvinistic faith. The
Kirk had removed from its members any assurance of eternal
salvation by the work of the Church and its sacraments. On
the contrary, a man's salvation depended upon himself: he must
prove himself to be one of God's elect—a congenial doctrine to
people who had always believed in self-reliance and a man's
importance to himself. God, majestic as He was, could be
reached by any man, however humble, without the mediation of
a priest; indeed, God is a Lord who requires an individual to be
a man in His presence, standing when he prays, not abjectly
kneeling, stating his own case manfully, as he did to his human
lord or laird.

The pride and touchiness of the Scot had already become
proverbial. There was something in his character like "quills
upon the fretful porpentine." The French had a saying, *ill est
fier comme ung Escossoys*, noted John Major in 1521.[3] Just as
the baron considered the king no better than himself, and would
fight and scheme to prove it, so every tenant had his pride that
was never far from touchiness. One reason for the revocation of

the French alliance may well have been the Scots' awareness that the French soldiers regarded them as "sauvages."[4] Contemptuous gibes frequently intensify pride and encourage boasting as a reaction.

The modern Lowlander is regarded as notoriously argumentative, and it may be, as some claim, that this trait developed as a result of the intense interest cultivated after the Reformation in theological points to which he listened for hours on end in his kirk. It may also be that this love of argument was only the verbal aspect of his self-assertiveness, his canniness, his pride in not being taken in. It has been suggested that the Scottish universities specialized in dialectic because it was already congenial to the minds of the students who attended them and to those of their Scottish professors.[5]

With all this spirit of freedom, this assertion of one's rights, this pride, a considerable question is raised by the apparently willing submission, after the Reformation, to severe church discipline. Several explanations may be offered for the paradox of the acceptance of discipline by a people who had resisted it for centuries. It might be said that the Scot had made his own free choice of a Kirk, and that the people themselves had had a hand in the decision; and so, convinced of its rightness and its independence from outside control and aware that it was of his own making, with his own sons in the pulpit, he now gave his loyalty to it, whatever the personal cost. Or again, no man is insensitive to the good opinion of his neighbors; and the Kirk, more than any institution Scotland had ever known, was in fact the organized community, whose voice carried irresistible weight. It could be said that a man's right to defend himself before the Kirk Session appealed to his sense of fair play. It may even be suggested that the canny Scot had long subconsciously recognized his own lack of discipline, and now that the minister made clear every week to him the ill effects of his impetuosity—not only to himself but to the Kirk and to the nation—he accepted the chastening rod for the good of his soul.*

* No one has suggested the selfishly pragmatic explanation that the great respect now accorded the minister, with the desire of a man that his own son might one day stand in the pulpit, might contribute to making the disciplinary system acceptable.

How good was the quality of the mind of the Scot? The answer to this question must not be confused by equating mental acuity with formal learning. The old-fashioned assumption that because a primitive people were illiterate they were therefore stupid and thick-witted has long since been refuted by anthropologists. An unlettered man may be shrewd, subtle of mind, perceptive, and logical. America's experience with democratic education is testimony to the changed opinion, for brilliant minds have been found in the families of illiterate immigrants, and Americans hold that most people are capable of thinking logically for themselves. This is part of the faith of democracy. It cannot, therefore, be assumed that because many, probably most, of the first Scots who went to Ulster were illiterate and came from the lower classes their mentality was of a low order.

The fact is that before the Reformation, and even in the next century after the number of schools had increased, the Scots had not been an intellectual people, no matter what the class. Chronicles of the period before 1600 so uniformly stress the narrowness of life and the appeal of bodily activity that one almost unconsciously slips into the assumption that mental powers were not respected and that a man who displayed a love of learning was held in contempt. Such an assumption is strengthened as one reads of the scorn of the nobles toward the artists with whom James III and his son surrounded themselves, of their feeling that a clerical life was a sorry one, to be followed only by weaklings, or of the feeble flickering out of an early Renaissance in Scotland. One is unprepared, therefore, for the sudden appearance of an enthusiasm for education that was almost a mania, and which extended to all classes.

This zeal for learning, especially its democratic aspect, now became another impressive characteristic of the Lowlander.* What the new order makes clear is that the Scot had, as he must

* David Riesman makes the point (*The Lonely Crowd* [New Haven, 1950], pp. 110-12) that few experiences are more significant to a people emerging from traditionalism than the discovery of the printed word. Literacy becomes both a hunger and an excitement, insatiable because it promises great rewards. Reading, and pondering what one has read, opens the mind to reason; it provides examples of standards other than the familiar; it offers new ideas, always the basis for criticism and freedom of mind. "Words not only affect us temporarily; they change us, they socialize or unsocialize us."

long have had, a fine, active mind—one that had been waiting only for stimulation. The Presbyterian Church, having discarded much ritual, laid its great emphasis upon the sermon. It is hardly an exaggeration to say that the sermon provided the necessary stimulus to the mind and was therefore a main cause of the new national respect for education.

To the modern man in a hurry it seems incredible that people were willing to make long journeys in all weather to devote practically a whole day to a series of sermons, each of which might last for two or three hours. What these people found in the parish kirk, quite aside from the satisfaction of their religious yearnings, was for the first time in their lives an appeal made directly to their minds. That a man could not yet read did not mean that he could not grasp the point of a theological issue; unlettered as he was, he could see what was at stake and could argue it with acumen. Theology was not a finespun argument about irrelevancies: it was a burning question about man's relation to God. One's immortal soul depended on it.* These were the days before journalism, the diffusion of literature, and the "mass media" of communication. To give one whole day out of seven to the topic that interested him most meant that one would continue to think and talk about it during the other days as well. The pulpit was a person's one source of mental excitement, and a man delighted in his new experience. Centuries of illiteracy had not dulled the shrewdness of the mind. The sermon and what it did to a man proved to be an oasis in a desert.

The educational system which the new Kirk developed adapted itself admirably to the very characteristics that have been noted. Schools were open to all; they were supported by the parish or by the common funds of the burgh. It is probably correct to say not only that Scotland was the first country to inaugurate public education but also that this democratic arrangement met no opposition from any quarter, least of all from the "aristocrats." Private tutors for children of the gentry had

---

* The Council of Trent, sitting at the very time of the Reformation in Scotland, counseled preachers of the Counter Reformation to avoid "the more difficult and subtler questions, which do not tend to edification" of ordinary folk. (See W. Sypher, *Four Stages of Renaissance Style* [New York, 1956], p. 243.) The Church of Scotland ministers categorically renounced such advice—to the infinite strengthening of their Kirk.

been few; it was no derogation of prestige for children of all classes to learn together at the school. Promising lads were encouraged to go on to the university, and they were more likely, by their very number, to be from farming families than from the gentry.

The pulpit, which now had enormous prestige, was open to any man who proved worthy. Two of the famous leaders of the Reformation, John Knox and George Buchanan, were sons of small farmers. They had made their way to the top by their ability. The appealing later picture of the "lad o' pairts" walking to the university town with his bag of oatmeal, which must last him for a whole term, on his shoulder and then making good in his studies, no matter how often he must trudge back to fill his bag, is based on solid fact. It likewise reveals the qualities of the Scot.

Zeal for education, however, must not be confused with a desire for liberal learning. In the seventeenth century the Scot revealed no desire to open his mind to the glories of literature and the arts or to the speculations of philosophy. The point of education was to train one to become a minister—or, failing that, a teacher who should train other ministers—and this meant expounding the Bible according to the reasoned theology of Calvin's *Institutes*. Universities continued to be training schools for orthodoxy, whose curriculum consisted of theology and dialectic. It would be only realistic to admit, moreover, that the motives which prompted some youths to seek a university degree were not purely those of saving men's souls. The learned professions now gave a man position, prestige, and power—and few are beyond the reach of personal ambition.

Scotland had its Reformation in the sixteenth century, but reversing the order of things in most European countries, it did not achieve its Renaissance until the eighteenth. The Scot had proved the acuity of his mind, but he had not yet accepted in all respects European standards about the content of an educated mind.

Some of the limitations of the mind of the seventeenth-century Scot were those of the times. Like most other Europeans, he believed that God had created the world only a few thousand years before, with each species of creature suddenly and uniquely formed and fixed, as the book of Genesis affirmed.   The hand of God could be seen in personal and national calamities, for God intervened in history now, as always, to punish sin.   Heaven and hell were tangible realities, whose details could be known from Scripture and whose glories or torments had been made even more vivid as the creative imagination developed them in thousands of sermons.   The Bible was the compendium of all necessary knowledge, the revelation of God's entire message: all other learning was therefore vain.   The veracity of the Bible was attested by its immediate applicability to life.   The Hebrews of the Old Testament had been much like the Scots in their constant warfare, their pride, their precarious life in a poor country with dangerous neighbors, their struggle against idolatry (for "Baal" read "popery").   The very images of the Scriptures applied as much to Scotland as to Palestine: the shepherds, flowers of the field, mighty fortresses, the woman who had lost a coin.   Scots were no more seafarers than the Hebrews; yet they fished, as did the men of Galilee, and they knew the danger of sudden squalls blowing down on their lochs.

The theological epistles of Paul, upon which Calvin had so largely drawn, gave the mind food for congenial thought.   Each man must, indeed, know the truth with his own mind.   The Almighty had certainly foreknown man's fate and predestined His own will to be accomplished—and the Scot felt reasonably sure that he was among the elect, under God's special protection. As the Westminster Shorter Catechism was to put it, in the middle of the century (1649), "Man's chief end is to glorify God and enjoy Him forever," and the Scriptures contain "the only rule to direct us how we may glorify and enjoy Him."

If some of the great discoveries of the sixteenth century were known in Scotland, there is no indication that these stirred the imagination or opened new horizons to the mind, even of the men in universities.   The earth might now be proved to be round, but that fact had no bearing on the matters that interested the Scot at the time.   He was not yet drawn to the New World, nor even to the world of imagination opened up by the explorers. As for cosmogony, common sense (and the Bible) told him that the sun rose and set, and if any Scots knew of Copernicus (1473-1543) or Galileo (1564-1642), the discoveries of these men apparently did not stimulate the men north of the Tweed. This was still a pre-scientific age in Scotland, with no laboratory in the whole country for experiments in physics, chemistry, and biology. The universities as yet produced no scientific theorists, for they remained primarily schools of theology. Alchemy, indeed, attracted a few speculators, among them King James VI, who wrote a treatise on this subject that might stand beside his other learned work on witchcraft; but James, proud of his learning, valued his knowledge of Hebrew and Latin more than the new discoveries in science. If science meant anything at all to the schoolmen, indeed, they thought in terms of Aristotle and Galen. For the average man, if the Bible and the minister did not inform him, it was satisfactory still to fall back upon the age-old testimony of the senses, upon old wives' tales, ancient saws, proverbial wisdom, and frank superstition—all of which had long flourished in Scotland.

One searches in vain the writings of the century following the Reformation in Scotland for any reference to the great European authors who were bringing literature to new heights—Shakespeare, Spenser, Bacon, the Elizabethan dramatists, Milton, and the Restoration poets in England; Corneille, Racine, and Molière in France; or to earlier authors, like Dante, Tasso, Ariosto, Petrarch, Boccaccio, Villon, and Montaigne. Painting and sculpture were all but unknown: certainly no artist practiced his craft in Scotland, and the dozens of portraits (*not* likenesses) of Scottish kings painted on the walls of Holyrood Palace were a job-lot performed at a reduced price by a fifth-rate itinerant. There was no theater in Scotland. Patrons for artists did not exist—and surely the Kirk would not be a patron, for it held that the eye and the other senses should not be distracted from the one essential matter of the hearing and expounding of God's Word. No collections or libraries had been formed in any baronial castle or in any burgh. Architecture was practical and mostly crude. Music produced haunting folk melodies and reels and marching tunes, but composers and opera were unheard of in that age that ran from Palestrina and Di Lasso to Purcell and

Lully. This is to say, then, that the Scottish people, with their minds on other things, had as yet missed not only the satisfactions but also the stimulation of all the fine arts flourishing elsewhere in Europe.*

The general absence of most of the influences which in other countries had accompanied the Renaissance need not be blamed upon the mentality of the Scots. Nor need it be attributed to a nay-saying religion, the obtuseness of Scottish noblemen, or dourness. Two factors especially combined to postpone the true Scottish Renaissance until the eighteenth century: the preoccupation of the Scots with other affairs in their most turbulent centuries and the poverty and isolation of the country.

The wars with England before the Reformation were succeeded by violent struggles to secure the independence of the Scottish Church from royal interference. From the time of Bruce in the thirteenth century to that of William and Mary at the end of the seventeenth, few years passed without armed conflict, which at times reached the point of a struggle even for survival. Scotland simply had no leisure class, nor any wealth to patronize the artist, nor any national triumphs like England's defeat of the Armada to give the people a burst of national zeal and creativeness.

Through these same years Scotland lay, geographically, on the northwestern periphery of "civilization." It was an isolated country whose people were poor; it was a realm that offered little incentive to the learned men, the authors and artists, the lively minds from other countries. Stimulus of new ideas comes from contacts, frequent and easily maintained, and the focus of such contacts is the teeming city, with its specialization and intermingling. Both contacts and cities were few in Scotland. Foreign traders were rare. The journey by sea to the small Scottish ports across the North Sea was too hazardous to establish ready channels of communication with continental sources of learning, and the constant Border troubles made peaceful access

* Whitehead called the seventeenth century "the century of genius" in Europe. It was the age that produced Kepler, Galileo, Harvey, Boyle, and Newton in science; Descartes, Hobbes, Locke, Spinoza, and Leibnitz in philosophy; Milton, Pascal, Racine, Molière, Rembrandt, and Velazquez in the arts. No Scottish name of the century can be placed alongside these or even with those of their lesser contemporaries in the realm of the mind.

to and from England minimal. Scots who went abroad to seek their fortunes were likely to remain abroad permanently; if they went to fight and came home as ex-soldiers, their purpose had been war and wages, not the accumulation of new ideas.

The seventeenth-century Scot thus stood outside the currents then playing over Europe, except in the one field of religion. Despite his isolation and his preoccupation with religion, however, he was by no means a complete conservative, if that word implies resistance to all change, simply because tradition is dear and change upsetting. Such conservatism one associates with downtrodden peasants, not with men who have personal pride. The Scot had to be convinced. He was too canny to give up a known good for an enticing vision. When he shrewdly estimated the change to be soundly beneficial he was ready enough to give up the traditional, as he showed when he supported a reformed Church, went in wholeheartedly for education, displayed an ambition to give up farming for a profession—and, most of all, when he went eagerly to find a better life for himself in northern Ireland. When, after a generation or two in Ulster, he moved on to the American colonies, the Tidewater citizens sometimes regarded him as positively radical. There he was to become a mainstay of the American Revolution; but at home he had never been a participant in any revolution—neither a Peasants' Revolt nor a Glorious Revolution nor any other. He fought to keep what he liked and to have the right to decide for himself.*

* Wallace Notestein's provocative *The Scot in History* devotes a hundred pages to an analysis of the character of the "early Scots." The subtitle of his book is "A Study of the Interplay of Character and History." From ballads and contemporary writing by and about the Scots, Notestein brilliantly records his estimate of Scottish national character before the Reformation. Among the favorable qualities he notes are their courage, endurance, loyalty to leaders, love of freedom, kindly hospitality, logic, realism, and a fondness for lively pleasures. Less favorable qualities include thievery, lawlessness and semi-anarchy, lack of discipline, revenge, cruelty, passionate impetuosity, a kind of meanness induced by poverty, and superstition. Notestein does much to explain the reason for many of the traits of both kinds.

Henry Jones Ford, in his *The Scotch-Irish in America*, quotes an estimate of the Scottish character by Heron. Although the analysis is that of a nineteenth-century author, Ford includes it in his discussion of "The Making of the Ulster Scot," and thus seems to regard it as applicable to the period around 1600. Heron says that the distinguishing features of the Scot were: ". . . an economy and even parsimony of words, which does not always betoken a poverty of ideas; an insuperable dislike to wear his heart upon his sleeve, or make a display of the deeper and more tender feelings of his nature; a quiet and undemonstrative deportment which may have great firmness and determination behind it; a dour exterior which may cover a really genial disposition and kindly heart; much caution, wariness, and reserve, but a decision, energy of character, and tenacity of purpose; . . . a very decided practical faculty which has an eye on the main chance, but which may co-exist with a deep-lying fund of sentiment; a capacity for hard work and close application to business, which, with thrift and patient persistence, is apt to bear fruit in considerable success; in short, a reserve of strength, self-reliance, courage, and endurance which, when an emergency demands . . . may surprise the world."

PART II: THE SCOTS IN IRELAND

6

The Plantation of Ulster, 1610 and After

THE SCOTCH-IRISH CAME INTO EXISTENCE because England tried to settle the Irish problem, a perennial nettle to royal politicians.

Throughout five centuries, ever since the Norman king of England, Henry II (1139-89), invaded Ireland, the English had tried repeatedly and constantly to subdue the island, whose people steadfastly resisted subjection. It became customary for the English king, after a successful campaign in Ireland, to give land there to Anglo-Norman families, hoping that they might, by living in the countryside, maintain and spread the English influence and so "domesticate" the wild Irish; yet it almost always happened that these families before many years intermarried with the Irish, taking sometimes their language, often their customs, and generally their patriotism, and thus joined with the Irish in resistance to English domination.

By the time of Queen Elizabeth (ruled 1558-1603) the Irish "problem" was no longer a sporadic one: it had become a steady drain on the royal exchequer, as on English manpower. A foothold for the English had been secured, but this was all. Around Dublin and its neighboring counties a Pale, or defended region, had been established: within that Pale, English control was relatively secure and English influence predominant. An Irish Parliament met in Dublin to carry out recommendations from London. But beyond the Pale lay most of Ireland, whose peasants spoke no English and lived a wretchedly poor agricultural life under their chieftains. Their culture, like their background and poverty, made them resemble the Highlanders of Scotland,

and civilized Englishmen regarded them, as they did the Highlanders, as little better than savages.

It was customary still to speak of the four traditional "kingdoms" of Ireland: Munster in the southwest, with such towns as
Cork, Tipperary, and Limerick; Leinster in the east, mostly inside
the Pale around Dublin; Connaught in the northwest, with Sligo,
Galway, and Roscommon; and Ulster, with its nine counties, in
the northeast, at one point only twenty miles across the channel
from Scotland.

In Elizabeth's day Ulster was not distinguishable from the
rest of Ireland in religion, language, clan rule, poverty, hatred of
the English, illiteracy, or primitiveness. Ulstermen were, like all
people beyond the Pale, "wild Irish." All of the twentieth century dissimilarities between the North of Ireland and the rest of
the country began with events shortly after 1600. One now
observes that the British flag flies over the North, while the
South is the independent republic of Eire; that the North is prevailingly Protestant and the South overwhelmingly Catholic; and
that the North derives wealth from its industrial activity while
the South remains agricultural. Among these distinctions, the
difference in religion is the clue to all the other divergencies.

When the Reformation was occurring in other countries, the
condition of the Roman Church in Ireland was as miserable as
it was anywhere in Europe. As Dunlop puts it, "outside the
Pale there was nothing worthy of being called a Church. To
say that the Irish had relapsed into a state of heathenism is perhaps going too far. The tradition of a Christian belief still survived, but it was a lifeless, useless thing."[1] Churches had fallen
into ruin, priests were few and often as ignorant and uncouth as
their parishioners. Edmund Spenser, who interested himself in
a solution of the Irish problem, said that "not one amongst a
hundred knoweth any ground of religion or any article of his
faith, but can perhaps say his Paternoster, or his Ave-Maria,
without any knowledge or understanding what one word thereof
meaneth. . . . Among the clergy you may find gross simony,
greedy covetousness, fleshly incontinence, careless sloth, and
generally all disordered life. . . . They neither read Scriptures,
nor preach to the people, nor administer the communion."[2]

Yet the Reformation did not come to Ireland. No Luther, Calvin, or Knox arose to lead it; Queen Elizabeth did not care to add religious problems to the ones already troubling the kingdom in Ireland; and the Church of England, now Reformed and Established within the Pale, made practically no effort to win the people by giving them religious instruction and ministry.* On the contrary, the Jesuits, with their characteristic zeal and power of organization, chose Ireland as one of the main centers for their missionary work of the Counter Reformation. Beginning in 1561 they preached to the people in their own tongue, performed pastoral duties with devotion, taught the catechism to the children, identified themselves with the patriotic struggles of the Irish against the English, and so won the hearts and loyalties of the people. They laid such a firm foundation for the resurgent Roman Catholic faith that three-fourths of the people of the South are now members of that Church.[3]

Elizabeth, realistically reconciled to the fact that Ireland would probably never be pacified by mere force of arms, tried the new method of colonization. Instead of sending over only a few noblemen to rule estates and then soon to become Anglo-Irish, taking the side of the people against the English, she planned to transplant hundreds of Englishmen to form a colony. The scheme involved driving away from their lands the native Irish and then granting these acres to English lords and gentry who would agree to bring over enough English settlers to establish the "plantation."† Her experiments were uniformly unsuccessful, although she tried them in Leinster and Munster in the 1560's and twice in Ulster in the 1570's. They failed partly because the Irishmen who had been driven away were so numerous that, from their hills and bogs, they would come back to raid, burn, and harass the new settlers; but they failed chiefly because not enough Englishmen could be induced to migrate to make a strong

---

* James Seaton Reid, the authority on Protestantism in Ireland, is highly critical of the indifference of the English to the opportunities for Reform in Ireland. He thinks the Irish could have been won to Protestantism rather easily. See his *History of the Presbyterian Church in Ireland,* I, 62 ff.

† Such colonization, of course, was nothing new in the world. It had been achieved with success by the Greek city-states, by Alexander the Great, by the Romans in the days of the Empire; and in Elizabeth's own time, the Spaniards and Portuguese were colonizing successfully in the New World.

Northern Ireland (Ulster)

military force at the same time they were becoming effective farmers. Discouraged English colonists usually went back home, leaving still another English landlord to cope with a recalcitrant Irish peasantry. The one value of these Elizabethan schemes was that they prepared the way for the successful Plantation of Ulster after 1610.[4]

None of Ireland was peaceful, but Elizabeth's worst troubles lay in Ulster. There Tyrone and Tyrconnell, the greatest clan leaders in the North (whom Elizabeth had tried to beguile to peace and co-operation by bestowing earldoms upon them), in 1595 led a grand alliance of chiefs and clans against the English. Essex, appointed as Lord Lieutenant to subdue them, could not, even with his twenty thousand trained troops, crush the rebellion. Upon his recall and disgrace, Elizabeth named Lord Mountjoy, who realistically engaged in a policy of frightfulness, destroying all the food, houses, and cattle he could find, as well as fighting in the field. Starvation and defeat made the Irish submit just as the Queen lay dying (1603). The depopulation of the region because of the wars made a new plantation scheme in Ulster appear more feasible.[5]

Even before the new King, James I (of England; VI of Scotland), had had time to make his plans for a new and more ambitious attempt at colonization, private enterprise began to show that successful plantation in Ulster was feasible. Along the east and south coasts of Down and Antrim, the two counties nearest Scotland, the wars had lightly touched the countryside, since the Irish chiefs did not extend their rule thus far. In 1603 Hugh Montgomery, a laird of northern Ayrshire (Scotland), learned that Con O'Neill, a chieftain of large properties in these two counties, was in prison. He contrived to communicate with him and to propose a bargain: he would effect the Con's escape and pardon if, in return, the Con would grant him half his lands. The escape and pardon were achieved, but King James would not ratify the assignment of the lands. Thereupon Montgomery brought to his aid another Ayrshire laird, James Hamilton, who had great influence with the King. A new agreement was drawn, giving each of the two lairds a third of the Con's property. King James knighted the Con and ratified the property agreement, on condition "that the lands should be planted with British Protestants, and that no grant of fee farm should be made to any person of meer Irish extraction."[6]   The Con later sold the rest of his estate to Montgomery and Hamilton.

Having now secured their large properties, in 1606 the two Scots began to induce tenants and other Scots from the southwestern regions to come over as farmer-settlers.   Since the distance was only twenty or thirty miles and the inducements were great, the risk was worth taking.   Harvests in both 1606 and 1607 in Ulster were so plentiful that, as the word spread, others "came over the more in number and the faster."[7]   By 1610 Montgomery could raise a thousand fighting men in his four parishes, and four years later he and Hamilton together could raise two thousand.   This indicates a total population of around eight thousand within ten years of the initial settlement, and shows the attraction to the Scot of the fertile lands of Ulster.[8]

Another example of successful private enterprise was given by Sir Arthur Chichester, English Lord Deputy for Ireland.   As a reward for his services in the wars he was granted in 1603 large tracts on the east coast of county Antrim, near the modern city of Belfast.   Determined to "plant" his estates, he brought farmers from his own county of Devon and attracted others from Lancashire and Cheshire.   His colonization so prospered that much of southern Antrim became English in character.   Other moderately successful plantations occurred in the inland county of Monaghan.

The testimony of these enterprises was not lost upon the shrewd Stuart King.   Following the defeat of the Ulster Irish in 1603 there had begun a series of complex maneuvers and intrigues whose upshot was that Tyrone and Tyrconnell fled to the continent in 1607, never to return to Ireland.   In the following year all the holdings of their clans in six of the nine northern counties were declared escheated to the King.*

* In feudal law, an escheat is the reversion of lands to the lord when, for whatever reason—such as lack of heirs or failure to pay proper feudal dues—the former holder of the lands is considered no longer to have a right to them.   If the law had been strictly followed, the Crown would have received only the freehold estates of the "disgraced" earls who had fled Ireland; but the argument was astutely advanced that in Ireland there had been no private property, since all clan lands "belonged" to the two great chiefs, such lands should now come to

James was an eager colonist. In 1606 he had approved the colony named for him at Jamestown in Virginia, and three years before this he had expressed his hope "that the sea-coasts [of Ulster] might be possessed by Scottish men, who would be traders as proper for his Majestie's future advantage."[9] With the example of the practicality of colonization in Ulster provided him by Montgomery and others and with his courtiers looking with hungry eyes upon the thousands of ownerless acres in the attractive Ulster countryside, James now decided upon an ambitious scheme of colonization in that region.

Many considerations may have presented themselves to his canny mind. If the colony were successful, he would have found a way at last to settle the constantly nagging Irish problem and so to spare him the expense of maintaining an army in Ireland. It seemed likely that industry might be stimulated in Ulster if the settlers were encouraged to raise sheep and flax; if this should occur, the realm would have increased its trade at no expense to the exchequer. It occurred to him that the two groups he especially hoped to interest, the London merchant companies and Scottish lords and lairds, would not only be grateful for his largesse but would benefit the state by their colonization. London was much overcrowded, with some 250,000 people living within her walls, whose congestion was thought to invite outbreaks of the plague (which had caused 30,561 deaths in London in 1603). As for Scotland, its poverty might be lessened by draining off some of its surplus population. No doubt the King also hoped to eradicate the barbarism of the "meer Irish."

James did not include the whole of the three million acres of escheated properties in his scheme. Private planters were already at work in the three counties of Antrim, Down, and Monaghan; and much of the newly won land was regarded as useless waste—bog, mountain, and forest—impractical for colonization. This still left half a million acres of farming land to be distributed among the participants.*

---

the Crown. The sub-chiefs were simply deprived on the ground that they were mere "tenants-at-will" of Tyrone and Tyrconnell.

* The whole of the six escheated counties—Donegal, Coleraine (now Derry), Tyrone, Armagh, Cavan, and Fermanagh—included 2,836,837 Irish acres, or in English measure, 3,785,057 acres. Ford (*Scotch-Irish in America*, p. 38)

By the King's design, the beneficiaries of his grant, who were also agents who would fulfill his purpose, were to be lords and gentry from England and Scotland, veterans of the Irish wars, the London Companies, the Established Church of Ireland, and Trinity College in Dublin. Half of the whole (about 250,000 acres) was to be parceled out among "undertakers" and "servitors." Notice of the allotment was to be given in England and Scotland, and any lord or gentleman might apply for a grant; if his application were approved, the undertaker would then agree to "plant" his new estate with Protestant farmers from either of the two countries and to build thereon a castle and a fortified enclosure called a "bawn." Servitors were to be Protestant military men who were given grants because of their meritorious service or because they might prove useful in future disturbances in Ulster. Their part of the agreement was the same as that of the undertakers, except that they were to build houses rather than castles and might take Irish tenants instead of bringing over English or Scottish Protestants.

One-tenth of the property was granted to twelve London Companies, the powerful guilds which consisted of the established businessmen of the capital. These Companies were, in effect, the "government" of London, for the municipal corporation was not then, as nowadays, regarded as a trustee for the general welfare, but as a mercantile body interested in trade for the benefit of the burgesses. The King and his Council were concerned with interesting this recognized power of merchant princes in the Ulster project. They had already undertaken the Jamestown plantation in Virginia and were ready to extend their enterprises. Their commitment resembled that of the undertakers with respect to transporting colonists and building castles and bawns.

The remaining four-tenths of the land went as follows: two-tenths for the support of the Established Church and Trinity College (this portion was chiefly land that had belonged to the old Church and which now could be used for the endowment of bishops and the parish clergy of the Episcopal Church, now

---

estimates that James's plantation scheme included 511,465 acres of cleared land, with bog and woodland in addition.

called the Church of Ireland); one-tenth for the establishment of forts and towns; and a final tenth to natives of "good merit." This last group was to be composed of Irish gentry who had been, or might be, of some service to the government and the Plantation. They would be permitted to take whatever tenants they pleased, and it seems to have been assumed that most of these would be native Irish Catholics.*

James soon added one other aspect to the project, in order to raise money for the Crown. In 1611 he instituted the new order of Baronet, a dignity between that of baron and knight, to be hereditary, though the holder would still be a commoner. A baronet, like a knight, would bear the title of *Sir*. Each recipient would pay for the dignity the sum of £1,000, nominally for the support of whatever soldiers might be required in Ulster; and each would now have the right to a coat of arms bearing the bloody hand of Ulster. The 205 English landowners who were advanced to this new dignity contributed to the royal exchequer the total sum of £225,000.†

Scottish participation in the Plantation, which does not seem originally to have been regarded as important by James's advisers, eventually became the mainstay of the enterprise. The English Privy Council took no steps to open the Plantation to Scottish undertakers until the plan was well along. In March, 1609, a letter to the Privy Council of Scotland informed its members that the King, "out of his unspeikable love and tindir affectioun" for his Scottish subjects, had decided that they were to be allowed participation. The Scots, it was pointed out, would have a great advantage, since they "lye so neir to that coiste of Ulster" that they could easily transport thither their "men and bestiall," or livestock.

The Scottish Privy Council immediately made public the

---

* The full plan was laid down in a paper received by the Lord Deputy for Ireland on March 6, 1608/9, entitled "Collection of such Orders and Conditions as are to be observed by the Undertakers upon the distribution and plantation of the escheated lands in Ulster." Its text can be found in Walter Harris, *Hibernica, or Ancient Tracts relating to Ireland* (Dublin, 1770).

† This was an impressive sum in 1611, and the whole idea bespeaks the ingenious thrift of the King (who was displaying a Scottish trait), as well as his shrewd estimate of what men would do for the sake of honor and prestige. See Insh, *Scottish Colonial Schemes*, p. 83.

news, inviting all those "quho ar disposit to tak ony land in Yreland" to present their applications. By September seventy-seven Scots had come forward. If their applications had all been accepted, some 141,000 acres would have been assigned; but the number was reduced to fifty-nine, and these by 1611 had been granted 81,000 acres in Ulster. Five of the fifty-nine were noblemen and the rest gentry; all of them were Lowlanders, and at least eighteen (and probably many more) were lairds from the southwestern counties of Scotland nearest to Ireland.*

King James, whatever his limitations, was a clearheaded man of business when he chose to apply himself. He was so much in earnest with regard to the settlement of Ulster that he took particular pains with the arrangements connected with it; and he was well acquainted with his "ancient kingdom of Scotland" and with its people. His "unspeikable love" for them may indeed have been strong, but his more calculating reason is evident in his comment about the nearness of Scotland to Ulster. It must have been clear to him that those parts of Scotland closest to Ireland, and which had had most intercourse with it through the years, were most likely to yield proper colonists. He resolved, therefore, to enlist the assistance of the great families of the southwest, trusting that their feudal power and influence would enable them to bring with them to Ireland sizable bodies of colonists. Thus grants were made to the Duke of Lennox, who had great power in Dumbartonshire; to the Earl of Abercorn and his brothers, who represented the power of the Hamiltons in Renfrewshire; and to men of the great houses in most of the southwestern counties.†

* See *Register of the Privy Council of Scotland*, VIII, 267-68. It was felt by some Englishmen that the Scots received the lion's share of the new lands; actually, however, they received less than the others. Their 81,000 acres were more than matched by the 81,500 that went to English undertakers and the 105,500 that were granted to servitors and "natives of good merit." Details are given in Hanna, *The Scotch-Irish*, II, 344.

† North Ayrshire had been already largely drawn on by Hamilton and Montgomery in their successful private enterprise in counties Down and Antrim; but one of the sons of Lord Kilmarnock, Sir Thomas Boyd, received a grant. From South Ayrshire came the Cunninghams and Crawfords, and Lord Ochiltree and his son. It was on Galloway men (from the southwest) that the greatest grants were bestowed. Almost all of the great houses of the time are represented—Sir Robert Maclellan, Laird Bomby as he is called, who afterwards became Lord Kirkcudbright; John Murray of Broughton, one of the Secretaries of State; Vans

James also knew better than his English courtiers the poverty of Scotland, the adventurous nature of the Scots, and the appeal of a good bargain. What tenant could resist the grant of a farm on "feu," a lease for twenty-one years or even for life, in almost virgin territory, when he had in Scotland a much shorter lease on difficult soil? The undertaker who received two thousand acres agreed to bring "forty-eight able men of the age of eighteen or upwards, being born in England or the inward parts of Scotland"; he was further bound to grant farms to his tenants in sizes specified; and he must have a stock of muskets and hand weapons to arm himself and his tenants.[10] It must have seemed evident to James that the hardness of Scottish life would induce more colonists to leave their country than would go from England, whose gentry and farmers were better established and who would have to make a longer journey, at greater risk, than the Scots.*

The assignment of lands to Scottish undertakers was to have permanent effect upon the subsequent character of Ulster, for those counties planted primarily by Scots continued to show a predominance of Presbyterianism, while those settled by Englishmen were normally counties in which the Established Church flourished. Of the six counties of the Plantation, Donegal and Tyrone were given almost wholly to Scots; Armagh and Derry were prevailingly English; Fermanagh and Cavan showed both Scottish and English influence. The other three counties of the province, though not part of the Plantation, likewise had been the scene of settlement, as already noted. Thus Down and Antrim contained the very successful colonies planted by the Scots-

---

of Barnbarroch; Sir Patrick M'Kie of Laerg; Dunbar of Mochrum; one of the Stewarts of Garlies, from whom Newton-Stewart in Tyrone takes its name.

* A contemporary Presbyterian minister in Ulster, Stewart of Donaghdee, found still other reasons for James's inclusion of the Scots in his project. He said, "The king had a natural love to have Ireland planted with Scots, as being, beside their loyalty, of a middle temper, between the English trader and the Irish rude breeding, and a great deal more like to adventure to plant Ulster than the English, to lying far both from the English native land and more from their humour, while it lies nigh to Scotland, and the inhabitants not so far from the ancient Scots manner; so that it might be hoped that the Irish untoward living would be met both with equal firmness, if need be, and be especially allayed by the example of more civility and Protestant profession than in former times had been among them." (Quoted in Hanna, *The Scotch-Irish*, I, 350)

men Montgomery and Hamilton, while Antrim also had Chichester's English colonists. Only Monaghan, of the nine counties,
remained truly Irish, for only one successful "foreign" settlement
was made therein.

King James had been explicit, by his limitation of grants to
Scots from "the inward parts of Scotland" (that is, the Lowlands),
to exclude all Highlanders from the Plantation. The records
show clearly the parts of the Lowlands from which most of the
early settlers in Ulster derived. Galloway, that region of the
southwest which included the shires of Ayr, Dumfries, Renfrew,
Dumbarton, and Lanark, provided the greatest number, for the
obvious reason that it was closest to Ulster. The counties around
Edinburgh (the Lothians and Berwick) came next in order, while
a much smaller contingent came from the district lying between
Aberdeen and Inverness in the northeast.[11]

Few ambitious enterprises develop precisely as planned.
Successful though the Ulster Plantation proved to be, the King
knew his disappointments. Some of the undertakers who had
received grants failed to implement their bargains, while others
were only halfhearted in carrying out what was expected of them.
Every ambitious undertaker needed more farmers than he had,
so that the competition for workers resulted in much moving
about in the early days of the Plantation. Despite the explicit
prohibition against the employment of "meer Irish," the temptation of hiring them for work on the estates was too great to be
resisted. This prohibition was openly flouted, and attempts to
enforce it were vigorously protested. Success depended upon
many contingencies: the enterprise of an undertaker, the attraction of his lands to prospective colonists, the personal bearing
of the undertaker as it inspired loyalty among his tenants, the
condition of affairs in the home country that might persuade a
man and his family to pull up their roots, and (later) the news
from Ireland itself and how the first colonists were faring.

News from Ulster was generally good in the early days.
Despite all the difficulties, reports from seven of the nine
counties were favorable. Monaghan and Cavan, as inland
counties most in contact with the rest of the Catholic interior,

failed almost from the start, the former having only one successful colony, and the latter soon collapsing altogether.*

The Plantation of Ulster succeeded. If it had not done so,
there would have been no Scotch-Irish, nor would Northern
Ireland now be British and Protestant. There were, however,
years of struggle and discouragement; at times it even seemed
as if the whole project must collapse. Reports made to the King
during the early years were full of complaints: many of the
undertakers were absentee landlords, who left affairs in charge
of agents who were dishonest; a number of men who received
grants, after visiting their lands, returned home and were now
trying to sell them; the quality of the settlers—especially of those
from Scotland—was regarded as poor; the Irish natives were by
no means dispossessed, but on the contrary their services were
being eagerly sought; fire-arms were few, and the prospects of
establishing an effective garrison against possible Irish uprising
were slight.[12]

The condition of the land itself varied, and this had an effect
on both the economic success of the newcomers and their state
of mind. Where war had not ravaged it and where the soil was
reasonably amenable to cultivation, there was good chance of
success. In many parts, however, the land was a desert. Between Donaghdee (county Down) and Newtown (in Armagh)
"thirty cabins could not be found, nor any stone walls, but ruined,
roofless churches, and a few vaults at Grey Abbey, and a stump
of an old castle at Newtown."[13] The war with Tyrone had been
conducted with such savage cruelty on both sides that great
tracts of land showed no cultivation, and some had been swept
almost bare of inhabitants.

Ulster became the meeting-ground, after 1610, of three people
of widely different culture and backgrounds—Scottish Lowlanders, English farmers and Londoners, and Irish natives. The
first and last groups are the principal actors in the story of the

* With few Scots and Englishmen, these two counties remained Roman Catholic. As the few colonists in Monaghan and Cavan gave up their enterprises,
lands gradually went back to Irish holders. When eventually Ireland was
divided between the Free State (now Eire) and Northern Ireland, these two
counties, together with Donegal in the remote northwest, chose to join the former,
thus separating themselves from what traditionally had been the Province of
Ulster.

Scotch-Irish.   Although many English undertakers took land and brought colonists, the English element was from the outset the smallest in number, though not always the least influential.   The twelve London Companies who had shared in the Plantation were given most of the county of Coleraine in the north.*   After a parish from county Tyrone had been added to it, the Londoners changed the name of the county to Londonderry.   The colonists brought in by the Companies were mostly Londoners of the Puritan persuasion.   Since many of them found the climate and the trials of farming in a rough country not to their liking, they returned to London.   Their place was taken chiefly by Scots and, despite its illegality, by Irish tenants.   Scottish influence soon became predominant here as in other counties.

Irish natives, by the very design of the Plantation, were to be regarded as little more than local annoyances to be subdued and controlled.   They were summarily driven off the lands they and their ancestors had farmed, however poorly, for generations, and were to have no right to their own institutions nor any voice in their government.   Even "natives of good merit" to whom a tenth of the area was to be granted, were shabbily treated.   By comparison with the others, their allotments were small—one grant consisted of only twenty-five acres—and without exception they were in the mountainous and more barren parts of the province.   Most of these Irish landlords were given only a life-interest in their estates, and although they often helped tide the Scottish and English settlers over their first hard years, little gratitude was shown them.   On the contrary, the Irish gentry were made to feel that their presence was being merely tolerated.   This was a shortsighted policy if the Privy Council had any expectation of winning over the Irish to a new state of affairs in Ulster.†

* These twelve Companies were the Mercers, Grocers, Drapers, Fishmongers, Goldsmiths, Skinners, Clothworkers, Merchant Tailors, Haberdashers, Salters, Ironmongers, and Vintners.

† George Hill, the foremost historian of the Plantation, is bitter in his account of the injustices done the Irish gentry.   He gives cases of men who in old age had sunk to being mere servants on lands they used to own, of daughters having to marry far beneath their position, and of sons who, unable to brook the new order of things, became Robin Hoods and made life difficult for the new settlers. (*Plantation of Ulster*, pp. 348-50.)

Despite every vicissitude, including massacres and war, the Plantation gradually grew strong and proved to be a success. If one cause more than any other can be singled out for its success, it would be the presence, the persistence, and the industry of the Scots in the region.   The Scottish source of supply of manpower made possible constant replenishment because of the nearness of Scotland to Ulster; the Scots came in numbers large enough to form neighborhoods; they were generally industrious, for all their backwardness in methods; and they clearly felt their prospects in Ulster superior to the ones they had left in the Lowlands.   Scottish undertakers also deserve credit for making the Plantation successful.   There were among them a number of defaulters and halfhearted planters, but again the nearness of Scotland made it possible for them to come over to supervise their Irish estates without absenting themselves too long from Scotland.   Their very presence worked upon the Scottish trait of loyalty to the chief to make their farmers feel that their interests, like their persons, were not forgotten.   One further influence mightily aided the Scottish success: the appearance of ministers from the Kirk of Scotland.   By their efforts with the transplanted Scottish farmers they achieved a kind of second Reformation among the Scots of Ulster and gave the people the sense of having their dearest institution at hand.*

A hoary institution of Scotland quietly disappeared from the scene in the colonization of Ulster: feudalism was not transplanted to northern Ireland.   This mark of the Middle Ages was to linger on in Scotland itself for another century, but the arrangements in Ulster, for all of their superficial resemblance to Scottish land tenure, were new bargains with new men, lacking the traditional usages of feudalism.   No attention was called to the end

---

* If this book were a full history of the Plantation of Ulster, it would show that many of the English settlements also prospered mightily.   English pioneers had two great advantages over their Scottish colleagues: they came from a more civilized country, whose agricultural methods were far in advance of those of Scotland; and they were fellow countrymen of the royal governors and the clergy of the Established Church in Ireland.   On the other hand, England was remote as a source of reinforcement and replacement; the contrast between the poverty of Ireland and the comforts of England was depressing; and the Scots, only a few miles from their own country, were needier, less aware of a comedown in external life, and more aware of what they had to gain by success.

of an era; but from now on Ulstermen, like their Scotch-Irish descendants, would feel a new freedom to strike their own bargains, a man deciding his future for himself. The passage to Ulster was a stride toward individualism.

7

Causes of the Scottish Migration

A. Economic

MEN MOVE TO NEW HOMES because of the attractions offered and because of the unsatisfactory life they are presently living, and sometimes for both reasons as well as for personal ones. As the folk saying has it, the donkey moves because of the carrot before and the stick behind. Both carrot and stick operated to move thousands of Scots across into northern Ireland in the seventeenth century.

There was no doubt, at home or abroad, that life in Scotland was hard and poor for most of its population. Incentives to emigrate must have been powerful if, as the estimates indicate, there were forty thousand able-bodied Scots living in Ulster after the first thirty years of the colonization project.[1] Into the general state of Scottish economic backwardness had appeared, in the years just before 1610, a new cause of hardship which, now that opportunity offered, was often determinative for the prospective emigrant. This new cause was the increasing hardship occasioned by the spread of a form of land tenure, the *feu*, which had the effect of dispossessing many farmers of their traditional lands.

A *feu* is a device whereby the landlord may acquire money in reasonably large sums: his tenant agrees to pay a fixed rent each year, with no obligation of services; in return the landlord gives him a lease for as long as he pays his rent. On the surface, it seems to be sound, practical, and even democratic, for it gives security to the farmer who rents the land, enables him now with free conscience to make improvements, and rids him of interruptions to his own labors to work on the landlord's property. The appeal of the *feu* to the landlord is clear: he has a fixed and increased income, for the payments of his tenants for the extended lease are fairly heavy; and he has fewer farmers to deal with and fewer quarrels to settle.

It was the average humble farmer who was hit by the new device. The situation in Scotland resembled the hardships of English farmers in a later period when landlords began to enclose land traditionally held, so that the squire might raise sheep for the profitable woolen industry. With the introduction of the *feu* (a definite, if unintentional, breach in the feudal system), Scottish tenants now saw lands which for generations had been leased to their families let out to others. If, by moving to some other locality, the dispossessed farmer could still find no land to rent, he was almost inevitably reduced to the position of becoming, at a great blow to his pride, a mere laborer or subtenant. Many of the dispossessed found their way to the towns, to increase there the already grim number of beggars.[2] Grant speaks eloquently of the hardships of dispossession as "only one note in the great minor chord of misery that rings through so many contemporary descriptions of the country-folk."[3] Sir David Lyndsay of the Mount, who flourished during the reign of James V (1513-42), lamented the fact that the tenure of *feuing* encouraged the dispossession of smaller tenants by those who were able to pay more.[4] "Kindly tenants" and old possessors were everywhere suffering, for in 1568 the proposal was made in Parliament that "no mailer, farmer, or other occupier of lands, who pay their duties," may be removed for a certain number of years, so that order may be taken for the relief of the poor and "the better forthsetting of the king's service."[5]

The position of kindly tenants became steadily weaker. If they had been the ones who were able to pay the *feu*-fees, Scotland might have developed something approximating the yeoman class in England; but kindly tenants were as little able to discover the money—were, indeed, quite as poverty-stricken—as other tenants. The *feus*, therefore, were chiefly acquired by great landholders, especially by ambitious lairds, in order to extend their estates; and the enlarged farms were now worked by hired laborers who had lost their status and independence as tenants.*

There are no figures by which the number of dispossessed may be estimated for the Lowlands. The process had gone on so slowly that it seemed to most farmers to be their individual problem, their personal crisis. There was no national movement of resistance to a development whose rationality was evident. By 1610, when the Plantation of Ulster was announced, many Scots felt not only the stick of poverty, lawlessness, and insecurity, to which they had grown accustomed; there was now the new goad of loss of status. It was, of course, not merely the dispossessed who were attracted to the generous lands visible across the Channel from the shores of southwestern Scotland. The old Scottish readiness to go abroad to seek one's fortune was stimulated by the advertisements of the planters. Country-folk far and wide entered upon the migration.

Any Scot who had the inclination might now take the short journey across to Ulster and there, on easy terms, acquire a holding of land reputed to be far more fertile and productive than any he was likely to know in his own country. More than this, he would be encouraged in his enterprise: the native Irish were to be driven back into the hills or expelled altogether, and there would be the protection of the English army, with a promise of peace and law. All this was a powerful attraction to men who wanted to better their lot.

B. Religious

Economic distress in the Lowlands and economic opportunities in Ulster were the predominant causes for migration during the first fifty years after the plantation scheme had begun in 1610.

---

* The origin of the *feu* is historically obscure. The king was using it late in the fifteenth century in order to increase his revenues. The Roman Catholic Church, as the greatest landowner in the country (it is estimated that it held from one-third to one-half of all lands in Scotland) and as the only consistent supporter of the king in his struggle with the barons, began to contribute a steadily increasing fund to the Crown; but when this proved insufficient, the king was encouraged to *feu* his lands. The same practice was soon followed by the royal burghs and by the Church itself. Parliament encouraged the practice in 1504, 1541, and 1584. For the background history of the *feu*, see, in addition to the sources already cited, Dickinson, Donaldson, and Milne, *Source Book of Scottish History*, II, 220 ff; and Pryde, "Development of the Burgh," in Dunlop, *Royal Burgh of Ayr*, 36 ff.

Thereafter, for the next thirty years, religious difficulties provided the chief incentive. Since religion was always prominent in Scotch-Irish history, some account must now be given of the religious developments in Scotland during the seventeenth century.

The reformed Kirk of Scotland led a tempestuous life for more than a hundred years after its establishment, never more violent than after the Scottish kings sat on the throne at Westminster. The son of Mary Queen of Scots (who fled Scotland in 1567) was James VI. A mere child upon his succession, he was trained by Protestant tutors and showed himself precocious, shrewd, and wily. He was content for Scotland to remain Protestant, for he saw the new Faith unifying his people, thus making rule simpler; but he also perceived that the General Assembly of the Kirk might become, by its authority and freedom of speech, a menace to the monarchical principle. England, he felt, had ordered its Reformation better by retaining bishops and a hierarchy. When, therefore, he ascended the English throne in 1603, he bent his efforts to the task of giving bishops to the Scottish Presbyterians.

Even as early as 1572, James's regent, the Earl of Morton, had made this attempt, partly to increase revenues and partly to make sure that Scotland should not fall under the rule of the Church, as Geneva had done. Andrew Melville, Principal of the universities of Glasgow and then of St. Andrews, opposed him, and in his Second Book of Discipline insisted that all ministers were equal (thus repudiating bishops) and that the temporal and spiritual jurisdictions were separate. To James, church government logically had no relationship to religious belief, and it had been the latter which precipitated the Reformation in Europe; but to Melville, church government had been ordained of God in the New Testament, and the king, who was "God's sillie [simple] vassal," must submit to it. James persisted, however, and succeeded in maneuvering the Kirk into making the moderator of each Presbytery (the regional governing body) perpetual in office. Then in 1610, following a neatly timed appeal for stronger action against Roman Catholicism, he called a General Assembly, whose members he himself had named. This body agreed to allow the consecration of perpetual moderators as bishops, at the hands of bishops of the Church of England. The popular outcry was bitter but unavailing.*

James now began to tread on even more dangerous ground, though he seemed always to sense just how far his Scottish subjects could be pushed without open rebellion. Deeply interested in fine points of church affairs, and priding himself upon his theological acumen, he undertook to "correct" Knox's hallowed Book of Common Order, so that it might be brought nearer to the English Book of Common Prayer. To have his two realms share religious observances would be a force for unification in the island. When in 1617 he returned for the first time to Edinburgh, he horrified the Presbyterians by bringing with him clergymen who wore the white (and Roman) surplice rather than the black Genevan gown, choristers who chanted, and courtiers who knelt at prayer. As he tried to make the people adopt these alien ways as well as other Anglican forms, they simply refused to conform. Neither his most imperious threats nor his Court of High Commission could produce any effect upon the stubborn nation-wide defiance of his orders. Thereafter matters continued in a stalemate until James's death in 1625.

Charles I (ruled 1625-49) shared his father's ideas about how the Church should be ordered, but lacked his sire's wiliness. Stubborn and tactless, he managed to alienate Kirk, people, and noblemen. The climax was reached in 1637, when he struck at the most sensitive spot in the heart of the people, their form of public worship. He required that Knox's order of service be supplanted by a new form, popularly called Laud's liturgy, full of High-Church Anglican forms. In the mistaken conviction that Charles was trying to revive Catholicism, an explosion was set off in St. Giles's in Edinburgh. According to tradition, this crisis was precipitated by Jenny Geddes, who threw her stool at the head of the Dean conducting the service, shouting as she

* The issue of having bishops was complicated by the doctrine of the apostolic succession. One can judge the effectiveness of the Reformation in Scotland by the passion of the people at James's triumph over the Kirk. Fifty years before no popular voice had been raised to defend the old Church against attack, but now throughout the Lowlands thousands spoke ardently in defense of the new one. Although most of the Highlands still remained, in a loose way, Catholic, the Protestant Presbyterianism of the Lowlands was general.

did so, "Traitor, dost thou say Mass at my lug [ear]?" Convinced that the Reformation was being undone by a return to popery, introduced by a king who clearly, to use Melville's words to James, had usurped the place of "Chryst Jesus the King, and his Kingdome the Kirk," the people overthrew the episcopacy in 1638 which James had so cleverly instituted. Their action was supported on both religious and patriotic grounds.

By this time Charles was in political trouble in England. The Scottish ministers, after negotiation with the Puritan leaders in England, drew up a Solemn League and Covenant, 1643, whose signers pledged themselves to mutual defense against all enemies, to root out prelacy, popery, superstition, and profaneness, and to maintain the privileges and rights of Parliament to meet together with the authority of the king. Charles, seeing the forces arrayed against him, unwillingly subscribed to the Covenant. Despite his concession, civil war broke out in England. The Puritans of that country hoped the Scots would join them in their fight against the King and the cavaliers, but on this issue Scotland, like England, was divided, and not many were willing to war against their own Stuart King. Despite their dislike of Charles's measures against the Kirk, the execution of Charles in 1649 was roundly disapproved in Scotland.

Cromwell was a bitter disappointment to the Scots. Because they would not yield to his Commonwealth government (which, unlike the King, was thoroughly English), Cromwell invaded Scotland in 1650, conquering its army at Dunbar. He then entrusted to General Monk the task of curbing the Scottish spirit. With English fortresses and a long chain of military posts across the Lowlands, the people for the first time in three centuries knew the pressure of a foreign yoke and a sense of national ignominy. The Kirk alone remained firm, as a thoroughly Scottish institution. From their pulpits the ministers continued to incite the people, and the General Assembly met continuously until 1653. Then Cromwell prevailed. The Scots, to their unutterable grief, saw venerated leaders of the Kirk driven from their places of meeting by English soldiers and led like criminals through the streets of Edinburgh.[6]

Certain Scots now began to hold conversations with Charles

Stuart, who promised, if restored to the throne, to uphold the Solemn League and Covenant. Shortly after his accession as Charles II (1660), however, he forgot his pledges and set out to bring the Presbyterian Scots to heel. Within two years he had begun a campaign to drive from their pulpits all ministers who would not conform to the ways of episcopacy. To avoid "conspiracy," he forbade family worship if one person outside the family were present, and all public meetings were strictly suppressed.

There followed now in Scotland the "killing times," when the resolute and fierce Covenanters of the Western Lowlands fought their guerrilla warfare against Charles's men. Refusing to accept episcopacy and determined to worship God after their own fashion, they left the towns to hold their meetings on hillsides and in secluded valleys. They carried arms to defend themselves against the soldiers who were sent to hunt them down. Many were killed on the moors; hundreds were cast into prison, others were tortured, and some were hanged; but nothing could tame their spirit. If martyrs are the seed of the Church, the Scottish Kirk now had its martyrs to increase its strength.

While this religious turmoil was raging bitterly in Scotland, there was comparative freedom of worship in nearby Ulster. It is small wonder that a new wave of migration to that haven of peace began, one which swelled mightily after the Covenanters, attempting a pitched battle, were decisively defeated at Bothwell Bridge (1679).

In the annals of the Scottish Kirk the Covenanters now have an honored place; yet every candid historian realizes that probably the majority of Scottish Presbyterians at the time were not of their persuasion, and that thousands regarded them as narrowminded, unruly bigots, who were not being "persecuted" but were rightly being punished for causing a disturbance. While the rest of the Presbyterians were experiencing no disruption of their worship and no qualms of conscience about "compromise," many of the Covenanters seemed actually to be enjoying their martyrdom and their violent insistence upon making the whole Kirk come round to their views. More than this, they often used physical force and persecution against those who opposed their intransigence. The fact remains that, in the quiet of later centuries, the "martyrs" have become a part of Scottish tradition and have been romanticized for their struggle against tyranny.*

The curious fact, to one who is accustomed to think of all religious persecutions and struggles for religious freedom as concerned with matters of faith and doctrine, is that the trials and sufferings of the Scottish Kirk (as well as of the Presbyterian Church in Ireland, shortly to be discussed) were not caused by differences on important points of creed. The crucial issue was church government. Presbyterians might have been as Calvinistic in their beliefs as they pleased if they had yielded to the monarchs and the supporters of the episcopacy by admitting bishops over dioceses. When James fumed that "a Scottish Presbytery as well fitteth with the monarchy as God and the Devil. No bishop, no King!", he was referring to the representative government of the Presbytery and the independence of its ministers. It may even be argued that the form of worship, the liturgy, which James and Charles tried so hard to alter, does not touch the fundamental matter of faith. Most of the difficulties of Presbyterians with Independents in the time of Cromwell would have been avoided if the Presbyterian form of government had been given up. Yet this very feature had endeared itself quickly to the Scots, and "persecution" by the Established Church consisted of trying to break down that attachment. As usually happens when force is applied to make people change their opinions—especially if it can be called persecution—the people simply became more strongly attached to their principles. The emotionalism connected with the Solemn League and Covenant is truly remarkable.[7]

The coming of thousands of Covenanters, as well as of their

---

* Sir Walter Scott, who was a scholarly antiquarian as well as a romancer, gives a very unflattering view of the Covenanters in his *Waverley*. A recent novelist, Josephine Tey, makes one of her characters say, "The Covenanters were the exact equivalent of the I.R.A. in Ireland. A small irreconcilable minority, and as bloodthirsty a crowd as ever disgraced a Christian nation. If you went to church on Sunday instead of to a conventicle, you were liable to wake on Monday and find your barn burned or your horses hamstrung. If you were more open in your disapproval you were shot. . . . It's the final irony . . . that a group whose name was anathema to the rest of Scotland in their own time should have been elevated into the position of saints and martyrs." (*The Daughter of Time*, [Penguin, 1954], p. 129.)

neighbors who wanted to be out of the way of all violence, strengthened the Scottish element in Ulster. Presbyterians after the middle of the century were dominant in six of the nine counties of the province and far outnumbered the Anglicans.

The Bloodless Revolution of 1689, which brought William of Orange to the throne, promised the Scots freedom in religious matters, and the promise was kept. The Presbyterian Church, without bishops, was now once more the Established Kirk of Scotland. In 1707 the Act of Union brought Scotland and England together in the United Kingdom, with the result of an immediate and vast improvement in the economic condition of the Lowlands.* The two main causes for migration to Ulster were thereby, in less than two decades, removed. The push and pull of the Scots toward Ireland practically ceased when Stuarts no longer sat on the throne.

* Union brought "unprecedented prosperity to Scotland," says Henry Gray Graham (*Social Life of Scotland,* p. 5).

8

The Pioneer Scots in Ulster, 1606-1634

THE QUALITY OF THE SCOTS who first came over to settle in Ulster was not, if some of the standard histories can be believed, of a high order. One learns upon investigation, however, that every historian who makes this assertion rests his judgment upon the statement of two early Presbyterian ministers in the region, one of whom was not even contemporary with the times. It is instructive to see precisely what these two men, whose remarks have become standard "facts of history," said and did not say.

The Reverend Robert Blair came to the Plantation in 1623 to become minister of the congregation at Bangor, county Down. In an autobiographical fragment, begun forty years later, when he was seventy years old, Blair wrote: "The parts of Scotland nearest to Ireland sent over abundance of people and cattle that filled the counties of Ulster that lay next to the sea; and albeit amongst these, Divine Providence sent over some worthy persons for birth, education and parts, yet the most part were such as either poverty, scandalous lives, or, at the best, adventurous seeking of better accommodation, set forward that way. . . . Little care was had by any to plant religion."[1]

The Reverend Andrew Stewart, minister at Donaghdee, county Down, from 1645 until his death in 1671, began in the last year of his life to write a history of the Presbyterian Church in Ireland. He did not know the first settlers from experience; his account has been supposed to have come from his father, who was also a minister in Ulster; but this gentleman died when his son was ten. Stewart's estimate is more often quoted than

Blair's. He wrote: "From Scotland came many, and from England not a few, yet from all of them generally the scum of both nations, who, from debt, or breaking and fleeing from justice, or seeking shelter, came hither, hoping to be without fear of man's justice in a land where there was nothing, or but little as yet, of the fear of God. . . . Going for Ireland was looked on as a miserable mark of a deplorable person—yea, it was turned to a proverb, and one of the worst expressions of disdain that could be invented to tell a man that Ireland would be his hinder end."[2]

What both of these statements are written to show is chiefly that the first settlers were not vitally concerned with religion and that when the Church arrived it transformed their characters. For the rest, the ministers assert that those who came were not gentry but rather "adventurers," that sober citizens back home at first looked askance at the wild risk of "going for Ireland," and that among the immigrants were many no better than they should have been. The same estimate could be given of the pioneers to Virginia, which was being colonized at the same period. None of the specifications can justify Stewart's invidious assertion that the people were "the scum of both nations."

Blair is no doubt quite accurate in his canvass of the motives leading to the migration when he names poverty, scandalous lives, and adventurous seeking of better accommodation as the chief reasons for leaving Scotland. So it had always been when Scots were going to France or Prussia in earlier centuries. Cautious citizens, particularly elders of the Kirk, rarely become pioneers (though they may follow when the way is paved), and such conservative folk would not approve a large exodus from the community. It is the foot-loose, those who have nothing to lose and much to gain, and (quite naturally) those who have not scrupulously kept all the laws—or who have felt the heavy hand of church discipline—who are most attracted to a new frontier. The first miners in California, the debtors sent to Georgia, the "criminals" deported to Australia, were likewise held in scorn by upright stay-at-homes. What they made of themselves, and what their sons became, indicate that, for all the hard things said about them, they were hardly "the scum of the nation."

Three facts throw doubt on the contumelious judgments of

Blair and Stewart. First, the colonists who were married brought with them their wives and families; next, within two years these very Scots had, by their industry, made such a success of the enterprise that thousands of their countrymen now followed them over to Ireland; and finally, as soon as ministers came to Ulster, the settlers welcomed them with open arms and shortly made their churches a replica of the strict moral environment that had now become normal in Scotland. Surely the pioneers were behaving rationally and naturally when they gave their first attention to farming, for otherwise there would have been no point in going to Ireland; but their eager welcome to the ministers indicates that there were not many more reprobates in the Plantation than in any other community.

Within twenty years the colonization had proved so substantial that a positive fever for emigration swept the Lowlands. Ships made the passage back and forth across the North Channel with the frequency of a ferry. Sir William Brereton, an Englishman traveling through Ayrshire in 1634, wrote: "Above ten thousand persons have, within two last years past, left the country wherein they lived, . . . and are gone for Ireland. They have come by one hundred in company through the town, and three hundred have gone on hence together, shipped for Ireland at one tide. . . . Their swarming in Ireland is so much taken notice of and disliked, as that the Deputy hath sent out a warrant to stay the landing of any of these Scotch that came without a certificate."[3]

Certainly a major factor encouraging the migration of Scots was their realization that if life in Ulster did not come up to expectations, one had only to come home, with only the rigors of the twenty-mile Channel to face, and possibly the crestfallen admission back home that one had not succeeded. Going to Ireland was not, as in the case of going to America, putting a mighty ocean between oneself and home. Brereton saw some of the disappointed and fainthearted returning, and remarked: "Some of them can give a reason why they leave the country. . . . Some of them complain of hard years, the better to colour and justify this their departure." He notes that even these admit that food is cheap in Ulster.[4]

Defections were far outweighed by arrivals. It was estimated by a careful commissioner that Ulster had approximately fifty thousand Scottish and English settlers by 1620, only ten years after the first Plantation. The estimates for 1640 are twice that number.*

In the main, the colonists must have been the right kind for their task, for they gave Ulster the reputation that would attract others to follow them. Moreover, most of them at once proceeded to build houses and provide food for themselves and their families. On the whole, the Scottish settlers seem to have done best of the newcomers and the London colonists the worst. Enthusiasm for colonization was in exact reverse to the home comfort and prosperity. Even the Scottish undertakers were poor men, many of them with estates deeply burdened with debt; they had everything to gain by going to Ulster. The inducement was even greater for their tenants. Besides, Ireland was near enough to see from Scotland on any clear day. If the King had enlisted men of the northwest of England to aid in the settlement of Ulster, as he did people of the southwest of Scotland, the history of Ulster might have been materially altered, with the English predominant. To London citizens, on the other hand, Ireland was a far-off savage country, for which they did not feel at all inclined to give up the comforts and the civilized activities of the metropolis. Thus the Londoners' colony was, for the first half-century at any rate, a failure, and the Companies let their lands to the "meer Irish," breaking the terms of their contract and involving themselves in ever-recurring quarrels with the authorities.[5]

Stewart of Donaghdee puts the issue on the higher standard

* Captain Nicholas Pynnar was commissioned in 1618 to make a detailed report upon every settlement in the Plantation. He found "at least 8,000 Men of Brittish Birth and Descent, to do his Majesty's Service for Defence thereof." Since his figure names only fighting men, the number would have to be doubled to embrace all the males, and doubled again to include all females. If, then, there were some 32,000 people in the six Plantation counties, it would not be uncautious to assume another 18,000 (at least) in the prosperous and quiet counties of Antrim and Down, where Montgomery and Hamilton had done their careful pioneering work, and in the Monaghan colonies. Pynnar's account is in the *Carew* MSS. See also Hanna, *The Scotch-Irish*, I, 545.

The estimates for 1640 are drawn from Lecky, *Ireland in the Eighteenth Century*, I, 83, 177-78, who cites Carte's figure of 120,000 and Latimer's of 100,000.

of living of the English, so that the latter would not migrate "except to good land, such as they had before at home, or to good cities where they might trade, both of which in those days were scarce enough here." He also notes that the marshiness and fogginess of Ulster were responsible for a disease, "a flux called here the country disease," which so affected the English settlers that many of them died. His comments indicate that there was more adaptability on the part of the Scots. It was clearly easier for people to make their adjustments to primitive conditions when they had come from a country whose standards had not been very different.[6]

The daily life of the new settlers is disappointingly reported by contemporary writers; indeed, so little is said about it that one is driven to conclude that there was nothing unusual about it in any way, since it resembled country life at home.

It had been stipulated in the original instructions that each planter (as distinct from the servitor and the native landlord) must build both a castle and a bawn. The castle was conceived by no one to be a towering edifice on a crag; it was to be a large and practical house of stone. Pynnar in 1619 describes several castles then being built. One is 32 feet high, 36 feet long, and 19 feet broad; another is "22 foot broad, four storeys high, whereof some part of the walls were standing before, and is now . . . well finished and slated;" one of the most impressive was that of Lord Aubigny: "This is five storeys high, with four round towers for flankers; the hall is 50 feet long and 28 broad; the roof is set up and ready to be slated. Adjoining one end of the castle is a bawn of lime and stone, 80 feet square, with two flankers 15 feet high, very strongly built."[7]

The enclosure known as the bawn was traditional in Ireland.* It had been customary to construct a cattle enclosure near residences in times of peace, and near the encampment in times of war, to guard the animals against wolves or other predatory animals, as well as against theft. The new settlers needed the bawn for the same reasons, particularly to preserve the cattle from raids by the dispossessed Irish. Each night, for safekeeping,

---

* According to Hill, the word "bawn" is the anglicized form of the Irish *bo-dhaigan* or *badhun,* a "cattle-fortress." See Hill, *Plantation of Ulster,* p. 82.

all cattle and horses were driven from pasture into the landlord's bawn. Only when there were enough settlers to form a substantial community could this precaution be relaxed.

The greatest uncertainty of life for the newcomers was, and remained for many years, the native Irish who had been driven from their lands to make the Plantation possible. Chichester, the Lord Deputy, had from the first tried to persuade the King to deal generously with the natives, to return much of the land to Irish gentry as landlords, and to permit the peasants to remain as tenants. Only thus, he felt, could the colonists avoid constant violence with the bitter exiles. King James, however, replied that he was engaged in a fight to eliminate barbarism within his dominions. He had tried unsuccessfully to plant the island of Lewis in the Hebrides after removing its barbarous natives; he was about to bring order to the Border shires of Scotland and England by severe punishment on all depredators; and he was making progress in bringing the lawless Highlanders under the King's law. His whole principle would be undermined by generous treatment of the barbarous Irish. The utmost concession he was willing to make to Chichester's insistence was to give niggardly grants to several of the Irish gentry and to allow servitors and Irish landlords to employ Irish tenants.

The settlers themselves undermined James's intentions. They needed workers, and the Irish were at hand, cheap. Chichester reported in November of the first year of the Plantation that the Scots were trying to get licenses to have the natives remain as subtenants, "which is so pleasing to the people that they will strain themselves to the uttermost to gratify them, for they are content to become tenants to any man rather than be removed from the place of their birth and education, hoping, as he [the English landlord] conceives, at one time or other to find an opportunity to cut their landlords' throats; for sure he is they hate the Scottish deadly, and out of their malice toward them they begin to affect the English better than they have accustomed."[8]

Few settlers, if they perceived at all the rancor in the hearts of the Irish, seemed to regard it as anything more than one of the hazards of life to be guarded against; there is no suggestion that their consciences troubled them about dispossessing the

Irish. The attitude seems to have been parallel to that of the pioneer on the American frontier: the rich lands are in better hands now, for they are being more carefully cultivated; moreover, the authorities have gone through the proper legal forms, and the pioneers now own the land they are working. To the morally sensitive of a later age it can be no surprise that the "natives" were moved by anger, injustice, and despair to fight back, and, when they found open warfare futile, to use treachery and guerrilla tactics.

Those natives who had received no land at all had to retire to the mountains and woods. They were known as widcairns, or wood-kerns (a "kern" originally meant a light-armed soldier), and they were feared and hated by all the settlers. Wood-kerns often operated in bands, under the leadership of fiery spirits among the youthful gentry and former nobility of Ireland, whose resentments and bravado made them Robin Hoods to their followers. They lived by plunder, since they now had no lands of their own. Stringent laws were enacted to curb them. The government offered large sums for their heads, and the colonists (like American pioneers with the Indians) were ferocious in dealing with any kerns who were caught. Bloodhounds were kept for tracing the "outlaws," and a captured kern was often shot without trial. If tried, the kerns were generally found guilty and, when sentenced, had halters immediately placed round their necks; they were then paraded through the street of the village to the place of execution and were hanged.[9] The policy of the government would neither pardon the kerns nor permit them to leave the country, except those who would bring in the heads of their kinsmen and associates. As none were found who would submit on such terms, the settlers themselves eventually petitioned that the kerns be allowed to emigrate from Ireland.[*]

[*] Hill says that Chichester eventually permitted the kerns "to go to Sweden, and enlist in the service of Gustavus Adolphus, the Protestant lion of the North— a service, however, which they hated, and from which they deserted at every possible opportunity to enter the armies of his opponents, the Spaniards. It is recorded in a State paper that the military escorts appointed to conduct these young Ulstermen to their several places of embarkation were charged not to pass, if possible, near any of their former homes, from a fear that they should be rendered even more reckless and desperate when gazing on their native fields and homesteads, then in the hands of strangers." (Hill, *Plantation Papers*, p. 30.)

Another constant danger to the settlers was wolves. Much of northern Ireland was heavily wooded, so that pastures near the forests were never safe. The ravages of wolves were so great in mid-century that Cromwell's government in 1652 offered a bounty of six pounds, then an enormous sum, for the head of every she-wolf. Payments of these bounties continued until 1710, and wolves were not finally eliminated in Ireland until 1770.[10]

The first task of each settler was to build a shelter of some kind. Most of the early houses were rude, rush-thatched huts, built as near the landlord's bawn as possible.* As soon as the pioneer had proved to himself that it was worth his while to remain, he improved his house. By 1619 Pynnar found already 1,897 "Dwelling Houses of Stone and Timber, after the English manner . . . besides very many such Houses in several parts which I saw not."[11] For reasons of defense and protection as well as from tradition, the houses of the farmers were together in a village, while the farmer's lands were divided into strips, separated from one another and generally intermingled with the lots of others, as had been customary in Scotland.

Two discoveries made by the Scots greatly assisted their enterprise and made farming in Ulster much more satisfactory than it had been in Scotland. First, they learned from the more advanced English tenants the art of draining bogs and swamps; and second, they now planted the potato, which had recently been introduced from America by Sir Walter Raleigh. The former was probably the greatest stride the Scots had ever taken in agricultural methods, for it made available much otherwise useless land, it induced a more careful cultivation, and it made possible settlement in plains rather than farms only on hillsides. The potato gave them a new and healthy staple of diet, one that was soon to become so indispensable not only in Ulster but throughout the whole country that it acquired the name of the "Irish" potato.

Sheep flourished on the Ulster meadows. From the beginning of the plantation the settlers made woolen cloth, which was easy to convey over the poor roads to seaport towns and which found

---

* Pynnar, reporting on the house and bawn of one John Hamilton, says that there is "also a village of eight houses adjoining the bawn . . . , a watermill and five houses adjoining it." (Ford, *Scotch-Irish in America*, pp. 117-18.)

a ready market abroad.   Most of the ready money of the colonists came from the export of cloth.

Despite all dangers from the natives—a threat that was not fully removed until the Battle of the Boyne in 1685—the colony prospered and the population steadily increased.   The first comers had proved by their very staying that life was better in Ulster than in Scotland.   Because the land had, during all the disturbances attendant upon pacifying the North, lain fallow, the crops of the first years were excellent.   Then, at this very moment, King James gave an unwitting incentive to other Scots to migrate. The very year of the Plantation was that in which he began to introduce his ecclesiastical reforms into Scotland, substituting the episcopal for the presbyterian form of church government. Many Presbyterian ministers found that their consciences could not endure this "reversion to popery," and so sought refuge and a new sphere of labor in the north of Ireland.[12]   Where a minister went, it was surely safe and respectable for his parishioners to follow, if they were so inclined.

The coming of the ministers seems, in retrospect, to have constituted the greatest spur to new migration and the greatest guarantee of stability in the early years of the Plantation.   The character of the colonists provided a challenge.   Stewart added to his other judgments on the settlers a statement that "on all hands atheism increased, and disregard of God, iniquity abounded with contention, fighting, murder, adultery, etc."   This is precisely what the first ministers of the reformed Kirk had found at the time of the Reformation in Scotland, and the dominie in Ulster would hardly have proved a true Scot without wanting to bring Christian order out of such moral chaos.

Blair, who had described the settlers as "drowned in ignorance, security and sensuality," nevertheless records that on the day after his arrival in Ulster he discussed religion with a group of Scots, spending several hours with them "in godly conference and calling on the name of the Lord."   He preached two sermons in one day, "one sermon on heaven's glory and another on hell's torments," and found his congregation much affected.[13]

Settlers welcomed the ministers and genuinely responded to their preaching.   Churches were established, and whenever more

ministers arrived they found ready congregations, eager to reproduce in Ulster the familiar forms and practices of the Scottish
Kirk. It required little effort on the part of the ministers to introduce the same strict discipline. Blair tells how he made evildoers publicly confess their sins. One of the illuminating accounts
is that of the Reverend John Livingston, who came to Ireland in
1630. Describing the discipline exacted by the Session of his
church, he says:

We [the Session] met every week, and such as fell into notorious
public scandals we desired to come before us. Such as came were
dealt with, both in public and private, to confess their scandal in the
presence of the congregation, at the Saturday's sermon before the
communion, which was celebrated twice in the year. Such as after
dealing would not come before us, or coming, would not be convinced
to acknowledge their fault before the congregation, upon the Saturday
preceding the communion, their names, scandals and impenitency
were read out before the congregation, and they debarred from the
communion; which proved such a terror that we found very few of
that sort.[14]

Just as the Scots had shown themselves eager for spiritual
guidance after the Reformation, so did the transplanted Scots in
Ulster. Blair and Livingston both speak of the extraordinary
fondness of the people for sermons and instruction. Livingston
says:

I have known them come several miles from their own houses to
communion, to the Saturday sermon, and spending the whole Saturday's night in several companies, sometimes a minister being with
them, and sometimes themselves alone in conference and prayer.
They have then waited on the public ordinance the whole Sabbath,
and spend the Sabbath night in the same way, and yet at the Monday's
sermon were not troubled with sleepiness; and so they have not slept
till they went home. In those days it was no great difficulty for a
minister to preach or pray in public or private, such was the hunger
of hearers.[15]

Ulster thus early received a puritanical and Presbyterian
character. Not only was the Church of Scotland Presbyterian,
with the strictest control of morals, but also the colonists in many
of the English settlements in Ulster were puritans. Ulster proved
a haven for ministers from both kingdoms who desired to escape
the episcopacy being promoted in England and Scotland by

Kings James and Charles. The Church of England, which became the Established Church in the whole of Ireland, was under the direction chiefly of puritan bishops, who brought in diligent pastors trained under the puritan influence.*

An effective compromise was devised whereby Presbyterian ministers in Ulster might accept ordination from a Church of England bishop with no offense to their scruples. Until 1642 Scottish ministers readily accepted this ordination, for it did not require them to use the liturgy, while it allowed them to remain Presbyterian and to receive tithes. Some of the bishops even consulted them about matters of church concern; in the convocation of the Established Church in 1634, several Presbyterian ministers were full members.[16]

Another arrangement quite different from contemporary practice was that laymen might be rectors in the Established Church. This meant, in practice, that they appointed clergymen as their vicars. It meant, further, that a rector who at the same time was a Scottish landlord would almost certainly be a Presbyterian and would appoint as his vicar a Presbyterian from Scotland. Thus James Hamilton, recently created Lord Clandeboy, brought in Robert Blair, who had resigned his position as professor in the University of Glasgow rather than submit to prelacy—and Blair received his ordination in the Presbyterian form at the hands of a bishop in Ulster in 1623.† Similarly in 1626 Josiah Welch, a grandson of John Knox, likewise resigned his professorship at Glasgow, settled at Templepatrick in Antrim, and was ordained by a bishop.

Everything conspired to give the Scottish Presbyterians a strong foothold in the colony. The first Presbyterian minister to come was Edward Brice, in 1613: he had left Stirlingshire because he opposed the motion to make Archbishop Spottiswoode

---

* They were drawn chiefly from Cambridge University, which even in Elizabeth's day had been a center of Calvinistic theology and puritan doctrine.

† When Blair was about to be ordained in Bangor, he told Bishop Echlin of Down that he could not submit to the use of the English liturgy or to the sole ordination of the bishop. Echlin replied, "Whatever you account of Episcopacy, yet I know you account a presbyter to have divine warrant; will you not receive ordination from Mr. Cunningham and the adjacent brethren, and let me come in amongst them in no other relation than a presbyter?" Blair adds, "This I could not refuse, and so the matter was performed." (Blair, *Autobiography*, pp. 58-59.)

permanent moderator of the Synod of Clydeshire.[17] He was followed by many others. In 1626 the ministers of Antrim and Down were numerous enough to establish monthly meetings, which resembled meetings of Presbytery, since they "consulted about such things as concerned the carrying on of the work of God." On one day each month there was public preaching, attended by great crowds: "in the summer day four did preach, and when the day grew shorter, three."[18] Revivals were held with much success, and sometimes, apparently, with the emotional effects that were to be observed as epidemics of abnormal behavior on the Ohio Valley frontier in America. At a revival conducted by one minister, according to Stewart, "I have seen them myself stricken and swoon with the Word—yea, a dozen in one day carried out of doors as dead, so marvellous was the power of God, smiting their hearts for sin, condemning and killing."[19] Blair was critical of this particular minister, because, "having a great voice and vehement delivery, he roused up the people and wakened them with terrors; but not understanding well the Gospel, could not settle them."[20]

By the time Archbishop Laud, under Charles I, inaugurated his program for strict conformity to High-Church Anglican practice, Presbyterianism had so strong a foothold in Ulster that his problem there was as difficult as it was in Scotland itself. Laud won a few battles, but he lost the war. Later in the century, an Anglican opponent of puritanism stated precisely what the Presterians had done in Ulster:

Hereupon followed the plantation of Ulster, first undertaken by the city of London, who fortified Coleraine and built Londonderry, and purchased many thousand acres of land in the parts adjoining. But it was carried on more vigorously, as more unfortunately withal, by some adventurers of the Scottish nation, who poured themselves into this country as the richer soil; and, though they were sufficiently industrious in improving their own fortunes there, and set up preaching in all churches wheresoever they fixed, yet whether it happened for the better or for the worse, the event hath showed. For they brought with them hither such a stock of Puritanism, such a contempt of bishops, such a neglect of the public liturgy, and other Divine offices of this Church, that there was nothing less to be found amongst them than the government and forms of worship established in the Church of England.[21]

9

The Hard Years, 1634-1690

TWENTY-FIVE YEARS AFTER THE FIRST SETTLERS had come to Ulster the colony seemed firmly established. So much land had been brought under cultivation that newcomers from Scotland, now eager to migrate, found it difficult to secure a farm.[1] Crops were good; the wood-kerns had been effectively silenced; and the natives were at least momentarily quiescent. There were always rumors of plots among the natives to sweep away the foreign settlers. In 1615, in fact, such a conspiracy had been discovered and suppressed with ruthlessness. The authorities were too alert and military precautions too extensive to admit any opportunity for a general rising, but they could not prevent marauding, and the colonists had always to be on the alert. As a report submitted to the government in 1628 put it: "The Irish, of whom many townships might be formed, do not dwell together in any orderly form, but wander with their cattle all the summer in the mountains, and all the winter in the woods. And until these Irish are settled . . . there is no safety either for their [the settlers'] goods or lives."[2]

Despite the possible danger from the natives, the very increase of the Scottish population was an element of security, and the presence of ministers, who had organized churches and introduced the familiar discipline, added an element of stability. The future augured well. From 1634 onward to 1690, nevertheless, life for the colonists in Ulster was to consist of a series of crises, some of them so prolonged and severe that the very existence of the Scottish settlements was threatened.

The trouble had two causes: religious exactions from England and native uprisings. It might be said that both of these had

their roots in religious differences and that both were in actuality
phases of the wars of religion that were desolating many countries
in Western Europe during the seventeenth century. This was
the very period in which the Rhineland was undergoing the
devastations of the Thirty Years' War, in which Gustavus
Adolphus and his Swedish army were scourging their neighbors,
in which England had her civil war and beheaded her king,
Scotland had her Covenanters, and France revoked the tolerant
Edict of Nantes. The account of the Ulster crises may well
start, therefore, with the first troubles over religion.

In 1633 two men received new appointments: Thomas Wentworth (later Lord Strafford) was made Lord Deputy of Ireland,
and William Laud became Archbishop of Canterbury. Each
man's work was an affliction to the Scots in Ulster.

Wentworth, although he had originally opposed the absolutist
policy of King Charles I, had no sympathy whatever with
Puritans, and when they increased in power and began to oppose
the King, Wentworth became a Royalist. He was an able man,
personally unselfish and honest, and intent upon giving Ireland
stability and prosperity; he was also imperious in his certainty
that his decisions were correct and was determined to punish
anyone, Catholic or Protestant, Irish or English or Scottish alike,
who opposed his policies. It was characteristic of him that, in
order to protect English manufacturers, he prohibited the making
of woolen cloth in Ireland; yet, recognizing the economic distress
this measure caused the people of Ulster, he spent much of his
own money to import flax seed from Holland, to build mills, and
to bring over skilled workmen from the Low Countries. The
linen industry he thus began was to become immensely successful as a source of real prosperity to Ulster.

Since the Anglican Church was now the Established Church
of Ireland as well and since he had no patience with Puritanism,
Wentworth laid down as one major aim of his policy the religious
conformity of all Ireland. Beginning with Ulster, in 1639 he
compelled all Ulster Scots over sixteen years of age to swear
that they would obey the King's royal commands and to declare
their disapproval of the recent Scottish rebellion against the
King's episcopal ordinances. All who refused to take this "Black

Oath," as it was called, were to be punished severely. This Oath resulted in a considerable exodus of Scots whose conscience would not allow them to subscribe to it: they went back to the mother country, where the "rebellion" of the Covenant of 1638 had successfully re-established Presbyterian practice.

Archbishop Laud had one sole purpose: to see to it that High-Church procedures prevailed in all of the King's dominions. To accomplish this purpose any means were permissible. His Liturgy, that "Popish-English-Scottish-Mass-Service-Book," as it was labeled, had already in 1637 precipitated the rebellion that resulted in the Scottish Covenant. Now in Ulster he replaced all Puritan bishops with his own men, requiring them to use their influence to make the Presbyterian ministers conform to the practice of the Church of England. Some of these ministers were deposed and excommunicated; all were required to approve the Thirty-Nine Articles or else to relinquish their charges. Wentworth supported Laud's stipulations. The result was considered to be persecution, and those ministers who would not conform had no recourse but to leave the country. For five years after 1636 most Scottish congregations in Ulster were without their ministers.*

Ulster Scots were as stubborn as any others. Efforts to make them conform to the Established Church brought forth resistance. Lacking their ministers, many Scots held religious meetings at night in secret, with a sermon delivered by one of their number. Those who lived near the seacoast frequently made the trip clear across the North Channel to Scotland in order to have their children baptized and to take communion. As many as five hundred crossed the sea on one occasion to celebrate the Lord's Supper under the exiled minister, Livingston, at Stranraer.[3] Some ministers ostensibly conformed and so retained their parishes, but they made a travesty of the regulations. Bishop Leslie of Raphoe complained that these ministers cut down the liturgy to the lessons and a few collects, and that during the

---

* One group of Ulster Scots, led by four deposed ministers, determined to migrate to America; but a fainthearted captain and a succession of terrible storms at sea forced the ship to turn back to Ireland. This might have become the first Scotch-Irish migration to America. See Blair, *Autobiography*, pp. 107-8.

reading of these the congregation walked about in the church-yard, rushing back into the church only when the sermon began.[4]

Severe as the religious restrictions were, Ulster flourished economically under Wentworth's administration. One of his final acts, however, was to have ominous results. When he learned that King Charles planned to invade Scotland in 1640 to punish those who had rebelled, Wentworth raised an army of nine thousand in Ireland to aid the king—and most of the number were Irish Catholics. Before the army could embark for Scotland, Wentworth was recalled by Charles to England to support him in the great contest that was beginning between himself and Parliament. The Irish Army was disbanded, but it was shortly to reassemble itself for a direr purpose, the extermination of the colonists.

Upon Wentworth's recall, religious liberty was re-established in Ulster by two Lords Justices, one of them a Puritan and supporter of Parliament and the other a realist who considered Laud's policy dangerous. Immediately many of the exiles returned to their farms, and a new wave of migration was beginning until it was suddenly checked by the Rebellion of 1641, when the Irish natives made their mightiest effort to drive out the aliens.

This Irish uprising had many causes. The most obvious one, which had rankled for a whole generation, was that Irish lands had been confiscated and that in the Plantation all of the best lands had gone to the intruders. Each year saw the settlers establishing themselves more firmly; their industry had cleared away many of the woods, drained the marshes, and built roads. The very prosperity of the colony deepened the sense of bitterness. Under the Jesuits the Irish people had become fervently Catholic; to them the Protestants of Ulster were heretics as well as interlopers. Rumor played its part in inciting the rebellion. The Scottish National Covenant of 1638 had pledged itself to root out prelacy and popery in Scotland; it was now reported that a Scottish army was about to descend upon Ireland to destroy Catholicism in that country. Puritans in the English Parliament were said to have boasted that neither a single priest nor a single Catholic would be left in Ireland. The opportune moment for an Irish blow seemed to have arrived: the English king was thoroughly embroiled with his own Parliament, and the Scots had proved by their rebellion in 1638 that revolt could be successful. The nine thousand Irish troops that Wentworth had raised the year before would make the nucleus of a formidable army. Lecky sums up the state of mind of the Irish at this moment: "Behind the people lay the maddening recollections of the wars of Elizabeth, when their parents had been starved by thousands to death, when unresisting peasants, when women, when children had been deliberately massacred, and when no quarter had been given to the prisoners. Before them lay the gloomy and almost certain prospect of banishment from the land which remained to them, of the extirpation of the religion which was fast becoming the passion as well as the consolation of their lives, of the sentence of death against any priest who dared to pray beside their bed of death."[5]

The rebellion began in October, 1641. It had been prepared so cautiously that the settlers were unready to meet it, and in the central parts of Ulster they were immediately driven from their homes and their property was seized. At the beginning the chief object of the rebels seems to have been plunder and the recovery of the land, but soon the war became as vicious and as cruel (on both sides) as other wars of this cruel century. Englishmen were the worst sufferers, not only because the Irish held them responsible for their worst miseries but also because their settlements lay in the regions first attacked. By the time the Scottish farms were reached, defenses had been prepared.

Fighting lasted for eleven years. England itself was too much involved with her own civil war to pay attention to events in Ireland. It is impossible to estimate even the approximate number of deaths resulting from the uprising, for the guesses run from 8,000 to 200,000. The soberest figure seems to be about 15,000, of whom a third lost their lives in the fighting and the rest died of privations.[6] It is probable that about a seventh of the total population of the colonists in Ulster had died.

The Scots were in an anomalous position throughout the insurrection. There was no doubt that they would fight against the Irish, even though these natives had shown themselves less hostile to Scots than to English. But the English themselves were now divided between Royalists and Parliamentarians, and the Scots found themselves unenthusiastic about either party. In Wentworth's time they had sided with the Puritans and had thus become a focus of Royalist hostility; but when the English Parliament ejected Presbyterians from the House of Commons, Ulster Scots turned against Parliament. When Charles I was beheaded (1649), Belfast Presbytery made an indignant protest; and in that same year General Monk, being sent over to command parliamentary forces in Ulster, actually formed a temporary alliance with an Irish rebel chief so that the latter might keep the field against Royalists and Presbyterians. Parliament even proposed in 1650 to remove the most dangerous leaders of the Ulster Scots south to Kilkenny, Tipperary, and Waterford. The project came to nothing, but it was a final cause of disenchantment of the Scots with the parliamentary side in the civil war.

Cromwell himself crossed to Ireland in 1650, and in one dreadful campaign crushed the opposition of Catholic and Presbyterian alike, ending the Irish rebellion and establishing the rule in Ireland of the English Parliament. What Cromwell did deserves to be ranked with the horrors perpetrated by Genghis Khan. His "pacification" of Ireland was so thorough that it left scars on that country which have never been forgotten or forgiven.

According to Sir William Petty, a statistician of that period, out of a population in Ireland of 1,448,000, three-sevenths, or 616,000, had perished by sword, famine, and plague. Of this number he estimates 504,000 to have been Irish. In addition to the dead there were extensive deportations of native Irish to the West Indies. Another 30,000 or 40,000 left the country to enlist in European armies. Petty says that before 1641 about two-thirds of the good land in the country was in possession of the Catholics, while by 1660 more than two-thirds had passed into the hands of Protestants. This was more than a devastation: it was a social revolution of the first order. The tribal organization of Ireland, which had shown vitality for more than a millennium, was now destroyed root and branch, never to return.[7]

At first Cromwell's government pressed hardly on the Ulster

Presbyterians, and many of the settlers were scheduled for transportation. Cromwell relented, however. His orders for transportation were not carried out, although lands seem to have been found for some of the Commonwealth soldiers in the northern counties.[8] To the surprise of the Presbyterians, government allowances were made to their ministers. Under Cromwell's stern rule the North of Ireland seems to have recovered steadily from the terrible blow of the rebellion that had begun in 1641.[9] The Lord Protector tolerated no squabbles between Episcopalians and Presbyterians. Peace had come, by superior force.

Ulster Scots, although they had endured hard times for two decades, had, in fact, suffered much less than either Irish or English, and now under Cromwell their settlements began to flourish once more. Whereas in 1653 only half a dozen Presbyterian ministers remained in Ulster, seven years later there were seventy regularly and permanently settled, having under their charge eighty parishes with a population of close to 100,000 (not, of course, all Scots). There was now no doubt that the Scottish element was predominant in the North. An Irish State Paper in 1660 says that "there are 40,000 Irish and 80,000 Scots in Ulster ready to bear arms, and not above 5,000 English in the whole province besides the army."[10]

Upon the restoration of King Charles II in 1660, there was not, as might have been expected, a reversion to hard times for the Presbyterian Scots. Their economy flourished mightily. A momentary setback for their Church occurred in 1661, when sixty-one of its ministers were ejected from their benefices; yet most of these were able to keep on with their parish duties even though shut out of parish endowments. Charles was too preoccupied with England to pay much attention to Ireland during the first decade of his rule; and for the twelve years after 1670 there was nothing that could be even remotely called persecution. On the contrary, the King showed himself so well disposed toward Ulster Presbyterians that in 1672 he granted their ministers a royal bounty, known as the Regium Donum.[11] Ten years later pulpits were closed again for two years, and as a result most of the ministers in the Presbytery of Laggan were disposed to emigrate to America "because of persecution and general poverty abounding in these parts, and on account of their straits, and no access to their ministry."[12]   But Charles died in 1685, before the emigration took place, and most of the annoying restrictions were removed.

During the years from 1660 to the end of the century the British element in Ulster rapidly increased.   Foremost in numbers were the Scots who came over to escape the "killing times" of the Covenanting troubles.   Whether themselves mostly actual Covenanters or rather those who desired to escape these violent religionists, the fact is that the southwestern counties of Scotland, nearest Ulster, were in disturbance while Ulster had peace and toleration.   The English element also increased, by the coming in of Dissenters.   Many Americans who consider their ancestors to have been Scotch-Irish are actually descendants of English settlers, especially from the counties between London and Wales and from the northern counties of England, who migrated to Ulster and there became members of communities where the Scottish influence was predominant.   When the movement to America began after 1717, many of these English Ulstermen joined their Scottish friends and neighbors in their removal to the New World.

Growing prosperity of Ulster in the latter years of the seventeenth century, its removal from the Cavalier relaxation of rigid morality, its prevailing Protestantism of the stricter Reform, and yet its freedom from control by an exacting State church, all exerted their attraction upon Puritans, Quakers, and other Dissenters.   The movement from the northern counties of England, especially Yorkshire and Durham, was fostered also by the lack of prosperity in the north of England, where in some areas the economic situation was not very different from that of the Lowlands of Scotland.   Ulster became, in these decades of friendly mingling of people of different backgrounds (though all Protestant), a kind of foreshadowing of what would happen to a much greater degree on the American frontier.

Prosperity such as no part of Ireland had ever known was maintained through most of Charles II's reign.   Cromwell had long since relaxed the restrictions on woolen manufactures imposed by Wentworth, and these now grew to such proportions that Irish woolens acquired a good name throughout Europe. The bounties Wentworth had given in the 1630's to encourage the cultivation of flax and the manufacture of linen were beginning to pay large dividends in both manufacture and trade. Economic setbacks occurred at times. In 1663 the English Parliament, with its large representation of country squires, grew so jealous of Ulster's trade that it forbade Irish ships to carry goods to any part of His Majesty's dominions. In 1666 it forbade the importation of Irish cattle into England and thereby ruined the cattle industry, one of the mainstays of Irish economy, though not the principal one in the North. On balance, however, Ulster was increasingly prosperous.

One of the most fortunate occurrences that happened to it came in the closing years of the century. In 1685 France revoked the Edict of Nantes, which for many years had assured religious liberty to the Huguenots. Historians estimate that some half-million of these Protestants left France as a result of the revocation of the Edict, to the benefit of the industry of the countries to which they migrated. Many of them (no figures are anywhere cited) came to Ulster, and since they, too, were Calvinists, for the most part they joined the Presbyterian Church and soon became a part of the Scottish communities. Their thrift and industry were beneficial; but their particular contribution was an improvement of the methods of manufacturing linen, for which the colony was already noted. Ulster's trade thereafter took another forward leap.

The three-year reign of James II (1685-88) and its immediate aftermath brought some of their hardest times to the Scottish colonists. James, an avowed Roman Catholic, appointed his brother-in-law Lord-Lieutenant of Ireland, and an ardent Irish Catholic, Tyrconnel, General of the Forces in the island. Englishmen were turned out of the army, Protestant regiments were disbanded, and Roman Catholic Irishmen took their place. It was openly stated that Tyrconnel's purpose was to drive all English and Scottish colonists out of Ireland, to destroy Protestantism in the country, and to restore the old faith. In alarm, hundreds of families left Ulster.

If James's hatred of Protestantism showed itself in Ulster,

it was even more evident in Scotland. His severe measures in the Lowlands no doubt played their part in stimulating a renewed migration to Ulster during the succeeding and benign reign of William of Orange. During Charles II's struggle to subdue the cantankerous Covenanters, his brother James (later the King) had been viceroy of Scotland and thus had a low opinion of these ardent Presbyterians. Now, as King, he sent as his special agent to subdue them James Graham of Claverhouse. Macaulay,[13] who says that "the administration of James was marked by odious laws, by barbarous punishments, and by judgments to the iniquity of which even that age furnished no parallel," notes that Claverhouse was a soldier of distinguished courage and professional skill, "but rapacious and profane, of violent temper, and of obdurate heart, who has left a name which, wherever the Scottish race is settled on the face of the globe, is mentioned with a peculiar energy of hatred."*

When in November, 1688, news came that William of Orange had landed in England, the mutual hostility between the two religions in Ireland was at its height. Protestants feared another uprising like that of 1641, for news had got about that a general massacre was planned for the night of December 9. The citizens of Londonderry, Enniskillen, and Coleraine, all in the northernmost parts of Ulster, closed their gates to government troops and made preparations for defense.

At this juncture King James, who had fled to France, decided to come to Ireland, join the forces he had brought with him from France with those of Tyrconnel, and try to regain his throne. Tyrconnel thereupon declared the northern Protestants rebels and sent an army to deal with them. Colonists in the line of march of the army pulled down their houses, burnt and destroyed what they could not take with them, and fled to the fortified towns. When James reached Dublin in March, 1689, Tyrconnel assured him that all Ireland was his except for the small corner

---

* It is reported that some of the mothers among the mountaineers of Tennessee and Kentucky, descendants of the Scotch-Irish, still threaten their children by saying, "Behave yourself, or Clavers will get you!" To the mothers, says Bolton (*Scotch-Irish Pioneers*, p. 300), "Clavers is but a bogey"; to their ancestors Graham of Claverhouse "was a very real cause for terror." The same threat of Clavers is reported in Black, *Scotland's Mark on America*, p. 12, and by Morrison, in the *Berea Quarterly* (October, 1908), 9.

in the north, which he felt could not hold out for many days against his army.

James's French army now marched northward to subdue these revolting towns. Londonderry county was truly desolate. One of the French officers said, "This is like travelling through the deserts of Arabia." Another said that in a journey of forty miles "only three miserable cabins" were left standing: "everything else was rock, bog, or moor."[14] The siege of Londonderry began on April 18 and, to the amazement of the attacking army, the town held out for 105 days. The endurance of the people of that city and the ingenuity of the untrained soldiers of Enniskillen, who constantly harassed the attackers, gave the lie to Tyrconnel's confident assertion of his army's power. Londonderry was relieved at the final moment by the arrival of supply ships, and the Enniskillen men gave a resounding defeat to the Catholic forces.*

Shortly after James's repulse in Ulster, William of Orange's army landed with ten thousand seasoned troops in county Down, Ulster. Marching south, he met James's army at the Boyne river. There on June 30 and July 1, 1690, the decisive battle was fought. William was completely victorious, James fled once more to France, and the "Glorious Revolution,"—which the English called "Bloodless," but was far from having been so for the Ulstermen—put William and Mary on the throne of England.†

William granted freedom of worship to the defeated Irish in the Treaty of Limerick (a concession soon and callously violated by England) and permitted Irish soldiers who desired it to go to France.‡

* It may well be that if these cities had not held out, James might have regained his English throne. Once he had eliminated resistance in Ulster, he could then have gone on to the Catholic Highlands of Scotland, which were to give such a romantic welcome to Bonnie Prince Charlie in 1745. With French, Irish, and Highland troops backing him, one can only speculate upon the outcome of his enterprise.

† One notes with some ironic amusement that William's victory at the Battle of the Boyne was received with transports of delight not only in England but in many of the capitals of the Continent, notably by the Pope of Rome and by the ardently Catholic court of Austria. The reason was not that William was a friend of either, nor that he had defeated Catholics, but that he was an enemy of Louis XIV, who had supported James and who was hostile to the Pope's political plans.

‡ About eleven thousand went; they formed the famous Irish Brigade of the French Army. Recruiting for this brigade went on steadily thereafter, and it is

The men of Ulster, despite all their losses, were much heartened by the outcome of the war. William was truly a Protestant prince, and he granted them complete freedom of worship. The era of religious wars was now nearing its end, and it may be said that William's actions marked the triumph of the first of the democratic liberties, freedom of religion. Not only had peace come to Ulster, but such a promise of civil security as it had never known. Once more the region had been decimated of "meer Irish"; their numbers were now too few and their spirits too broken to undertake any further resistance against the intruders. The Irish had to write off as lost to them the northern counties.* Time was required to regain the prosperity Ulster had known in the previous decade, but everything conspired to rebuild this prosperity.

Those Scots who, with many of their ministers, had fled to Scotland at the approach of Tyrconnel's army, now began to return. It was apparently difficult to persuade all of the ministers to venture back after three generations of recurrent hardships; but younger men were found to replace the fainthearted. During the last decade of the seventeenth century Ulster received one final wave of immigration from Scotland, of men attracted by the offer of farms that had been laid waste during the trouble under James II. This newest accession to the population was a valuable one. Archbishop Synge, the Anglican divine, in 1715 estimated that fifty thousand Scots had come over to Ulster in the decade between 1690 and 1700, attracted by the cheapness of farms and by the new opportunities for trade. It was also noted that these latest arrivals were among the most substantial of all the colonists, as far as property was concerned, that Ulster had received from Scotland.[15]

The Presbyterian Church once more went forward. "In 1697 the five presbyteries were increased to seven, and there

---

estimated that during the next fifty years more than 450,000 Irishmen died in the service of France. (Woodburn, *The Ulster Scot,* p. 170)

* Henceforward Ulster was recognized as British and Protestant, and in six of its nine counties was so to remain. Ulster is in the present century considered by the Republic of Eire as *terra irredenta* because it remains part of Britain; but the southern Irish often welcome the fact of its industrial prosperity, and thousands of them go north to improve their standard of living.

were now two sub-synods and one General Synod. A few years later, in 1702, the congregations were rearranged and nine presbyteries were formed. . . . There were now nearly 120 congregations and over 100 ministers."[16]   Since many of the recent arrivals had been Covenanters, the tone of Ulster Presbyterianism, already prevailingly puritan, took on the added strictness and rigidity of that persuasion.

10

Intermarriage with the Irish

WHEN PEOPLE OF DIFFERENT ETHNIC BACKGROUNDS settle down beside each other for any long period of time, the chances are good that intermixture, if not intermarriage, will take place—unless there are prejudices so profound that they overcome the powerful drive of sexual desire and the casual results of propinquity. Before the first sizable emigration of Ulster Scots to America began in 1717, Scots had been living for a century close at hand with the Irish, thousands of whom were subtenants on the same farms. The question therefore arises whether the Scots intermingled with the Irish. Are the Scotch-Irish ancestors both Scots and Irish?

This question has aroused hot debate, with its partisans on each side refusing to give an inch. Those who answer Yes are chiefly polemicists of (southern) Irish descent, resentful of the implication that the Scots so disdained the Irish that they would not consider marriage with them. Those who answer No are mostly Presbyterian panegyrists, who indignantly reject the notion that their ancestors might have consorted with Irish Roman Catholics. The question cannot, unfortunately, be settled by documentary evidence. The only way intermixture could be definitely proved or disproved would be by the examination of marriage records in Ulster between 1610, when the Plantation began, and 1775, when the last great wave of Ulstermen came to America; and such records do not exist. Arguments on both sides therefore rest upon logic, circumstantial evidence, and what stands to reason.

At first glance, the argument for intermixture appears strong. Human nature and the strength of the sexual impulse, combined with a hundred years of close proximity of the two people, would normally result in mingling. Since the first large-scale migration to America did not occur until 1717, the Scots had by then lived for more than a century and for some four generations in Ulster; those who crossed the Atlantic as late as 1775 were often products of six generations or more of Irish life. Can it be conceived, one asks, that during so long a period two neighboring groups of people could keep themselves isolated and separate from each other, when they lived and worked side by side?

When James I had parceled out the escheated lands of the Irish lords, the native Irish had been neither exterminated nor driven off to other parts of Ireland. On the contrary, as has been shown, some of the Irish gentry were given new leases, and in defiance of the agreement thousands of Irish peasants were employed on the farms of the planters. Here was opportunity for daily contact, often of the closest and most intimate sort. There have been few cases in history in which people of the same color, the same language, and a similar occupation and standard of living, have lived side by side for generations without assimilation. America itself is the best evidence of what such proximity and opportunity produce, for most of its immigrant stocks have now lost their national identity.

It cannot be denied that, at the outset, the native Irish resented the intrusion of Scottish (and English) interlopers on their ancestral lands, nor that their resentment exploded in 1641 in bitter insurrection. Yet throughout their history the Irish have shown the ability to absorb foreigners, even when they have come as conquerors. Captive Ireland more than once took captive its captors and turned them into patriots more Irish than the Irish. The most notable instance occurred in the very century of the Plantation, with Oliver Cromwell's men. Cromwell had made a shambles of the island; he and his Puritan soldiers had massacred the inhabitants of Drogheda, desolated the land, killed and deported almost half the population, and left a bitterness in Irish hearts. Yet when the army was disbanded, hundreds of Cromwell's Roundheads settled down in Ireland and married Irish women. Within a short time their children were not Anglo-Irish, but Irish.* By contrast, the Scots had come not as conquerors in arms, but as peaceful farmers. It is at least conceivable that young Scots over the years, as bitter feelings died down, might also have recognized the charm of Irish girls and the practicality of having an Irish wife.

No formal obstacle stood in the way of intermarriage. Until the very year of the Plantation a law had forbidden union between Protestants and Catholics in Ireland—a testimony to English efforts to segregate and subdue the Irish. This ban was lifted in 1610, "to the great joy of all parties," as the historian of Irish Presbyterianism notes.[1] If there was actually "great joy," it must have been because the wish to intermarry existed.

Economic and social distinctions of any importance did not interpose barriers between the union of individuals of each stock. For all the temptation to descendants of the Scotch-Irish to think highly of their ancestors, it is plain from what has been said that Scotland was so poor that its farmers had migrated to Ulster to better their wretched lot. Little is gained by calling the newcomers "the scum of the nation," and the natives "meer Irish," except to indicate that poor people of one country met poor people of another. Scottish methods of farming were almost as primitive as Irish methods; both people had been called barbarians by the English. Property and social distinctions were lacking to both Scots and Irish.

The most persuasive evidence of intermingling is found in the prevalence of North Irish names among the Scotch-Irish of America. On the records of the Scotch-Irish Society one finds O'Neills, MacMahons, O'Donnells, and many other characteristic Irish names. More than this, it is known that many immigrants modified their names after living in America, transforming the Irish into a Scottish form, so that O'Neill became MacNeill, O'Donnell changed to MacDonald, and so on. Often, to give the name an English form, the prefix was altogether dropped, still further obscuring the ancestral origin. Thus Duffie may

---

* As Lecky (*Ireland in the Eighteenth Century*, II, p. 404) remarks, "the conquest of Ireland by the Puritan soldiers of Cromwell was hardly more signal than the conquest of these soldiers by the invincible Catholicism of the Irish women."

once have been O'Duffy or MacDuff, and Daniel may have been O'Daniel or MacDaniel.[2]

Finally, it is argued, if the Scots lived their faith to any degree and their Presbyterian ministers preached the word assiduously, as they did, it is unlikely that no Irish converts would be made— and with the religious barrier removed, what could stand in the way of marriage? It is equally unlikely that cases of love between a Scots youth and an Irish girl never led the latter to take her husband's religion for the sake of a happy marriage. Practicality can also be adduced: some farmer, needing a wife and unable to find one among his own group, might well make a sensible marriage with an Irish woman of worth; likewise, some Irish woman, recognizing realistically that the Scots were in Ulster to stay, that Irish land was permanently alienated, that peace was more important than constant strife, that Scots were, after all, decent fellows, and that Jock himself was an attractive lad, might break with Catholicism and take steps to become part of the Scottish community.

Against all these persuasive arguments are arrayed others to contend that very little intermixture occurred. No one would deny that some illicit unions were formed or that an occasional legal marriage took place. What is emphatically denied is that enough mixture occurred to make any real impression on the Scottish heritage, whether biological or cultural. The two main deterrents, say the proponents of this point of view, would have been religion and pride.

Enough religious antagonism still persists in the world to convince one of the intensity of feeling it can arouse; and the seventeenth century marked the peak of heated religious emotions. This was the period of religious wars, nowhere more bitter than in Scotland. When the Lowlanders first came to Ireland the Reformation was at its zealous climax in the Lowlands. During the century of migration to Ulster the efforts of the four Stuart kings to bend the religious Scots to their ecclesiastical will had only strengthened the stubborn resistance of the Scots and made them more loyal than ever to their Kirk. Martyrs had died in the holy cause, especially in the southwestern Lowlands, nearest to Ulster. This partisan spirit, concentrated upon

religion, was the heritage of the Scots who went to settle among the Catholic Irish, and popery was the almost unforgivable sin.*
Intermarriage with Roman Catholics would be treacherous, sinful, and degrading.

The Irish, on the other hand, were by now quite as ardently Catholic as the Scots were Presbyterian. The Reformation may have swept other countries, but it did not touch the Irish, for the Jesuits had done their work well. They had made ardent Catholics of indifferent ones. Irish patriotism was linked with Catholicism, for the English were not only oppressors but Protestants: they had tried to extinguish both Irish political liberty and the Roman Church. As the Church fought back, it became a symbol of the struggle for Irish freedom, the focus of hostility to all these foreign settlers who had robbed the Irish of their lands, slaughtered Irish folk with ruthless barbarity, and were now treating the survivors like dogs. An Irish martyr was a Catholic martyr, and martyrdom regularly inspires an intenser loyalty.†

On both sides, therefore, the religious difference between Scots and Irish was an unsurmountable barrier. One side, it is contended, could no more have intermingled with the other than Jew with Samaritan or Moslem with Christian.

Pride would also play its part in maintaining the separation. The Scots came to take lands that had always been Irish. Because power was on their side, they felt the superiority of their position and the inferiority of the natives; and because the Irish naturally showed a belligerent resentment, the Scots had to maintain a perpetual guard. Irish people were enemies to be watched, not neighbors to be married; they were all the more dangerous, indeed, because they were always at hand, and in numbers. An instructive parallel suggests itself: there was almost no intermingling between American pioneers and Indians. It is true that race and language may have been crucial barriers

---

* An article in the *Edinburgh Review* as late as 1869 speaks of "the intense hatred of Popery that has always marked the Scottish mind," as if the author, Chalmers, were stating a truism in need of no proof.

† Max Weber (*The Protestant Ethic and the Spirit of Capitalism*, trans. Talcott Parsons [London, 1930], p. 87) remarks that "Catholicism has to the present day looked upon Calvinism as its real opponent."

here; but race is not necessarily a deterrent to miscegenation, as can be seen in Negro-white relationships in the old South. Why, then, were there singularly few cases of American frontiersmen having children by Indian women? For precisely the same reason Scots did not consort with Irish women: Indians hated the whites and kept their women at home; Indian women shared all the prejudices of their culture; the white man's social taboos regarded intermingling with aversion; and (here the argument draws on modern psychology) when one subconsciously realizes that he has wronged another by taking away his birthright, he hates the one he has wronged more intensely than would be possible for any other reason. All of these deterrents, it is said, were at work in Ulster.*

King James, in casting about for a people to make good settlers for his Plantation, ones who would make and keep Ulster Protestant, designedly chose his own countrymen, and among these, the Lowlanders. He knew their pride as Scots, who had fought for six centuries to maintain national independence. He knew the stubbornness of their Presbyterianism—and was to know it even better. He guessed rightly that he could count on their upholding, supporting, and maintaining his Crown against the opposition of Irish Catholics in Ulster.

The pride of the Irish was equally intense. Vainglorious intruders were lording it over Ulster, living on lands that had been Irish from time immemorial, battening on discriminatory laws, while the Irish were contemptuously pushed off into the worst acres of bog land and were hired only as a last resort. Every Catholic Mass, especially if it had to be celebrated in secret, was a reminder of the burning indignity of the Irish position. With a nature already given to passion, the Irish would have made life miserable for any woman who allied herself with the other side or for any man who showed himself so treacherous.

Other evidence substantiates the argument that practically no

---

* John Harrison (*The Scot in Ulster*, p. 30) says that, from his intense study of Irish State Papers of the seventeenth century, "One thing is very evident—that the English and Scots of the time looked on the Irish just as the white settlers regard Kaffirs in Cape Colony. In the official documents they are invariably termed the 'mere Irish.' They were treated as an inferior and subject race, who would do a graceful act if they would only disappear from history."

intermarriage occurred. The Scots usually came over to Ulster with their wives and families, or, if unmarried, had only to travel a short distance back to the old country to find a wife. There was thus no scarcity of women of their own kind to compel a man to take an Irish bride. It has often been pointed out that the presence of English women in the American colonies was a chief reason for the prejudice against intermingling with the Indians, whereas the absence of Spanish and Portuguese women in the colonies to the south was the primary cause for intermixture.

Ministers of their own faith accompanied the Scots, to give the colonists a sense of having their most familiar and most cherished institution with them; and no one could be more zealous than a Scots divine in disapproval of any traffic with the Catholics. Northern Ireland is still, after three centuries, not Irish in the sense of religious, economic, and political assimilation. In some remote villages of Ulster even yet the dialect is Scots. Probably the most convincing point against intermarriage is that wherever the Scotch-Irish settled in America they built their churches in the faith of Scotland. Intermarriage on a large scale inevitably brings assimilation; yet there was no such thing as a Scotch-Irish Catholic church in the colonies.

Lecky, the eminent Irish historian, states most succinctly the consensus of scholarly opinion when he says: "Most of the great evils of Irish politics during the last two centuries have arisen from the fact that its different classes and creeds have never been really blended into one nation, that the repulsion of race or of religion has been stronger than the attraction of a common nationality, and that the full energies and intellect of the country have in consequence seldom or never been enlisted in a common cause."[3]

If one must give his verdict, the weight of evidence seems to be on the side of little intermixture. The Scotch-Irish, as they came to be known in America, were overwhelmingly Scottish in ancestry and Presbyterian in faith. To the extent that occasional intermarriage occurred, the Irish partner seems almost invariably to have been absorbed into the Presbyterian element.*

* For a further discussion of this question, see Appendix I, p. 327, "The name 'Scotch-Irish.'"

11

The Character of the Ulster Scot

FOR AN UNDERSTANDING OF THE SCOTCH-IRISH in America, the important question is whether the Scot in Ulster differed in any clear way from the Lowland Scot at the time of the migration to America. Were the Scotch-Irish true Scots in culture and outlook, in character and temperament, or had the experience in Ulster significantly changed them?

In three important aspects of life the Ulsterman of 1717 was recognizably different from his cousins in Scotland: social distinctions had changed their character; his loyalties were now centered in Ulster rather than in Scotland; and his religion had subtly hardened.

The quiet and unheralded disappearance of feudalism at the inception of the Ulster Plantation had done more than mark the end of an ancient institution. By releasing men from attachment to a particular locality for life it had given individuals a freedom of choice as to where they would live, for whom they would work, whether they must follow the age-old occupation of farming. The growth of the woolen and linen industries offered considerable alternatives to traditional agriculture, while the very prosperity of manufacture and trade provided the inducements to desert tenant farming. There were, quite simply, no traditional families in the new Ulster, and consequently no ties to bind a man to lord, laird, and locality. In any community there might be families from various parts of the Lowlands; this in itself meant that leadership would have to reveal itself by a person's performance, not by his family's accustomed status through the centuries.

The complete disappearance of feudalism can best be perceived by the unchallenged assumption, within the very century of migration from Scotland, of a man's right to leave his farm to become a factor in the woolen and linen industries or to set up a business for himself in a town. Here were, for the Scot, distinctly new economic phenomena: free labor, freedom of movement, the opportunity to achieve a new social status. These are everywhere regarded as the first steps toward the emergence of new order of capitalism. More than this, society in Ulster was not based upon kinship, on the place a man's family had always held in a traditional community. Such links to the conservative past had been broken by crossing to Ireland. Now a man was a free agent. Society consequently began to develop new distinctions based upon property, income, and leadership, all of which are marks of the modern rather than the feudal world. Even the word "laird" disappeared from the Ulsterman's vocabulary, and with it the idea of an ascribed status of social relationships.[1]

It would be too much to suggest that ambition had as yet become a dominant motive of life, as it is in capitalistic society; yet the very transferral from Scotland to Ulster proved that men responded to the economic motive. If, therefore, new opportunities appeared whereby one might gain increased income, a better home, and new comforts in life, these attractions provided an incentive unknown in contemporary Scotland. Many of the people responded. As their wealth increased, they were recognized as substantial citizens. New men became elders in the church and leaders in the community; business enterprise required traveling and the broadening of horizons. Quite simply, many people who in Scotland would have remained tenant farmers, and thus members of the lowest social class, now in Ulster rose in the social scale and were accorded all the more prestige because of the very limited number of men in the highest positions of traditional class society, the lords and gentry. In fact, Ulster made her own gentry, although they might have been thought upstarts by the conventional gentry of England and Scotland at the time.

This social transformation showed itself clearly during the period of migration to America. Thousands of those who went to the New World were so poor that they had to pay for their passage by becoming indentured servants for a period of time; these people were generally those who had remained tenant farmers in Ulster. But numbers of those who left had so risen from the ranks that they were, by any standards, middle class: they could pay their own fare and have enough left over to purchase land in the New World. Because they were known as substantial citizens in their Ulster communities, they normally assumed similar leadership in the farming communities established on the American frontier. Their example and their success induced emulation. The seed of ambition had been well planted on Ulster soil; it was to bear fruit in America.

The second difference that distinguished the Ulsterman of 1717 from the Scot was the shift in loyalty to place. British historians often write of the "Ulster Scot." This designation, while it accurately notes the ancestry of the people, is misleading, for the Ulsterman of Scottish descent was now a person of a new and different nationality. While his experience in northern Ireland and his Presbyterianism led him to make a clear distinction between himself and the native Catholic Irish, nevertheless the home of the Ulstermen was in Ireland, not Scotland. Having lived for generations in Tyrone or one of the other northern counties of Ireland, they knew no other homeland. When they left for America, the Irish countryside lingered in their memory as familiar and dear because of personal associations. It was in Ireland that they had had their troubles and had won their struggles. Here their fathers had made their farms and built their homes, shed blood for the defense of their families, developed their industries; here generations of their people were buried.

Scotland, on the other hand, was a folk memory and little more, since few of the Scotch-Irish immigrants to America had ever seen it. The Scottish tales of their elders were vivid and could arouse the imagination; but the people were Irish—with a difference. The situation was parallel to that of the second and third generations of immigrants to America: these are no longer Polish or Greek or German, but American. In this sense, then, the Ulstermen of Scottish descent were not truly Ulster Scots, but people of a new nationality with its own traditions and culture and points of reference. That many American colonial officials called them Irish did not offend them, unless by that designation they were confused with the Catholic Irish. They were only dimly concerned with contemporary developments in Scotland, unless these impinged upon their common Presbyterian faith.

The difference in nationality was still further marked because of the intermarriage in Ulster of people of Scottish ancestry with those who had come from England. The puritan from Yorkshire or Somerset now living in Derry or Down would find a Presbyterian church more congenial to him than the Anglican church, and so would identify himself with the Scottish element. Children in a home with parents or grandparents from both British countries were unlikely to develop a purely Scottish patriotism. What they knew best and loved was northern Ireland.

A third distinctive characteristic of the Ulstermen who became Scotch-Irish was the quality of their Presbyterianism. While Scotland itself, in the determinative years of the seventeenth century, was developing degrees of religious usage ranging from rigid narrowness to a more genial acceptance of necessary compromise, Ulster Presbyterianism remained almost uniformly puritan and conservative. Some have said that the experience in Ulster not only strengthened the religious conviction of the Presbyterians; it actually made them bigots. Such derogatory terms do little more than emphasize a particular frame of mind, one in which religion is considered highly important, providing criteria by which other aspects of life may be judged. Ulster Presbyterianism tended to resemble more the Covenanting faith of the western Lowlands (from which, indeed, it drew many of its elements) than the less exigent faith of other parts of Scotland.

Church discipline, wherever the Presbyterian Church existed in Ulster, was not for an instant relaxed; if anything, its intensity increased during the seventeenth century. Such minute control of personal life could not have persisted without general approval of the members of the Church. In Massachusetts, where the same control was shown, there are records of individual rebelliousness and protest; no such protest is recorded in Ulster. One is reminded of the control of the Amish and Mennonites over their members. No doubt this surveillance and the people's submission to it contributed to the sense of community in a land where the Presbyterian faith was neither Established nor held by the natives.

The justification of the Church's oversight of personal behavior was clear to all thinking Ulster Calvinists, whether Presbyterian or Puritan. Like Augustine before him, Calvin had made quite clear that Original Sin is the heritage of every man. As the Shorter Catechism put it, in its implacable way, "All mankind, by the Fall, lost communion with God, are under His wrath and curse, and so made liable to all the pains of this life and to hell forever." If a saving remnant is to be freed from this guilt, it is the duty of the Church not only to show men the plan of salvation but also, by admonition, instruction, example, and reproof, to do its best to keep people in the strait and narrow path. Then, too, from a purely worldly aspect, man's brute propensities and his desires of the flesh are dangerous for the whole community. They lead to discord and strife—to the disintegration of that order necessary for social living. If men are to receive the necessary discipline, only two institutions can exert it: the Church and the State. The latter, however, consists of worldlings; it includes many whose convictions are tenuous; it compromises on essentials; and nothing in Scottish tradition had ever favored submission to close control by the State. The Church, therefore, remained as the logical institution to exert the necessary oversight and correction.

So said Calvin and the dominies and the Kirk Session, and the ordinary person did not contest the logic. He submitted, and found for himself the best degree of personal freedom he could manage. Discipline was minute. Each Session made and enforced its own rules. The history of the Presbyterian Church in Ulster is full of the details.[2] One example will suffice. The church at Templepatrick ruled that a person who complained of the behavior of another must accompany his bill with a shilling, which would be forfeited "if he proves not his point" ("This is done to prevent groundless scandal"); a beer-seller who let people get drunk would be censured; parents who allowed their children to "vague or play" on the Sabbath would themselves be held to have profaned the Sabbath; no child might be baptized until the good character of the parents was attested. Public penitence was required of evildoers; for example: "John Cowen shall stand opposite the pulpit, and confess his sins, in the face of the public, of beating his wife on the Lord's Day."

If Presbyterians had not been made already stern and dour by their travails both in the old country and in Ulster, their church discipline would have conduced to the development of such qualities in their character.

Certain aspects of the Presbyterian faith bore fruit on the American scene. These were not distinctive qualities of Ulster Presbyterianism, but of Calvinism wherever it is fervidly held. They are here noted because the Scotch-Irish had thoroughly absorbed the attitudes of mind and brought them to the American colonies, where their practical effect was to be observed in American political life.

Calvinism was strongly opposed to the principle of absolutism in government, and this at the very moment when absolutism was ascendant on the European scene. The century of the colonization of Ulster, the seventeenth, was the great Age of Absolutism, with Louis XIV on the throne of France, the Stuarts ruling England, and Hobbes among others providing the philosophical justification for the powerful monarch. Civil and political distractions of preceding ages might probably have been enough to account for the rise of absolutist principles; but in this religious century it was useful to quote St. Paul's affirmation that "the powers that be are ordained of God" and that the Christian must cheerfully submit to the magistrates.

John Calvin provided an answer to this whole principle by insisting upon the sovereignty of God, before whom all kings are minions. He followed Paul in requiring passive obedience "if we are inhumanly harassed by a cruel prince; if we are rapaciously plundered by an avaricious or luxurious one; or if we are persecuted on account of piety, by an impious and sacrilegious one."[3] But then he made a great exception that practically does away with the rule: "If they [the magistrates] command anything against Him, it ought not to have the least attention; nor in this case, ought we to pay any regard to all that dignity attached to magistrates." Presbyterians in Scotland followed the exception, not the rule, in their resistance to James and Charles, and Ulster Scots relied upon the exception in resisting Wentworth and the Black Oath he tried to require of them.

It cannot be maintained for a moment that what Calvin and his followers were asserting was any principle of freedom of conscience, religious liberty in general, and least of all the rights of the individual as later centuries were to define these. The history of Geneva under Calvin and of Scotland after the Kirk became established shows that toleration was not regarded as a virtue; on the contrary, it betokened slackness. Presbyterians, like a majority of Western Europeans in the seventeenth century, believed firmly in an Established Church; and the principle that prevailed after the Peace of Westphalia (1648)—*cuius regio eius religio:* the church of the ruler becomes the Established Church of a country—seemed a fair compromise to end the wars of religion. Nevertheless, in the outcome, Calvin provided a basis for the coming revolution against absolutism. The new sects arising after the Reformation were fighting for their very existence; their belief that they were following the will of God received logical support from Calvin's (to them self-evident) affirmation that God is King above all kings. Melville followed Calvin in stating what seemed incontrovertible, that King James was God's "vassal."

What the Scots at home had convinced themselves of, and what the Ulster Scots acted on, was the superiority of the Presbyterian Church to any order a king might make that curbed or thwarted it.* This conviction had implications few bothered

---

* The working of the thoughtful Presbyterian mind on the subject of absolutism and freedom can be seen from the record of the examination of a minister, John Dick, by the Commission of Glasgow in 1684.

"Being asked if it was lawful to bear arms, he answered he thought it lawful for the defense of religion,—that is, when people are oppressed for adhering to their principles, pressed to deny them, and killed for not denying them,—and for personal defence against robbers and murderers. He was further asked, 'But what if the king should carry on a course contrary to the Word of God, may he be opposed by arms?' He answered, 'He might, when no other means would prevail.' The bishop . . . said, 'But I'll make it plain to you from the Word of God, that though the king carry on a course contrary to Scripture, he ought not to be

in those trying times to think out: if one Church may revolt justly, so may another for the same reasons—and that way might easily lie anarchy.   The only alternative might well be a compromise that would allow religious liberty to all, with agreement among competing religions to accept a government with no voice in religious matters.   Here is religious freedom, as the Americans were to discover it.   Ulster Presbyterians were a minority under English rule; their demand for liberty of worship, as a minority, must put them in America on the side of those who demand liberty of worship for all denominations.

Still another implication of the action of the Scots in resisting the king was that there is a justification for revolt against authority.   If at the moment that justification lay only in religion, in another age, when another interest was predominant, there could be justification for other kinds of revolution.   Indeed, once the yeast of logic begins to work, the principle of revolution may also be applied to the individual, who can now claim his "rights of conscience" against the Established Church, even when that Church is the Kirk itself.   Almost as soon as the eighteenth century opened, the government of England began to pass legislation that discriminated against the Ulstermen.   They opposed the laws—and made their protest effective by emigrating to America.   This was resistance to the government by peaceable means.   But when the English government passed still further discriminatory laws and the American Revolution began, the Scotch-Irish showed by their fighting that they now subscribed to the principle of armed resistance to a government they considered unjust.*

Experience in Ulster in several ways prepared the character

---

opposed.'   John, interrupting him, said, 'The world will never do that, for it is setting Scripture against itself, and the like of that was never heard.'   Then it was asked if he would kill one of the king's guards if he found them in the way. He answered, he was of no such murdering principles.   They were very close upon him as to his praying for the king; and, after many questions this way, they asked, 'Can you now pray for him?'   He said, 'I can, as he hath a soul, and hath not sinned the unpardonable sin; but to pray for him as he is king, and for the prosperity of his courses, I cannot do.' "   (Wodrow, *History of the Sufferings of the Church of Scotland*, III, 368-69)

* It might be noted that the Reformation itself was a rebellion against the absolutism of the Roman Catholic Church and of the Pope, even though the Reformers established another absolutism in place of these.

of the people for the life they were about to begin on the American frontier. They lived on land in both regions that had often been forcibly taken from the natives. The confiscation itself was declared legal by the authorities, and the actual settlement was made by Scots in the conviction, no doubt, that the land was now rightfully theirs. When the natives, whether Irish or Indian, refused to accept either the legality or the settlement, preferring rather to fight back by whatever means they could devise, the settlers fought equally hard to retain the homes and farms they had made by their own labor. They learned from hard experience that one must fight for what he has; that turning the other cheek does not guarantee property rights; in short, that might makes right, at least in the matter of life and land ownership. The streak of cruelty already noted as a part of Lowland Scots character was, if anything, intensified by the conditions of daily life cheek by jowl with enemies. A man must be hard as well as ingenious to survive and to keep his own in an iron age.

It is worth noting that in all the contemporary accounts of the Ulster Plantation, the troubles with the Irish, and the establishment of the Presbyterian Church in northern Ireland, the life and character of the women are never mentioned. If women are referred to at all, it is only in a census, a requirement for an oath, a casual statement that they were also present. One must conclude, by this negative evidence, that the status of women, whether legal or actual, improved not a whit during the seventeenth century. No property was ever given them in the Plantation; no suits were brought for or against them at law. They were disciplined in the churches; but their life must otherwise have been the traditional one of subordination to men in a patriarchal society, doing the household work and sharing the work in the fields. Neither is there any record of complaint by them against their lot: they had never known any other. There were no schools for them, either in Scotland or Ulster, for they could not become ministers or attend the universities. Their only school was the hard one of being helpmeet and companion to a strong man. The success of Ulster and of the Scotch-Irish settlement in the back-country of America is the silent but eloquent tribute to the hardiness of the Ulster woman.

Once again the character of the people must be seen in the light of their times. Eulogists have attributed to the Scotch-Irish in America a democratic fervor which, according to some authors, the people brought with them to the colonies and which actually produced the democracy of the American Republic. Whatever truth there may be in the ascription of influence on American thought and practice, it cannot be said that the Scots who left Ulster for the New World were democratic. Belief in democracy is the result of several prior commitments: to freedom of thought, to a belief in reason, to individualism, to a stress upon opportunity in politics and economic life, to an ambition to improve one's standard of living, and to the right of people to a voice in their government. If these be conceded as some of the prerequisite convictions for a democratic faith, Ulster Scots by 1700 can be said to have been on their way toward only two of them: individualism and a desire for a better life. They were not yet such individualists that they had begun to demand the right to think for themselves about religion or to rebel against the control of their personal lives by the Church; but they were individualistic enough, and desirous enough of improving themselves, to have left home to seek a better life elsewhere, and to want an education for their sons so that these youths might become leaders.

It has been argued that the Presbyterian Church provides democratic experience by its representative government and its higher church councils, in which ministers and laymen deliberate on terms of equality. There is some truth in this, although American Presbyterians misunderstand Scottish and Ulster practice of the time. Whereas a Presbyterian congregation in the United States elects its representatives to be elders of the local Session and deacons to care for its business affairs, the minister of the Scottish Kirk usually named his elders, and the Session selected the deacons. This gave the congregation its representatives, but it practically assured the minister of control. The Session selected one of its number to accompany the minister to the higher courts of Presbytery (regional) and Synod (a combination of Presbyteries), where each commissioner's vote was equal. This, too, was representative government, but it was government by the spiritual elite. Presbyteries named commissioners to the highest court, the General Assembly.

In the light of contemporary practice, therefore, it cannot be truthfully maintained that the average Ulsterman had had much experience in speaking his mind on important issues in a democratic assembly of his church. On the other hand, it was democratic to encourage any bright youth, no matter what his family background, to go on to the university and become a minister; yet here Presbyterianism was hardly different from Catholicism, for the priesthood was constantly recruited from the "lower orders." It was even more democratic (in contrast with Catholic practice) for a congregation to call its own minister rather than to have him appointed by a bishop. Presbyterian church courts rigorously maintained their right to legislate for church members, with no veto or oversight by the State. It was this freedom from royal domination that had been at issue in King James's determination to give bishops to the Kirk, for otherwise he could have no voice in church policy.

It must be suggested, accordingly, that authentically democratic principles, when the Scotch-Irish exhibited them in America, were rather the result of their experiences on the colonial frontiers than the product of their Scottish and Ulster heritage.

The subtle psychological effects of one's religious beliefs are debatable. Max Weber suggests that the doctrine of predestination created in Calvinists an "inner loneliness," as a component of his sense of duty, his tendency toward asceticism, and his self-reliance. To the extent that a man looks only to his God and his inward conscience for his standards, the point may be valid and may contribute to an understanding of the Scotch-Irish.[4]

Ulster Presbyterians, like Scottish ones, were devoted to education, and as Scotch-Irish they transferred this zeal to their settlements in America. One must not be misled, however, by the word: education among the people of 1717 was not liberal in the modern sense, even when it was most triumphantly classical. The great purpose of learning was still religious—to open the pathway to the ministry and to enable a person to read the

Bible. There was no ideal of going to the university in order to develop a genuinely free and open mind, to have one's life enriched by the best that had been thought and said and created in philosophy, literature, and the fine arts. The great age of science in Europe no more touched Ulster than it affected Scotland. Scotch-Irish people brought with them to America few of the enthusiasms that had made Italy, France, the Low Countries, and England fill the pages of intellectual history with names of great creators in the realm of the mind. Years had yet to pass before any Ulsterman became famous in intellectual and creative fields.

Nevertheless, the pressure to become educated, by their own definition, was constant. Formal teaching was almost entirely in the hands of the ministers, who did a thorough and conscientious job, but who saw to it that the end of all learning was religious instruction. Informal teaching in the homes, however limited, had the Bible and catechisms as textbooks. A remarkable testimony of the general literacy of the people is provided by an address to the Governor of Massachusetts in 1718, in which 319 members of an Ulster community requested permission to settle in the Puritan colony. All but 13 of the 319 had appended their names "in fair and vigorous autograph." The historian who records this fact comments: "Thirteen only, or four per cent of the whole, made their 'mark' upon the parchment. It may well be questioned, whether in any other part of the United Kingdom at that time, . . . in England or Wales, or Scotland or Ireland, so large a proportion as ninety-six per cent of promiscuous householders in the common walks of life could have written their own names."[5]

One quality in which the Scots of the time were adjudged defective was also apparently undeveloped by the Ulstermen: they seemed unmindful of man-made beauty or of any need for it; and, if their silence on the subject is indicative, they took the beauties of nature for granted without mention of them. An Englishman who visited the prevailingly Scotch-Irish village of Pittsburgh on the American frontier in 1784 made a telling remark: he said that the people there lived "in paltry log-houses, and as dirty as in the north of Ireland, or even Scotland."[6] An

English observer in Ulster remarked that if a Presbyterian "builds a cottage, it is a prison in miniature; if he has a lawn, it is only grass; the fence of his grounds is a stone wall, seldom a hedge." He further noted that Presbyterians in those parts have "a sluggish imagination: it may be awakened by the gloomy or terrific, but seldom revels in the beautiful."[7]

Manners varied with social class, improving with the rise from tenant farming; but Ulster had had no association with the Cavaliers of the seventeenth century nor with the urbanity that might emanate from the presence of large and fashionable cities and watering-places. In the humbler walks of life manners were quite as uncouth as they were in contemporary Scotland (and elsewhere). One of the chief complaints of the New Englanders against the Scotch-Irish who settled among them was their almost complete indifference to cleanliness. The account of the personal habits of an industrious Presbyterian community is frank: "Wash-bowl and pitcher were no part of the common set-out of the newly-married pair. In the more progressive families an iron skillet in the kitchen sink opened up a chance for parents and children to wash their hands and faces in the morning, a chance, I take it, that rarely hardened itself into a rule for either. Ablution of the whole body even once a year, or ten years, or a lifetime, was a thing practically unknown for three generations of our ancestral fathers and mothers." Pigpens and barns were in close proximity to houses, so that "the two were scarcely discriminated from each other." In church there was the "stench arising from crowded religious assemblies, often prolonged for hours and hours." To their New England neighbors the Scotch-Irish immigrants seemed "to the last degree uncleanly and unwholesome and disgusting."[8]

A kindly English traveler in Ulster told of stopping one day at a roadside cottage for a meal; he asked for eggs, as safer than the unknown contents of the family stew-pot. The housewife cheerfully roasted two eggs for him in the ashes of her fire, but when he asked whether they were done, "she took a long pin with which she had been picking her teeth and thrusting it into the side of the egg:—'Ah; weel-a-wot, surr,' proceeded she, presenting it to him: 'it's as weel done an egg as ony in Christendom.'" Bread, with butter dexterously spread with her thumb, "after the custom of the people," completed his meal.[9]

The Ulsterman, when he was about to become a Scotch-Irishman, was no longer a Scot in character and temperament. Pride, noteworthy in the Scots, had become intensified by living as a royal colonist in a conquered country among a people held in general contempt. Conflict with the Irish, especially during and after the insurrection of 1641, toughened and hardened a character that had never been soft, with an added iron provided by steady church discipline. Some critics felt that Ulster had developed industrious and frugal habits not yet common to Scotland, but that it had also tended to develop penuriousness.

On the other hand, this man of a new nationality acquired an adaptability the native Scot had no need to learn. To move away from all familiar places and customs to an entirely different country necessarily meant adjusting oneself to new circumstances and surroundings—and this was but the first step in continuous adjustment. Alongside the Ulster colonist lived not only the unfriendly Irish but also the English Puritan, Dissenter, and Anglican, and later the French Huguenot. New influences gave a new spur and direction to his activity, for manufacture, trade, and commerce were open to him while the contemporary Lowlander was still usually only a traditional tenant farmer. Business, like intermarriage with descendants of Englishmen, enlarged the view. Most of all, his freedom to decide where he would live and what occupation he would pursue encouraged both self-reliance and adaptability.

It had initially been a risk to go to northern Ireland; it was a greater risk to go to America. But it was taken by thousands of Ulstermen. What makes the character of the Scotch-Irish interesting is the degree to which their acquired adaptability would show itself in the New World, and the points on which they would not compromise.

PART III: THE SCOTCH-IRISH IN AMERICA

12

The Migration

BETWEEN 1717 AND THE REVOLUTIONARY WAR some quarter of a million Ulstermen came to America.* On several occasions during the preceding century, when life in Ulster had momentarily seemed unendurable, there had been talk of emigration to the American colonies. In 1636, for example, a group of clergymen actually started out with a large number of their parishioners for New England but were turned back by violent storms. Fifty years later, in 1684, members of the Presbytery of Laggan intimated to their fellow Presbyterians that, "because of persecution and general poverty abounding in those parts and on account of their straits and little or no access to their ministry," they intended to remove to America, as some did.[1] Others went in small numbers, so that by the time the Great Migration began in 1717, a few Ulstermen were present in at least half of the American colonies, often alongside immigrants who had recently come directly from Scotland. The reasons for the Great Migration were mainly economic, though in the first years religious considerations played some part.

The hope entertained by King James that the settlement of northern Ireland would prosper materially had, by 1700, been realized. Green asserts: "In its material result the Plantation of Ulster was undoubtedly a brilliant success. Farms and homesteads, churches and mills, rose fast amid the desolate wilds of Tyrone. . . . The foundations of the economic prosperity which has raised Ulster high above the rest of Ireland in wealth and intelligence were undoubtedly laid in the confiscation of 1610."[2]

* For estimates of the number of immigrants from Ulster to America, see the NOTE at the end of this chapter, pp. 179 ff.

It was, paradoxically, the very success of the Plantation that led to events which caused many of the Ulstermen to leave their homes for the New World. The English Parliament began to grow alarmed by the competition of Irish goods with English ones and to impose restrictive measures that caused great distress in Ulster.

The root of the matter was that England could not make up its governmental mind about the status of Ireland. That country was not, like Scotland after 1707, a sister kingdom whose rank was co-ordinate with that of England. Nor was it wholly a colony, in the sense that Virginia and Barbados were colonies, for the monarch termed herself Queen of "Great Britain and Ireland." The Navigation Act of 1660 had placed Irish ships on an equal footing with those of England and the colonies, and it was distinctly provided that enumerated articles could be traded directly between Ireland and the colonies. Thus at the outset Ireland enjoyed the same privileges in colonial trade as did England; and, conversely, Ireland was also subjected to the same restrictions as were English traders. Still further, Ireland had a Parliament of her own.

Yet Ireland's status was hybrid. Its province of Ulster, though an English "plantation," was also a rival whose economic interests were distinct from those of England. The generous provisions of 1660 were gradually withdrawn. The Staple Act of 1663 prohibited the direct exportation from Ireland to the colonies of anything but indentured servants, horses, and provisions; a further act of 1671 limited the importation to Ireland of colonial goods.[3] Such restrictions, though exasperating, did not at the moment seriously affect the welfare of Ireland, since its chief product, foodstuffs, might still be exported.

It was when Ulster developed, in rapid succession, two new industries that the pinch came. Both woolen and linen manufacture grew apace in the closing years of the seventeenth century, bringing remarkable prosperity to northern Ireland and arousing uneasiness among English competitors.

Out of the swamps of the Laggan Valley had arisen the town of Belfast, whose admirable location gave Ulster a sheltered seaport for her growing trade. Sheep flourished in all of the northern counties, and the manufacture of wool was the logical result. The competition of Irish cloth seemed unendurable to English cloth interests. They brought pressure to bear upon Parliament, and in 1698 petitioned the King for protection. At his command the subservient Irish Parliament in Dublin in 1699 passed the Woollens Act, prohibiting the exportation of Irish wool and woolen cloth to any places except England and Wales. This prohibition left the foreign and colonial markets wholly to the English, who could then set their own price. Here was a crippling blow to the most prosperous industry of Ulster.[4]

The setback to economic prosperity in northern Ireland did not immediately prove disastrous because a second industry, linen, was just then developing. This industry had been greatly stimulated by new methods introduced by the Huguenots recently arrived in Ulster. King William III in 1689 had invited a colony of these French expatriates to settle in northern Ireland, partly in gratitude to the Huguenots in Holland who had sent a regiment to help him against James II and who had played a role in the decisive battle of the Boyne. Knowing their industrious habits and their ingenuity, and having the welfare of his whole domain at heart, William sagely induced a number of them to settle at Lisburn (county Antrim), a few miles upstream from Belfast. There they stimulated the cultivation of flax and initiated the large-scale manufacture of linen, which soon became a very profitable enterprise, taking up the slack caused by restrictions on woolen export. They organized the industry on a domestic basis, with piecework distributed widely through the homes of the region, thus giving employment to many women.

The rapidity with which the new industry grew indicates the place the Huguenots made for themselves in Ulster. Their Calvinism made them welcome to Presbyterians and Puritans, and their proverbial thrift and application inspired emulation. Irish linen soon entered the English and foreign markets, somewhat restoring the prosperity of Ulster. Before King William's death in 1702 linen exports amounted to £6,000 annually.[5] Yet for all the progress of the linen industry, the development of Ulster had been seriously set back by the Woollens Act. The tenor of restrictive legislation was to place Ireland in the position of being a foreign power, not a colony, and certainly not an integral part of Britain.

What had happened, however, was that the substantial leaders of Ulster had put their primary economic faith in manufacture and trade—and their success in life now depended upon two unknown and uncontrollable factors: the arbitrary acts of the English Parliament and the ups and downs of the foreign market. Periods of depression inevitably came, and their appearance throughout the eighteenth century can be accurately dated by periodic spurts of emigration to America from Ulster. Arthur Young, after his tour of Ireland from 1776 to 1778, analyzed the effect of economic depression on Ulster, saying: "It is the misfortune of all manufacture worked for a foreign market to be upon an insecure footing; periods of declension will come, and when in consequence of them great numbers of people are out of employment, the best circumstance is their enlisting in the army or navy; and it is the common result; but unfortunately the manufacture of Ireland is not confined, as it ought to be, to towns, but spreads into all cabins of the country. Being half farmers, half manufacturers, they have too much property in cattle, &c., to enlist when idle."[6]

Added to the curtailment, in its lusty infancy, of the woolen trade, and to the periodic depressions that affected the linen industry, a third and more immediate economic cause stimulated the first great migration of 1717. This was the suffering caused by rack-renting. This practice, whose name has a dire ring which subtly suggests conscious cruelty, was simply that of a landlord's raising the rent when a lease on his land had expired. From his point of view, and certainly from that of present-day practice, his act was both understandable and economically sound: the lease had expired, many applicants wished the land, and consequently a wise property owner should make the best possible bargain. Money was scarce in Ireland, even among landlords. One can hardly blame them for wanting as much income as they could get from their estates.

The common term of a lease in Ulster was for thirty-one years —considerably longer than was customary in Scotland. This fact, as noted, had been one of the great attractions drawing Scots to the Plantation. More than that, rents during the closing years of the seventeenth century had been quite moderate, for there was then still plenty of land, and owners were trying to induce more Scots to come over and settle. Because of long leases the tenants had felt stimulated to improve their holdings, extend their cultivation into waste lands, apply new methods, and become thriftier farmers than they had ever been in Scotland. During the second and third decades of the eighteenth century, however, thirty years after the large migrations resulting from Covenanter troubles and from the desire to live in prosperous Ulster, thousands of leases expired. Thereupon the rack-renting began.*

Unexpected results came to landlords from the practice. Farmers, feeling a sense of injury and stubbornly refusing to accept what they regarded as an outrageous departure from just and traditional practice, resisted the rack-rent. The highest bidder for the new lease was therefore often a native Irishman. The intransigent and dispossessed farmer had an alternative of leaving the country, to go either to Scotland or—especially after the first contingent of 1717 had shown the way—to cross to America. The native Irish, on the other hand, had no desire to leave their own country, and saw in the present situation an opportunity once more to hold Irish land. Combining with six or seven of his countrymen, an Irish tenant would offer the highest bid and so receive the tenancy. Shortly thereafter, while the unsuccessful Protestant bidder might be clearing frontier lands in Pennsylvania, his Irish successors were now ready to abandon the lands they had obtained at an impossible rental. Never over a third, and often not over a fifth, of the profit went to the tiller of the soil, and the slightest misfortune reduced the profit to the laborer below the point of subsistence.[7]

It has been stated that "almost every civil war, rebellion,

* Landlords could generally count upon securing a higher rent, if not from tenant farmers, then from men willing to run a cattle farm. The government had recently abolished the old "tithe of agistment," a special tax on every animal raised. This abolition in large degree undid the harmful effect of the Woollens Act, making sheep-raising profitable; it rendered pasturage so much more lucrative than ordinary tillage that many landlords throughout the North of Ireland began to consolidate their farms and expel their tenantry at the expiration of leases.

insurrection, and disturbance in Ireland, from the time of the Tudors downwards, arose more or less directly from questions connected with the possession of lands."[8]   The land question assuredly played a large part in driving Presbyterian Ulstermen to take the drastic step of removing to America.   Archbishop William King, a churchman who loved Ireland, writing in 1719 just after the first wave of Scotch-Irish emigrants had left for America, was convinced that the land question was the real cause of the exodus.   He wrote:

Some would insinuate that this is in some measure due to the uneasiness dissenters have in the matter of religion, but this is plainly a mistake; for dissenters were never more easy as to that matter than they have been since the Revolution [of 1688-89] & are at present: & yet they never thought of leaving the kingdom, till oppressed by excessive [rents?] & other temporal hardships: nor do only dissenters leave us, but proportionately of all sorts, except Papists. The truth of the case is this: after the Revolution, most of the kingdom was waste, & abundance of the people destroyed by the war: the landlords therefore were glad to get tenants at any rate, & set their lands at very easy rents; they invited abundance of people to come over here, especially from Scotland, & they have lived here very happily ever since; but now their leases are expired, & they obliged not only to give what was paid before the Revolution, but in most places double & in many places treble, so that it is impossible for people to live or subsist on their farms.[9]

Jonathan Swift, writing in 1720, considered landlords as tyrants who, by "screwing and racking" their tenants, had reduced them to a worse condition than peasants in France or vassals in Poland.   Property owners, he said, were pressed by debts incurred often in London or on the Continent.   They felt forced to exact the last penny from their tenants, and too often turned a thrifty Scotch Protestant farmer from the land he had, by incessant toil, brought into good condition so that the land might go to two or more Catholic families who could only live together in poverty.[10]

Although Swift showed understanding for the reasons motivating the rack-renters, few contemporaries and few later historians expressed sympathy for their position.   Their treatment of tenants was called arbitrary and was regarded as evidence of their cupidity. What made matters worse, to contemporary opinion, was that landlords lived abroad, rarely even visiting their estates. Absentee landlordism was insult added to the injury of rack-renting. To men of the time, unused to impersonality in business affairs, a landowner had a moral obligation to know his tenants and deal personally with them. Merely to turn over his affairs to an agent offended human dignity; and the agent, whose tenure depended upon keeping his employer in funds, had perforce to tighten the screw of the rack upon the tenants.

Rack-renting had dire results. Whole villages lost their Protestant element by migration to America. Presbyterian farmers who remained in Ulster now had the lurking fear, amounting almost to a certainty, that they too would lose their lands when leases expired. Within a single generation the mood of Protestant Ulstermen had changed from optimism to gloom.

Impartial observers commented upon what had happened within a century. In 1610 Ulster had been a wretched wilderness. Thereafter it had been transformed by the coming of frugal, industrious farmers from Scotland and England. Lands were cleared, production was increased, methods were improved. Mud hovels and wattled huts were replaced by substantial, if rarely handsome, houses. Thrift was regarded as a virtue. It had been the industry of the farmers that had brought prosperity to Ulster and increased the value of the land by their careful cultivation. It seemed unjust, merely because leases had expired, that they should be rewarded by having their rents doubled. In the minds of most contemporaries a landlord should have some sense of *noblesse oblige*; people had not yet acquired the modern, detached idea that an individual should consider only what would materially benefit himself.

Here, then, lay the offense of the rack-renters. As it was said, the landlords, "unwilling to share the benefits with the farmers, and only to raise their rents in a moderate degree, . . . extracted from them all they possibly could, irrespective of their improvements and what the tenants had done to make the property valuable."[11] Instead of making an effort to reach an arrangement which would have been just to both parties and instead of considering the welfare of the whole community, the landlords, as soon as leases expired, invited proposals for new leases on their lands.   That the invitation brought bidders from outside the local community left a rankling sense of injustice to men who were still accustomed to a sense of personal relationship in economic matters.   It seemed to them unfair that another person, especially an outsider and an Irishman, should bid for the possession of their own improvements.

It is possible that even this accumulation of economic disabilities and woes might not have resulted in the exodus that began in 1717.   The final blow was a succession of calamitous years for farmers.   During the 'teens, there were six years in succession that were notable for insufficient rainfall (1714-19). So continuous a drought ruined crops, discouraged farmers, and so curtailed the supply of flax that weavers of linen cloth were desperate.   The cost of food for townspeople soared.*   In 1716 sheep were stricken with a destructive disease known as rot. Severe frosts over northern Europe during the same decade crippled the supply of food.   During the spring and summer of 1718 "a slow confluent smallpox" raged over Ulster in a malignant form, while the next three years brought fevers in the winter months.[12]

The "stick behind" was well plied, therefore, by economic circumstances; but to these were added, at the very same time, religious disabilities.

In the second year of the reign of Queen Anne (1703) an Act was passed requiring all office holders in Ireland to take the sacrament according to the prescriptions of the Established Church.   The weight of this requirement in Ulster fell most heavily upon the substantial members of the Presbyterian Church, who in the normal course of events would be candidates for magistracies and other civil posts in the region.

* Failure of the potato crop was not a cause of the Scotch-Irish migration, as it was of the Catholic Irish migrations of 1845-47. The "Irish" potato has a curious history. It was indigenous to South America and was introduced to Europe only in the sixteenth century. It soon became a staple, especially for the Irish. According to tradition, little or nothing was known of it in New England when the Scotch-Irish introduced it there in 1718. The people of Worcester, it is said, feared it was poisonous. See Green, *Scotch-Irish in America*, p. 6; Parker, *History of Londonderry*, p. 49; William Lincoln, *History of Worcester, Massachusetts* (Worcester, 1837), p. 49.

This "Test Act" has been called persecution, and so it seems to those accustomed to the religious freedom of the twentieth century. For the period, however, it was nothing unusual. Most statesmen of Europe at the time agreed that the best interests of the State were served by having all people worship in the same way and that this way should be that of the Church established by the government. In Queen Elizabeth's day all persons had been commanded to attend church on Sundays and holy days; in these services the Book of Common Prayer was required. Religious wars on the Continent in the seventeenth century had been resolved on the workable principle that the people of any state were required to take on the religion of their monarch (*cuius regio eius religio*). Scotland at her Reformation had established a State Church. The nonconforming Parliament in England in the 1640's had tried to impose Puritanism on the nation. It was the aim of Presbyterians in Ireland to ask, as soon as they were sure of their strength, that the army should be under Presbyterian influence only. The same strong spirit of uniformity prevailed in puritan New England.

Although Ulster Scots had suffered religious restrictions, especially in the days of Charles II and James II, they had made their adjustments to these, and their Church was now flourishing. Many bishops of the Established (Episcopal) Church in Ireland had shown themselves especially tolerant. In Queen Anne's time (1702-14), however, the High-Church party was dominant, and its bishops were determined to bring about complete conformity. They made use of an Act that had been aimed primarily at the Catholics of Ireland, but which by strengthening could be turned against Presbyterians. The impression was given in discussions before the Irish Parliament (no member of which might be a Catholic) that the new measure was aimed only at Catholics; and on this supposition some of the lay members of Parliament objected, on the ground that the Roman Church had already been checked.* But the majority of the members

---

* Thus John Mitchel: "I might indeed suppose that Popery had been already sufficiently discouraged, seeing that the Bishops and regular clergy had been banished; that Catholics were excluded by law from all honorable or lucrative employments; carefully disarmed, and plundered of almost every acre of their ancient inheritances." (McCarthy, *The Reign of Queen Anne*, II, 170)

yielded to the argument that a good deal more yet remained to be done for the discouragement and eradication of popery, and so the Test Act was passed. It was then used unscrupulously as a weapon to place Presbyterians on the same level of disability with the Roman Catholics.

Presbyterian ministers were almost everywhere turned out of their pulpits or threatened with legal proceedings. Since ministers no longer had official standing, the legality of marriages they performed was now denied. Because the sacramental test was made a condition of holding any office, civil or military, above the rank of constable, reputable Presbyterians had to make a choice between their consciences and their offices. Those who remained true to conscience were at once cut off from the army, the militia, the civil service, the commission of the peace, and from seats in municipal corporations. In some parts of Ulster the people were not permitted to bury their dead unless an Episcopalian officiated at the funeral and read the burial service of his Church. In other places they were compelled to hold the office of churchwarden and take certain official oaths foreign to their consciences. Children could no longer be taught by tutors of the Presbyterian faith, for all dissenters were debarred from teaching school.[13]

The results of these Tory and High-Church measures were not only a blow to the esteem of weighty citizens of Ulster and to Presbyterianism. Local government also suffered. At Belfast the entire Corporation was swept out; ten of the twelve aldermen of Londonderry were ejected. In their place were put men who were inexperienced, youths, and persons of little repute, whose chief recommendation was that they went to church. What rankled most was that the Act, in its practical administration, favored Roman Catholics. In the eyes of High Churchmen, Catholic priests were lawfully ordained, whereas dissenting ministers were mere "sanctified upstarts," not in the line of apostolic succession. It was announced that children of all Protestants not married by rites of the Established Church should be regarded as bastards; and "many persons of undoubted reputation, were prosecuted in the bishops' courts as fornicators for cohabiting with their own wives."[14]

This Test Act was more than unjust; it was demeaning, and it was stupid. In the truest sense of the word, the Ulster Presbyterians had always been loyal. They had maintained the authority of the king, had not supported the Parliamentary side in the civil wars, had protested the beheading of Charles I. They had defended their province against the last effort of the native Irish to recover their lands; and they had helped make the Ulster Plantation not only a success but a prosperous part of the realm. The wise policy of William III was now overturned because of the persistent narrowness of a clique in Queen Anne's government. To alienate substantial citizens in a valuable province, for no better reason than to please a group of prelates, was silly.*

The Presbyterian Synod at first determined to stand by the defendants who resisted the Act, but they were soon dissuaded— and by financial arguments. The Regium Donum, that annual grant from the government which Charles II had bestowed upon nonconformist clergymen in Ulster in recognition of Protestant loyalty, was suspended. Presbyterian businessmen, fearful of a revival of animosities in Ulster if too great an issue were made of the Act, threatened to withhold their contributions to the Church. It seemed wise, therefore, to make the necessary submission and hope for lenient administration of the Act, despite its indignities.

When the Whigs returned to power in 1709 they immediately endeavored to repeal the Act. With the bishops practically unanimous against repeal, however, it was not possible to carry the measure of repeal through Parliament. The only mitigation that resulted immediately was the sending of an archbishop to

---

* James Anthony Froude, who had, before devoting himself to history, been educated for priesthood in the Church of England, castigates the Test Act. He calls the action of Ulstermen between 1685 and 1690 heroic, and remarks, ironically, that this "was an insufficient offset against the sin of non-conformity." "When the native race made their last effort under James II. to recover their lands, the Calvinists of Derry won immortal honor for themselves, and flung over the wretched annals of their adopted country a solitary gleam of true glory. Even this passed for nothing. They were still dissenters, still unconscious that they owed obedience to the hybrid successors of St. Patrick, the prelates of the Establishment; and no sooner was peace re-established than spleen and bigotry were again at their old work." (Froude, *The English in Ireland*, I, 129, 130)

Ireland who would modify some of the excesses of the first years of the Act. Gradually thereafter other modifications were made.*

One effect of the Test Act was to silence the dissuading voice of the ministers when, in 1716 and 1717, talk grew more frequent and serious about removing to America. Indeed, no element of the Presbyterian community in Ulster could argue against the move, for all classes had suffered. The first migration, then, was touched off by a combination of drought, rack-renting, diminished trade in woolen goods, depression, and now religious discrimination and "persecution." The exodus was not a mere vagary of emotional people; on the contrary, among the first emigrants were ministers, ready to lead their congregations to the New World.

The pull of America had in recent decades become increasingly powerful. English colonists by 1717 had lived in the New World for a century. Some of their colonies were flourishing, many were optimistic. Reports of opportunities for enterprising settlers were circulating widely in the Old World: Penn had advertised the attractions of his colony by personal journeys to Europe, and agents of other colonies were abroad. Presbyterian ministers had gone to America as long ago as 1683, and there were Scots and even a few Ulstermen in New Jersey, Delaware, Maryland, Virginia, and South Carolina. To go to America would not be to go to a howling wilderness.

When the fourth successive year of drought ruined the crops in 1717, serious preparations began to be made for a migration. Ships were chartered, consultations were held, groups were organized, and property was sold. More than five thousand Ulstermen that year made the journey to the American colonies.

Reports coming back to Ulster from these first emigrants were highly favorable, especially those that came from Penn's colony. Land was cheap, authorities well disposed, the country vast, its soil fertile beyond all expectation. More than this, the

---

* The first formal act of modification was the declaration (11 George II, chapter 10) of the government that Presbyterian marriages were legal. In 1755 dissenters were again permitted to hold commissions in the militia. From the beginning of George II's reign in 1727, the highest authorities in the Established Church of Ireland and in the State were generally favorable to Presbyterians. The Test Act itself was finally repealed in 1782.

colonies wanted men. There were but two real drawbacks—the perils of an ocean crossing and the expense of that passage. The former was very real, and no one minimized the fearfulness of being at sea in a small vessel, overcrowded, subject to epidemic (smallpox particularly), on a journey that might require three months; but chances for survival of the passage were high, and the hardy could soon shake off the memory of a nightmare. As for passage money, the practice of indenture had long been a familiar device, and few who had made up their minds to go would be deterred by the prospect of having to work at first for a master in America until the term of indenture was up. On the contrary, this period might prove a valuable apprenticeship, giving the newcomer an opportunity to learn American ways, ascertain where lay the best lands, and accumulate a supply of necessary implements and animals when he was free to farm for himself.°

Once the way to America had been shown by the pioneers of 1717-18, going to America became easier for later emigrants. At times the zeal for migration became almost a mania, in the unaccountable manner of fads. The movement resembled an undulant fever, reaching its climax in those years when economic conditions pressed hardest in Ulster. There were five great waves of emigration, with a lesser flow in intervening years. An analysis of the tides of 1717-18, 1725-29, 1740-41, 1754-55, and 1771-75 provides, in effect, a chart of the economic health of northern Ireland.

1717-18. This first movement, so significant as a path-opener, had as its immediate cause the years of drought; but it was the opinion of Archbishop King and Dean Swift that not even the dire effects of bad crops and high prices would have been enough to make the people move if they had not had the added goad of rack-renting, still such a novel practice that it caused intense resentment. In a letter of 1718 to the Archbishop of Canterbury, King summed up the causes and tried to persuade his colleague to use his influence to arouse the English conscience to a realization of the effects of what was happening. He charged: "I find likewise that your Parliament is destroying the little Trade that

° For a fuller account of indentured servants, see below, pp. 174-79.

is left us. These & other Discouragements are driving away the few Protestants that are amongst us. . . . No Papists stir except young men that go abroad to be trained to arms, with intention to return with the Pretender. The Papists being already five or six to one, & a breeding People, you may imagine in what conditions we are like to be."[15]

In addition to the 5,000 or so who went in 1717, there is no means of knowing how many other Ulstermen left in this first wave. King, always observant, said in 1718 that "last year some Thousands of Families are gone." Jonathan Dickinson reported from Philadelphia in 1717 that there had arrived "from ye north of Ireland many hundreds in about four months," and that during the summer "we have had 12 or 13 sayle of ships from the North of Ireland with a swarm of people." To New England ports between 1714 and 1720 came 55 ships from Ireland, one with 200 passengers from Londonderry, another with 150 passengers, "some with smallpox."[16] Whatever the total number, their experience conquered the doubts of many skeptics in Ulster, making it easier for later dissidents to follow them.

1725-29. The second wave was so large that not merely the friends of Ireland but even the English Parliament became concerned. Parliament appointed a commission to investigate the causes of the departures, for they had reached proportions that portended a loss of the entire Protestant element in Ulster.[17]

Letters from immigrants themselves spoke of rack-rents as a determining cause of this second wave; but the *Pennsylvania Gazette* mentioned these as only one of the "unhappy Circumstances of the Common People of Ireland" that had resulted in so great an exodus. An article in that journal (November 20, 1729) reported "that Poverty, Wretchedness, Misery and Want are become almost universal among them; that . . . there is not Corn enough rais'd for their Subsistence one Year with another; and at the same Time the Trade and Manufactures of the Nation being cramp'd and discourag'd, the labouring People have little to do, and consequently are not able to purchase Bread at its present dear Rate; That the Taxes are nevertheless exceeding heavy, and Money very scarce; and add to all this, that their griping, avaricious Landlords exercise over them the most merciless Racking Tyranny and Oppression. Hence it is that such Swarms of them are driven over into America."

Swarms there were, so great that Secretary Logan of the Pennsylvania province wrote: "It looks as if Ireland is to send all its inhabitants hither, for last week (in 1729) not less than six ships arrived, and every day, two or three arrive also. The common fear is that if they thus continue to come they will make themselves proprietors of the Province. It is strange that they thus crowd where they are not wanted. . . . The Indians themselves are alarmed at the swarms of strangers, and we are afraid of a breach between them—for the Irish are very rough to them."[18]

Contemporary evidence of conditions in Ulster at the time makes vivid the underlying reasons for the migration of 1725-29.* Archbishop Boulter wrote in three letters in 1728:[19]

(March 13) "The scarcity and dearness of provision still increases in the North. Many have eaten the oats they should have sowed their lands with. . . . The humor of going to America still continues, and the scarcity of provisions certainly makes many quit us. There are now seven ships at Belfast, that are carrying off about 1,000 passengers thither; and if we knew how to stop them, as most of them can neither get victuals nor work, it would be cruel to do it."

(July 16) "We have hundreds of families (all Protestants) removing out of the North to America; and the least obstruction in the linen manufacture, by which the North subsists, must occasion the greater number following; and the want of silver increasing, will prove a terrible blow to that manufacture, as there will not be money to pay the poor for their small parcels of yarn."

(November 23) "We have had three bad harvests together. . . . Above 4,200 men, women and children have been shipped off from home . . . above 3,100 this last summer. . . . The humour has spread like a contagious distemper, and the people will hardly hear anybody that tries to cure them of their madness.

---

* Jonathan Swift wrote in his *Irish Tracts* of this time: "Whoever travels through this country . . . would hardly think himself in a land where either law, religion, or common humanity was professed," with the old and sick "every day dying and rotting by cold and famine and filth and vermin."

The worst is, that it affects only Protestants, and reigns chiefly in the North, which is the seat of our linen manufacture."

1740-41. The second wave had so well established the Scotch-Irish in the southeastern tier of counties in Pennsylvania that their influence even in political affairs in the Quaker commonwealth was becoming impressive. Famine struck Ireland in 1740 and was certainly the principal occasion for the third large wave, which included numbers of substantial Ulstermen. An estimated 400,000 persons died in Ireland during 1740-41; for the next decade there was a tremendous exodus to America.[20]

This third wave marked, on the American side, the first movement of Scotch-Irish in any numbers beyond the confines of generous Pennsylvania to the southwest. Following the path through the Great Valley, many Ulstermen now went into the rich Shenandoah Valley of Virginia, whose southern extremity opened out toward North and South Carolina. Arthur Young, writing in 1779, estimated that between 1728 and 1750 Ulster lost a quarter of her trading cash and probably a quarter of her population that had been engaged in manufacture.[21] His comment, if accurate, suggests the caliber of men now leaving the country.

1754-55. The fourth exodus had two major causes: effective propaganda from America and calamitous drought in Ulster. A succession of governors of North Carolina had made a special effort to attract to that province colonists from Ulster and from Scotland. That two of these officials were themselves Ulstermen lent persuasiveness to their invitation and appeal. As drought ravaged the countryside, testimony of Scotch-Irish success in America struck a particularly responsive chord in hearts back home. Governor Dobbs of North Carolina, whose colony immigrants had now begun to reach by way of the Valley of Virginia, declared that as many as ten thousand immigrants had landed in Philadelphia in a single season, so that many were "obliged to remove to the southward for want of lands to take up" in Pennsylvania.[22]

At this moment, however, the Scotch-Irish pioneers had their first taste of real trouble with the Indians. The French and Indian wars broke out in the colonies and were to last for more than seven years. For the time being, these violent disturbances effectively dried up the source of new immigration. More than this, Ulster was just now undergoing a true economic recovery. Her prosperity was so pronounced that the vacuum left by emigrants began to be filled by arrivals of people from the south of Ireland and from Scotland. Her population began to increase apace; indeed, it was the pressure of numbers, combined with a new economic depression, that caused the final large wave of migration.

1771-75. Young, writing in 1779, when the outbreak of the American Revolutionary War had eliminated the possibility of further emigration, said that the people of Ulster had by 1770 become very poor, living chiefly "on potatoes and milk and oat bread," and that their little farms had been divided and sub-divided until "the portions are so small they cannot live on them." More than this, the shipowners at the ports of Belfast and Derry were in distress because their "passage trade, as it was called," which had long been a regular branch of commerce, was now cut off.[23]

There was, however, a special reason for the departure of this final wave. In 1771, when the leases on the large estate of the Marquis of Donegal in county Antrim expired, the rents were so greatly advanced that scores of tenants could not comply with the demands and so were evicted from farms their families had long occupied. This aroused a spirit of resentment so intense that an immediate and extensive emigration was the consequence. During the next three years nearly a hundred vessels sailed from the ports in the North of Ireland, "carrying as many as 25,000 passengers, all Presbyterian."[24] Froude gives an even larger figure: "In the two years which followed the Antrim evictions, thirty thousand Protestants left Ulster. . . . Ships could not be found to carry the crowds who were eager to go."[25]

One scholar asserts, though without evidence, and probably erroneously, that this final removal consisted chiefly of substantial emigrants. Noting that 17,350 Ulstermen migrated to America in 1771-72, he says that "almost all of them emigrated at their own charge; a great majority of them were persons employed in the linen manufacture, or farmers possessed of some property which they converted into money and carried with them. Within the first fortnight of August, 1773, there arrived at Philadelphia 3,500 emigrants from Ireland."[26]

The inclination to migration came not only from conditions in Ulster; there was also the constant stimulus of widespread propaganda—broadsides, letters from the colonies, pamphlets—especially on the part of shipowners, emigration agents, and well-to-do people in America who wanted indentured servants or settlers on their properties. Shipowners did not wait for passengers to appear, but sent scouts through the towns and villages to paint a glowing picture of America and to encourage the hesitant. Emigration agents were much more methodical. In certain cases very extensive tracts of American land had been granted to a single individual: for example, William Beverley received from Virginia 118,481 acres and Benjamin Borden more than 500,000 (in the 1730's). It had been stipulated that the recipient fill his land with a specified number of settlers before his patent was made final; accordingly he either went himself or engaged others to go for him to canvass the countryside of Ulster, trying to secure the best possible colonists for his tract.

Agents for procuring indentured servants were great promoters of colonization among the poorer people. Thousands of the Scotch-Irish began their New World careers as servants. In 1728 it was estimated that "above 3,200" persons had come from Ulster to America in the previous three years, and "that only one in ten could pay his own passage." A contemporary Irish writer calculated that from 3,000 to 6,000 emigrated annually from 1725 to 1768; naval records reveal that 5,835 "Irish servants" landed at Annapolis in the thirty years after 1745.[27]

The best advertisement for the colonies, however, was clearly the success of the pioneers. Messages they sent back home inevitably had the effect of removing the last psychological barrier from the minds of many already inclined to leave. Going to America came to mean, by the middle of the century, not launching out into a vast unknown, but moving to a country where one's friends and relatives had a home. It meant more: it offered the very exciting chance to own one's own land instead of holding it on a lease that might end in rack-renting; it meant a heady freedom from religious and political restrictions; it even promised affluence and social prominence to those who were truly ambitious. Every group who went made it easier for others to follow. And so by 1775 probably 200,000 Ulstermen had migrated.

Throughout the fifty-eight years of the Great Migration, religious liberty had been a motive only at the beginning. It is nevertheless significant, both for Ireland and America, that those who left Ulster were almost all Presbyterians. Members of the Established Church rarely went, nor did Roman Catholic Irishmen. Young wrote: "The spirit of emigrating in Ireland appeared to be confined to two circumstances, the Presbyterian religion and the linen manufacture. The Catholics never went; they seem not only tied to the country, but almost to the parish in which their ancestors lived."[28] He thus repeats in 1779 what Archbishop King had noted in 1718, during the first wave.

The English historian Froude says that the migration from Ulster "robbed Ireland of the bravest defenders of the English interests, and peopled the American seaboard with fresh flights of Puritans."[29] In his rather exaggerated estimate, it was the shortsighted policy of England and the cupidity of the landlords that damaged Ulster and gave added power to the Revolutionary cause in America, thus ultimately losing England her colonies. He says:

Twenty thousand left Ulster on the destruction of the woolen trade. Many more were driven away by the first passing of the Test Act. . . . Men of spirit and energy refused to remain in a country where they were held unfit to receive the rights of citizens; and thenceforward, until the spell of tyranny was broken in 1782, annual shiploads of families poured themselves out from Belfast and Londonderry. . . . Religious bigotry, commercial jealousy, and modern landlordism had combined to do their worst against the Ulster settlement. . . . Vexed with suits in ecclesiastical courts, forbidden to educate their children in their own faith, treated as dangerous in a state which but for them would have had no existence, and associated with Papists in an Act of Parliament which deprived them of their civil rights, the most earnest of them at length abandoned the unthankful service. They saw at last that the liberties for which their fathers had fought were not to be theirs in Ireland. . . . During the first half of the eighteenth century, Down, Antrim, Armagh, and Derry were emptied of their Protestant families, who were of more value to Ireland than California gold mines.

In the early years of the migration many of the more substantial citizens of Ulster resented the work of ship captains and agents who tried to persuade the poorer people to leave for America. They felt sure that most stories of great plenty in the colonies were delusions and that offers of "great estates to be had for going for" were simply falsehoods. To them it seemed little short of degrading that a person would sell himself as an indentured servant in order to pay his passage. As Archbishop Boulter put it, referring to those who had left in 1728, "Of these, possibly one in ten may be a man of substance, and may do well abroad; but the case of the rest is deplorable. The rest either hire themselves to those of substance for passage, or contract with the masters of ships for four years' servitude when they come thither; or if they make a shift to pay for their passage, will be under the necessity of selling themselves for servants when they come there."[30] The archbishop decidedly underestimated the opportunities for a person with nothing but his healthy body and his optimism. Experience in the New World was to refute his gloomy estimate.

He was almost certainly correct, however, in his surmise that few could pay for their passage. The practice of indenturing oneself as a servant was common throughout the period of colonization in America. Abbot E. Smith, an authority on the subject, estimates that "not less than a half, nor more than two-thirds, of all white immigrants to the colonies were indentured servants or redemptioners or convicts," and that, beginning in 1728, "by far the greatest number of servants and redemptioners" came from Ireland.[31] It would seem, therefore, that more than one hundred thousand Scotch-Irish came to America as indentured servants.

To the modern ear, selling oneself implies disgrace, as if one were enslaved for a period of years; yet the practice of indentures supplied the American colonies with many of their best settlers.[32] In a sense, the contract of indenture was no different from the long-established practice of apprenticeship, at least in the restrictions it placed on the servant. It carried no stigma of slavery. Although a member of the gentry would have considered himself demeaned to acknowledge his impecunious state by signing articles of indenture, the lower orders, from whom the bulk of America immigration was drawn, considered it both practical and respectable.

The procedure was simple. A person, by agreeing to have his services sold in the New World for a period of time to some master, would be conveyed across the ocean at no cost to himself. When the ship arrived at the American port, a sale was announced, and those colonists who wanted servants looked over the newcomers and bid for them. The term was generally four years, although sometimes it went to seven. A young person, even after four years as a servant, would still be in the prime of life and ready for pioneering. Contracts were carefully supervised by colonial officials, under regulations laid down by the assemblies. In addition to his food, clothing, and shelter for the period of indenture, the servant generally was to receive a specified set of tools, a sum of money, and possibly even cattle and weapons at the expiration of his term. Then he was entirely free to make his own way in the world.[33]

The need of colonists for helpers was so great that the trade in indentured servants was highly profitable to a shipowner or an agent. Lure of profits often led to illegitimate activities. The poor and ignorant in the old country were induced by false tales of the New World to commit themselves to indenture, and frequently boys and girls were kidnaped and sent off under duress to the colonies. The best classes participated in this vicious business. Agents who legally solicited business were generally termed "drums," while those who brought too much pressure to bear were known as "crimps."[34] Kidnaping occurred generally at seaport towns: an eager youth, especially if newly arrived from rural regions, was invited to inspect the ship, was offered (drugged) wine, and waked up when the ship was under weigh; in cruder cases, young men and women were physically overpowered and shanghaied.[35]

Despite the abuses, the indenture system helped bridge the ocean for the lower social classes, and gave American colonies what they most needed—manpower.* Pennsylvania probably made more intelligent use of the indentured servant than most colonies. The form and scale of her agriculture made possible employment of these servants in both household and the fields. The Quaker colony carefully regulated details of the contract. A servant pledged himself to give industrious labor and to avoid vices which might interfere with proper discharge of his duties. The master on his side promised fair treatment, food and lodging, and, on completion of the period of indenture, stipulated rewards. In 1700 the Pennsylvania legislature named these as "two compleat suits of apparel," a new axe, one "Grubing Hoe," and "one Weeding Hoe." More than this, under Penn's own regulations, the freed servant was entitled to fifty acres of land. A Pennsylvania servant was thus able to start out as a free man under excellent conditions. In fact, some immigrants with sufficient means for an independent estate indentured themselves in order to learn the methods of the new country.[36]

The condition of the indentured class in actual practice has been variously described. Europeans who wanted to discourage emigration to the New World from their own countries claimed that the servants "groan beneath a worse than Egyptian bondage." The immigration agent, on the contrary, pictured indenture as a short and comfortable stage in the transition to freedom, one materially profitable to the servant because of what he learned and what he received at the end. There was undoubtedly a tendency to overwork servants in some southern colonies where, on plantations, Negro slaves worked side by side with white servants. The Negro was a permanent piece of property and must be conserved; the servant was a temporary investment to be exploited to the full. Escapades of the servant were generally punished by whipping, and if he ran away he had to recompense the master for the cost of apprehending him and then serve double time for his absence. But these punishments were no better or worse than those for freemen at the same period. His legal position gave the servant some protection against cruelty and exploitation, and courts were entrusted with

* In Maryland the number of servants was for a time in the seventeenth century six times that of free men, and in Virginia the proportion was also high. Pennsylvania ranked next. (Kirkland, *History of American Economic Life*, p. 32)

protection of his rights. Whatever his treatment, he could look forward to a career of freedom and independence, not to a lifetime of exploitation.[37]

In a sense, then, indentured servants were among the first real settlers of America. As Herrick puts it: "The early explorers could get settlers only by appealing to gold as a lodestar, and settlers came out expecting to amass wealth and return. This phase of colonization had passed (by 1687). In general it may be said that the working classes emigrate only after the ground has been broken by the adventurers."[38]

Even if one-tenth of the Scotch-Irish immigrants were, as Archbishop Boulter had said in 1728, men of substance, the migration from Ulster would have been unusual; and if Spencer's estimate that most of those who left in the final wave were persons of property, the class of immigrants would have been extraordinary. What mattered, however, was not the property a man came with, but his qualities of character and self-reliance, his ambition to make good, his adaptability in crises. As pioneers the Scotch-Irish proved their mettle. They arrived, moreover, at the period when the American colonies most needed them. Until 1680 English immigrants had been almost the only settlers in the colonies, but after that date English migration sharply declined until 1768. Most provinces south of New England therefore welcomed colonists from non-English backgrounds— German peasants from the Rhineland in Pennsylvania, for example, or French Huguenots in New York and South Carolina. For thirty years or more even these were few. Then, in 1717, the Scotch-Irish tide began to flow toward the New World, continuing in spate for the next six decades. Increased German immigration began in the same year. America was to be strengthened by a new kind of settler, the "typical" pioneer who went beyond the outer fringe of civilization to establish himself on the frontier.

NOTE

The Volume of the Migration

Two obvious questions about the migration from Ulster to America are impossible to answer exactly: how many came

and how large was the Scotch-Irish element when the colonies
became independent.   There are no adequate statistics either
in Britain or America for population and immigration during the
colonial period.   Records which cite figures are fragmentary,
and figures given do not always agree.

The conventional estimate of the total immigration of Scotch-
Irish into America is 200,000, although Hansen's figure is around
225,000, Dunaway gives 250,000, and Barck and Lefler suggest
"perhaps 300,000."[39]   The lowest of these figures would mean
that an average of some 3,500 people reached America from
Northern Ireland in each of the fifty-eight years between 1717
and 1775.   The highest estimate implies an annual average of at
least 5,175.   Hansen thinks that around 4,000 came annually,
and remarks that this "emigration from Ulster was as much a
feature of American history in the eighteenth century as Irish-
Catholic emigration in the next and had a much greater effect
on the development of the country."

For the peak years of the migration, any of these estimates
would be moderate; there is general agreement that more than
6,000 came in some years.   The scholar must make his judgment
of the total on partial evidence.   In the following paragraphs
are given samples of the kind of evidence available, some of it
already cited in the text.   The samples could be multiplied.   My
own conclusion is that the figure of 200,000 is most nearly accurate.

1717.   Archbishop King reported that "some Thousands of
Families are gone,"[40]   Jonathan Dickinson of Pennsylvania noted
the arrival of "many hundreds from Northern Ireland in about
four months," "a swarm of people."[41]   Boston records showed
fifty-five ships from Ireland in six years, one with 200 passengers,
another with 150.[42]

1725-29.   "Between the years 1725 and 1727 there are records
of about 5000 persons emigrating from Ireland including 3500
from Ulster."[43]   Archbishop Boulter, writing in 1728, said that
"above 3,100" people "have been shipped off from home . . .
this last summer."[44]   Logan noted that in Philadelphia in 1729
"last week not less than six ships arrived, and every day, two or
three arrived also."[45]   The *Pennsylvania Gazette* stated that in

1728 "in New Castle government there arrived forty-five hundred persons, chiefly from Ireland; and at Philadelphia . . . 1155 Irish."[46] A news item dated August 14, 1728, from New Castle, read: "There is come in this last week about 2000 Irish People, and abundance more are daily expected. In one Ship about 100 of them dyed in their passage hither. It is computed that there is about 6000 come into this River since April last."[47] Smith mentions a scrap of paper, whose source is unknown, which has been preserved by the Historical Society of Pennsylvania. It cites figures of "Passengers & Servants imported from Ireland" into Philadelphia—in June 1729, 1,856; in 1731, 322; in 1734, 755; and in 1735, 343.[48]

1729-68. Arthur Young, economist and statistician, estimated in 1779 that between 1729 and 1750 Ulster lost a quarter of her population that had been engaged in manufacture.[49] A writer in the *Dublin University Magazine* asserted that "from 3,000 to 6,000 annually emigrated" from Ireland in the years from 1725 to 1768, although this writer of 1832 gives no proof of the accuracy of his figures.[50] It was said that the Presbyterian population of Ireland declined by one-half between 1718 and 1775—a statement that offers a clue but not a definite figure.[51]

1768-1800. Newenham in 1805 surmised that 200,000 people had emigrated from Ireland during the last half of the eighteenth century; and, during the three years 1771-73, "by exact statistics, 28,600."[52] The *Gentleman's Magazine* in 1774 quotes exact figures, asserting that 6,222 immigrants from Ireland had come to America between August 3 and November 29, 1773; while in five years between 1769 and 1774 there came to America 152 ships with passengers from Londonderry, Belfast, Newry, Larne, and Portrush, with a total tonnage of 43,720. The note is added: "the number of emigrants is supposed fully to equal the number of tons of shipping."[53] Futhey reports that between 1772 and 1775 nearly a hundred vessels sailed from ports in Northern Ireland, "carrying as many as 25,000 passengers, all Presbyterian."[54] Froude says there were 30,000 Ulster emigrants to America in these years.[55]. Naval records show that 5,835 "Irish servants" landed at Annapolis in the thirty years after 1745, and eighty-three during the same period in Virginia.[56]

The question of numbers assumes added interest if it is asked what proportion of the population in the newly formed United States of America was Scotch-Irish. If as many as 200,000 immigrants came over from Ulster, there were obviously considerably more Scotch-Irish in America than this by 1789. The birth rate was high (from five to ten children in a family was normal), and thousands of Scotch-Irish had now been in America for two generations or longer, adding yearly to the population.

The 1790 census counted the white people in this country as 3,172,444; estimates of how many of these were Scotch-Irish range from 6.7 per cent to 16.6 per cent. The higher figure, that of John Fiske, is nothing more than a guess, for this historian of an earlier generation offers no evidence for his estimate, merely saying that one-sixth of the colonial population in 1776 was Scotch-Irish.[57] The lower estimate is highly suspect because of the method by which it was derived. The Census Bureau in 1909 made a study of family names as reported in the first census of 1790, suggesting that these names would reveal at least something of the national origin of the people.[58] On this basis, the Bureau found that 83.5 per cent of the 1790 population had English names, 6.7 per cent Scottish (with another 1.6 per cent having Irish names). Since Ireland outside Ulster had by 1790 sent few immigrants to America, and since Scots were few in the United States (many of them having left the country during the Revolution), it could be assumed that the 6.7 per cent would fairly represent the Scotch-Irish element.

There are two great flaws in the thesis of the Census Bureau. The first is that an arbitrary decision has to be made (and an amateur one was certainly made) as to what nationality is represented by the name. There might, of course, be little difficulty with such names as Ian MacIntosh or Malcolm Knox; but who could spot, as distinctly Scottish, such eminent eighteenth-century names as Adam Smith or John Witherspoon? The other difficulty with the thesis is that during the century there was a widespread tendency in America to Anglicize difficult foreign names, and to change the spelling and even the form of names. Thus Schwartz became Black, Heidt became Hite, O'Donnell became McDonald or McDaniel or Donald or Donnell, and so on.

The American Council of Learned Societies and the American Historical Association in 1931 published a report of a Committee on Linguistic and National Stocks in the Population of the United States. This committee refined upon the thesis of the Census Bureau of 1909, using all the expert advice available.[59] Its conclusions were that in 1790 the white people in the United States of English descent numbered 60.9 per cent, those of Scotch descent 8.3, those bearing distinctive names of Ulster 6.0, and those with names characteristic of "the Irish Free State" 3.7. Since it would be impossible for all Scotch-Irish people to bear names distinctive of Ulster, and since thousands of them certainly had truly Scottish names, it might be contended that the just estimate of the Scotch-Irish element in the population of 1790 would be 14.3 per cent—combining the Scotch and Ulster names.

Using the lowest figure suggested (6.7 per cent), this would give a Scotch-Irish total of 212,554. Using the figure of 14.3 per cent, the total would be 453,655. Using the highest figure suggested (16.6 per cent), the total would be 528,731. It would be safe to say only that considerably more than a quarter of a million Americans in 1790 had Scotch-Irish ancestry. Certainly this element, next to the English, was the largest nationality group in the country, with the Germans next. (The Census Bureau's 1909 figure for German names in 1790 was 5.6 per cent; the Council of Learned Societies' figure for them was 8.7 per cent.)

13

Scotch-Irish Settlements

THE FIRST SCOTCH-IRISH ARRIVALS in America were not, like the colonists at Jamestown and Plymouth a century earlier, crossing the sea to a wilderness peopled only by Indians. News from each colony had penetrated every part of the British Isles; ship captains could offer shrewd advice; agents for companies and proprietors talked earnestly with prospective settlers. While information was often inaccurate, it was generally known to leaders of the first Ulster emigrants of 1717 that the American provinces differed widely in degree of development, population, economic enterprise, and welcome to newcomers.

In planning their removal, leaders hardly considered the southern provinces, Virginia and the Carolinas, for impoverished Ulstermen would see nothing attractive in a region of plantations and slave-owning, where the Church of England was established. Maryland had been founded for Roman Catholics, was principally a plantation colony, and now had an Established Church; it was therefore no place for Presbyterians who wanted small farms. New York's governors were reportedly hard on dissenters, and her lands up the Hudson were owned in great estates. Eliminating these, there remained the Middle colonies and New England. Much might be said for both. Reports from Penn's settlements were enthusiastic as to the quality of land and the treatment of colonists; moreover, an invitation to settle there had come from the Secretary. The attraction of New England, especially to ministers who advised those about to leave, was its

Calvinism; then, too, its people were numerous and industrious, its tidy towns civilized and prosperous.

In a sense, the emigrants of 1717 would be explorers whose report on their experiences could guide those who came after. The Ulstermen who went to Boston found unexpected difficulties and a welcome that lacked warmth. Those who followed them in the next two years were made to understand that they were not at all welcome. The people who entered America by the Delaware River, on the other hand, found a land of the heart's desire. Their enthusiastic praise of Pennsylvania persuaded others to follow them, and then still others, until by 1720 "to go to America" meant, for most emigrants from Ulster, to take ship for the Delaware River ports and then head west. For the entire fifty-eight years of the Great Migration, the large majority of Scotch-Irish made their entry to America through Philadelphia or Chester or New Castle.*

With these towns as their starting point and the western frontier their destination, the immigrants, as they poured in, found their path of progress almost laid out for them by geography. The Great Valley led westward for a hundred miles or more; then when high mountains blocked further easy movement in that direction, the Valley turned southwestward across the Potomac to become the Shenandoah Valley. From the southern terminus of the Valley of Virginia, it was a short trip, by the time the pioneers had reached it, into the Piedmont regions of the Carolinas, where colonists were now warmly welcomed. Within this seven hundred mile arc of back-country, therefore, from Philadelphia as far as the upper Savannah River, most of the Scotch-Irish made their homes.

The present chapter is a chronicle of the three major concentrations of Scotch-Irish people—in southeastern Pennsylvania, in the Valley of Virginia, and in the Piedmont of the two Carolinas—whose timetable reveals the pilgrims' progress:

* Despite the absence of reliable statistics, it seems clear that well over three-quarters of the immigrants from Ulster entered America by these ports. Even indentured servants found more welcome here than elsewhere. New York, Charleston, Boston, and Annapolis would probably follow, for the Ulstermen, and in that order. See the NOTE at the end of the preceding chapter for figures of immigration.

	PENN.	VIRG.	N.C.	S.C.
First effective settlements	1717	1732	1740	1760
Beginning of steady inflow	1718	1736	1750	1761
First frontier county organized	1729	1738	1752*	1769
First inland Presbyterian church	1720	1740	1755	1764*

By 1776, when the Revolutionary War had effectively stopped immigration, possibly nine-tenths of the Scotch-Irish in America were living in these regions.†

The course of migration from Ulster to America was closely paralleled by a large migration from Germany. Both started in 1717, the German immigration coming principally from the Rhineland Palatinate. Like the Scotch-Irish, most Germans entered by ports along the Delaware. From that river, through Pennsylvania, and on to South Carolina, the advance of the Germans accompanied, slightly preceded, or slightly followed, that of the Ulstermen; thus every chapter on Scotch-Irish settlement must have its German paragraphs.

A. SOUTHEASTERN PENNSYLVANIA

It would have been difficult to imagine anywhere, in the world of 1717, conditions more attractive to discontented inhabitants of the Old World than those which prevailed in the province of Pennsylvania. Here immigrants would find a hearty welcome from officials, readiness to assist newcomers in their

* The province of North Carolina organized a frontier county before 1752, but not for Scotch-Irish settlers. The problem of dating the first inland Presbyterian church organized in South Carolina depends upon the precise definition of "inland"; the date here given is for the first church in the up-country west of the Fall Line.

† This estimate of numbers is debatable. If the findings of the 1931 committee of the American Council of Learned Societies be accepted, and if (a very dubious condition) the Scottish and Ulster elements shown by that committee be combined—because of the difficulty of distinguishing Scots from Ulster and Scots from Scotland—the following percentages would result in the census of 1790:

Maine	12.5	Pennsylvania	19.6
New Hampshire	10.8	Delaware	14.3
Vermont	8.3	Maryland	13.4
Massachusetts	7.0	Virginia	16.4
Rhode Island	7.8	North Carolina	20.5
Connecticut	4.0	South Carolina	25.0
New York	12.1	Georgia	27.0
New Jersey	14.0	Kentucky and Tennessee	17.0

(See *Annual Report of the American Historical Association*, 1931, Vol. I, p. 124)

search for lands to farm, easy financial terms for the purchase of land, a countryside fertile beyond belief (especially by comparison with Ulster), an equable climate, an ordered community with courts and a high reputation for honesty and justice, towns and villages in which one could acquire necessary supplies, complete religious toleration, with neither Established Church nor compulsory tithes.

Of all these allurements, the most enticing in the early days of migration was the combination of a liberal, fair government in a land that seemed miraculously productive. Pennsylvania, among the last of the original colonies to be founded (Penn received his charter in 1681), had by 1717 been proving for thirty years its stability and prosperity, its practical liberality and hospitality. Nothing like the generosity of its appeal was known in other colonies. William Penn, in the very foundation of his province, displayed qualities that mark him as a farsighted statesman.* Sincere religious conviction underlay many of his liberal policies; common sense dictated others; and whether the desire for profit may or may not have dominated his arrangements, they proved economically practical.

Penn himself and his friends, by personal appeals, pamphlets, and broadsides, set forth to Europeans the advantages of his province. Its rich and virgin soil, its healthy climate, its advantageous geographical position in the midst of the English colonies in America—all of these external circumstances offered promise of economic success for a man who was willing to work and of prosperity for the province as a whole. Beyond these material advantages Penn guaranteed in his charter a government based on almost universal male suffrage (unknown at that time in the Western World) and a humane penal code. As a pacifist and Quaker, he made no provision for a militia or any military establishment; as a man of good will, he announced his intention to deal honorably with Indians and win their friendship. But beyond all of these marks of a generous spirit, he guaranteed in his charter complete freedom of conscience. An

---

* Contemporary governors of other provinces, though they must have regarded Penn as capable, had no high regard for his political arrangements. These were so far out of tune with contemporary opinion that they seemed, to royalists, highly dangerous, if not positively subversive, to sound government.

uncompromising defender of the cause of religious toleration and a member of a sect that had suffered because of nonconformity, he felt a profound sympathy for Europeans who were then enduring religious disabilities.

It was understandable that fellow-Quakers from England should be the original settlers of his province. They founded the City of Brotherly Love and soon had settled in the attractive regions around the quiet village of Philadelphia (the modern counties of Bucks, Montgomery, Delaware, and Chester). Penn now quickly turned his attention to attracting other settlers. His shrewd eye turned first to west Germany, for that region had by no means recovered economically from the devastations of the Thirty Years' War. The religious settlements that followed the Peace of Westphalia (1648) had left thousands of devout Protestants, most of them belonging to small Pietist sects, under the exactions of established State churches which to the simple peasants were alien and unscriptural. Penn's personal appearances in the Rhine country convinced the leaders of these people of his complete sincerity and of the honesty of his accounts of the province in America. Led by their ministers, great numbers of Mennonites, Dunkards, Amish, Schwenkfelders, and others began to come to Pennsylvania in 1683.[*] In their New World homes, starting first at Germantown, they found that Penn had been as good as his word; Pennsylvania was in truth a land of milk and honey.

Three decades after these first German settlers, the first Scotch-Irish also found in Pennsylvania a Promised Land. Where in Ulster they had known famine, here it seemed unlikely that crops could ever fail; moreover, game was so abundant that no man need lack for meat. There was wood in plenty for making one's houses, furniture, and implements, as well as for fuel

---

[*] Francis Daniel Pastorius, who had become a Friend, in 1683 brought thirteen families from Crefeld, Germany, to settle in Pennsylvania. Pietist groups soon followed. Pietists, in effect, desired to secede from the "world," so that they might lead holy lives in simplicity with a community of their fellow-believers. After Penn's Rhineland visit of 1677 there appeared in London a brief description of his new province, "Some Account of the Province of Pennsylvania in America." The translation of this booklet into German and its publication in the same year in Amsterdam made excellent advertisement for the colony. For Penn's plan of government, see *Collection of the Works of William Penn* (London, 1726), 2 vols.

more efficient than peat. Where in Ulster the Test Act had made life miserable for Presbyterians, who had to pay tithes to a Church not their own, in Pennsylvania religion was free. Political disabilities upon dissenters did not exist.*

To the extent that religion had been among the motives for migration, the first Ulstermen could be doubly assured. Already in 1706 there had been enough Presbyterian ministers and churches in the vicinity of Philadelphia to warrant the organization of the first Presbytery in the New World. Presbyterianism had, indeed, been founded on the continent in 1683 in the neighboring Eastern Shore of Maryland by a Scotch-Irishman, Francis Makemie. English, Scottish, and Welsh settlers in the Lower Counties (Delaware), the "head of Chesapeake" (Maryland's northeastern county of Cecil), and in and around Philadelphia had also formed Presbyterian congregations. By 1717, when the Scotch-Irish migration began, there were thirteen organized Presbyterian churches in the vicinity.

Upon disembarking at New Castle, Chester, or Philadelphia, only indentured servants were likely to linger in the towns. The immigrants had come to be farmers, not artisans or hired workers. They must, of course, get their bearings, find out where land was available, equip themselves with what they could afford in the way of implements and livestock; and the "respectable folk" among them secured land patents—a formality soon to be overlooked by impetuous and impecunious arrivals. All were eager to get to the frontier, then only thirty or forty miles west or north of Philadelphia; there was no point in trying to purchase more expensive tracts in existing neighborhood of Quakers and

---

* Although the early Scotch-Irish, engrossed in establishing homes and farms, showed no immediate concern with practical politics, this later became a major interest. (See below, chapter 16.) It is therefore worthy of mention that Penn's charter had already, long before 1717, begun to be modified in remarkably liberal fashion. The privilege of initiating legislation, at first reserved to the Governor and Council (upper chamber), was soon conceded, and without reluctance, to the Assembly. In 1701 the Council had entirely disappeared, as a superfluous body. The laws of Pennsylvania were thereafter passed by an elected and representative assembly. The constitution itself might be amended as necessity arose. (See Thayer, *Pennsylvania Politics*, ch. 3.) By the middle of the eighteenth century the Scotch-Irish, then agitated by Indian troubles, entered politics and were able, because of these liberal arrangements, to achieve political power in the Province.

Germans. Only a few chose to settle near their fellow-Presbyterians in adjoining counties of Maryland and Delaware.

The Scotch-Irish could not have the frontier lands to themselves. Arriving simultaneously with them, as noted, were
Germans, now chiefly Lutherans and Reformed in religion, not
Pietists as the earliest immigrants had been.* Pennsylvania now
became the scene of an alternating and parallel movement of the
two peoples which, if it could have been viewed by some mirac-
ulous slow-motion camera, might have resembled the stately
rhythm of a formal dance. Scotch-Irish went to one part of a
river valley, Germans to another; then the next year's arrivals
advanced beyond the settlements to repeat the process. In the
great valley of the Susquehanna, westward motion was delayed
until homemakers had fanned out to the hills in the north; but
soon the river was crossed, and the rhythm was repeated. (By
1732 the same process began to exhibit itself in western Maryland
and the Shenandoah Valley of Virginia, and after 1750 was
carried on southward into the Carolinas.) A map in any given
year might show a preponderance of Scotch-Irish in one section
of the county and Germans in another or a whole (modern)
county with one people or the other predominant.†

There was inevitably a measure of necessary contact between the two peoples, but it soon became apparent that this
would be held to a minimum. The language barrier was a
formidable one, even if there had been incentives to intimacy.
Religion, cultural attitudes, social heritage all were different.
Temperamental traits were so divergent between the two peoples
that many colonial commentators noted them. It was usual to
expect Germans to be orderly, industrious, carefully frugal; they

* The number of German arrivals was in some years quite as numerous as the
Scotch-Irish. Between 1727 and 1754 it seems to have averaged about two
thousand a year; thereafter it diminished, and was notably smaller than the great
years of Ulster migration in 1771-75. Whereas the Germans arriving before
1717 had come primarily for religious reasons, later migrations consisted mainly
of farmers who, although they took religion seriously, saw an opportunity for
improved economic conditions. See Faust, *The German Element in the United
States*, I, chs. 1-3.

† Even in the twentieth century, despite all the changes that have occurred
in two hundred years, the results of this alternating pattern can be discerned:
one county will have a predominance of German names and of Lutheran or
Reformed churches, while its neighbor will show a large number of Scotch-Irish
names and of Presbyterian churches.

rarely had trouble with Indians; if they interested themselves at all in politics, it was usually on the local level. Scotch-Irish, by contrast, were regarded as quick-tempered, impetuous, inclined to work by fits and starts, reckless, too much given to drinking. No contemporary observer praised them as model farmers. Their interest in politics on the Provincial level was soon to become active, even tempestuous; and their fame as Indian fighters was to become almost as notable as their reputation for causing trouble with the Indians.

It is hardly too much to say that neither Germans nor Scotch-Irish liked each other, wanted the other as near neighbors, or engaged more than was necessary in social intercourse with the other. It is surprising, indeed, that with such differences, dissension and conflict between the two people was not more frequent than it was. Occasional election disputes sometimes caused serious ill-will. Feuds in (present) York County reached such a point that in 1749 the Proprietors instructed their agents not to sell any more land in that area to Ulstermen, and to try to persuade them to move on westward to the Kittatinny Valley.[1] There were occasional outbreaks of ill feeling in (modern) Dauphin and Adams counties.[2] But the usual rule was simply for one people to avoid the other. In the next century it was stated as incontestable "fact" that "the white races in Pennsylvania were remarkably unmixed and retain their original character beyond that of any State in the Union. These distinctly marked races are the English, Scotch-Irish, and German."[3]

The initial welcome given the Scotch-Irish by Pennsylvania authorities was genuine. James Logan, the Provincial Secretary, actually invited the first group of Ulstermen to come to the colony, for they were his "brave" fellow-countrymen.[*] He wrote in 1720: "At the time we were apprehensive from the Northern Indians. . . . I therefore thought it might be prudent to plant a settlement of such men as those who formerly had so bravely defended Londonderry and Inniskillen as a frontier in case of any disturbance. . . . These people if kindly used will

[*] Logan was born at Lurgan, near Belfast in Ulster, of Scottish parents, in 1674. While engaged in trade between Dublin and Bristol he met William Penn, who invited him to become his secretary. Logan accepted and arrived in Philadelphia in 1699. He died in 1751.

be orderly as they have hitherto been and easily dealt with. They will also, I expect, be a leading example to others."[4]   He accordingly gave them an extensive tract of land in Chester (now Lancaster) County—and they immediately named their settlement Donegal, after the home county in northern Ireland.

Logan's good opinion of the Scotch-Irish shortly changed, for their character as pioneers, though certainly brave enough, exhibited traits offensive to the meticulous Secretary.   Only ten years after his first statement, he wrote that "a settlement of five families from the North of Ireland gives me more trouble than fifty of any other people."   And further: "It looks as if Ireland is to send all her inhabitants hither; for last week not less than six ships arrived, and every day two or three arrive also.   The common fear is, that if they continue to come, they will make themselves proprietors of the province."   He was not far wrong in his prediction on this last score, for the Quakers lost control of the Assembly in 1756.   Logan also found the Scotch-Irish "troublesome settlers to the government and hard neighbors to the Indians."[5]

The Secretary even refused for a time after 1729 to issue land patents to them, but this simply confirmed the Scotch-Irish in their "audacious and disorderly" habits.   They now increasingly settled on land without bothering to secure legal rights to it. Here was the beginning of the practice that was henceforward to become familiar on every later American frontier—squatting. The inrush was so swift that officials could not be everywhere to supervise it, and, by the time they arrived, the land had for so long been cultivated by squatters that they assumed they had established a right to it and bitterly resisted any effort to expel them.

Illegal though squatting was, and however exasperating to officialdom, the practice was humanly understandable.   To Logan's challenge of their taking land without purchasing it, the Scotch-Irish made a simple reply: "the Proprietary and his agents had solicited for colonists and . . . they came accordingly."[6] Land was abundant and no settlers were living on it; to the Ulstermen it was only reasonable that they should have it if they were willing to clear the forests and make farms on it.   In 1726

Logan estimated that a hundred thousand acres were in the possession of people who had no shadow of right to settle upon them.[7]

Because poverty was a principal cause of migration, many Scotch-Irish lacked money to pay even the small price the Penns asked for farm lands.* The earliest advertisements offered lots of five thousand acres at a purchase price of only £100, with a quit-rent of one shilling for each hundred acres. A renter might secure fifty acres for himself and another fifty for each servant he brought over, paying a rent of only a penny an acre.[8] These reasonable sums were later reduced but were still too much for most immigrants to afford. Indentured servants who had served their time and now had a small sum of money were not inclined to use it for the purchase of land when they knew that their fellows on the frontier had got away with squatting. They knew that by luck and persistence they could take western land for no payment whatever.

Administrators in Philadelphia, however, long continued their effort to make squatters pay and conform to the law. Provincial Secretary Richard Peters even tried to dispossess squatters—and learned what many a later official discovered. Several times Peters burned down the cabins of squatters, trying to overawe illegal settlers by appearing with surveyors, sheriff, and other officials; but when these retired, the cabins were rebuilt and the land was farmed again.[9] Sometimes the intimidators were themselves intimidated by an ugly show of force. "A body of some seventy [squatters] joined circlewise around Mr. Parsons' instrument, and began narrowing in upon it, the front ones on foot, the rear ones on horseback," until the officials thought it expedient to retire. As Secretary Logan reported, the squatters "alleged that it was against the laws of God and nature, that so much land should be idle, while so many Christians wanted it to labor on, and to raise their bread."[10] Another official expressed his belief that, if the Scotch-Irish were driven back from their frontier farms and forced to settle among the Germans and

---

* It will be recalled that Archbishop Boulter estimated that only one Ulster emigrant in ten was a man of substance, and that "the case of the rest is deplorable." (Boulter, *Letters,* I, 226)

others to the east, "there will be next to a Civil War among them."[11]

Officials found it impossible to force all the thousands of new arrivals to take out regular warrants or licenses; there were too few officers and too many immigrants. When eventually surveyors arrived to run the lines required by the Provincial government, their presence was regarded as a harbinger of eviction, and settlers more than once drove them off by force. Some of the people no doubt knew that legal formalities were required and that land was not free; but many seemed to be under the honest impression that they might settle anywhere west of occupied land, without let, hindrance, or cost. When they had lived for many months as squatters, undisturbed on land they had cleared and planted, many resolutely declined to tolerate warrant, survey, and patent, "especially shunning papers that called for payment of any ground-rental or quit-rent to the Proprietors."[12]

Travel from the river ports to the frontier was by foot for most of the pioneers and on horse for those who could afford to purchase an animal. Frontier Pennsylvania at first had no road that could have accommodated a wheeled vehicle even if the immigrants, newly arrived by ship and eager to make a home, had been able to spend time and money to construct wagons or carts. Occasionally even a cow served as pack animal to carry the family belongings. The colony soon undertook the construction of a road leading westward from Philadelphia; but the pioneers were always pushing beyond its terminus.

It is not the purpose of this survey to give a detailed account of the exact location and progress of each Scotch-Irish settlement,* yet a glance at the map reveals better than words the rapid

* County historical societies in Pennsylvania have generally done admirable work in discovering and preserving records of early settlers, with deeds, plats, wills, and the like. Addresses, some scholarly, some merely appreciative, reveal details of the character and social life of the pioneers. There are, in addition, dozens of local histories—of counties, valleys, cities and regions. The careful historian, Wayland F. Dunaway, has written an admirable general history of *The Scotch-Irish of Colonial Pennsylvania,* making use of all these sources. The Presbyterian Church, through its historical foundation in Philadelphia, has also done notable work, not only on the religious life of the Scotch-Irish settlers but also on other phases of their character and social life. Later chapters of this book attempt summary generalizations that recognize the significance of the Scotch-Irish in the Province of Pennsylvania, while endeavoring to place them in the larger context of the entire migration.

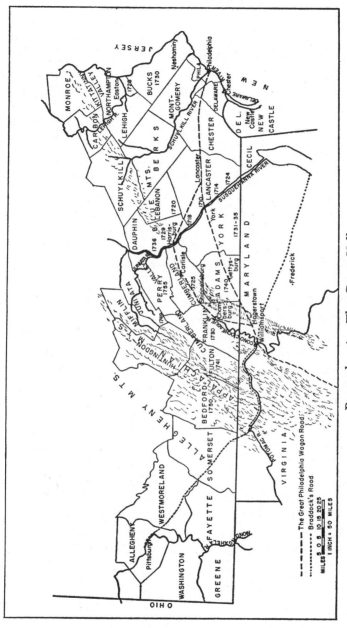

Pennsylvania: The Great Valley

filling up of the countryside. The geographical feature that most distinguishes southeastern Pennsylvania, the Great Valley, sweeps in a wide and gentle arc from the Delaware River toward the southwest. The Appalachian range makes a kind of natural outer boundary to a region containing some of the richest farmlands of the continent. Through this Great Valley flow rivers large and small, with the Susquehanna almost bisecting the region. Pioneers had only to traverse gently rolling hills to find themselves in still another smiling valley. This southeastern quarter of Pennsylvania nearest the Delaware ports was naturally the first part of the Province to be settled. With Penn's capital as the hub, Scotch-Irish and German pioneer settlements went, almost like spokes on a wheel, to the beckoning frontier, until they had reached the rim, the Appalachians.

To the three original counties along the Delaware (Philadelphia, Chester, and Bucks) the proprietors thought it wise in 1729 to add a fourth, Lancaster. Here was evidence not only of the path taken by settlers, but of the density of their numbers. For many years Lancaster embraced the whole of Pennsylvania west of Chester. The map shows the dates only of first Scotch-Irish settlement. It can be seen how the Scotch-Irish followed the river valleys (where German settlers had not forestalled them), keeping north of the disputed border line of Maryland.* The provincial government organized still further counties as the frontier was filled up: York in 1749, Cumberland in 1750, and Bedford in 1771, not to mention other counties to the north of Philadelphia.

Only one "spoke" of Ulster migration radiated directly northward from the hub. Certain groups of Scotch-Irish in the years from 1728 to 1730, before the path westward had become almost *de rigueur* for their fellow-countrymen, followed the Delaware River up into (present) Bucks and Northampton counties. This region had the advantage of being accessible by ship; but English

---

* The boundary was finally fixed in 1767, when Mason and Dixon completed their four years of work on the historic line; and, as a chronicler of Lancaster county notes, the Scotch-Irish were sent by the Proprietors toward the Maryland border, where "these sturdy, brave and independent men from a turbulent homeland" might be "almost happy in constituting the frontier line against encroaching Maryland Catholics." (Klein, *Lancaster County*, I, 82)

and German settlers dominated this portion of Pennsylvania and early had taken up the best lands. Yet this district is famous in Scotch-Irish annals as the home of the Tennent family, where, at Neshaminy, William Tennent opened his Log College, forerunner of all Presbyterian institutions of higher learning in the country. (See below, p. 277.)

As long as the Ulster settlements were in the present counties of Chester and Lancaster,* pioneers were within reach of markets and supply centers at Philadelphia. When later migration pushed on westward, however, the frontier village of Lancaster rapidly grew into an important town, specializing in crafts and trades useful to pioneers. It became the point of departure for immigrants headed toward western Maryland and the Valley of Virginia; it was also a supply point for those hardy individuals who engaged in fur trade beyond the mountains even into Ohio. Not only did artisans set up shop in Lancaster to cater to the pioneers; here also were markets to which herds of cattle later were driven from as far away as North Carolina. Quaker merchants of Philadelphia saw the promise of the town and established branches there; these businessmen soon became so prominent that they could almost control the economic activities of the flourishing town.[13] Lancaster may have been, in mid-century, the largest inland town in all the colonies.

A particularly useful and practical citizen of the frontier was John Harris. A native of Yorkshire, he established his homestead beside the Susquehanna in 1705. Between 1720 and 1730 Scotch-Irish had settled along the eastern bank of the river both south and north of him. The foothills of the Appalachians to the north indicated that further waves of newcomers must seek land across the wide river to the westward. Harris, who had already thriftily opened a trading post at his seat, now instituted a ferry service, to transport families and goods of pioneers to the west bank. Harris's Ferry was to become an indispensable

---

* In Chester County, the Germans filled up the eastern section, while the Scotch-Irish spread over the whole western part, from the Maryland line to the Welsh mountains. In Lancaster County the Germans were chiefly in the north and the Scotch-Irish in the south and along the southern part of the Susquehanna, around Pequea and Tulpehocken. See Egle, *History of the Commonwealth of Pennsylvania*, pp. 526, 820.

link in the "Great Philadelphia Wagon Road" extending eventually all the way down to upper South Carolina, and before long the busy river place became Harrisburg.

Across the Susquehanna, the first Scotch-Irish settlements were in the upper portion of the Cumberland Valley nearest Harris's Ferry.   Chroniclers speak of the Scotch-Irish who arrived in Cumberland during the decade after 1725 as folk "of the better sort . . . a Christian people."[14]   The rich and gracious Cumberland Valley now became the center of attraction for several decades.   Dunaway calls it the most important single Scotch-Irish center in America—"the seed-plot and nursery of their race, the original reservoir which, after having filled to overflowing, sent forth a constant stream of immigrants to the northward and especially to the South and West.   For a generation other racial groups were but scantily represented here."[15]   Franklin County received its first Scotch-Irishmen between 1728 and 1740, and York, whose initial settlers consisted of "families of the better class of peasantry," between 1731 and 1735.[16]

By the time the Cumberland Valley was in process of settlement, the uneasiness of the Proprietors was increased.   Lands were now being farmed in the valleys of far-off (modern) Perry, Juniata, and Fulton counties, and even beyond.   The steady stream of immigrants each year meant numerous Scotch-Irish squatters in Indian territory.   Impatient protests from tribal chiefs came to the Proprietors in Philadelphia.   From the beginning of the Province, Penn and his agents had always been scrupulous about purchasing Indian lands before permitting any white settlement within a region; but the trouble with the Scotch-Irish was that they did not wait for permission to settle where they chose.   Three times, to the exasperation of the Proprietors, they had been forced to purchase lands to provide for settlers they had already come to regard as obstreperous, yet still the squatters pushed on.*   Neither proclamations of the Governor nor laws

---

* After the initial treaties, the proprietors in 1736 purchased land directly west of the Susquehanna toward the mountains; in 1737 they bought, by the "Walking Purchase," a large tract from the Shawnees and Delawares around the Lehigh River; in 1749 still more territory toward the west was purchased. The principal encroachments of the Scotch-Irish squatters occurred along the

of the Province had the slightest effect upon the trespassers. There is no evidence that the Scotch-Irish appreciated the scrupulosity of the Proprietors in trying to extinguish Indian rights before permitting settlement. If the settlers were even aware of Indian feelings at the encroachment, or imaginative enough to perceive that there might be a limit to the red man's patience, their land-hunger apparently silenced their scruples. Logan had early spoken of the "rough treatment" given Indians by the Scotch-Irish. The impetuosity of these pioneers helped light the torch of Indian resentment. The flame broke out in 1754—and for the next century and a half hardly a year passed without Indian troubles, whose cause was always the encroachment of pioneers who, like the Scotch-Irish, wanted land, whatever the Indian's claim to it might be.

If impetuosity early proclaimed itself as a dominant trait among many Scotch-Irish, so also did their restlessness. In contrast to the Germans who, once they found a home, tended to remain fixed, the Scotch-Irish never seemed satisfied. Needless to say, many of the Ulstermen remained where they made their first homes; but thousands of others seemed to feel a compulsion to move again and again. Long before fertile areas in the Susquehanna and Cumberland valleys had been filled up, scores who had settled here had, for one reason or another—or for no reason at all, so far as observers could perceive—moved on down the Great Valley into Virginia, and thence into the Carolinas. It began to be said that no Scotch-Irish family felt comfortable until it had moved at least twice; they "seem to have had a psychological repugnance to making permanent homes until they had moved several times."[17] One result of this mobility was that excellent land in Pennsylvania which had originally belonged to Ulstermen now came into the hands of Germans. This was true in Cumberland County as early as 1757-60;[18] it became even more evident in the region around Lancaster. Scotch-Irish

---

Juniata and its tributaries, in the Great and Little Coves formed by the Kittatinny and the Tuscarora hills, and at the Big and Little Connolloways. See Egle, *History of the Commonwealth of Pennsylvania*, p. 78; and Sutherland, *Population Distribution*, p. 154. For an account of Pennsylvania's colonial policy toward the Indians, see the 18th *Annual Report* of the Bureau of American Ethnology, pt. 2 (1896-97), pp. 568 ff.

influence, and often their Presbyterian churches, yielded to Germans and their denominations.*

It was partly this restlessness (to which attention will several times be called hereafter), but even more the constant influx of new arrivals from northern Ireland, that accounted for the settlement of the back-country of colonies south of Pennsylvania. Beyond the Cumberland Valley high mountains loomed in the west. Latecomers from Ulster (and Germany) therefore followed the extension of the Great Valley southwestward until they had crossed the narrow belt of Maryland into the province of Virginia. Only after the years of Indian fighting ended in 1764 did any but the hardiest pioneers push beyond the Appalachians to settle in the neighborhood of the future Pittsburgh in western Pennsylvania.

B. THE VALLEY OF VIRGINIA

Two counties in the Valley of Virginia, Augusta and Rockbridge, claim to be the most Scotch-Irish counties in the present United States. It is said that they have more Presbyterians within their borders than members of all other denominations together. Telephone books list names beginning with "Mac" in a separate category from those under "M". While it is true that the Cumberland Valley of Pennsylvania is one seedbed of Scotch-Irish, the central part of the Valley of Virginia is another, its stock derived by transplantation from Ulstermen who came down from, or at least through, Pennsylvania.

The contrasts between the two important colonial provinces are instructive, as they relate to the filling up of the frontier. Penn's province was full of small farmers from Northern Ireland and Germany within fifty years of its foundation, while Virginia for a century and a quarter after Jamestown was primarily a plantation colony, dominated by gentry in the Tidewater. Its western regions, especially the fertile lands of the Shenandoah

---

* The Scotch-Irish did not always choose the best agricultural lands available to them. Limestone regions, which Germans made into the most productive farms of colonial times, were not at first held in high esteem by Ulstermen. They seemed to prefer slate hills, where there was an abundance of pure springs, and where the air of the hills and the rolling countryside may have reminded them of their native scene in North Ireland. (This is the suggestion of Rupp, *History and Topography of Dauphin*, p. 541.)

Valley, were almost empty. Penn had seen immediately the advantage of a large population of industrious farmers, whose initiative and success would conduce to the prosperity of the Province. It was only at the beginning of the eighteenth century that the rulers of Virginia began to think of inviting immigrants into the back-country—and then primarily as a military safe-guard.*

Even when Virginia wanted settlers, the Council thought in terms of companies rather than of individual farmers. In 1701 great tracts, from ten to thirty thousand acres, with exemption from taxes for twenty years, were offered to companies who would bring in settlers, the stipulation being that within two years there should be one able-bodied and well-armed man ready for defense for every five hundred acres, with a fort built in villages near the center of the tract. In 1705 fifty acres were offered free to any person who would settle in the up-country.[19] Such offers brought no results, so far as the Valley was concerned, for the Shenandoah was as yet unknown and unexplored, too far away from any available supply of settlers to be practically accessible.

The year 1730 was the effective date of the opening of the Valley of Virginia, for by that time three simultaneous developments had occurred: the Great Valley of Pennsylvania had been largely settled and pioneers were already crossing southward into Maryland's up-country; a particularly heavy migration of Scotch-Irish and Germans occurred during the decade after 1727, and the newcomers found the most attractive Pennsylvania lands already taken, or too costly; and a new land policy was instituted by the governor of Virginia, William Gooch—the granting of great tracts of Valley land to individual enterprisers. These land grants were made at the precise moment when colonists were at hand, looking out for farms upon which to settle.

It seemed at first as if Germans might pre-empt the entire Valley. Already they had taken up most of the land in the

* The turning point of Virginia's western development may be said to have begun in 1701 with the passage of an "Act for the Better Strengthening the Frontiers and Discovering the Approaches of an Enemy." The purpose of the Act was to attract settlers by generous terms for land they might take, their main obligation being to establish forts and means of defense. (Hening, *Statutes-at-Large*, III, 204 ff.)

The Valley of Virginia, with Adjacent Present-Day Counties

western part of Maryland between the Pennsylvania border and the Potomac. Along the Monocacy River in (modern) Frederick County and westward in the area around Hagerstown (now Washington County), the whole countryside was German. A small group, led by Jacob Stover, penetrated in 1726 to the Shenandoah Valley itself, settling on the south branch of the Shenandoah River; and in 1730 another group, led by Adam Miller, took farms near present Luray.* But the important event

* While there were "very few" German settlers in this Massanutten section

in Valley settlement occurred when Governor Gooch of Virginia in 1730 granted forty thousand acres to John and Isaac Van Meter, of Pennsylvania. Starting at the Potomac River, the grant extended southward to embrace most of the three modern counties of Jefferson (West Virginia), Frederick, and Clarke. The Van Meters shortly sold their warrant to Joist Hite,* a German or Hollander, who in 1732 not only established his own estate on the Opequon just south of present-day Winchester but also brought in sixteen families. While it is true that a number of Scotch-Irish soon came to Hite's lands and that a sufficient number of Quakers from around Philadelphia and Chester arrived to found several Meetings in the neighborhood, the German element was for many years completely predominant in the Valley just below the Potomac, as it was in Maryland north of that stream. Not much later, still other German immigrants pushed beyond the Hite grant into the region around Strasburg (now in Shenandoah County) and Harrisonburg (Rockingham County).†

It was the second and third grants by Gooch, both made in 1736, that brought the great Scotch-Irish movement to the Valley and assured the predominance of this Ulster element in the central and southern reaches of that Valley. These grants were much larger than the 1730 patent which Hite had taken.

The first of the two 1736 grants went to William Beverley (also spelled Beverly), of Essex County, a man prominent in

before 1729, by 1733 there were fifty-one Germans, in nine "plantations," in the region. See Waddell, *Annals of Augusta County,* pp. 22-23.

* His name has many spellings; in addition to the one given, the most common ones are Jost Heydt, or Heidt, or Hight.

† The grant to Hite caused litigation that dragged on for decades, for Gooch had given land already claimed by Lord Fairfax. King Charles II, fifty years before Hite's time, had made a stupendous grant of more than five million acres to Lord Culpeper, from whom it descended to Fairfax. This donation embraced the whole "Northern Neck" of Virginia, including everything from the Chesapeake Bay in the east to the headwaters of the tributaries of the Potomac, in the present state of West Virginia. Later surveys showed that the Fairfax grant embraced 4,142 square miles east of the Blue Ridge, 2,111 in the Valley, and 2,147 in the mountainous area west of the Valley. Hite's grant clearly overlapped Fairfax's; but whereas Fairfax had made no early effort to secure settlers in the Valley part of his grant, Hite did precisely this. Colonists were often in a dilemma: some secured deeds from Fairfax, some from Hite. Heirs of the two patentees carried on the litigation long after the two principals were dead. See, among other accounts, Couper, *History of the Shenandoah Valley,* I, 398-99, and Kercheval, *Valley of Virginia,* pp. 154-56.

colonial affairs.   Gooch gave him a patent for the "Manor of Beverley," comprising 118,491 acres "lying in the county of Orange, between the great mountains, on the river Sherando [Shenandoah]."   This splendid gift overlapped some of the German settlements (in present Rockingham County), but it principally covered the excellent farm lands in the northern part of the modern county of Augusta, including the cities of Staunton and Waynesboro.*

Several years before Beverley received his land, certain families of Scotch-Irish people had settled in that area.   By local tradition, the first establishment was that of John Lewis, to whose name attaches a dramatic tale: he had, in Ulster, killed his brutal and merciless landlord, and so had fled as a refugee to Pennsylvania in 1731.   Thence he had come to Hite's settlement along the Opequon in 1732, and soon thereafter to the neighborhood of (modern) Staunton.   At least three other Scotch-Irish families were settled in that region in the same year.†

Only a few months after making the grant to Beverley, Governor Gooch issued a patent to Benjamin Borden (also spelled Burden), of New Jersey, an agent of Lord Fairfax.‡   The grant was for some half-million acres along the headwaters of the Shenandoah and James rivers, beginning at the southern border of Beverley Manor, and thus including the southern part of present Augusta County and almost the whole of Rockbridge (around Lexington).   One of the stipulations was that Borden should have a hundred families settled on the land before he could receive title.   Within two years he had succeeded to the

* A meticulous map of the Beverley Patent, showing all the original grantees from 1738 to 1815, is included as an end-paper in Wilson, *The Tinkling Spring, Headwater of Freedom.*

† The Kerr family contests the Lewis priority in Augusta, claiming that James Kerr had arrived in 1730.   The other Augusta "first families" are those of Gilbert Christian and John Campbell.   See Wilson, *The Tinkling Spring,* pp. 11-12.

‡ A diverting legend attaches to the Borden grant.   It is told that this New Jersey merchant, a frequent visitor to eastern Virginia, had met John Lewis in 1736.   Accompanying him to his Valley home, he spent some months in hunting. He caught and tamed a buffalo calf, which, upon his return to Williamsburg, he presented to Governor Gooch.   This official "was so much pleased with his mountain pet that he directed a patent to be issued authorizing Burden to locate 500,000 acres of land on the upper waters of the Shenandoah and James rivers." (Lewis, *History of West Virginia,* p. 69.)

extent of ninety-two cabins and so in 1739 received his clear patent.[20]

Between 1732 and 1738-39, when the Beverley and Borden patents were officially confirmed, a considerable number of Scotch-Irish settlers had come down from Pennsylvania into the region. In practice, all of these pioneers must be termed squatters, for authority was two hundred miles away at Williamsburg, and the settlers had simply made their homes without legal formalities. After the appearance of the two patentees, immigration continued, with squatting; but now the "better" families took pains to have their lands surveyed and their purchases confirmed. It appears that both Beverley and Borden dealt amicably with those already established upon their lands, for both men were intent upon filling their grants with settlers. Beverley gave legal title to those living in his Manor at the rate of one English pound for forty acres.[21]

These first settlers, beyond the reach of law and officials, succeeded in keeping peace among themselves by developing a kind of customary "law." Simply by use and wont, they agreed upon several kinds of "rights" which they themselves recognized as valid. There was the "corn right," which entitled the planter to approximately a hundred acres of land for each acre he had planted. (A variation of this was the vaguer "taking up land," which meant building some kind of lodging and raising a grain crop of any kind, however small.) Next was the "tomahawk right," established by deadening a few trees, generally around a spring, marking one's initials upon the bark of trees, or blazing a few trees along the line of claim. The "cabin right" (more vaguely) was based upon the settler's having built a log cabin upon the tract he claimed. If another pioneer wished to settle within a neighborhood, he must, in this authentic folk society, buy up the "rights" from the "owner."[22]

Germans also soon came to the Beverley and Borden grants, but this region was within ten years after 1736 so predominantly Scotch-Irish that it was known as the "Irish Tract."[23] The Scotch-Irish dominance of the territory is evidenced by the remark of two Moravian missionaries traveling from Georgia northward in 1749; they wrote of their great relief when "we passed confidently and safely through the Irish settlements."[24]

Shenandoah lands presented to the settlers a prospect quite as beckoning as any they had known in Pennsylvania. Most of the Valley of Virginia was a vast prairie, showing to pioneers a vista of fertile territory, making settlement easy and rapid. The prairie had been created by the Indians, who used the whole Valley for hunting. At the close of each hunting season they set fire to the open ground, thus keeping it from reverting to woodland. This was done to attract the buffalo, an animal that shunned forest and lived on grasslands.[25]

Both Beverley and Borden were indefatigable in their efforts to procure settlers, and both men were fortunate in their first colonists. Lewis, despite the legal cloud hanging over his name, was a person of the finest qualities; and Borden secured one of his ablest settlers, Ephraim McDowell, by a lucky chance in a casual conversation engaged upon during a visit to Lewis. McDowell's son John, a surveyor, assisted Borden in making his location, and the McDowell family soon became distinguished in the Valley.

An enterprising agent, James Patton, served both Beverley and Borden in their effort to attract colonists. A native of Ireland and "bred to the sea," Patton had served in the Royal Navy. He later became owner of a ship of his own, carrying on trade between Britain and the Rappahannock River. He is said to have crossed the Atlantic twenty-five times, carrying abroad cargoes of peltries and tobacco, and returning with Ulstermen.[26] By far the greatest number of Scotch-Irish settlers in the two great tracts, however, entered Virginia by way of Pennsylvania. They were not only newcomers from Northern Ireland, who followed the path of their predecessors westward from the ports on the Delaware, but included many who had lived, and had even been born, in Pennsylvania. As younger sons, ambitious men, or those dissatisfied with the "crowding" in a growing region, they were looking for better opportunities elsewhere.

It was the third wave of emigrants from Ulster (1740-41) which swelled the number of settlers in the Valley. The winter of 1739-40 was known in Northern Ireland as "the time of the black frost," because of the unusually dark appearance of the ice and the almost total absence of sunshine. The calamities of this winter touched off a large migration, whose members generally went through Pennsylvania without a pause, to seek lands in Virginia. The southern limit of the Borden grant was soon traversed, and the Scotch-Irish had now reached the James River around (modern) Buchanan and Fincastle, in Botetourt County. Still others crossed the first range of Alleghenies to settle the valleys of Highland and Bath counties, beside the rivers to which they gave the homely names of Cowpasture, Bullpasture, and Calfpasture.

Virginia authorities, like those in Pennsylvania, took notice of the rapid filling of the Valley and tried to provide for the legal and civil needs of settlers by the creation of county institutions. Before 1738 Orange County, with its county seat in the Piedmont, embraced not only most of the Valley but also much of what is now West Virginia. Legal matters arising in the affairs of Valley settlers required a long and trying trip across the Blue Ridge to the east. In 1738 the authorities formed two new counties: Frederick in the north, with Winchester as its center; and Augusta in the south, to include the Beverley and Borden region. Both of the new counties extended westward into howling wilderness, theoretically as far as the Mississippi, where Virginia's claim ended—although beyond the Alleghenies there were, as far as anyone knew, only Indians and wild beasts, with a few French explorers and traders.[27] Although Augusta County was organized in 1738, it was not until 1745 that the governor made the organization effective, with the appointment of twenty-one justices of the peace, a sheriff, and other officers for the vast county. By 1750 the county seat was established at Stanton, or Staunton, as it was afterwards spelled.

Not only did the early establishment of civil institutions lend stability to the Scotch-Irish settlements of the Valley; churches also were organized early. Despite the fact that the pioneer Presbyterian, Makemie, had preached on the Eastern Shore of Virginia in the years after 1683 and that Scots had a Presbyterian congregation near Norfolk, the faith of the Scotch-Irish was not represented anywhere in the colony in the 1730's. The Presbytery in Pennsylvania had written to the Presbytery of Dublin in 1710 that "in all Virginia there is but one small congregation at Elizabeth River, and some few families favouring our way in Rappahannock and York."[28]

Presbyterians in the Valley of Virginia petitioned Donegal Presbytery in eastern Pennsylvania to supply ministers to fill the needs of the Scotch-Irish settlers. Their plea arrived just at the moment when the Great Awakening was stirring not only Presbyterians but most other denominations to take active steps in meeting religious needs of the people. Donegal Presbytery was eager to satisfy the Virginians, and by 1740 the first Presbyterian pastor since Makemie's death in 1708 came to settle in "the Triple Forks of the Shenando." There John Craig organized the Augusta Stone Church and the Tinkling Spring Church. Soon afterwards both Augusta and (modern) Rockbridge counties were dotted with Presbyterian churches. By the time of the Revolutionary War there were twenty-three of these congregations in the Valley of Virginia.

Although the Church of England was established in Virginia, religious liberties granted to settlers in the Valley were considerable. Neither Germans nor Scotch-Irish could be expected to conform to the doctrines and ritual of the Established Church. The issue of religious liberty was not raised at the time of the influx of Valley settlers, but neither was there any effort to curtail the free exercise of religion according to conscience. Certain Presbyterians in Pennsylvania, however, felt that the issue should be openly raised and settled, so that future Scotch-Irish Presbyterians in Virginia might know what to expect. At a meeting of the Synod of Philadelphia in 1738 a memorial (inspired by John Caldwell, grandfather of John C. Calhoun), drawn up for presentation to Governor Gooch, specifically requested religious toleration in Virginia. Gooch replied: "As I have always been inclined to favour the people who have lately removed from other provinces, to settle on the western side of our great mountains, so you may be assured, that no interruption shall be given to any minister of your profession who shall come among them, so as they conform themselves to the rules prescribed by the act of toleration in England, by taking the oaths enjoined thereby, and registering the places of their meeting, and behave themselves peaceably towards the government."[29]

No difficulty was experienced by the Presbyterians, therefore, in the exercise of their religion. It is true (as will be seen in the later chapter on politics) that the parish organization, stemming from the Establishment, was set up in the frontier communities to provide for the needy and for other local and eleemosynary purposes; but Presbyterians of the Valley calmly accepted this arrangement, elected their own members to parish councils, and ran local affairs as they saw fit. Within a few decades Virginia had disestablished the Church and proclaimed religious freedom.

The never-ending stream of Scotch-Irish continued to pour southward into the Valley. By the 1740's they had reached the James River and had crossed it, at Looney's Ferry (modern Buchanan). The path thereafter for thirty miles south was easy. When the present site of Roanoke was reached, the Valley, as such, came to an end. The home-seeker was now faced with an alternative: he might turn southwestward and proceed through a narrower arm of the valley, toward the formidable Appalachian range; or he might head in general southward, through very hilly country, toward North Carolina.

The first alternative had only one real advantage: once its trees were cut down, the valley land was rich and accessible. Its disadvantages in the 1740's were numerous: the country to the west was unexplored and must soon lead to a mountain wall; the constricted limits of the valley could not support enough farmers to justify effective civil institutions; and pioneers who thought of their sons realized that they must look elsewhere for farm lands. The southwestern valley, in short, appeared to be a cul-de-sac. Its nearest reaches, under the leadership of James Patton and others, were soon occupied, in the present counties of Montgomery, Pulaski, and Wythe. By 1775 there were even settlers on the banks of the Holston and Clinch, and it was now well known that eastern Tennessee and Kentucky lay across the mountains. Churches were organized, and the settlements, increased by arrivals from the Tidewater and Piedmont, were flourishing.[30] The southwestern valley was to become a veritable highway after the Revolutionary War, as Virginians moved west to Kentucky.

In the 1740's, however, the first alternative was rarely chosen. The overwhelming majority of Scotch-Irish pioneers chose an easterly path when they reached the site of modern Roanoke. Word had spread abroad that land in the Carolinas was available in hundreds of thousands of acres. The colonies to the south of Virginia eagerly welcomed settlers, and first reports on soil, civil and religious liberties, and peaceful Indians were highly favorable. The main stream of movement therefore flowed toward the Carolina Piedmont.

Both Scotch-Irish and Germans by the thousands, having traversed the Great Valley and the Shenandoah, went eastward through the Staunton River gap of the Blue Ridge, swung southward again close to the Blue Ridge, crossed the rugged territory of the Blackwater, Pigg, and Irvine streams, until, beyond the Dan River, the path opened out into the wide spaces of the Carolina Piedmont. Few of these eighteenth-century pioneers dropped out of the procession between Roanoke and the Dan, in order to make homes in the hilly country of that part of southern Virginia. Their destination was the province of North Carolina.

C.   THE UPPER CAROLINAS

The third great region of Scotch-Irish settlement was the Piedmont country of North and South Carolina. Coming later than the Pennsylvania and Virginia waves, the sweep into the Carolinas resembled them in general character, despite the decided difference of terrain. In the provinces to the north there had been a valley, whose retaining walls made the progressive waves of settlement almost methodical in their advance, newcomers simply passing beyond land already taken until the Great Valley was "filled." By the time North Carolina was reached, however, the mountains had swung far to the west. The movement of people was now into open Piedmont, stretching in all directions for scores of miles. Scotch-Irish newcomers, encountering no natural restraints to confine them, spread outward like a stream inundating a plain.

Until 1729, both North and South Carolina had been owned by great English Proprietors, few of whom had taken active steps to develop their American holdings—certainly not to the extent that Penn had done. It was after the cession of these proprietary estates to the Crown in 1729 that the frontier regions began to receive active attention from government. Until then, in both regions, settlement and rule were entirely in the coastal plains. Aristocratic planters, with slaves and indentured servants to perform menial tasks, tried to live like lords in the New World. The Church of England was, of course, established, and familiar English institutions were introduced for the comfort of the gentry. Occasionally there were small accretions to the Carolina population, especially in South Carolina—numerous Huguenots after the revocation of the Edict of Nantes in 1685, certain "dissenters" from England and Barbados, a congregation from Dorchester, Massachusetts. Charleston (Charles Town, as it was then called) was a thriving port. In both North and South Carolina, however, the fall line of the rivers marked the end of civilization, and beyond it to the west, in the Piedmont, Indians roamed at will.

Official indifference to the up-country gave place, after 1730, to a policy of definite encouragement to settlers. The doors of both provinces were now thrown open to Protestants of all nations. Several governors even took active steps to induce groups of European Protestants to come to the two Carolinas. For twenty years the new policy was moderately successful, especially in South Carolina. Here many Palatine Germans settled around Orangeburg, Congaree, and Wateree; certain Swiss newcomers established themselves along the Savannah River; a few Ulstermen came to Williamsburgh. The triumph of the period from 1730 to 1750 was the large migration (this time especially to North Carolina) of Highland Scots. "The '45," as it was called, had failed in its attempt to bring the Stuarts back to the throne; after the defeat at Culloden, Stuart supporters were severely repressed; and hundreds of Highland families, including that of Flora Macdonald herself, came to America. Landing near Wilmington, they came up the Cape Fear Valley to establish them-

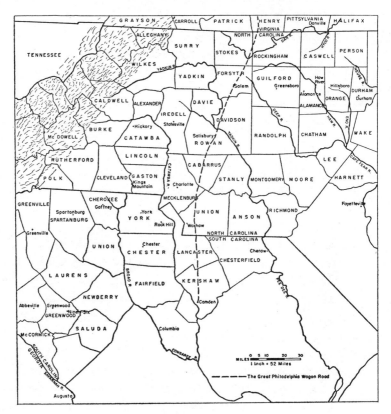

The Carolina Piedmont

selves in sizable colonies from the coast to the region of Fayette-ville.*

All of this influx in the twenty years after 1730, however, had come by sea, and either remained near the coast or was concentrated in the lower river valleys. Hardly any of the newcomers penetrated the actual Piedmont. If a diagonal line had been run in 1750 northeastward from (modern) Aiken, South Carolina, through Columbia and Fayetteville, to Wilson, North Carolina,

* It must not be supposed that these Scots had friendly contact or even sympathy with their fellow-Presbyterians when the Scotch-Irish shortly began to pour into the up-country west of them. At the Revolution, on the contrary, Scots and Scotch-Irish often were to be found fighting on opposite sides. The two peoples were now foreigners to each other, in language, dress, background, and experience. See below, ch. 16.

few of these ship-borne settlers would have been found west of it. The fall line was still the limit of civilization.

Yet while official attention was still centered on the east, a few hardy souls from the Valley of Virginia had found their way into the up-country of North Carolina. These families who came in between 1740 and 1750 were harbingers of what was to prove one of the mightiest migrations in colonial times. So great was the tide pouring in from the north that, by the outbreak of the Revolutionary War, the North Carolina back-country had at least sixty thousand settlers, while that of South Carolina had eighty-three thousand—almost four-fifths of the colony's white population.[31] Certainly some of this up-country folk in both colonies had moved in from the Tidewater counties; but the tremendous bulk of the people were "transfers" from Pennsylvania, Maryland, and Virginia—a few Swiss and Welsh, large numbers of Germans, but more Scotch-Irish than all others put together.

Why did these thousands come south? Many of them, of course, were immigrants newly arrived in America from Ulster, following the usual course to Philadelphia and then through the Great Valley. Finding this more densely settled land too expensive, they had pushed on until they reached North Carolina. Other thousands, however, were making a second—or even a third or fourth—complete move. Their reasons were varied. A second generation of young Scotch-Irishmen was growing up, with the normal compulsion of young men to make their own way in the world. As Pennsylvania's population steadily increased, both from immigration and a high birth rate, the demand for land drove prices to a point beyond the ability of youths to pay; thus sons in a large family were impelled to move where land was still cheap and plentiful. Agents from Proprietors in the south had much to do with the removals. Just as spokesmen for Hite, Beverley, and Borden had advertised their grants in the 1730's and 1740's, attracting many settlers to Virginia, so now the agents of Lord Granville came to hymn the advantages of living in North Carolina.

Already, too, there were rumblings of Indian unrest at the mid-century, with threats of serious trouble to come; by 1753 the western frontiersmen in Pennsylvania were complaining in exasperation that the provincial authorities, safe in Philadelphia, were supinely ignoring the danger in the west. After 1754 there was the reality of Indian terror, not only in Pennsylvania but also in the Valley of Virginia, to send settlers to seek other homes. And always there was the Scotch-Irish restlessness, to which attention has been called: impatience with social restrictions that attend the development of stable community life, the lure of striking out on one's own in a land where one can live "free," the conviction that farthest pastures are greenest. Some simply went because others went. As a Moravian observed, "The migrations of men are like the movements of a flock of sheep, where one goes the flock follows, without knowing why."[32]

Even if Lord Granville's agents had not been active, it is probable that the newcomers would settle first on his lands, simply because these lay astride the most traversible path from the Valley of Virginia into central North Carolina. Here the forerunners had come in 1740 and 1745, to make their farms along the banks of the Hyco, Eno, and Haw rivers.[*33] Granville alone of the Proprietors had not ceded his land to the Crown in 1729; he still reserved his rights as owner of the soil over an area covering nearly half the colony.[34] Here were thousands of neglected acres to be had for the taking, and beyond them, to the west and southwest, was the rich bottom land of the Yadkin and Catawba river region, leading onward to the border between the two Carolinas. This mesopotamia became the home of a great concentration of Scotch-Irish, and the highway leading to settlement in South Carolina's piedmont.[†]

* The first actual settlement of Scotch-Irish in North Carolina was not in the Piedmont, and arrived by sea rather than by way of Pennsylvania. On November 29, 1735, Governor Johnston informed his Council that Arthur Dobbs (later to become governor of the province), "and some other gentlemen of distinction in Ireland," and Mr. Henry McCulloh, a merchant of London (later agent for Lord Granville), had written him "respecting their intention of sending over to this province several poor Protestant families with design of raising flax and hemp." They asked for a grant of sixty thousand acres of land in New Hanover County. Their request was granted, and next year (1736) the settlers arrived at their land on the Black River (now Duplin County), where they organized themselves into two congregations, Goshen and the Grove. (*Colonial Records of N.C.*, IV, 72-73) It is not stated, however, what the size of this colony of "several" families was.

† The (modern) counties receiving the largest numbers of Scotch-Irish settlers were Orange, Alamance, Guilford, Caswell, Rowan, Iredell, Cabarrus, Mecklenburg, Lincoln, and Gaston.

Three North Carolina governors enthusiastically encouraged the immigration from the north—men who had a special interest in attracting settlers with a Scottish background to expand the population and economic development of the province. Gabriel Johnston, governor from 1734 to 1751, was a native of Dumfriesshire in Scotland; Matthew Rowan, president of the Council in 1753-54, was an Ulsterman; so also was Arthur Dobbs, governor from 1754 to 1765. Dobbs, born in Carrickfergus in Northern Ireland, had long been intensely interested in exploration and colonization. Coming to North Carolina, he associated himself with the Scots agent of Granville, Henry McCulloh; through his exertions, three colonies of Ulstermen came to North Carolina, in 1751, 1754, and 1755. By 1754 Dobbs had been made governor of the Province. The years from Johnston's appointment in 1734 to Dobbs's retirement in 1765 were precisely the period of the Province's enormous growth. Through these officials, "their relatives, friends, connections, and acquaintances in the north of Ireland and the south of Scotland, North Carolina was, perhaps, better known than in any other part of the old world."[35]

Details of the filling up of the countryside are illuminating. When Johnston took office the population of North Carolina was about fifty thousand; when he retired seventeen years later it was ninety thousand.[36] As he reported in 1751, "Inhabitants flock in here daily, mostly from Pennsylvania and other parts of America who are overstocked with people and some directly from Europe. They commonly seat themselves toward the West and have got near the mountains."[37] President Rowan wrote in 1753: "In the year 1746 I was up in the country that is now Anson, Orange, and Rowan counties. There were not then above one hundred fighting men; there is now at least three thousand, for the most part Irish Protestants and Germans, and daily increasing."[38] Counting one fighting man as representative of a family of five, the population in the western region had probably increased from five hundred to fifteen thousand within seven years.

Governor Dobbs wrote in 1755 of seventy-five families who had settled on land he owned in North Carolina: "They are a colony from Pennsylvania of what we call Scotch-Irish Presbyterians who with others in the neighboring Tracts had settled together in order to have a teacher, i.e., a minister of their own opinion and choice."[39] He testified to the size of what we have called the "fourth wave" of immigration from Ulster, noting that as many as ten thousand people from the North of Ireland had landed at Philadelphia in a single year, many of whom, he said, were "obliged to remove to the southward for want of lands to take up" in Pennsylvania.

As in both Pennsylvania and Virginia, Germans were a considerable part of the newcomers. As usual, they tended to keep themselves separate from the Scotch-Irish. In the county of Orange, organized in 1752 because of the swelling population, the Scotch-Irish settled chiefly in the east, and the German Lutherans west of the Haw River.[40] A large concentration of German Moravians was to be found in the western reaches of the county (now Forsyth). When the United Brethren purchased here their great Wachovia tract in 1752, Bishop Spangenburg referred to it as "probably the best left" in the province.[41] Here their colony of Bethabara was formed in 1753. The bishop was wrong in his supposition about the best land left, however, for later Germans found much fertile territory around Salisbury in the Catawba Valley.

Although there were enough Germans to continue the Palatinate stream into the piedmont of South Carolina in the next decade, the flow of Germans into America began to diminish around mid-century, and soon had dwindled to a trickle. The Carolina piedmont as a whole was much more thoroughly Scotch-Irish than German.

The years immediately following 1754 saw a shift in the source of the Scotch-Irish immigration into North Carolina. It was in that year that the French and Indian wars began in earnest in Pennsylvania, and Indian depredations made it perilous for people to traverse that colony's Cumberland Valley on the way south. Governor Dobbs said that the Indians had put a "total stop" to the influx of Pennsylvanians. The Valley of Virginia was nearer, however, so that when Indians descended upon settlements there to burn, pillage, and murder, the exodus of Scotch-Irish thence was hastened. "In one week of October, 1756, three hundred persons went by Bedford Court House [in Virginia] on their way to Carolina, and five thousand more 'had crossed James River, only at one ferry, that at Goochland Court House.' "[42]

North Carolina likewise had its Indian troubles during the 1750's, though later than those in the north and never reaching the proportions they assumed in western Pennsylvania or even in Virginia. The principal tribes of the North Carolina piedmont at this time were the Cherokees and Catawbas.* Both had been friendly enough to the whites in the early days, the Catawbas remarkably so. Cherokee amity had recently been secured through the expert diplomacy of Governor Glen of South Carolina, in whose province were large areas of Cherokee lands. In 1754-55 Glen had persuaded these Indians to yield to the Crown an enormous tract of their territory for some $300 worth of presents.[43]

Cherokees returning from the fighting in Pennsylvania, and probably incited by the French, in 1756 created a series of incidents in upper Carolina. Mismanagement of the affair, rough retaliation, and hot tempers now resulted in what is generally known as the Cherokee Uprising. Depredations were committed upon outlying and scattered settlements; and while North Carolina settlers felt nothing like the panic of their kinsfolk in Pennsylvania and Virginia at the Indian "menace," many of them prudently moved eastward to safer homes. The number of taxables in Rowan County, in the center of the trouble, was reduced by half between 1756 and 1759; but in Orange County, to the northeast, settlements were exempt from Indian raids.[44] By 1761, after an impressive show of force by the authorities, the Cherokees retired to the west, having lost five thousand of their people, including half their warriors.[45] Thereafter the forward march of the pioneers was resumed.

---

* The Catawbas from the first arrival of the whites showed them unusual friendliness. Rights says: "They aided in the [1711] campaign against the Tuscaroras in the east and served as a barrier against tribes of the west. The flood of immigration that poured into the Piedmont area after 1700 was little opposed by the friendly Catawba." He also notes that they were hereditary enemies of the Cherokee. (*The American Indian in North Carolina*, p. 125) About 1738 a great epidemic of smallpox decimated Catawba villages and also caused havoc among the Cherokee. (Milling, *Red Carolinians*, p. 237) This may have deterred the latter from the risk of war and the loss of further warriors.

As in Pennsylvania and Virginia, North Carolina officials were concerned to provide civil institutions for settlers in the west. In 1746 all the counties in the province were in Tidewater country, with Edgecombe, Craven, and Bladen extending as far west as North Carolina claimed territory—that is, through the whole reach of Tennessee to the Mississippi. In that year, however, Granville County was cut off from Edgecombe, to become the first county of the Piedmont. By 1752 it was considered expedient to organize Orange County, whose territory had for several years been attracting Scotch-Irish and German settlers. Within another decade this single frontier county had the largest number of taxables of any county within the province,* and by 1770 it was necessary to cut off the western section of Orange to form the new county of Guilford. In the southern part of the province, Anson County, extending westward along the South Carolina boundary line, beyond the Yadkin River, was organized in 1749. Like Orange, and even earlier, it had to be subdivided: in 1762 its western portion became Mecklenburg, one of the greatest centers of Scotch-Irish concentration.†

In the central section of the Piedmont frontier region, Rowan County, beyond the Yadkin, was created in order to meet the needs of settlers around Salisbury. Thus, because of a phenomenal growth of population, North Carolina had added five Piedmont counties within the twenty-one years between 1749 and 1770.

Inevitably, all this flow of people from the north soon traversed the Piedmont of North Carolina and swept into the province to the south. No natural barrier separates the two Carolinas, and it is probable that most of the land-hungry travelers were unaware that they had crossed a boundary line when they came into South Carolina's piedmont. The history of the filling up of the southern province's frontier lands is in many respects a duplication, a decade later, of the North Carolina story.

---

* "Its number of taxables increased from twenty to about four thousand during its first twenty years," says Lefler (*History of North Carolina*, I, 96). Orange County had been formed from parts of Granville, Johnston, and Bladen.

† Mecklenburg County, around Charlotte, was to make a name for itself in 1775 by its call for independence from Britain, and, during the Revolutionary War, by the sturdy fight of its Scotch-Irishmen against the redcoats.

As early as 1750 a few families who had come down from Pennsylvania and Virginia were located in the up-country one hundred miles from Charleston.* South Carolina might during the ensuing decade have had a large immigration from the north if the Cherokee Uprising had not broken out in 1756, with much of the actual fighting done in South Carolina. These years of strife with the Indians were nothing like so costly in lives as in Pennsylvania: only 150 or 200 white persons were killed. But it is estimated that by 1761 South Carolina had spent more than £100,000 to defeat and then to pacify the Cherokees.[46]

The effective settlement of the South Carolina piedmont, therefore, began only after 1761. Simms says that in 1756 there were only some twenty-five families in the whole up-country, although three of these families had penetrated as far as the Savannah River near Abbeville.[47] After 1761 the inrush began, coming through central North Carolina, into the region between the Pee Dee (Yadkin) and Catawba rivers, with the Waxhaws making a kind of central distributing point. As in the north, the Scotch-Irish were greatly preponderant, with Germans now few in number. From the Waxhaws settlements spread through the (modern) counties of Lancaster, York, Chester, Fairfield, Union, Newberry, Abbeville, and Edgefield. "No colonial area," according to Bridenbaugh, "expanded with the rapidity of the back parts of Carolina after the defeat of the Cherokee in 1761."†[48]

So many thousands of people headed in the same direction, all coming from the north, could not fail to make something more than a beaten path. Their common route, indeed, became one of the most impressive highways of colonial times, The Great

* "Colonel Clarke, with a party of Virginians, settled in that year on the Pacolet. Other parties subsequently joined him, dotting with civilization the forests along the Fair Forest and Tiger rivers. A few other parties, here and there, with these constituted the only white settlements of the back-country until 1755, the year when Braddock was defeated." (Simms, *History of South Carolina*, p. 120)

† Bridenbaugh, stressing the source of the immigration that filled the back-country, suggests that this region of the Carolinas might with propriety be called "Greater Pennsylvania." Writing of South Carolina, he says, "In the newly settled Rocky Mount district in 1767, a missionary found people already crowded together, 'thick as in England.' John Stuart wrote from Charles Town in 1769 that 'the Country near the line is very full of inhabitants, mostly Emigrants from the Northern colonies.'" (*Cities in Revolt*, p. 127)

Philadelphia Wagon Road, as it was called in the north, or "The Great Wagon Road from the Yadkin River through Virginia to Philadelphia distant 435 Miles," as Joshua Fry and Peter Jefferson meticulously labeled it on their "Map of the Most settled Parts of Virginia" (1775).

It began, naturally enough, at the colonial metropolis, Philadelphia, starting on the western bank of the Schuylkill. By the 1720's it reached out only to the settlements in Lancaster County, for there the Susquehanna made a natural end of the track. This section of the road was steadily widened and improved, for it was the most used, and it now passed through the thriving frontier market town of Lancaster. At the Susquehanna the main road went through York and Gettysburg, and so across the Monocacy River in Maryland to Williamsport on the Potomac; but a much-traveled northern branch of it led up from Lancaster to Harris's Ferry (Harrisburg), to traverse the Cumberland Valley and lead through Chambersburg to Williamsport. The ferry here crossed the Potomac into the Shenandoah Valley. By the middle of the eighteenth century a number of towns and villages had grown up along the road in the Valley of Virginia—Martinsburg, Winchester, Stephensburg, Strasburg, Woodstock, and Staunton.

At the James River, Looney's Ferry at modern Buchanan took passengers across for the short trip to the end of the Valley at the site of Roanoke. There the Road turned briefly eastward through the Staunton River gap of the Blue Ridge, crossed through hilly country over such minor streams as the Blackwater, Pigg, Irvine, and Dan, and entered North Carolina. In this province it traversed the Moravian settlement at Wachovia, on a branch of the Yadkin, and then followed the open country between the Yadkin and Catawba rivers. In 1760 it had reached Salisbury. When the South Carolina piedmont was thereafter opened up, the Road went on through the Catawba Valley to the settlements around Pine Tree (modern Camden), thence southwestward beyond the Congaree to Ninety-Six and Augusta. From Philadelphia to the original terminus, Wachovia, it was 435 miles; extended to its full length, to the Savannah River, it was almost 700.[49]

It is not surprising that the Scotch-Irish in the Carolinas formed neighborhoods. Governor Dobbs had noted in 1755 that these people, "whom we call Scotch-Irish Presbyterians," settled near each other "in order to have a teacher, i.e., a minister of their own opinion and choice."[50] Dobbs may not have been correct in assigning the reason for close settlement; there is, indeed, evidence to indicate that the founding of a church sometimes persuaded new families to settle in a particular neighborhood. Many historians, however, have been struck by the tendency of the people not to isolate themselves. "In the selection of a site for settlement," says Meriwether, "the back countryman was nearly always influenced by the distance from other settlers. He was rarely found more than ten miles from his fellows."[51]

The farms were of considerable size. In Orange County, North Carolina, more than three-quarters of the property holders owned between 100 and 500 acres of land; only some 5 per cent had farms smaller than 100 acres, and only 5 per cent had more than 1,000 acres.[52] In the Granville District of upper North Carolina, "the regular grant was 640 acres."[53] Holdings in South Carolina were generally smaller, partly because the Province had allowed a bounty of a hundred acres for every man, with fifty more for each woman and child.[54] The average here seems to have been around 175 acres.

Such figures make clear that in the Piedmont of both Carolinas the Scotch-Irish were farmers, not plantation owners. With their divergent origins, background, religion, and economic interests, the up-country people were regarded with ill-concealed distaste by most of the eastern planters, who still controlled affairs in both provinces. It was felt by South Carolina gentry of the coastal region, for example, that after their expense in quieting the Cherokees, they should not have to tax themselves to provide courts and other conveniences for these up-country "ruffians."[55] With such an attitude, the officials sent into the frontier country were often lax in performance of their duties or, much worse, unjust and exigent in their taxation, and even unfair in their exercise of "justice." In both North and South Carolina, consequently, there were "Regulation" movements (noted in detail below, in chapter 16), which marked the growth of sectional feeling in the two provinces.

Despite this, the merchants of Charleston saw opportunities for business with these disdained people in the hinterland. Since the rivers that begin in central North Carolina flow southeastward to the coast of South Carolina, Charlestonians saw to it that a road was constructed to lead up to meet the extension of the Philadelphia Wagon Road. Merchants from Charleston, having already set up stores in outlying settlements of the low country, now began to provide markets for the corn and cattle of up-countrymen. "North Carolina butter made by the Scotch-Irish at Rock River sold in fifty- and one-hundred-pound kegs at Atkins and Weston's warehouse on the Cooper."[56]

Once more, in the settlement of the Carolinas, the restlessness of the Scotch-Irish may be observed. Nash tells in detail of a family which moved in 1751 from Berks County, Pennsylvania, to the region of the Eno River in North Carolina.[57] Their motives were loss of crops by an early frost, death of the oldest child, and glowing accounts sent back from the Eno by former neighbors. Another family, the Pettigrews of Abbeville, South Carolina, had made a twenty-eight-year pilgrimage from Ulster before their final settlement. Arriving at New Castle in 1740, the original American Pettigrew, well educated and a friend of Benjamin Franklin's, moved to a frontier tract of three hundred acres in Pennsylvania. Well established there, he sold his property when Indians began their depredations and went to the Valley of Virginia. "Uprooting his family again after three years, he settled in North Carolina, stopping there until rumors of Arcadia enticed him to the trail again in 1768. After four years on Long Cane Creek, in South Carolina, he moved again, but this time only a mile or so down the trail."[58] In another instance, "Andrew and John Pickens served as justices of the peace at the first court of Augusta County, Virginia, in 1745; six years later they had located at the Waxhaws below the South Carolina boundary; and in 1762 John and Andrew, Jr., received warrants to parcels of land in the Savannah Valley."[59] Such cases could be multiplied.

The descendants of these restless Scotch-Irish people crossed the Appalachians and led the way, not only into the frontier regions beyond the mountains, but thence eventually across the Mississippi even to the Pacific coast.

D. Indian Menace to Settlement

The Great Migration of the Scotch-Irish (and Germans) from its beginnings up to 1754 had been a steady and almost wholly peaceful advance through frontier regions, with only natural barriers to impede it. In 1754, however, that peace prevailing throughout all regions of settlement was rudely shattered. Indians now began violently to oppose the white people who had penetrated into their territories. The next ten years were marked by bloodshed, bitterness, constant anxiety, cruelty, and death to men, women, and children. Immigration from Ulster, as from Germany, almost ceased. Frontiersmen were fighting for their very existence in Pennsylvania and Virginia. It would be well over a century before Americans would cease to speak of the "Indian menace" on the frontier.

It may seem remarkable that, with constantly increasing numbers of intruders into Indian lands from 1717 to 1754 and with the importunate Scotch-Irish in the van, there had not already been Indian disturbances on a major scale. That these did not occur can be attributed principally to two fortunate circumstances, which a reflective Ulster Presbyterian might have regarded as predestined: the wise and pacific Indian policy of Pennsylvania and the absence of Indian settlement in the Shenandoah Valley.

Quakers in Pennsylvania from the very outset had determined to deal with the Indians as friends and equals. All land on which settlement was likely to occur was purchased from the tribes beforehand, and not for a pittance, but at a fair price. The government in Philadelphia built no forts, established no militia, trained no scouts and Indian fighters. This attitude of complete friendliness rested upon religious conviction and moral conscience; and, as often happened in Quaker experience, honesty and fair dealing proved practical, for it spared the colony expense and fear. The Scotch-Irish could have chosen no happier place for their initial settlements.*

Virginia also had a long record of peace with Indians. Few remained anywhere east of the Blue Ridge, while in the Valley itself there were only two small Indian settlements, a Shawnee town near Winchester and a Tuscarora village about thirty miles north (in present Berkeley County). The whole valley was regarded as a hunting ground, and Indians who used it generally had their permanent homes farther to the south or west. Shawnees did, in fact, cause considerable trouble to the first settlers in their part of the Valley, but when white settlements steadily increased in number after 1736 the Indians quietly moved away. These initial harassments, however, had warned pioneers of the necessity of erecting a number of small forts and stockades—a policy Governor Gooch had stipulated when he made his grants to Beverley and Borden. Indian hunters were a familiar sight to first settlers in the Valley. The Catawbas, whose largest village was in South Carolina, continued to come north to hunt in the Valley until the buffalo disappeared and other game became scarce.

Farther south, as has been noted, the Catawbas had always displayed remarkable friendliness to the whites,[60] while the Cherokees, a more numerous and aggressive people, were at first kept quiet by the astute diplomacy of Governor Glen of South Carolina, who visited among them, treated them with respect, and finally, in 1754, purchased most of their lands in the western part of his province.[61]

Despite the remarkable peacefulness of the Indians during the first half of the eighteenth century, however, colonial governments of the provinces south of Pennsylvania could envision

* The Quaker attitude is exemplified in a letter addressed by a Philadelphia Friend to other Friends settling in 1738 on Hite's lands in the Shenandoah Valley: "I desire that you be very careful—being far and back inhabitants—to keep a friendly correspondence with the native Indians, giving them no occasion of offence. . . . My counsel and Christian advice to you is, my dear friends, that the most reputable do with speed endeavor to agree with any purchase your lands of the native Indians. . . . Consider you are in the province of Virginia, holding what rights you have under that government; and the Virginians have made an agreement with the nations to go as far as the mountains and no farther, and you are over and beyond the mountains, therefore out of that agreement." (Lewis, *History of West Virginia*, p. 72.)

at least the possibility of future trouble. Pioneers were insatiable in their land-hunger; at any moment a rash act by the volatile Scotch-Irish might touch off a conflict.

Unimaginative as Tidewater officials often seemed, it would require small perception to realize that no people would remain forever patient as its lands shrank, even by legitimate purchase. White population steadily increased, white pioneers constantly moved farther into Indian territory. Inexorably the Indians had been bought off, pushed back, persuaded to retire; but might there not come a time when they would retreat no farther from their ancestral lands? Capitals of all the provinces were on the Atlantic coast or near it, so that Easterners were unlikely to be attacked; but the prosperity of every colony now depended upon its increasing population, whose farms and plantations every year extended farther to the west. The Great Migration of the mid-century was an economic boon, but it might well portend the end of Indian patience. If violence should develop, the Easterners naturally felt that it were well for the frontiersmen to do the fighting. Few colonial administrators of the South could have failed to envisage the pioneers as a source of protection to seaboard settlements; they therefore encouraged precautionary measures.

Pennsylvania alone refused to admit the possibility of conflict. Officials in Philadelphia lamented the rashness of Scotch-Irish settlers in pushing constantly into Indian territory, for each westward thrust made it necessary for the government to purchase more land from the Indians. Incidents were occurring with increasing frequency, so that officials were kept busy restoring the peace and making amends to tribal chieftains. When reports reached the capital that the French beyond the Alleghenies were inciting Indians against the English colonists, Quaker officials either ignored them or treated them as irrelevant to their own province.

White men in the Shenandoah Valley in 1753 learned that emissaries had come to Indians from tribes west of the mountains, inviting Shawnees and Tuscaroras to move west. This news excited suspicion that a storm of some sort was brewing and that it might be wise to take extra precautions.[62] In that same year Indians made several raids on white settlements in Pennsylvania. The storm broke in 1754 in both colonies, with hostilities spreading far and wide. During the ensuing decade the opinion that "the only good Indian is a dead Indian" began to fix itself as a truism in the mind of the American pioneer.

The war itself is known in American history as the French and Indian War. By European historians it is conceived entirely as one phase of a larger conflict, primarily between the French and English, with Prussia and Austria also involved—a Seven Years' War fought in Europe as well as America. The issue in the New World, as the French saw it, was British colonial expansion westward into lands held by the French for three-quarters of a century. The issue, as the English saw it, was France's ambition to become the primary power in North America: she already owned Canada and was claiming the whole Mississippi and Ohio valleys. To American colonists, however, and especially to those on the frontier, the war was one against murderous Indians who, as allies of the French, did most of the fighting in which the pioneers were engaged. Few colonists could yet foresee the day when population might expand across the mountains into the remote regions claimed by the French; what they could plainly see was that their lives and their homes were daily endangered by Indians on the warpath. The French had had little difficulty in persuading Indians to be their allies, for they promised, if successful, to push the English colonists back to the seacoast and to restore to the Indians their former territories.

The story of the war is familiar. In 1753, when Governor Dinwiddie of Virginia demanded that the French retire from the headwaters of the Ohio (territory then claimed by Virginia, though located in western Pennsylvania of today), the French replied by building Fort Duquesne at its forks, near Pittsburgh, the key to the whole Ohio Valley. Although England withheld her declaration of war against France until 1756, she sent General Braddock in 1755 to recover the land claimed by the English at the forks of the Ohio. Braddock's tactless disregard of colonial advice and his ignorance of Indian methods of warfare shattered his red-coated army. The Indians, stimulated by the utter defeat of the British, now broke loose upon frontier settlements all the way from Canada to southern Virginia. "It is incredible," wrote a French captain, "what a quantity of scalps they bring us. . . . These miserable English are in the extremity of distress."[63]

Accounts of the depredations on frontier homes and settlements give us a sense of the terror that was now struck throughout the formerly peaceful countryside. The initial shock to the white man was the Indian mode of fighting: "his method of making war is never open and manly. He skulks in ravines, behind rocks and trees; he creeps out in the night and sets fire to houses and barns; he shoots down, from behind a fence, the ploughman in his furrow; he scalps the women at the spring, and the children by the roadside, with their little hands full of berries."[64] War, as the Indian fought it, was no gentleman's sport, as it still tended to be in Europe. To see one's home burned, one's wife with a battered head, one's children mercilessly killed; to realize that capture was worse than death, since it meant inhuman torture; to perceive that there could nevermore be peace and safety until the Indians had been completely defeated and driven out—all this made the Scotch-Irish rise almost to a man in the imperiled regions.

In Pennsylvania, because of official inaction, the pioneers had to take matters into their own hands. The Quaker hierarchy, having utterly neglected any preparations for defense, was still unwilling to vote adequate men and supplies even after the war had begun, since this went against conscience. Braddock wrote the governor of Pennsylvania in February, 1755, of his astonishment at seeing "one of the Principal Colonies preserving a neutrality when his Majesties Dominions are invaded, when the Enemy is on the Frontier."[65] Despite his protest and the shock of defeat and death, despite the massacres, despite even the overwhelming sentiment of the people for a declaration of war, the Quaker Assembly still held back. It was only in 1756 that the governor took matters into his own hands and proclaimed war; and in that same year the Quakers lost their control of the government of Pennsylvania.

In the set battles of the war, English redcoats did most of the fighting; but the war was, for the pioneers, much more than a series of formal battles. It was a succession of raids and retaliations, in which no white man for years could afford to be off his guard. The Scotch-Irish in Pennsylvania and Virginia did most of this kind of fighting. To one living two centuries later, it is not difficult to perceive the state of mind on each side. The Scotch-Irish, by their constant incursion into western territory and their often complete insensitivity to Indian rights and feelings, were destroying the Indian way of life and making the future seem bleak indeed. On the other hand, the pioneer had made a home in what, to him, had been wilderness and empty land; he had no intention of retiring supinely from what he had created with his own toil. Because his settlements were nearest the Indians and most subject to forays, he had personal reasons for bearing the brunt of years of guerrilla fighting.

The Scotch-Irish soon got over any Old World notions of the "proper" way to fight; they quickly adopted Indian methods. If the savage butchered the white man, the only way to fight back was to butcher the Indian, to scalp him, to burn his villages in surprise attacks. There is no doubt that this is brutal and that whatever finer sensibilities the people may have possessed frequently became dulled.* Chivalry and honor the Scotch-Irish now felt to be fantastic whims if applied to a savage opponent. The policy of appeasement so long followed by the Quakers seemed now mere obstinate stupidity; in its place the rule must be blow for blow, death for death—and woe to the vanquished. The Scotch-Irish carried the war informally into the Indian's territory and wrought desolation at every opportunity.

Easterners in the English parts of Pennsylvania and Virginia could now clearly distinguish between the characteristics of back-country settlers. Germans, in general, especially those in Pennsylvania, retired rather than fight Indians; many of these Rhinelanders were as pacific as the Quakers and the others had taken pains to obtain Indian consent to their settlements. Scotch-Irish, on the other hand, were known to be excitable and hotheaded. Tidewater people generally saw them as "invincible in prejudice,"

---

* Chambers, writing a century later, said: "One of the great evils of war, is its corruption of human nature, and hardening the heart to all the sensibilities of humanity." (*A Tribute to the Principles . . . of the Early Settlers of Pennsylvania*, p. 73)

frequently rude and lawless, implacable to enemies. Yet, as a later historian of the Braddock expedition put it, "they hated the Indian while they despised him. . . . Impatient of restraint, rebellious against anything that in their eyes bore the resemblance of injustice, we find these men readiest among the ready on the battlefields of the Revolution. If they had their faults, a lack of patriotism or of courage was not among the number. Amongst them were to be found men of education, intelligence, and virtue."[66] Ministers fought along with their congregations. Many accounts tell of sermons preached with the minister, gun at hand in the pulpit, keeping watch through the church door for signs of Indians.

The simple fact is that the Scotch-Irish contributed greatly to the ultimate defeat of the Indians and to the end of French control of the Ohio Valley.

The tide of war turned in 1758. In that year Prime Minister Pitt sent over a contingent of troops large enough, when aided by the colonial militia, to capture Fort Duquesne. As this was the key point of French defenses in the whole region, the French now retired not only from the Forks of the Ohio but from forts lying west of it. In 1759 Wolfe took Quebec from Montcalm, and by 1760 the British were in possession of the whole of Canada. Through the Treaty of Paris in 1763 France ceded to Britain all of its American possessions east of the Mississippi, including Canada.

Any expectation of Pennsylvania and Virginia settlers that the capture of Fort Duquesne and the signing of the treaty had ended Indian hostilities was rudely shattered in 1763. In that year Pontiac's War began. The Ottawa chief had convinced Indians of many tribes of the necessity, if the relentless advance of the white man was to be stopped, of uniting in a massive attack on the English colonies. Mutually hostile tribes joined in the fight. This renewed war, desolating in itself, was doubly grim because of Indian fury descending upon the whites at a moment when they hoped peace had been secured. In Pennsylvania two thousand whites were killed and as many more had to flee eastward; in Virginia the Shawnees completely annihilated a settlement on the Greenbrier River, massacred many at Kerr's Creek, and renewed terror throughout the central part of the Valley.

Frontier regions were again desolated. Francis Parkman writes: "The country was filled with the wildest dismay. The people of Virginia betook themselves to their forts for refuge. But those of Pennsylvania, ill supplied with such asylums, fled by thousands, and crowded in upon the older settlements. The ranging parties who visited the scene of devastation beheld, among the ruined farms and plantations, sights of unspeakable horror, and discovered, in the depths of the forests, the half-consumed bodies of men and women, still bound fast to trees, where they had perished in the fiery torture."[67]

Pontiac's War was finally ended after two well-led expeditions into the Ohio country. Two results of the Indian wars, one immediate and the other soon to become apparent, should be noted: the Scotch-Irish had proved their fighting mettle and they had shown a bold independence in action that to many conservatives seemed ominous to political stability.

In every province where there had been Indian trouble the Scotch-Irish fighters had revealed themselves to be able soldiers, rough, ingenious, adaptable, ready to endure hardship. They could be counted upon to fight for all they were worth in a cause in which they believed. Many were soon to demonstrate all their fighting qualities in the larger War for American Independence. More than this, they had displayed willingness to take matters into their own hands, without waiting for guidance and command for authorities. In most cases the results justified their independence of spirit.

In 1763, however, an ugly incident in Pennsylvania revealed the other aspect of Scotch-Irish impetuosity. With Pontiac's men on the rampage and the Quakers in Philadelphia again pursuing a pacific policy, a group of young Scotch-Irish rangers in Dauphin County heard a rumor that the peaceful Conestoga Indians of Lancaster County (adjoining Dauphin to the south) had given secret aid to the hostile Indians. Without waiting to hear all the evidence, these "Paxton Boys"—so-called because they lived in Paxtang township—descended upon the Conestoga settlement and killed twenty of the Indians. This Conestoga Massacre (December, 1763) was barbarous slaughter, but it found wide justification among the Scotch-Irish. More than frontier justice was involved: by killing Indians their lands were freed for settlement by white men. Here was introduced an ambiguity in Indian relations that was to be apparent many times as the white man went west.[68]

Close upon the heels of this incident came an even more ominous demonstration of Scotch-Irish political recklessness. The frontiersmen drew up a formal Remonstrance against the disabilities they felt they endured; but instead of merely sending it quietly to Philadelphia, they gathered an armed crowd of determined men to accompany their emissaries. Easterners regarded this as a dangerous mob, possibly a rebellious one that might attack the capital and forcibly overthrow the government. The crisis passed without a fray, but henceforward few conservatives could avoid an uneasy feeling that the Scotch-Irish might well, with their radicalism and their explosive tempers, undermine the stability of settled institutions.

The violence of Indian disturbances in Pennsylvania and Virginia were, as has been seen, among the causes of Scotch-Irish migration to the Carolinas. There only the Cherokee Uprising had disturbed the peace; and despite many anxious moments for settlers, the loss of life and property even in the worst years, 1756-61, was much less than it had been farther north.*

The French and Indian War had broken the rhythm of the Great Migration. By the time the Indians had been driven back, few Germans from the Rhineland seemed interested in coming to America. Another eighty years were to pass before a new and large German accretion was added to the population of the New World. Ulstermen, however, seemed only to have been waiting

---

* The Indian menace east of the Appalachians was not permanently ended even with the events of 1764. Raids still occurred. As late as 1774 Lord Dunmore had to call upon men of the Shenandoah Valley to fight Indians at Point Pleasant—a battle primarily of Scotch-Irish against Indians. A decade later in southwestern Virginia (now Tazewell County) came the Indian raid that killed most of a family, but displayed the courage of Mary Moore of Abb's Valley, who survived capture and life with the Indians. (This story is well told in Foote, *Sketches of Virginia*, I, 505-24.)

for fighting to end. Emigration to America was resumed in the 1760's, and the greatest tide of all came in the four years immediately preceding the War of the Revolution.

In the story of the Scotch-Irish the decade of the 1760's marks a turning point, as it does in American history. Before 1763 settlement was confined to the region east of the Appalachian range which swept southward from Pennsylvania to Georgia; after that year a vast territory changed from French to British hands beyond these mountains, and settlement within it would not be long delayed. The final shrinkage of Indian lands in the east had been accomplished, and the killing assault on the red man's way of life was now to begin in earnest beyond the mountains. Henceforth Indian sovereignty would be a myth.*

The trans-Allegheny region of the Ohio Valley and the territories south of it were not immediately penetrated by settlers at the conclusion of the French and Indian wars. A royal proclamation of 1763 ordered that no white settlement should be made beyond the mountains, in the new territory acquired by Britain. At the time, this seemed a realistic boundary line, with white settlers to the east and Indians to the west; and it remained a practical one until after the War for Independence had been won, although eastern Tennessee and Kentucky had already by then received their first white settlers. After 1782, however, it seemed as if a considerable part of America was determined to go west; and in the vanguard of the pioneers were the restless Scotch-Irish.

It is with this westward sweep that the account of the Scotch-Irish ends. Whether in eastern Tennessee, in Kentucky, or in western Pennsylvania, there were among the first arrivals Americans of all sorts. Across the mountains began a new phase of American history, for here people of many national backgrounds met and merged as they had never done in the east. From the Appalachians westward to the Pacific Ocean the pioneer was simply an American, not an Englishman, Scotch-Irishman, or German, nor even primarily a Pennsylvanian or Virginian

* Guess remarks: "The Catawbas of upper South Carolina pathetically symbolize the attrition. Once roaming the whole length of the river which bears their name, they agreed in 1763 to a fifteen-mile-square holding, diminished in modern times to a 625-acre tract in York county." (*South Carolina*, p. 67)

or New Englander.* Nothing like the familiar concentration of Scotch-Irish in one neighborhood and Germans in another settlement took place in the West; on the contrary, there began the intermingling and intermarriage that now is characteristic of the American people.

Few aspects of American history have become more familiar than this "winning of the west" and settlement of the frontier. There would be little point in still another account of it. Let it suffice to say that the Scotch-Irish element made itself strongly felt in the first sweep beyond the mountains. This would be so, if for no other reason, because this people were settled in the largest numbers just east of the mountains. The frontier on the other side was most accessible to them; they were adept in conquering the wilderness and fighting the Indians; and thousands of them were ready to move. In southwestern Virginia they had already before the outbreak of the Revolution reached the Cumberland Gap leading toward the west, and from Virginia to Kentucky and Tennessee was a short move. North Carolinians had found the way through their mountains into Tennessee as early as 1771. In both of these new territories immigration poured after 1782, until Kentucky was ready for statehood a decade later, and Tennessee by 1796. It is worthy of note that in the histories of neither state is ethnic or national background ("racial" stock) of the first settlers often stressed, but rather Kentucky's connections with Virginia and Tennessee's with North Carolina.

Western Pennsylvania exhibits as clearly as any other transmontane region not only the western push, but the merging of the Scotch-Irish with other Americans until they were no longer a distinctive people.

Among the first settlers in the area around Fort Pitt (now Pittsburgh) were people from Maryland and Virginia. Their path, even from Tidewater and Piedmont regions, was not a difficult one, for they had only to follow the road marked out by Braddock in 1755—from Baltimore along the Potomac as far as Cumberland in western Maryland, and thence northward

* There are, of course, exceptions to this generalization. Certain immigrants of the mid-nineteenth century settled in colonies and sometimes retained their ethnic identity for a generation or more. This was particularly true of some of the Scandinavians and to a lesser extent of certain Germans.

through the Monongahela Valley to the settlement around Fort Pitt at the junction of the Ohio and Allegheny rivers. Scotch-Irish Pennsylvanians found their way through the mountainous regions, along passes familiar for decades to fur traders. Because these Scotch-Irish of the Cumberland Valley were the largest and nearest source of supply, it is not surprising that they soon outnumbered people of other stocks in western Pennsylvania.*

By 1790 Pittsburgh had become a flourishing town in the midst of a growing region of farmers and an active supply point for the constant stream of Americans on their way into the Ohio Valley. Pennsylvania historians say that the whole territory was prevailingly Scotch-Irish, an assertion strengthened by the preponderance of Presbyterian churches in the vicinity. While it is the contention of this book that the people no longer thought in terms of their ancestral origin, it is tempting to see Scotch-Irish characteristics at play in one of the first notable events of the history of western Pennsylvania, the so-called Whisky Rebellion of 1794.

Only five years after the United States government was established, the farmers of this region, like their fathers of the East, once more defied constituted authority. They rebelled against taxes levied on their principal product and almost their only source of money, whisky. The notoriety attending this Rebellion convinced legislators in the national capital of the growing importance of the West in the life of the country. For many years thereafter the issue of roads and canals to link East and West dominated national politics. More and more Americans, as settlers poured into the Ohio Valley, could foresee the future development and significance of that part of the United States. Pittsburgh became known as the Gateway to the West for the Middle States.

* Germans participated hardly at all in this first surge to the West. Not only had German immigration to America dwindled; but more than this, the Germans seemed content with the quiet and orderly life of their farming communities in the East. They had found in America what they were seeking; it could hardly be bettered by moving. Indian trading had rarely appealed to the Germans, and still less (especially to those of pacifistic sects) Indian fighting. Pennsylvania Germans were, quite simply, the best farmers in the new Republic, and owned the best farm lands. What more could the West offer? See Sutherland, *Population Distribution in Colonial America*, p. 149.

If people of Scotch-Irish origin were largely responsible for opening this gate westward, it was Americans who went through it. The Scotch-Irish, as such, were now a subject matter for historians and antiquarians.[*]

E. SMALLER SETTLEMENTS OF SCOTCH-IRISH

All of the thirteen original American colonies received Scotch-Irish settlers. By comparison with the main stream that flowed through Pennsylvania, the Valley of Virginia, and the Carolina Piedmont, however, Scotch-Irish settlement in other colonies was insignificant in numbers. The strength of Presbyterianism in many of the colonies (New Jersey, for example) was not, as might be supposed, evidence of Scotch-Irish settlement; on the contrary, most of these churches had been founded by English and Welsh Presbyterians and many by immigrants directly from Scotland.

A clear distinction should be made at this point between colonists from Scotland and those from Ulster, for the two have often, to the complete distortion of events, been thought identical. It has already been noted that by 1717 Scots and Ulstermen were two different nationalities. Extensive emigration from Scotland to America occurred during the eighteenth century, possibly a fourth or a fifth as large as that from Ulster; but the reasons for Scottish emigration were distinct. Before the union of the two Crowns in 1707, many Scots were exiled as criminals and many more came as indentured servants or as merchants to America. After the Union, since Scots had equal rights with Englishmen, including the right of moving to the colonies, thousands came over to escape the grinding poverty at home. Defeat of the Highlanders in 1746, after the collapse of the Stuart cause, with the determination of the government to "civilize" these people, caused a large exodus; and the enclosure of lands, the dispossession of tenants, and the consequent dissolution of ties of personal

---

[*] Dunaway is among those who regard "racial" origins as still important. He says: "Prevailingly Scotch-Irish by 1790, this territory became increasingly so in the next generation and formed a second reservoir of this race, which overflowed northward and westward as time passed. . . . Southwestern Pennsylvania became in time the principal stronghold of this race in the commonwealth." (Dunaway, *Scotch-Irish of Colonial Pennsylvania,* p. 85)

loyalty binding man to chief, sent thousands of others to America. The pull from the colonies was, as usual, the opportunity for a better life. At times during the nineteenth century there came to be a positive "rage for emigration" throughout both Lowlands and Highlands.

Scots in America from the first showed traits clearly different from those of the Scotch-Irish. Scots were seldom explorers, Indian fighters, or frontier traders; they played only a minor role as pioneers, preferring to settle in the east and to carry on business enterprises. Their greatest difference from their Ulster cousins, however, was seen at the time of the American Revolution: whereas the Scotch-Irish were usually ardent patriots and notable fighters in the cause of the colonies, the Scots were, with notable exceptions, Loyalists faithful to the Crown. Only in their Presbyterianism and a few of their traits of personality did they resemble the Scotch-Irish. In North Carolina the Highland Scots for a long while retained their Gaelic language and even their Highland dress.[69]

(1) New England

Since New England was Calvinist and Puritan, it might have seemed logical that Presbyterians from Ulster would be drawn to that region. New Englanders were godly in their morality, were growing in population, and were developing a lucrative trade; they had proved themselves by the time of the Scotch-Irish migrations to be stable, thrifty, and prosperous.

To Massachusetts, indeed, the Ulster Scots had first turned their eyes, and long before the Great Migration of the eighteenth century. After the harrowing days of 1636 in Ulster, when it seemed that the very Plantation might fail, a group of Presbyterian ministers wrote to the church leaders in Massachusetts inquiring about the possibility of settling with their congregations in that colony. Cotton Mather gives an account of this episode, although, because the ministers were Scots and sent their letter of inquiry directly from Scotland, he seems unaware that the project concerned a migration from Ulster. He says:

There were divers gentlemen in Scotland, who, being uneasy under the ecclesiastical burdens of the times, wrote on to New England the inquiries:—whether they might be there suffered freely to exercise their Presbyterial church government? And it was freely answered—that they might. Thereupon they sent over an agent, who pitched upon a tract of land near the mouth of the Merrimac River, whither they intended to transplant themselves. But although they had so far proceeded in their voyage as to be half-seas through, the manifold crosses they met withal, made them give over their intentions; and the providence of God so ordered it that some of these very gentlemen were afterwards the revivers of that well-known *Solemn League and Covenant,* which had so great an influence upon the nation.[70]

The "manifold crosses" to which Mather refers were a series of storms which so endangered their frail ship, *Eagle Wing,* that she had to put back into port if all lives were not to be sacrificed. The attempt to settle in New England was to be long postponed.

In the years between 1636 and 1717 New England became acquainted with Scots and Ulstermen, many of whom were landed upon its shores involuntarily. When Oliver Cromwell, having subdued England, turned his attention to Scotland in order to make the recalcitrant Presbyterians submit to Parliament, he defeated them disastrously at Dunbar in 1650. Thereupon he transported at least two shiploads of Presbyterian prisoners as unwilling indentured servants to Massachusetts. Some 250 of these exiles reached Boston early in 1652.[71] Throughout the remainder of the century occasional indentured servants came to Boston from Ireland, some of them from Ulster, but many of them Catholics from the south. The Puritans liked neither Scots nor Irish, partly because of their religion and their different national backgrounds but more especially because of their illiteracy, their physical dirtiness and slovenliness, and their notable divergence from Puritan customs, habits, and outlook. As household servants Scots were esteemed the best by the New Englanders, Irish Catholics the worst, and Ulster servants as satisfactory.[72]

Although Puritans had shown distaste for aliens, one of the first expeditions of the Great Migration directed its course to Massachusetts Bay. Early in the spring of 1718 several hundred people in the Valley of the Bann, south of Coleraine in Ulster, sent an agent to Boston. These people wished to remove to the

Puritan colony. The agent brought to Governor Shute an engrossed parchment to assure him of the good faith and "earnest resolve" of the emigrants. The governor encouraged the proposal, and the colonists, having converted their property into money, embarked in five ships for Boston, arriving on August 4, 1718. A Bostonian of the time noted contemptuously that "a parcel of Irish" had arrived, the "parcel" consisting of between six and eight hundred persons. (The designation of the newcomers as "Irish" was inexact, and not merely because of possible confusion with the Catholic Irish. A good number of them, including those with the most favorable economic position, were actually natives of Scotland, having come to Ulster only during the Covenanter troubles from 1685 to 1688. They were Ulster Scots, but more Scottish than Ulstermen.)

Their reception at Boston was grudging in the extreme. They apparently expected (although there is no proof that they had made inquiry on the matter) that they would be allowed religious freedom. They were shortly informed, however, that citizenship would not be granted in any Puritan colony except by membership in the established church, the Congregational. Only a few colonists expressed willingness to forsake the Presbyterian form. Governor Shute generously granted the rest a "township right," permitting them to occupy any suitable area, twelve miles square, on the frontier, and recommended to them the region around Casco Bay, near the present city of Portland, Maine.

About a quarter of the people thereupon went to Casco Bay in the late fall. The Maine winter was more severe than the people had ever experienced in Ireland; several of the families had to remain all winter upon their ship, and all suffered from hunger and privation. When spring came, they were determined to seek a settlement in a warmer and less exposed location. A few remained behind, to establish themselves in other parts of Maine, in the region around Wiscasset. The rest, however, upon landing at Haverhill, on the Merrimac, learned of a fine tract only fifteen miles to the northwest, in what is now southern New Hampshire. Having examined the place, a pleasant valley notable for its nut trees, they determined to settle there, changing its name from Nutfield to Londonderry, to remind them of Ulster and of the siege in which their families had distinguished themselves thirty years before. Here they were joined by most of the other colonists, who had spent the winter near Andover.

On the frontier, away from the Puritans, they founded their own church and developed a thriving community. In 1723 they built a house for their minister, and in the next year a church. By 1729 they had founded four schools in their township. An evidence of the fecundity of the people is seen in the fact that during the next half century they made ten other settlements in New Hampshire, two in Vermont, one in Pennsylvania, and two in Nova Scotia.

Fifty of the families of 1718, however, instead of going to Maine and then to New Hampshire, went directly from Boston to the frontier post of Worcester. Here there had been many recent troubles with Indians, and the new arrivals were given a cordial welcome because they strengthened the defense of the post. Initial cordiality, however, turned shortly to extreme dislike and then to open hostility. The focus of the prejudice, whatever its other bases, was the difference in religion. When the Presbyterians lost their first minister, they were persuaded to give up their own church and unite with the Puritans, upon the clear understanding that the pulpit might occasionally be filled by a Presbyterian. This agreement was not carried out; on the contrary, the Scotch-Irish found themselves paying tithes to support a minister and a church not their own. Upon their petition for relief from the tithe, the township abruptly denied the Presbyterians their right to independence from the "establishment." Immediately many families left for the frontier, but those who remained determined to build their own church. When the building was partly finished, the Puritans dismantled it, sawed up its timbers, burned or carried off the materials.[73] The exodus now became general. Scotch-Irish from Worcester were consequently the founders of several new frontier colonies: at Pelham and Coleraine, thirty or forty miles west of Worcester; at Blandford, west of modern Springfield; at Warren (formerly Western), near the border of Worcester County, and in Otsego County in New York.

Treatment of the Scotch-Irish by New Englanders was little different from that accorded other outsiders by the Puritans. The policy of the New England colonies was clearly one of exclusion of all who differed from them in religion and in national background. At the insistence of Charles II, church membership had disappeared from the qualifications for suffrage, but orthodoxy took its place. New England remained so homogeneous throughout the seventeenth century that aliens who arrived were conspicuous. Their presence was tolerated, but not their divergence. Newcomers were assimilated as rapidly as possible to local culture—or were made uncomfortable.*

A "nativist" feeling was reinforced by economic considerations. In the years before 1714 Boston had a serious problem of the unemployed poor, and the selectmen had hardly arranged for their care, at the cost of higher taxes, when the first Ulstermen appeared. Their numbers were so great at a time when prices were rising rapidly that authorities feared lest "these confounded Irish" should eat the Bostonians out of house and home.[74] Many of the immigrants promptly went on the rates, to the understandable annoyance of the citizens. From 1701 to 1715 over 230 aliens had been warned to leave town immediately; during the next five years, when the Ulster immigration began, more than 330 were warned.[75] Among these were 49 miserable passengers who arrived on a single ship from Northern Ireland. The treatment may have been harsh, yet it is understandable that the Bostonians should not wish to encumber themselves with the growing expense of caring for dependents who were not citizens. Again in 1723 hundreds of Scotch-Irish arrived; to forestall future trouble with these people, it was ordered that all who had

* New England received many non-Puritans during the second half of the seventeenth century, but none of them established a community of their own. In 1651 a ship of Scots and Ulstermen landed at Boston; in 1654 a group of "Irish" (Ulster) redemptioners came to the same port. Cromwell's 250 Scottish prisoners arrived in 1652 to be sold as servants. Governor Belcher in 1751 reported that a thousand people from Ulster had come in during the preceding decade—although it is not clear whether he may not have been including in that number the original six to eight hundred already discussed above. Of a total population of ten thousand in 1751, New Hampshire reported that one thousand were "Irish." Efforts of Anglicans, Quakers, and Baptists to form communities in colonial New England are commonplaces of American history. See O'Brien, "Irish Pioneers in New England," *Journal* of the Am. Hist. Soc., XVIII, 127; and *Documents relating to the Province of New Hampshire*, IV, 532-33.

arrived since 1720 should register with the Town Clerk for purposes of a survey.[76]

Feeling against "foreigners" became so intense by 1729 that "a mob arose to prevent ye landing of Irish," and the watch had to be strengthened to preserve order in the town. During the decline of trade in the next decade, again new arrivals were warned out of town, and one ship captain was forbidden to land any of his "Transports."[*][77]

Wherever the Scotch-Irish went in New England it was made abundantly clear to them that they were unwelcome. The final offshoot of the original group settled in Voluntown (now Stirling) in northeastern Connecticut, where they may have been joined by others from New Jersey. When these Presbyterians called their first minister in 1723, the town council met and presented a Remonstrance against the minister, "because he is a stranger; and we are informed that he came out of Ireland; and we do observe that since he has been in town that the Irish do flock into town; and we are informed that the Irish are not wholesome inhabitants."[†]

Boston was the only New England port to receive any impressive number of Ulster immigrants. A few came to Newport, Rhode Island, in the 1740's, and during the last great surge of migration, it was reported that 717 Ulstermen arrived there in the single year 1773.[78] In contrast with the South, eighteenth-century New England did not need, and could not use, large numbers of indentured servants. Even when the religious ardor of Puritanism began to decline, the cultural homogeneity of the region made immigrants unwelcome and uncomfortable. It is understandable, therefore, that the Great Migration from Ulster should affect New England but slightly. No accurate estimate of the total number of immigrants (including indentured servants) to the Puritan provinces can be made; it is possible that, counting the servants who came as early as 1650, as many as twenty thousand Ulstermen came to New England. Of them all, only

[*] Smith notes that the number of indentured servants entering New England "was negligible after 1645,"—another evidence of the feeling of nativism. (Smith, *Colonists in Bondage*, p. 337)

[†] This church nevertheless struggled along until 1779, when it became Congregational, "probably a mark of ultimate assimilation of the Scotch-Irish by the New Englanders." (Hanna, *The Scotch-Irish*, II, 22)

the Londonderry settlers of 1718 flourished as a Presbyterian community; the random indentured servants and other immigrants were soon assimilated.*

(2) *The Middle Colonies*

Presbyterianism throughout the eighteenth century was strong in all of the Middle colonies—New York, New Jersey, Pennsylvania, and Delaware; as for Maryland, the denomination had its first organized churches in the New World in this province. Since by 1800 the Presbyterian Church in America was preponderantly Scotch-Irish in membership, it might be concluded that large numbers of Ulstermen made their homes in the Middle colonies. The actuality is precisely the opposite. Except for Pennsylvania, these provinces attracted fewer Scotch-Irish settlers than any other region of America.

It is useful to recall at this point the variety of background and designation among the followers of John Calvin. On the European continent, Calvinists called their churches "Reformed" and generally organized them along national lines—Dutch Reformed, German Reformed, and French (Huguenots). In the British Isles the designation used by Calvinists referred either to church government or to rigor of moral codes. Thus, Calvinists who stressed representative government by elders in church courts were Presbyterians; those who preferred rule by each separate congregation were Independents (or, as Americans came to call them, Congregationalists); and the rigid moralists were Puritans. There might be combinations of these—Presbyterian puritans, Congregational puritans, and more rarely, congregations ruled by elders but not by presbyteries.

In the migrations to America all of these persuasions were represented. Most New Englanders were Congregational puri-

---

* Perry observes that New England seems to be fatal to the Presbyterian form. "Presbyterianism came to us early; it came strong; it reinforced itself from time to time with new and large recruits, but it could not root in Yankee land." He remarks that, although Presbyterian churches were founded over and over again, "the presbyteries have run one steady and inevitable course toward extinction." When he wrote in 1891, he commented that "there is one nominal presbytery in New England today doing duty only on the official records of the church, denominated 'Boston,' but it was utterly unrepresented in the General Assembly last week. . . . It has a name to live, but it is dead." (Perry, *The Scotch-Irish in New England*, p. 50)

tans. Charleston and Savannah had Independent Presbyterian churches. Dutch and German Reformed churches followed their members to the colonies. But the traditional Presbyterian government was congenial to those settlers who had been Presbyterians in England, Wales, Scotland, and Ireland, and to the Huguenots from France.

For thirty-five years before the Great Migration from Northern Ireland began in 1717, the Presbyterian Church in the Middle colonies had grown quietly and steadily. Among its congregations were a few persons from Ulster—an occasional merchant or trader on the Eastern Shore of Maryland, a family or single person who had come as an indentured servant to Pennsylvania or Delaware. But these were far outnumbered by Presbyterians with a different background, especially in the English tradition of the faith. As it began, so it continued throughout the eighteenth century, always with the great exception of Pennsylvania. The account of Scotch-Irish settlement in the other Middle colonies is a short tale soon told.

New York. Despite its size and its growing importance throughout the eighteenth century, New York rarely attracted Ulstermen. After the English took over the province from the Dutch in the 1660's, many years were to pass before New York was able to draw numerous colonists of any sort. Governor Dongan reported in 1687 that in the preceding seven years not more than twenty families had entered the province from England, Scotland, and Ireland together.[79] Matters shortly improved, however, and the Dutch element became steadily outnumbered by the arrival of Englishmen, New Englanders, Huguenots, and Germans.

The Presbyterian Church in the province had its start on Long Island. Here came certain Presbyterians from England and, because of its nearness to Connecticut, many Puritans from New England. In several instances the Calvinists in a neighborhood found it expedient to compromise by organizing a Presbyterian church to be served by a Puritan divine. The arrival of Huguenots in Westchester County meant the organization of other Presbyterian churches, so that by 1700 there were thirteen of these around the small town of New York, though none within it. There the Anglicans were hard upon dissenters, and their harshness was supported by the attitude of the royal governors of the time; indeed, the High Churchman, Lord Cornbury, in 1706 ordered the arrest of the notable Presbyterian minister, Francis Makemie, for preaching in the town without a license.

When the Great Migration from Ulster began, therefore, leaders saw nothing to attract them to New York. Its land policy was not generous; its country regions along the Hudson were taken up in great estates; and no especial effort had been made by officials or agents to attract colonists from Northern Ireland. By the time the province of New York began to show its real promise, Pennsylvania had already become the lodestone for immigrants from Ulster. Colonial records indicate that only three small colonies of Scotch-Irish settled in New York throughout the eighteenth century.*

Sir William Johnson in 1741 brought in sixty Scotch-Irish families to settle at Warrenbush, in the interior county of Otsego; and these were joined shortly by a few of their compatriots and by some thirty emigrants from the Scotch-Irish community of Londonderry, New Hampshire. A second clustering occurred around 1750, near Goshen (in Orange County, about forty miles northwest of New York City) and at Wallkill (in the county significantly named Ulster, just north of Orange). A third settlement, made up chiefly of Scotch-Irish who had migrated from New England, was to be found near Salem and Stillwater, in Washington County near the Vermont border.[80]

These were all—a few hundreds in comparison with the thousands of Scotch-Irish added annually to the population of Pennsylvania, Virginia, and the Carolinas.† Their number was increased by the arrival of indentured servants, though here again New York had not the drawing power of provinces to the south. The greatest use for the labor of servants was always to be

---

* It is interesting to note, however, that many Germans, whose countrymen likewise had found Pennsylvania attractive, discovered in central New York a most desirable haven. New York is the single province in which Scotch-Irish settlement did not parallel German settlement in the same region.

† Scottish migration to New York exceeded that from Ulster. Ford suggests that "emigration from Ulster to the interior counties of New York was incidental to emigration from Scotland, which usually took in Ulster ports on the way." (Ford, The Scotch-Irish in America, p. 258)

found upon southern plantations and the prosperous farms in Pennsylvania; thus both Philadelphia and Charleston outstripped New York as ports of entry for indentured servants from Northern Ireland. The growing town on Manhattan Island, like other American towns, needed as servants chiefly girls to work in a household or men with some special skill as blacksmiths, carpenters, weavers, tailors, or cordwainers. As the century advanced, and especially during the final wave of migration touched off by severe economic depression in Ulster, the number of artisans coming to New York increased. A report in 1774 noted that "many Irish are come here,"—a statement confirmed by the frequency of Scotch-Irish names appearing in advertisements.[81]

New Jersey. The province of New Jersey became one of the strongholds of Presbyterianism in colonial America, but it was Scots, not Ulstermen, who made it so. In 1682, upon the death of Sir George Carteret, several prominent Scots joined in the purchase of his interest in the proprietorship of East Jersey. Their extensive advertisement of the colony at home attracted many Lowland Scots, especially those who at the very moment were involved in Covenanter difficulties. Settling near Perth-Amboy, they soon spread throughout the colony. Still other Scots, chiefly Presbyterian Highlanders, came thither after 1746 because of their embroilment with the losing cause of the Stuarts. The success of these first Scots in New Jersey led to a substantial migration of others of their fellow-countrymen between 1760 and the outbreak of the Revolution.

Few Scotch-Irish were to be found as settlers in New Jersey, and again because the main stream of migration flowed through Pennsylvania and because the province was not a favorite market for indentured servants. In a large sense, however, New Jersey played a considerable role in the history of the Scotch-Irish in America. The Scottish Presbyterians of New Jersey, seeing the need for training ministers of their persuasion, founded at Princeton in 1746 their College of New Jersey, the first true Presbyterian institution of higher learning in the colonies. From this college ministers went out to congregations of Scotch-Irish people even as far south as Georgia, and to it came young men from these back-country settlements to receive their training. Thus, although the province of New Jersey had not provided an actual home for many Ulstermen besides the occasional indentured servants, it became a kind of spiritual center for Scotch-Irishmen throughout America.

Delaware. The settlers in the three counties of Delaware were first of all Swedes and thereafter prevailingly English. Here again the Presbyterian element, with English and Welsh backgrounds, was considerable; before the Scotch-Irish migration began there were enough churches of the denomination to unite themselves into New Castle Presbytery. By 1717 Delaware lands were well settled, with no truly frontier regions to attract colonists. Because the port of New Castle was the first to be reached by ships entering the Delaware Bay, the colony served as a major gateway for Ulstermen on their way to Pennsylvania. Inevitably a considerable number of them remained in Delaware, particularly those who had come as indentured servants and whose four years in that capacity had made them prefer the security of civilized life to pioneering in the west. Only a limited number of newcomers, however, could be absorbed in Delaware's two northern counties; and the southernmost, Sussex, not only had the reputation of having an unhealthy climate, but was also feeling the economic depression of neighboring counties on Maryland's Eastern Shore.[82]

Maryland. The Chesapeake Bay not only divides Maryland geographically; it also separates two kinds of Scotch-Irish settlers. Those on the western side of the bay came primarily as indentured servants, most of them arriving during the last two decades of the Great Migration. Those on the Eastern Shore were early arrivals and were among the very first to intermingle with settlers of different origin and background.

Social history of the Eastern Shore before 1717 is illuminating. The geographical course of the peninsula from south to north is likewise the course of the order of settlement. The Eastern Shore begins in the south with Virginia counties, whose soil and landscape are almost identical with those of the adjacent Maryland counties. In its northern reaches the peninsula is shared by Maryland, Delaware, and Pennsylvania, near whose junction settlers of varied backgrounds met and merged. Not long after

Jamestown, Englishmen laid out plantations on the Eastern Shore to raise that crop of all crops in the seventeenth century, tobacco. They bought slaves and acquired as many indentured servants as they could afford; their plantations soon covered the Maryland as well as the Virginia parts of the Eastern Shore.

By the 1650's English Presbyterians were living in this region in numbers large enough to attract notice. Since few Presbyterians of that period could have afforded to purchase a plantation or would have felt at home in the society of planters, it seems probable, despite the lack of precise information, that these people were mostly indentured servants whose term had been served out. Observers speak of them as merchants, traders, middlemen, and artisans of various kinds. Their services in these capacities would be highly useful in the plantation economy.

Scots also came to the Eastern Shore as indentured servants in the latter half of the century. The usual motivations were at work, chief among them, the lure of possible wealth in the tobacco colonies, grinding poverty at home, Covenanter and other religious troubles. To read of the Scots on the Eastern Shore is to perceive the first steps of the Scottish people toward the reputation they were soon to enjoy for business canniness. There is the record, for example, of a Scot who, after serving his indenture, became first a surveyor, then the founder of iron works, and finally a builder of flour mills. All of these useful enterprises brought him sufficient income for the purchase of a large estate and earned him considerable prestige in the province.[83]

Two contemporary statements likewise reveal the acumen of the Maryland Scots. Governor Nicholson wrote in 1697 that a decade or so before, six or seven hundred of these people "had settled in Somerset county, and had gone in for the manufacture of woollen goods" much needed in the area.[84] It was also said by "a Traveller" that some of the Scots around Snow Hill were engaged in an illicit, but profitable, trade in tobacco.[85] This seems entirely probable. Before the Union of 1707 between England and Scotland, the Crown forbade traffic in tobacco between the colonies and Scottish ports; but merchants of Glasgow, Dumfries, and Leith need not have felt moral scruple in engaging in an enterprise forbidden by their ancient enemies, especially a lucrative one.

It is impossible to say how many indentured servants from Ulster also came to the Eastern Shore; some were certainly there, and possibly as many as from Scotland. Sir Thomas Laurence, Secretary of the province, said in a report of June 25, 1695: "In the two counties of Dorchester and Somerset, where the Scotch-Irish are most numerous, they almost clothe themselves by their linen and woollen manufactures, and plant little tobacco."[86] Altogether there were enough Presbyterians in the region to create a demand for a minister; and it was here that the first Presbyterian churches in the American continent were organized by a minister from Ulster, Francis Makemie, in the years after 1683.*

The opening years of the eighteenth century saw a gradual exhaustion of soil on tobacco plantations both on the Eastern Shore and across the Chesapeake. With this decline of prosperity based upon the staple, those enterprises which had supported English and Scottish traders and manufacturers also suffered. Inevitably the population declined as people began a steady movement northward on the Eastern Shore. Economically, it was a movement from plantation services to small farming; geographically, it was a movement toward the "Head of Chesapeake," where the Susquehanna empties into the bay, and where both Pennsylvania and Delaware make boundaries for Maryland's northeastern county of Cecil.

A glance at the map will reveal the significance of this region in Scotch-Irish history. Cecil County lies only a few miles west of the first major port in the Delaware basin, that of New Castle;

---

* Makemie was not the first Presbyterian minister in America. At least three others had preached to English and Scottish Presbyterians in Maryland before 1683, although none of them organized churches as did Makemie. The Reverend Francis Doughty came into the Maryland part of the East Shore from the Virginia county of Accomack around 1657. In the next decade "a Presbyterian divine of militant memory," the Reverend Charles Nicholet, preached "a politically-minded sermon before the House of Burgesses." On the western side of the Chesapeake, the Reverend Matthew Hill preached to an English congregation. Writing from Charles County, on the neck of land between the Potomac and Patuxent rivers in 1669, he stated that "there are many here of the reformed religion, who have a long while lived as sheep without a shepherd, though last year brought in a young man from Ireland, who has already had good success in the work." (Andrews, The Founding of Maryland, p. 305; Hanna, The Scotch-Irish, p. II, 7)

it touches the (modern) Pennsylvania counties of Chester and Lancaster in the very region where Ulster immigrants were given their initial grant by Secretary Logan; the Susquehanna River, along whose banks in Pennsylvania the Scotch-Irish were soon to settle in numbers, is the western margin of Cecil County. Newcomers from Ulster, landing at New Castle, ignorant of Provincial boundaries, and heading toward frontier lands, would pass in numbers through Cecil. Many of them, indeed, finding here not only available land, but also fellow-Presbyterians, made this their home. What is more significant is that there took place considerable intermingling of the three prevailing stocks, English, Scottish, and now Scotch-Irish. They were small farmers with common problems, speaking the same language, sharing the same faith, shaping their civil institutions and community life. Intermarriage among the young people soon followed. The clannishness that kept Scotch-Irish from intermixture with their neighbors the Germans in Pennsylvania, Virginia, and the Carolinas, was absent in northeastern Maryland. By the middle of the nineteenth century the intermingling of peoples, together with the constant mobility of Americans, had resulted in the practical disappearance of a separate Scotch-Irish strain in Cecil County—as also in nearby Chester, Lancaster, and York counties in Pennsylvania.

One of the clearest evidences of what had happened to the former concentration of Presbyterians in the central parts of the Eastern Shore is the fate of the churches there. When the Synod of Philadelphia was organized in 1717, one of its four component Presbyteries was to be that of Snow Hill, the district where Makemie had founded five churches. This Presbytery, however, was now so depleted in numbers by emigration that it could not function, and most of its churches wasted away to nothing.*

* The antiquarian, W. S. Ray, makes the important point that North Carolina derived many of its Piedmont settlers from the Eastern Shore of Maryland. He has traced the families of eleven signers of the Mecklenburg Declaration to homes in Cecil County. He thinks also that, with the decline of prosperity in the Snow Hill area, a considerable number of the people went directly to the Carolinas: "The records disclose that often members of the same family would go one way while others went another; one neighbor to Pennsylvania and another to Carolina." He does not solve the problem of the path by which these people reached the Carolinas, nor where they settled in the four decades between the

If the Eastern Shore of Maryland was significant in the social history of the earliest Scotch-Irish, the lands west of the Chesapeake were representative of Tidewater regions in that they received large numbers of later indentured servants. While English immigration to the colonies declined sharply after 1689, the need for servants in the southern colonies continued to increase. The slack in the English supply was taken up by the Scotch-Irish and Germans, with the former providing "by far the greatest number." Maryland plantations received their greatest accessions of servants in the years between 1750 and 1775, when some 25,000 (among whom were some convicts) came into the province. Records at Annapolis show that 5,835 came directly from Ireland; it is impossible to judge how many others, starting from Ulster, came to Maryland by way of Bristol or some other English port.[87]

After the usual four years of indenture, the servants were then free to make their own life in America. It was almost certain that the freed servant, if he had ambition, would not remain in Maryland, unless he had developed some special skill as an artisan. The available farm lands in western Maryland had long since been settled by Germans moving south from Pennsylvania. The best possibilities for the ex-servant, therefore, lay in the Piedmont of Virginia and the Carolinas, especially the latter, to which thousands of Scotch-Irish were then on their way.

(3) *The Tidewater South*

It has been seen that Virginia, North Carolina, and South Carolina drew thousands of Scotch-Irish to their back-country. The seaboard, on the contrary, with its plantation economy and its Established Church, made little appeal as a region of permanent homemaking. One might profitably begin there in indentured service, however. Of the three provinces, South Carolina probably had more Ulstermen near the coast than either of the other two. Presbyterianism was well represented in the Tidewater of both Carolinas by 1750, but it was Scottish in both cases. Although Scottish immigration to America does not con-

---

decline of Snow Hill and the settlement of the Piedmont. Nor is it clear how many of the families he traces had come originally to the East Shore directly from Scotland and how many from Ulster. (Ray, *The Lost Tribes*, pp. 518 ff., 535-37)

cern us, Presbyterianism does; and it is worth noting briefly why Scots were located in the Tidewater.

Around 1683 several Scottish noblemen and gentlemen incurred the royal displeasure of Charles II by their opposition to his "prelacy." They thereupon purchased a large tract of land from the Lords Proprietors of South Carolina and sent over a number of their countrymen who were suffering from governmental pressure because of their faith. Their reception in the province was scarcely cordial, yet their colony survived, with the addition of other Scots in later years. By 1700 there were enough dissenters of the Reformed faith in the capital city of the province, Charleston, to found a church and call a minister. Because the members included Presbyterians, Huguenots, and Puritans from New England, it was decided that the church should be ruled by elders (presbyters) but remain independent of any connection with an organization, whether the Church of Scotland or the Congregational establishment in New England. Most of its early ministers were drawn from the Church of Scotland.* Five Presbyterian churches had been formed in the neighborhood of Charleston by 1710.

In the fifty-eight years of the Great Migration, an occasional shipload of immigrants from Northern Ireland found their way to Charleston. The details are scanty, and it seems that most of them were indentured servants. Howe, the historian of the Presbyterian Church, says that "many" Scotch-Irish people came to the colony, but found the Congregational Church the only religious organization using their form of worship. In these churches the newcomers found a welcome; "but, desiring ministers of the Westminster Confession, they soon broke away to set up a Presbyterian Church in a small wooden edifice in 1731."[88]

In this same decade other Scotch-Irish settlements were made around Williamsburgh and Kingston. "On October 27, 1732, a ship arrived from Belfast with eighty-five passengers," and in 1737 the Reverend John Baxter reported that he "had brought in forty-three persons from Belfast."[89] There were Presbyterian churches at Cainhoy, on Edisto Island, on James Island, and on

---

* The most notable of these was the Reverend Archibald Stobo, who served from 1700 to 1740. He was one of the ancestors of Theodore Roosevelt.

John's Island by 1710; a church was founded at Charleston in 1734 and one at Beaufort in 1756. Walterborough had a congregation in 1728 and Williamsburgh by 1736. Dr. Stobo served not only the Independent Church at Charleston but the Presbyterian congregation at Wilton (Colleton) by 1704.[90] The very presence of so many Presbyterian churches argues a considerable settlement of people of this faith, and one must suppose that many of them were Ulstermen.

By 1763, when the province had become interested in attracting settlers into the up-country, a bounty was offered to stimulate immigration. This consisted of a "headright" of a hundred acres for each man, with fifty acres for each woman and child.[91] The government, moreover, supplied the arrivals with "the most indispensable implements of agriculture."[92] This bounty was offered just as the Scotch-Irish from Pennsylvania and Virginia had reached the upper Piedmont by way of North Carolina. There was now a valid reason for sailing straight from Belfast to Charleston, instead of landing at Philadelphia and traversing the seven hundred miles of the Great Wagon Road. "Scarce a ship sailed" from any port in Ireland for Charleston, we are told, "that was not crowded with men, women, and children." But McCrady notes that the Scotch-Irish who came in from the north, "who had some experience of America and were also first on the soil of this region . . . were more favorably located than those who came afterwards through the port of Charleston."

The outbreak of the War for Independence in the next decade put a stop to practically all immigration to America. South Carolina's Scotch-Irish population thereafter grew by natural increase rather than by additions from Ulster.

The province of North Carolina was so little known and undeveloped in the seventeenth century that it attracted no immigration from either Ulster or Scotland. The turn in its affairs came after the cession of its lands from the Proprietors to the Crown in 1729 and particularly after the vigorous Scot, Governor Johnston, came to office in 1734. He saw an excellent opportunity for building up the population of his sparsely settled province by inviting to North Carolina those Highlanders who were suffering from the aftermath of Prince Charles Stuart's defeat at Culloden in 1746.

As early as 1729 a few families of Highlanders had settled on the Cape Fear River. Here they found a genial climate, fertile soil, and mild and liberal government; all of this they reported to their friends in Scotland. One of the settlers, Neal McNeal, visited the homeland in 1739 and brought back with him a shipload of 350 Highlanders. Despite their extraordinary appearance, dressed as they were in their "peculiar costume," the House of Commons of the province passed a series of resolutions exempting the settlers from taxation for ten years and appropriating £1,000 for their subsistence.[93] It was after Culloden (1746), however, that the great flow of Highlanders to North Carolina began. Landing either at Wilmington or Charleston, the Scots quickly found their way to kinsmen along the Cape Fear. Within a few years their settlements were thickly scattered throughout the territory now embraced in the counties of Scotland, Robeson, Richmond, Bladen, Anson, Cumberland, Harnett, Moore, Sampson, and Hoke. With a keen appreciation of its commercial advantages they selected a point of land at the head of navigation of the Cape Fear where they laid out a town, first called Campbellton, then Cross Creek, and finally Fayetteville.

Still others came, especially after 1769, from the Western Isles. At the time of the Revolution these Scots were generally Loyalists. The Governor of North Carolina wrote to the King in 1775 that he could raise in the colony an army of three thousand Highlanders. It is therefore reasonable to suppose that the Highland Scots population of the province was not less than fifteen thousand.[94]

Nothing in the Tidewater region of North Carolina drew any of the Scotch-Irish of the Great Migration, nor is there in the colonial records mention of the coming of but one group of Ulstermen to the coastal region. As has been seen, their entry was into the central part of the province, by way of Virginia, from 1740 onward, and especially after 1750. The Revolutionary War proved, if proof were needed, that the Scotch-Irish were no longer Scots, for the two elements of North Carolina's population were generally ranged on opposite sides, the Highlanders fighting for the Crown and the Scotch-Irish around Mecklenburg putting Cornwallis' men to fight.

The only Scotch-Irish in Tidewater Virginia were indentured servants or those who had completed their indentures and had taken land in the interior. Once more, Scots were present in the region. They had begun to come to Virginia between 1670 and 1680 to establish themselves along the Elizabeth River, near Norfolk. Little is known of them except that they were numerous enough to form a congregation and eventually to persuade a Presbyterian minister from Ulster to come to them. By the end of the seventeenth century other Scots, with possibly a few Ulstermen, had appeared on both sides of the Chesapeake Bay to the north. On the west shore there were Scottish settlements in Lancaster and Northumberland counties (between the Rappahannock and Potomac rivers), and also near Alexandria; on the Eastern Shore they settled in Accomack County, not many miles from their Scottish neighbors in the Maryland counties. It is likely that they, too, engaged in surreptitious tobacco trade with Scotland and in the manufacture of woolen and linen goods.[95]

Georgia was the last of the thirteen colonies to be founded. By 1733, when Oglethorpe began his settlement, the migrations from Ulster had long been under way, and the pathway through Pennsylvania had become the route for immigrants to follow. Georgia at this time would, in any case, have held few attractions for the Scotch-Irish. It was much too near the Spanish border of Florida, where fighting proved to be frequent between the first Georgia settlers and the Spaniards and Indians. Its reputation as a colony established to receive convicts from England, and its development as a plantation colony with slaves, were also factors that could not appeal to men from Ulster. In Georgia, as in the two Carolinas, Scots rather than Scotch-Irish predominated among the first non-English settlers. As in both of these provinces to the north, Highlanders came to make settlements in Georgia, though prospects here were too discouraging to stimulate a real migration.

Georgia's development came late. By 1752, when the trustees surrendered the colony to the Crown, there were still only about twenty-four hundred people in the entire colony. Gradually Georgia began to achieve stability, especially after peace had come to its southern area and Savannah had been founded as a flourishing seaport. In the last decade before 1776 the Scotch-Irish tide, having rolled through the Carolina Piedmont, now crossed the upper valley of the Savannah River and began to settle in Georgia. This last of the colonies is, therefore, the only one of the thirteen in which the back-country received an earlier development than the coastal region. When the first census of the United States was taken in 1790, Georgia had a population of eighty-two thousand, of whom fifty-two thousand were whites; and 90 per cent of these lived in the up-country farms rather than in the plantations of the lower counties which had comprised Oglethorpe's original colony.

14

Frontier Society

FOR MANY AMERICANS THERE EXISTS a mental image of a "typical
pioneer," living with his large family in a log cabin set in a
space he had cleared in the forest. There he led a rough but
simple life, hunting and trapping, farming with crude implements and wasteful methods, and occasionally having to fight
Indians. He drank a great deal of corn whisky, scorned refinement, loved practical jokes, danced vigorous reels and hoedowns
to a scraping fiddle, and enjoyed such rough sports as fights with
his bare fists. Yet at bottom his character was sound and his
impulses were right. He and his kind, according to this image of
pioneer life, conquered the wilderness and laid the foundations
of democratic faith and practice.

Frederick Jackson Turner and his successors suggested that
each time the pioneers moved another stage farther west one
more layer of civilization was stripped off, one more tie that
bound men to European standards and institutions was loosed.[1]
They believed that the unique experiences of frontier life called
into being qualities of character and, more significantly, democratic ideas, which together have made later generations Americans rather than transplanted Europeans.

In both the image of the typical pioneer and in the Turner
thesis the Scotch-Irishman plays a significant role. He is regarded as America's first true backwoodsman, showing the way
to the winning of the west, leading the vanguard of those who
cross the Alleghenies to open up for settlement that great valley
in the heart of continental United States. It must therefore
be asked whether the Scotch-Irish pioneers actually lived in the
rough, hardy, but upright manner regarded as typical; and

whether, in addition, they were among the shapers of an almost anarchic democracy, anti-intellectual and equalitarian in its results.

It is curious to observe that most histories of the American frontier begin with the movement into the Ohio Valley, after the American Revolution, as if the preceding 150 years of settlement in the wilderness from Maine to Georgia had had no such effects as making the pioneers strip off European habiliments, while leaving them crude in manners and democratic in outlook.[2] The almost mystical influence of frontier life could apparently begin to exert its force only when the colonists had gained their independence and had moved away from the Atlantic seaboard. Yet here is a confusion. Since the Scotch-Irish migration had occurred before the Revolution, it should logically show the social characteristics, say, of New England or New Jersey rather than those of Kentucky and Ohio. On the other hand, because Scotch-Irish settlement was always in the back-country, far away from the seaboard and its European connections, it should produce the typical pioneer characteristics of manners and outlook. The Frontier School of historians do not resolve this dilemma. They seem only occasionally to regard the Scotch-Irish in colonial times, while east of the mountains, as representative of the new type of American character; yet after 1783, when many moved west, the wild frontier began, according to the theory, to exert its mysterious influence.

It would seem wise to consider the social life of the Scotch-Irish as it actually was, rather than to view it as either confirming or refuting a thesis.

Ulster itself had constituted something of a frontier environment in 1610, for there were homes to make and wild natives to subdue; but by 1717 Ulster was "civilized," even in the eyes of the English Parliament. Ulstermen believed in orderly government and courts; they knew and respected standards of morality and propriety with the same degree of rigidity and laxity apparent in any society; they accepted without challenge the existence of monarchy as the proper form of government and of social classes as the right ordering of society. They came to America to escape none of these, but because times were hard in

Ireland whereas America seemed to be a land of endless opportunity. As has been noted, they objected to certain governmental policies, bitterly resenting the restrictions on trade and on Presbyterian magistrates; but it would be a serious distortion of history to claim that the exodus from Ulster was a crusading search for freedom. On the contrary, all of the evidence shows that the people hoped to find social institutions in America very much like the ones they were leaving.

These they did find, in the settled areas around their ports of debarkation. When they took farms in the wilderness they set to work forthwith to establish familiar institutions.

Their immediate task was, of course, to build a home and plant a crop as soon as possible. In these first days and months every family in the community lived under conditions roughly similar to those of their neighbors. The life of newly arrived frontiersmen was the same practically everywhere, north or south, and whether the people had come straight from Europe or had moved from a community along the American seaboard. Crude and makeshift arrangements did not first begin on the western side of the Alleghenies. The important question seems to be how long these arrangements were tolerated—how strong the impulse was to change them into something resembling settled life. In the following account, which happens to be a description of pioneering in New Hampshire, one has the details of the early days of people on a frontier; it might have been an account of pioneers in Virginia or Pennsylvania, in Scotch-Irish settlements or in English ones, in early colonial regions or in the much later settlements around the Ohio country.

They frequently lie out in the woods several days or weeks together in all seasons of the year. A hut composed of poles and bark, suffice them for shelter; and on the open side of it, a large fire secures them from the severity of the weather. Wrapt in a blanket with their feet near the fire, they pass the longest and coldest nights, and awake vigorous for labour the succeeding day. Their food . . . is salted pork or beef, with potatoes and bread of Indian corn; and their drink is water mixed with ginger; though many of them are fond of distilled spirits. . . . Those who begin a new settlement, live at first in a style not less simple. They erect a square building of poles [that is, a log cabin], notched at the ends to keep them fast together.

The crevices are plaistered with clay or the stiffest earth which can be had, mixed with moss or straw. The roof is either bark or split boards. The chimney a pile of stones; within which a fire is made on the ground, and a hole is left in the roof for the smoke to pass out. Another hole is made in the side of the house for a window, which is occasionally closed with a wooden shutter. In winter, a constant fire is kept, by night as well as by day; and in summer it is necessary to have a continual smoke on account of the musquetos and other insects with which the woods abound. The same defence is used for the cattle; smokes of leaves and brush are made in the pastures where they feed by day, and in the pens where they are folded by night. Ovens are built at a small distance from the houses, of the best stones which can be found, cemented and plaistered with clay or stiff earth. Many of these first essays in housekeeping, are to be met with in the new plantations, which serve to lodge whole families, till their industry can furnish them with materials, for a more regular and comfortable house; and till their land is so well cleared as that a proper situation for it can be chosen. By these methods of living, the people are familiarised to hardships; their children are early used to coarse food and hard lodgings; and to be without shoes in all seasons of the year is scarcely accounted a want. By such hard fare, and the labour which accompanies it, many young men have raised up families, and in a few years have acquired property sufficient to render themselves independent freeholders; and they feel all the pride and importance which arise from a consciousness of having well earned their estates.[3]

Characteristic (and practical) frontier actions occurred among the Scotch-Irish as elsewhere: neighborly help was expected and given in log-rolling, house-raising, tree-felling. No doubt one cabin so much resembled every other that a visitor would have supposed that no social distinctions could exist. Coming with few household goods or implements, each family must camp out until the cabin could be built. With the preliminary preparations made, erection of a house usually required but a day, with a rough division of labor among the helpers. With the walls up, a man could at his own leisure construct his furniture, shape his wooden dishes and buckets, build a stone chimney, and make a floor to cover the bare earth. The indispensable equipment of every pioneer consisted of rifle, pouches, powder horn, axe, and hoe; beyond these a man's acquisitions marked his economic progress.

Many Scotch-Irish have left memoirs of these earliest days, with all the earthy details still vivid in their memories. It is actually the testimony of these accounts that has led to the impression of the rough crudity of all true pioneer society. What is sometimes forgotten is that the people regarded such conditions as a temporary, if necessary, makeshift, to be endured until a better life could replace it—and "better" meant having the institutions and established order of civilized Ulster. Progress to that order could be marked in almost precise stages: first, the building of a church and securing a minister—and if a school could be managed, so much the better; second, the appearance of a store and possibly a tavern, as links with settled communities in older parts of the country and with the outside world; and third, bringing the neighborhood under the jurisdiction of a court, near enough to assure effective law and order.

The American pioneer, whether Scotch-Irish or any other, must begin as a jack-of-all-trades. Almost the only professions represented among the early Ulstermen were the ministry and teaching, usually performed by the same individual. In the later settlement of the south, surveyors and then lawyers were especially useful: squatting, verbal agreements, and guesswork as to boundary lines resulted in conflicting claims, and the Scotch-Irish were often regarded as "a very litigious people." Farming, of course, was the major concern of everyone, often even of the minister. Individual farmers who developed particular skills were called upon by neighbors who needed specialized work done; the obligation would be repaid by return service in another specialty, by extra help on farm chores, or (rarely) by money payments. Some of these specialists might choose to set up shop in a village or town, when settlement increased. The most usual and necessary of crafts were those of the blacksmith, wheelwright, wagon-maker, joiner, cooper, weaver, fuller, tailor, hatter, rope-maker, and wine-maker.

More significant for American life than the familiar details of pioneering is the gradual modification of concepts of social distinctions. What occurred among the Scotch-Irish between 1717 and the end of the century was an augury, almost a pattern, of things to come in the United States.

When the Great Migration began in 1717 no one in his right mind, either in the British Isles or in the colonies, questioned the fact of social superiority and inferiority. Some families were wellborn, some were "middling," and most belonged to the "lower orders,"—and so it had been since the beginning of time. Such distinctions seemed clearly to be in the natural order of things. The stability of society derived from this order: people always knew where to look for leadership, and the training in responsibility was assumed in families of property, education, and background. The system of social classes was not immutably rigid, for men might occasionally rise, and persons of "family" often shirked their duties; but in the main the system worked.

Coming to America meant for Ulstermen months of primitive living, yet it would not be long before the social distinctions of the old country would manifest themselves, not only in the leadership assumed by "substantial" men but by the rapid material progress they made. They had started with the advantage of more money than the average immigrant had to spend on implements and livestock. They could not, at the outset in the wilderness, be above the hard manual labor required for making a farm; but they were intent upon having homes equal, even superior, to the ones they had left. Why else had they come to the New World? Such men were not so enamored of adventure that they wished to live as on a permanent camping trip. If they could afford to buy the labor of indentured servants or to hire young helpers, they could clear more ground than their neighbors, extend their homes, and improve their grounds.

Within months the old social distinctions were visible to all. Substantial men were not called aristocrats; the Old World vocabulary changed in America, and the ancient word "peasant" disappeared altogether; but the social order remained. Any community could name its good families, its middle group of respectable people, and the lower orders who ranged toward the shiftless. It was observed that in colonies where frontier counties were organized, the Scotch-Irish invariably chose gentlemen from the good families to represent them in the Assembly. If a church were organized, these men were made elders. It was they who pressed for civil institutions and economic betterment of the community.

Social status in a Scotch-Irish community was revealed by objective criteria, such as the size and condition of the dwelling, care of the farm, work done by women in the family, personal character and morality, or even diversions engaged in.

The quality of a family's home quickly revealed status. On arrival at the site chosen for the farm, the first shelter could be only a hastily constructed lean-to; this soon was replaced by an "open Logg Cabbin," consisting of a roofed structure closed on sides and back, but open on the front to the elements. If a man endured such an arrangement for many months, the neighborhood knew instantly where to place him in the social order—as it did the man whose permanent cabin was most ambitiously laid out and most neatly constructed.

A glance round a farm after two or three years would reveal the man's social standing. Good, respectable families had their fields unencumbered with stumps, more land cleared each year, clean crops and careful farming. The cow was the most valuable domestic animal, and the observer could see whether enough cattle were being raised to send east to market for cash or goods.* Other animals in variety were further clues to the standard of living in the family. Pigs were certain to be found on every farm, for the Scotch-Irish quickly lost their ancient prejudice against pork, the preferred meat on most American frontiers.† Sheep, so plentiful in Ulster, were rare on frontier farms, for they required either shepherds or fences, and labor was not available for either; but the presence of even a few sheep bespoke the quality of clothes the family would wear. As for food, no pioneer need ever want, even before his first crop was harvested. Forests teemed with game, wild fruits, nuts, and berries, and the

---

* For well over a hundred years—indeed, until the 1890's—it was a familiar sight to see droves of cattle on their way to markets in Philadelphia, Baltimore, Charleston, and other ports and markets. The drover, generally a younger son, would arrange to reach the farm of an acquaintance by nightfall, and there find water and pasture for his cattle and hospitality for himself and his helpers.

† Scots had for centuries surprised the English by their aversion to pork. Highlanders apparently did not conquer their prejudice until after 1746. Scott's novels contain many references to this dietary peculiarity. See, for example, *The Fortunes of Nigel*, II, 161, 347; and *Waverley*, I, 362.

streams with fish. It marked the quality of the family, however, if it long depended chiefly on what nature offered, instead of cultivating a garden that contained not only the staples of the Old World, but the attractive vegetables of the New—corn, sweet potatoes, new varieties of beans, squash, and pumpkins.*

An almost absolute clue to status was afforded by the women in a family. Were the wife and grown daughters permitted to work in the fields? If so, that family belonged to the lowest class. All women worked, and worked hard; but the proper place for a woman of good family or of respectability was in the home. Marriage was early, for a bachelor could hardly survive in a frontier community without a wife, unless he left home to become a perpetual explorer, hunter, trapper, or Indian trader. Domestic economy depended upon the women: cooking, baking, the making of clothes, washing, milking cows, making butter, spinning, weaving, pickling, all the other manifold duties of a housewife, in addition to being mother to eight or ten children, nursing them, caring for them through illness without a doctor, and teaching them if a school were not available. How efficiently and successfully a wife and mother accomplished her endless tasks was, justly or unjustly, considered a mark of status. Not even in the most trying days of early settlement, however, would a man who valued his social position permit field labor for his wife and daughters.†

It could well be reasoned that the informal, but very real, social class system of the Scotch-Irish was based upon character. One of the strongest checks on laxity of behavior had been removed upon the American scene: the farm village. In Ulster, as almost everywhere else in the British Isles, tenants on an estate lived in houses close by each other along a village street, each tenant going thence every day to work on his own plot of land. This close proximity had the inevitable result of making every man aware of his neighbors and their opinion, for each person

---

* For the potato, see above, 164n.

† Almost every historian who comments upon domestic life on the frontier includes a well-deserved eulogy upon the courage, fortitude, and even heroism of the frontier wife. Dunaway (*Scotch-Irish of Colonial Pennsylvania*, p. 189) justly says: "On some towering mountain peak of Pennsylvania, the Commonwealth should erect to [the Scotch-Irish woman] a monument as a worthy memorial of her character and deeds."

was in truth his brother's keeper. In the New World, however, the farm village was characteristic only of New England. Among the Scotch-Irish, and thereafter across the frontier to the end of the Great Plains, it seemed more practical for each farmer to live near the center of his own land. Until the prairies were reached, a man's land had to be cleared out of the forest, and with his hunting grounds might include three hundred acres or more. A village could come into being only when specialists—a store-keeper, lawyers, a smith, a tavernkeeper, the minister—were present, or when a courthouse marked the final arrival of civilization. For families living alone on an isolated farm, it would be easy to fall into compromises, to let standards deteriorate, in short, to become shiftless in the absence of daily surveillance by close neighbors. Families who, removed from watchful eyes, still upheld the best standards they knew, had proved their worth.

More than this, life in the wilderness offered special temptations to laxity. Long accustomed to the use of whisky in Scotland and Ireland, the pioneers quickly learned how to turn their new crop, corn, into whisky. Stills abounded, for in whisky the Scotch-Irish found their first product easily marketable and easily conveyed in compact form to trading centers. With no voice yet raised against drinking, with plentiful supplies of whisky in every home (even the homes of ministers), and with corn liquor the one social drink expected at every social gathering, many people became hard drinkers. Here again, character and self-control revealed the man: sobriety (not abstention) distinguished itself from occasional drunkenness, and this in turn from "drinking too much."

Diversions afforded still another criterion of social class. Pioneer reminiscences devote many pages to the vigorous athleticism of most frontier sports, all of them ones that brought people together—for the men, wrestling, competitive shooting for a mark, racing; for the women, quilting parties and co-operative work at the men's house-raisings, corn-huskings, and harvest-times. Strenuous dancing marked most festival occasions. Imperceptibly, as pioneers moved farther away from settled communities, many of their diversions degenerated into crudity. Travelers in Kentucky and the Ohio Valley were often shocked at the wrestling matches in which men gouged out each other's eyes, at brutal fist fights, at such sports as "gander-pulling," in which a live fowl was suspended by its legs from a limb, while men on horseback galloped by and tried to twist the head off the creature's greased neck. From every part of the frontier came stories of wedding celebrations, to which the whole community had been orally invited: the occasion generally began with the young men racing for a bottle of whisky, the winner having the right to be the first to kiss the bride; and it ended with the "bedding" of the couple, accompanied by ribald good wishes for the beginning of a large family and finally by a "shivaree" (charivari)—a raucous serenade on pots and pans.

This widespread crudity was explained and justified by comments on the boisterousness of high animal spirits, the youth of the pioneer, the need for uproarious relaxation after a day's or a week's steady and monotonous labor on an isolated farm. Out of such occasions seem to have grown many traits commented upon with distaste by European travelers: the American addiction to practical jokes, the tall tale, the preference for exaggeration rather than understatement in humor.[4]

In this realm of amusements there was also an opportunity for social distinctions, for what was congenial to ordinary folk was often not "proper" for their betters. An elder's family might well participate in many of the amusements, however vigorous; but a subtle line was drawn where behavior seemed to be in bad taste. The appearance of village life—the goal, it may be repeated, of all ambitious Scotch-Irish pioneers—provided a steady pull away from the excesses of folk hilarity. Indeed, the two poles are clearly seen: at one extreme the wild frontier, always moving beyond the reach of established institutions and their restraints; at the other extreme the settled village, drawing people toward refinement of manners.

These contrary influences no doubt occasioned a serious tension for many individuals, especially the younger ones. On the one hand, there was the desire to become respected and substantial citizens by the traditional standards of education and community responsibility. The church, as the dominant social institution, with all of the prestige of authority and continuity and with its customary surveillance of one's personal life, abetted parental influence in drawing youth to the high standards expected of the best families and the respectable. On the other hand, the challenge of launching out for oneself, of making one's own way by conquering his own difficulties, combined with the pressure of population on the supply of attractive land in the East to lure one away to the new frontier. There the restraining hand of church and community watchfulness would be removed; one need not be actually rebellious to understand the appeal of deciding for himself and the appeal of good-natured, if crude, practices.

Excitement and adventure as contrasted with routine were also aspects of the tension. Hunting and tracking game, which had been necessities for survival at the beginning, soon became favorite pastimes. Scotch-Irishmen learned Indian methods of forest-craft as quickly as they had learned Indian methods of fighting, and many of the men became expert hunters, even addicts, who preferred life in the woods to the tameness of life in a village. Moving west to unknown country, with a possibility of danger from wild beast and Indian, was preferable for many young men to safe security.

Life in Scotch-Irish communities, therefore, though it differed in detail from life in Ulster, continued to reflect for many years the familiar social distinctions between families. Gradually, however, especially as people moved beyond Pennsylvania and Virginia into the Carolinas, class lines became blurred and criteria for distinguishing them vague. By the end of the eighteenth century there were even those who expressed resentment against emphasis on family and what it implied of social superiority. The Scotch-Irish did not cause this social transformation; many deeply regretted it; but it was among them that the old standards of social class began to be eroded. No democratic theory attacked the old system. It was weakened by the fact that people by the thousands were constantly on the move.

Stable social classes flourish only when residence is continuous in a community, so that men agree upon what brings prestige and position; when upper classes are fairly exclusive in their marriages; when sons are indoctrinated with the idea that they have not only rights but also obligations of leadership and responsibility; and when tradition guides institutions into conservative channels. The mobility of the Scotch-Irish simply swept away all of these foundation stones of the class system for thousands of the people. However much the first settlers expected to reproduce the standards of the Old World, there was always a drift of the restless and a pull of the young and ambitious to a new settlement, and beyond that to a still newer one. Every fresh move meant that life had, at least momentarily, to be primitive again—chopping trees, making first crops, living in camp. Maturing youths married their available neighbors and could not wait for persons of good family to appear. In a new frontier region there is no school for children, no church for anyone. Weddings, baptisms, and funerals, if they can be performed by anyone, must depend upon the arrival of an itinerant preacher, who might be illiterate and wholly unlike a Presbyterian divine. If not even an itinerant is at hand, then at least the baptisms and funerals can wait. Where, under such frontier conditions, are class distinctions, especially if the young folk and the restless move off to repeat a process so corrosive to tradition?

There was, indeed, a certain tug in the direction of preserving the old system. The age of a settlement, nearness to economic markets, the presence of an organized Presbyterian Church, established courts and civil institutions, the growth of villages and towns—all of these were conserving influences. Yet they could not exert their steadying force upon the thousands who came in each year from Ulster looking for cheap lands, nor upon the ambitious young people of the prolific Scotch-Irish who felt that they must strike out for themselves. At any given moment in the latter half of the century, settlements could be found in every stage of "civilization," with each newest stage suspending and modifying old standards. In 1765, for example, communities in Pennsylvania and Virginia had become stable, orderly, accustomed to social and economic amenities; here class distinctions were visible. In the Carolinas, however, the social order was still in the making, with Regulation movements in both provinces a political indication of unstable institutions. The observer here would find not the amenities of orderly life but various degrees of pioneering crudities.*

The half century during which Scotch-Irish immigration and settlement occurred, therefore, sounded the knell of social classes based upon family background. It was the constant movement of people into new territory that caused the erosion of traditional distinctions, and it was among the Scotch-Irish that it first occurred on a large scale. Among the older settlements in the East —in Boston, Philadelphia, the Tidewater, Charleston, for example—the respected distinctions not only persisted but continued to be regarded as part of the natural order; but henceforward the class system, so calmly accepted in 1700, was bound to disintegrate under the steady movement of swelling numbers to new lands of the West.

The experience of the Scotch-Irish in this matter of classes was doubly interesting. It was true that, with them, the old order faded away; but it was also with them that a new order appeared and one that came to be fairly representative of American life. People always make social distinctions. They are always conscious of prestige, even though the attainments that bring prestige change over the years and change radically. What disappeared among the Scotch-Irish and among most Americans thereafter was the idea of *permanence* of social distinctions, the

* The most graphic account of the shocking effect upon a conventional mind of this primitive life is that given in the Journal of the Reverend Charles Woodmason. This Anglican itinerant traveled constantly among settlers of the South Carolina up-country from 1766 to 1768. Discounting to the fullest Woodmason's belligerent attitude toward dissenters, his naïveté, bias, and prejudices, one can still perceive the almost elemental nature of much of the life in the region at that time.

Population increase had far outstripped institutions. There were families, of course; but many couples lived together and had children without being married —for who was there to perform the ceremony? No courts were present to secure justice nor were there schools or churches. Lawlessness, vile manners, ignorance, and slovenliness were commonplace, with people unaware of how far they had sunk from "civilized" life. To Woodmason it seemed not a hopeful sign that Presbyterians and Baptists were at work among these people, but rather as an evidence of Satan's presence to pervert men from the true (that is, the Anglican) faith. Yet it was simple tragedy that so many of the people had moved so far, and so often, from civilized society that thousands had never even heard of God, religion, or church. Often where religious institutions had made their start, bigotry and denominational animosities were so rampant that one sect would try to drive another from the region. (See Woodmason, *The Carolina Backcountry on the Eve of the Revolution.*)

belief that families must be given deference simply because they have always had it. What was retained among the Scotch-Irish and later Americans was acceptance of social distinction, even social class, based upon whether an individual family, in this generation and for this generation alone, achieved the qualities that were admired, respected, and honored at the time and place.

A shift had been subtly and imperceptibly made from the criterion of family heritage to that of individual achievement. One's own strength of will, self-control, inward determination, were now the primary factors determining status in a community. The goals worth achieving were to change in the nineteenth century from those of the eighteenth: wealth meant more in the later period than living like a "gentleman," for example. Yet an unbiased examination of any predominantly Scotch-Irish community from Pennsylvania to Georgia in 1800 would reveal the reality of class distinctions. These would simply not have been the same ones men's grandfathers would have honored in the same community fifty years before.*

Scotch-Irish settlements east of the Appalachians marked, in effect, a turning point in American life. They were a field, as the Tidewater was not, in which opposing values found full play, with those who chose one set remaining in the settled communities and those who chose the other set going on farther west. Those who stayed showed their belief in stability, viable institutions, community control of morality, amenities of social intercourse, decency and order, the worth of tradition. Those who moved away preferred instead the values of individualism, adventure, independence of action, making their own way in the world, taking risks. The region of Scotch-Irish settlement, simply by its geographical location, was both the last bastion of traditional standards and the threshold across which Americans could pass to more egalitarian ways of life.

* In such a characteristic Scotch-Irish town or village of 1800, the upper class would almost certainly consist of those who were educated, members of the Presbyterian Church, financially capable of having servants, engaged either in gentleman-farming or in an enterprise in which manual labor was not involved, with leisure for riding and visiting and reading, opposed to enthusiasms whether in religion or politics, and moral with a puritanical rigidity. Memoirs preserved in county historical societies throughout the whole area of Scotch-Irish predominance attest the validity of this picture.

As the Frontier School of historians have noted, each new move to the West strengthened the democratic impulse as it weakened traditional distinctions. It has become commonplace to remark that in the wilds the judgment of a man was not made on the basis of his antecedents but upon his virility, courage, and ingenuity. Book learning and intellectuality were no longer the criteria for respect, but rather physical qualities. Neighborliness was essential for survival in a wilderness; no family could hold itself apart; marriage was necessary, and one's choice was more and more likely to be made on the practical basis of availability and personal characteristics, not upon who one's family might have been in the East. Where people share comradeship in protecting themselves against Indians, and neighborliness in house-raisings, where all join to find diversion, where neither church nor sedate older people are present to emphasize tradition, a rough equality is bound to exist.

Children and grandchildren of the original Scotch-Irish settlers in America were always among the leaders in the move to the new West; but they were no longer Scotch-Irish in their social characteristics and outlook. Just as they were likely to become Methodists and Baptists instead of remaining Presbyterians, so they were likely to marry persons whose background may have been English or German. The memory of Ulster and its respectabilities and distinctions meant little or nothing to these constant pioneers. They were Americans.*

One problem that beset the lives of immigrants to America in the nineteenth century was spared to most of the Scotch-Irish: except in New England, and rarely elsewhere, they never felt themselves to be a "minority group." Beginning in 1846, with

---

* The temptation to ascribe social characteristics to a specific cause is difficult to resist. It is here that the Frontier School of historians has been most at fault, for these scholars have attributed many American national characteristics to the influence of frontier life, as if this alone were the explanation. In the same fashion, certain social scientists have named the Industrial Revolution as the cause of "mass society," supposedly an American characteristic. They name as trends within this mass society a decline of kinship ties, the growth of specialization, of secularism and rationality, of associations formed for specific purposes rather than of communities, of mobility. (See, for example, Leonard Broom and Philip Selznick, *Sociology* [2d ed.; Evanston, 1958], pp. 35-39) Frontier life was essentially individualistic and thus diametrically different from a mass society; yet it, too, stimulated mobility and a decline of kinship ties, two of the supposed results of the Industrial Revolution.

the first mighty influx of Irishmen escaping from the potato famine, and continuing until 1921 when Congress effectively closed the door to mass immigration in this country, newcomers poured into the United States. The first years for these immigrants after 1846 were, in the majority of cases, spent in the cities and settled regions of the East, where American culture had long since taken shape. Immediately the immigrant was confronted with standards, values, and mores unlike his own—often radically different from his own. An individual's mind is free only when he does not have constantly to make personal judgments of right and wrong, only when he accepts, as second nature, the standards of his culture. These later immigrants, however, were "marginal men," caught between two cultures in conflict for their loyalty: the familiar culture of their childhood, deeply ingrained in their souls, and that of the country to which they had come with high hopes. If the immigrant conscientiously retained the old standards, he saw his children accept the new, so that the conflict was sudden, sharp, and centered in his very home. His life was, in effect, a battleground on which he must be perpetually on guard—and worse, he must decide both tactics and strategy for himself, for he was not now fully a member of any society whose culture he could wholly accept. He was on the margin of two cultures and two societies, pulled sentimentally and by his conscience toward one and by his hope and commitment of life toward another.

Durkheim calls this state of mind *anomie*—normlessness, an absence of clear standards to follow.[5] Anomie was an experience unknown to the Scotch-Irishman, for he moved immediately upon arrival to a region where there was neither a settlement nor an established culture. He held land, knew independence, had manifold responsibilities from the very outset. He spoke the language of his neighbors to the East through whose communities he had passed on his way to the frontier. Their institutions and standards differed at only minor points from his own. The Scotch-Irish were not, in short, a "minority group" and needed no Immigrant Aid society to tide them over a period of maladjustment so that they might become assimilated in the American melting pot. Like all people, whether immigrants or stay-at-homes, they must have known individual discouragement and disappointment; some may even have had a heightened feeling of inner loneliness, a quality of mind Weber attributes to most Calvinists who reflect upon the implications of the doctrine of predestination.[6]   But to the extent that their neighbors shared similar experiences and attitudes, without pressure from other Americans to be different, the Scotch-Irish were not anomic, were not marginal men.   They were, on the contrary, full Americans almost from the moment they took up their farms in the back-country.[7]

15

The Presbyterian Church

THE COURSE OF PRESBYTERIANISM in America between 1717 and 1789 neatly reflects the transformations of the mind and the social life of the Scotch-Irish as they became Americans. The eighteenth century in the colonies was a period whose currents of thought had inevitable effects upon church as well as state. Presbyterianism changed much during the century, and in three aspects its changes were significant for the Scotch-Irish: the church became Americanized; it enlarged its conception of service to the common man; and it made tentatives toward democracy. Yet during the very century that saw its increase in vision and effectiveness, the Presbyterian Church lost its hold upon thousands of Scotch-Irish for whom it had been a birthright. The causes of this defection likewise reflect the realities of life in the American back-country at the time.

The Scotch-Irish immigrant to America was a Presbyterian. He may not have been always pious and zealous; but the Presbyterian Church had long been his peculiar institution, his mark of distinction from other people in Ulster, his proud heritage from the days when his ancestors had stood up to kings and oppressors. It had watched over his morals with meticulous care. Its ministers were educated men, graduates of a university, always respected, however tyrannous or ungracious their lives. The church demanded of its members scrupulous knowledge of the Bible and the catechisms, regular attendance at worship, attention to long theological discourses. The ministry was the highest calling that could come to a youth. That there were wayward members, who found irksome all these duties and this oversight, goes without saying. The church in Ulster, however, proved once more the validity of the observation that loyalty is given most readily where much is demanded and expected.

To transplant Ulster Presbyterians into the New World should, accordingly, have meant to transplant their church with them. The will to do so was present. It was the usual practice for several members of the same congregation to leave the old country together. On the long voyage across the ocean, fellow-passengers normally came to have a sense of community, even though they had been strangers before. Upon arrival in America, shipmates normally went together to the same frontier neighborhood to make their farms. Here, then, were the elements of a congregation, and here also was the desire for a church, the institution that above all represented stability and tradition.

One thing was lacking: a minister. In a very few happy instances the minister from Ulster came over with his flock; a church was formed and soon became the center of community life, as it had been at home. Settlers flocked into America by the thousands, however, while only a handful of ministers came. The result was a serious and immediate setback for every aspect of religion. Without the influence of a church, and in the daily exigencies of conquering a wilderness, moral sensibilities might easily become dulled: life was hard and sometimes cruel; determination to succeed could result in bickering and ill will; hard drinking and coarse manners found little check. Often the "better element" in a community encouraged the construction of a meetinghouse, or meeting in homes or even barns, so that worship, conducted by an elder or some respected neighbor, might be held. Without a minister, however, no congregation could flourish.

Here was a central problem that beset Presbyterianism among the Scotch-Irish throughout the colonial era—the numbers, training, and attitudes of its ministers. During the first generation of immigration, certainly until 1738, the problem was acute. With all the thousands of Ulstermen in Pennsylvania by that time and with all of their scores of neighborhoods only thirteen churches had been organized among them, and some of these lacked ministers. At no time in their lives could people have stood in greater need of true pastors. It requires little imagination to perceive the effects upon men and women of loneliness in the vast silence of forests, of the absence of familiar social and moral landmarks, of the inevitable pain and sorrow, of the daily need of encouragement and assurance.* Yet pastors were few. The root of the problem was that they must come from abroad; and the concomitant difficulty was that the Church required a highly educated clergy.

Above all else, the Presbyterian minister must be thoroughly trained. It would be foolish to suggest that Presbyterians of the early eighteenth century were notably intellectual; but from the time of Calvin and Knox the Church had demanded learning as a requisite for ordination. Presbyterians, therefore, from ingrained conviction, long familiarity, and personal preference, expected their ministers to deliver scholarly, logical, and theological sermons. It was unthinkable that a young man might enter the pulpit without a thorough familiarity with Hebrew, Greek, and Latin, as well as divinity. The supply of Presbyterian ministers must come from the small number of university graduates— and for the Scotch-Irish in America this meant chiefly graduates of St. Andrews, Aberdeen, Glasgow, or Edinburgh. Before the migration, these Scottish universities could meet the needs of Ulster; but the exodus from that region did not release ministers from parishes there: it simply increased prodigiously the number of congregations requiring a pastor.

The Macedonian call from America must now reach the ears of university graduates who also had calls from parishes in Scotland and Ulster, nearer home, in familiar surroundings, and with fixed salaries (provided in Ulster almost wholly from the Royal Bounty). (This *Regium Donum* is discussed above, p. 126.) To accept a call from America meant launching out into the unknown, to minister to congregations scattered over many miles of wild country, to desperately poor settlers unaccustomed to the idea of paying a regular salary. Even if a stipend were mentioned in the call, it could be paid only in kind, so that, as many ministers found, they must also farm and do secular work in

---

* It is pathetic to note that more than one Ulsterman claiming to be a minister was found, upon presenting himself to the Presbytery in Philadelphia, to be "a renegade who had forged his credentials." (Trinterud, *The Forming of an American Tradition*, p. 36)

order to live.   In short, a clergyman who went to America must
feel true missionary zeal.

The needs of the frontiersmen could not possibly be met by
the Presbyterian Church already existent in the colonies before
the Great Migration from Ulster began.*   This church, different
as was the background of its English and New England ministers,
took notice of the arrival of Ulstermen and made at least a gesture
to help them.   The Synod in 1722 introduced a quasi-itinerant
system, whereby pastors should not only care for their own
charges but should extend their labors into adjacent regions as
far as they were able.   This was an admirable conception; but
in practice it was powerless to meet the need when Scotch-Irish
were arriving by shiploads and were pushing many miles into
the interior, away from the Eastern communities in which all the
few ministers of the Synod lived.†[1]

Religion could flourish among the Scotch-Irish only if there

* Presbyterianism in America, as already noted, had its official inception
with the work of Francis Makemie, a minister ordained by the Ulster Presbytery
of Laggan.   Makemie had come to America in 1683, doing work on the Eastern
Shore of Maryland, where he founded five churches.   In 1704 he persuaded
Presbyterian and Independent ministers of London to send two ministers to
America and to assume their support for two years.   During the same period,
English, Welsh, and Huguenot Presbyterians in the Middle Colonies had organized
congregations and secured ministers, mostly from New England.

Under the stimulus of Makemie, seven ministers in Maryland, Delaware, and
Pennsylvania met at Philadelphia in 1706 to form the first Presbytery in the
New World.   With the arrival of other ministers and the growth of new congregations, it became possible in 1717 to form a Synod, to be composed of four
Presbyteries: Long Island, Philadelphia, New Castle (Delaware), and Snow Hill
(the Eastern Shore of Maryland).   The last of these proved too weak to
survive.   Seventeen ministers were on the roll of the first Synod.

† Upon the arrival of even a few ministers from Ulster and their admission
to the Synod, divergences of opinion began to appear, bordering at times on
acerbity.   English Presbyterianism, never bound in any common organization
with the Scottish Kirk, had inevitably developed, over a century and a half,
attitudes and preferences of its own.   Puritans from New England, trained at
Harvard and Yale, filled several Presbyterian pulpits, and their attitude toward
Scots and Scotch-Irish often seemed to reflect the old disdain of Englishmen
(now "new" Englanders) for the "wild Caledonian barbarians."   There may even
have been a fear on the part of these ministers of English background that, if
ministers from Scotland and Ulster became ascendant, the Church in America
might attach itself to the Kirk abroad, as a superior judicature.   (This is the
suggestion of Trinterud, *The Forming of an American Tradition*, p. 36.)   One
of the first major controversies in the Synod was whether ministers should be
required to subscribe, with no right of reservation on any point, to the Westminster Standards of the Church.   This issue was settled in 1729 by compromise.
(Klett, *The Scotch-Irish in Pennsylvania*, p. 37)

were ministers in every community. Calvinists in New England had met precisely this situation by founding colleges of their own to train ministers on this side of the ocean—Harvard in 1636 and Yale in 1701. A promising step in this direction was taken by a Presbyterian, the Reverend William Tennent, in 1726. This minister from Ulster, a graduate of Edinburgh University, founded a school at Neshaminy, Bucks County, in eastern Pennsylvania. It consisted of nothing more than a log cabin adjoining his manse; but here he devoted his spare time to teaching eager young Scotch-Irish boys. Tennent was a fine scholar, and his curriculum of Greek, Latin, theology, and the "arts and sciences" was rigorous. A small, steady stream of ministers was graduated from his academy, which came to be known facetiously as the Log College.[2] Here was a practical solution to a crucial problem; but it was only a small beginning, a tiny ray of hope.

The difficulty was not wholly the lack of ministers. It may be doubted whether, even if the supply had been adequate, the set of mind characteristic of the clergy at that time could have answered the true spiritual needs of pioneers. In all major denominations of the 1730's it seemed as if clergymen had lost sight of the meaning of such words as "pastor" and "minister" and had come to feel that formal discourse in the pulpit, together with a proper direction of church services and sacraments, comprised their whole duty.[*] The Age of Enlightenment and of Reason had begun, with its disdain for "enthusiasm": any display of deep and fervent piety was suspect. Since the clergy came from the universities, they often reflected this attitude of intellectuality and detachment. More than this, the three denominations most concerned with Americans of the time were Established Churches, either in Britain or in the colonies. It may be suggested that the very monopoly of Establishment conduces to inertia, unadaptability, and contentment with the formal proprieties of things as they are.

The attitude of the clergy had its effect upon the people. Religion in America in the 1730's seemed to lack vitality. New England Puritanism had lost its early zeal and spirit; Anglicanism

[*] Benjamin Franklin remarked of a Presbyterian divine in Philadelphia that he spent most of his time in polemical preaching against other churches or in defense of his own.

tended to become increasingly a polite and decent social formality; Presbyterian ministers from Scotland were likely to represent
the "Moderate" movement of the time, and those from Ulster,
polemic orthodoxy. The mood that had produced the Protestant
Reformation only two centuries ago had almost vanished. Spiritual needs of the people were no fewer, but empty pews testified
to the failure of the churches to meet these needs.* Could a
Presbyterian minister of the time speak to the intensified needs
and yearnings of the Scotch-Irish pioneer?

Suddenly, in 1738, a religious transformation began to take
place. John and Charles Wesley had recently been stirring up
the Church of England; now their collaborator, the fiery evan-
gelist George Whitefield, made the first of his seven visits to
America. Traveling from Georgia to New England, he spoke
with compelling force directly to the hearts of men, not to their
minds. With him "the Great Awakening" began to sweep the
colonies. Whitefield had no qualms about offending good taste:
religion to him was of such consuming importance that nothing
else mattered. He made vivid God's love, the reality of sin, the
agony of hell, the bliss of heaven. Creeds did not concern him;
the condition of a man's soul did. Wherever he went, whether
in towns or in the back-country, he drew enormous crowds, who
heard him with almost desperate eagerness. He figuratively set
colonial America ablaze with religious fervor, drawing into his
evangelical orbit dozens of ministers who had caught a new
vision of their calling. Whitefield probably excited more interest
than any other contemporary, and certainly he furnished more
themes for discussion and argument.

Few denominations were more drastically affected by the
Great Awakening than the Presbyterian. Conservatives were
contemptuous of Whitefield's pulpit pyrotechnics, dubious of the

---

* In the Anglican Church, the Reverend Thomas Bray, aware of the failure
of his church to reach and hold those whose forebears were Anglican, and
convinced also of missionary needs in America, took the lead in founding both the
SPG (Society for the Propagation of the Gospel in Foreign Parts) and the SPCK
(Society for the Promotion of Christian Knowledge). Scores of clergymen were
sent to the colonies by these two organizations. Their work, however useful,
was often marked by the same formalism, insistence upon rote memory, and
traditionalism that was characteristic of ecclesiastical training at the time. Few
of the clergymen seemed to sense that a backwoodsman or an Indian was a very
different person from an English villager who had never been out of his parish.

validity of the sudden conversions he achieved, and sure that the church would degrade itself by diluting its message and making religion "easy" for the common man. Other Presbyterians, however, regarded Whitefield as a true and timely prophet. He had shown the church that it must be active in going out to the people, speaking to them in their own language, in order to seek and save the lost sheep. By 1745 this divergence of opinion had reached a stage of such virulence that the Presbyterian Church underwent a schism. Those opposed to the new evangelical attitudes and methods were called the Old Side, and those who favored these, the New Side or, contemptuously, the New Lights.

The points at issue concerned more than fervor and methods. The nature of the church was involved. Old Siders were, to borrow a phrase from another denomination, High Churchmen. There was a right way of doing things, one hallowed by tradition and experience. What was true and proper for the fathers was still true and proper for the church in America. When every condition of life in a new country seemed to undermine the established order of faith and morality, surely the church should be a rock and mighty fortress, unyielding and changeless. Why give up the wisdom of centuries for a fad? Old Siders agreed that the church must offer the opportunities for salvation, by providing churches; but it was man's duty to seek the church, not the church the man. New Siders, on the contrary, said that the validity of the church rested upon New Testament teaching and experience. Christ himself and his apostles had gone out into the byways and hedges to win souls; as they tried to be all things to all men, so must their successors in the modern world.

Another matter at issue was the proper spiritual experience of a Christian and the function of a minister in stimulating that experience. Foote states the question thus: "whether true spiritual exercises implied or admitted great excitement,—whether conversion was a rapid or very gradual work,—whether evidences of grace were decisive or necessarily obscure,—whether true revivals were attended with great alarms, deep convictions, great distress and strong hopes and fears,—whether a collegiate course of education was a necessary preparation for the ministry of the gospel,—and whether personal experience of religion should form part of the examination of candidates for the ministry."[3]

These questions all turn, not upon fundamental Christian doctrine, but upon the manner in which religion should be experienced and promoted. Put bluntly, the argument was whether the Presbyterian Church should continue in its accustomed ways or recognize the fact that America needed new and different ways. Some later commentators have seen these issues of 1745 as only "differences between tweedle-dee and tweedle-dum;" to Presbyterians of that time they were so vital that "men would have been crucified for these points of difference."[4]

New Siders recognized their first task as evangelical—to see to it that the thousands of Scotch-Irish people in the backcountry should have their spiritual needs ministered to. Missionary work for the first time began actively to be carried on, first near at hand in the Pennsylvania settlements, then in all the frontier regions being filled up in Virginia and the Carolinas. The number of new congregations founded grew by leaps and bounds. The rigid formalism to which Presbyterian ministers had normally tended began to yield to a vital personal faith that gave men a sense of urgency. The church was undergoing transformation from Old World standards because of New World realities.[*]

It was in this setting that Tennent's Log College experiment began to bear remarkable fruit. New Siders realized that the church could never accomplish its task so long as it had to depend upon ministers trained abroad; they also saw that such ministers would naturally lean toward conservative Old Side attitudes. In 1746, therefore, the New Side Presbyterians of New Jersey founded at Princeton a college, patterned after Harvard and Yale, whose purpose should be to train and send forth a host of American ministers. In one sense, the founding of the College of New Jersey was the Presbyterian Church's declaration of independence from Scotland and England. To

---

[*] The modern reader must recall the dignity of a Presbyterian divine in his Genevan gown, stocks, and possibly wig; speaking from an enclosed pulpit; accustomed, simply *ex officio*, to respect and authority. Old Side ministers were quite right in supposing that both dignity and authority might be lost by New Side methods. This, indeed, was part of the transformation that the church was undergoing in becoming American.

the extent that the college succeeded in its purpose, America would train its own ministers in American ideas for American parishes.

New Side ministers, recognizing the church's requirements for education, now began to conduct school classes in their manses. Having got a start in such informal schools, bright youths could then go on to the large "academies" that soon began to be a part of the Presbyterian landscape in the colonies. Some of these academies achieved a considerable reputation in their time—for example, Samuel Blair's at Fagg's Manor and Robert Smith's at Pequea, both in Pennsylvania; John Brown and Robert Alexander's in Augusta, Virginia; David Caldwell's "Log College" in North Carolina. Even the Old Siders were impelled to found Newark Academy. Before many decades some of the academies grew into true colleges. Throughout the colonies it was well known that Calvinists, whether the Puritans of New England or the Presbyterians, took the lead in promoting higher education. *

The bitterness of dissension that divided the Presbyterian Church gradually abated, and by 1758 the breach between Old Side and New Side was formally healed. Aware, the Synod said, of "the divided state of these colonies," and the "abounding of profanity, luxury, infidelity, error, and ignorance," it was well for the church to be united. Neither side had "won", but the church that came together in 1758 was considerably different from the church that had split in 1745. No longer did there seem to be English, Scots, and Scotch-Irish "wings" or interests; all were American. All agreed that, whatever methods were proper, the church must make a strenuous effort to provide for all its people. Presbyterians in America were now committed to missionary enterprise, carried on almost wholly by American funds and by a native-born clergy, more and more of whom were coming from humble homes.[5] It was further agreed that it was

* The Presbyterians of the piedmont section of Virginia founded the second Presbyterian college, Hampden-Sydney, in 1776, on the model of the College of New Jersey. Pennsylvanians began in 1780 the institution that was to become Washington and Jefferson. Several academies were founded by action of Presbyteries rather than by individuals; thus, Hanover Presbytery in Virginia in 1774 ordered an academy to be founded at Timber Ridge, and called the Reverend William Graham to preside over the institution that later became Washington and Lee.

the duty of the church to provide educational facilities for its young men.

In spite of all the expansion of education and the remarkable missionary accomplishment, the church could not begin to meet the religious needs of the two hundred thousand Scotch-Irish who by 1776 were filling the back-country and steadily increasing their large families. Certainly the church was vividly aware by now of the spiritual needs of the people. Presbyteries ordered pastors to leave their congregations to make missionary journeys among the settlements—preaching, performing marriages, administering the sacraments, consoling the ill and bereaved. Young men who wished to enter the ministry were not ordained until they had visited the frontier. So persistent were the calls that a good part of the time of each Presbytery's meetings was taken up by consideration of appeals from Scotch-Irish settlements. Yet the Church's best was not enough: thousands of the Scotch-Irish people were without the care of a church or a minister, and had been for years.

What Presbyterians could not do, Baptists accomplished. All the ardor and adaptability displayed by the former following the Great Awakening could not overcome the major obstacle of insufficient numbers of ministers. One fundamental Presbyterian commitment stood in the way: the clergy must be well educated. Baptists had no such requirement. To them the gospel was simple, uncomplicated, within the reach of all. Neither Christ nor his disciples had been university men, and his final command had directed ordinary persons to preach the gospel to all men. More than this, it required no complex organization to form a Baptist church; the approval of no Presbytery or other ecclesiastical court was involved. A group of like-minded Christians could form a congregation and select as their minister a dedicated Baptist who felt the "call." He was forthwith a minister, endowed, as he felt, by God's grace to perform all the functions of his office. While Presbyterians were spending six years or more at great expense getting ready to preach, Baptists were already at work—and more of them every year.

At times the zealous young Baptist ministers and missionaries and exhorters could not even read or could read only haltingly;

but they knew many passages of the Bible from memory and could speak directly to the hearts of their ready listeners about the great issues of life and death, sin and hell, faith and heaven. The form of Baptist government no doubt made easy the work of the ministers, for there was no House of Bishops or hierarchy to discipline the ardor, correct the theology, and limit the activities of the zealot. If the sedate proprieties of the more established faiths were often offended by the preaching of these enthusiasts, if discourses were unpolished and frequently uncouth, if immersions became scenes of intense emotionalism, to many pioneers the deep earnestness of the "preacher" was more than enough to compensate for any lapses of taste they may have perceived.*

At the close of the colonial period the Presbyterian Church was still predominant among the Scotch-Irish, but its monopoly was fast being undermined. The following table, showing the number of ministers at work in the four major denominations in 1776, reveals the advantage the Baptists had already gained.

	NEW ENGLAND	MIDDLE & SOUTH	TOTAL	PER CENT†
Congregational	1650	113	1763	35
Episcopalian	127	1136	1263	25
Baptist	217	391	608	12
Presbyterian	51	462	513	10

* Some of the New Side Presbyterians, seeing the success of the Baptists and ascribing that success primarily to the licensing of "uneducated" men as ministers, suggested that the Presbyterians do the same. They made no headway. Again in 1783 the request was made of the Synod of New York and Philadelphia, and again it was refused. In 1785 the Synod answered in the negative "by a great majority" the question, "Whether in the present state of the Church in America and the scarcity of ministers to fill out numerous congregations, the Synod or Presbyteries ought to relax, in any degree, the literary qualifications required of entrants into the ministry." It was even proposed to raise these standards and to require both a liberal arts education and a two-year divinity course; but this was laid over and rejected the following year. (*Records of the Presbyterian Church in the United States of America, 1706-1788*, pp. 499, 511)

† This table is adapted from Weis's *Colonial Churches and the Colonial Clergy*, p. 17. According to Weis's count, there were 734 other ministers in the colonies, with the next four denominations being, in order, the Reformed, Moravian, Lutheran, and Roman Catholic.

It is not certain whether a census of church membership, if one could be compiled, would demonstrate the same order as that in the table. Thompson says that Presbyterians were outnumbered only by Congregationalists, but he does not reveal his sources for the statement. (Thompson, *Presbyterian Missions*, p. 36)

The success of the Baptists was phenomenal, not only among Scotch-Irish and other frontiersmen, but among those who found the older churches cold and representative of the privileged classes. The ardor of the Great Awakening gradually cooled in the East, but it continued to glow at white heat among the Baptists. Late in the eighteenth century the Methodist Church, reflecting the zeal of the Wesleys and the far-sighted direction of its first American bishop, Francis Asbury, began to share the Baptist success.* After independence, when the Appalachians began to be traversed and the Ohio Valley to be filled, the progress of these two denominations was accompanied by methods truly sensational. Whitefield's meetings may be said to have been forerunners of the "revival meeting," which both Baptists and Methodists eagerly adopted; but by 1802, in Kentucky, the revival had led to the still more fervid and dramatic "camp meeting." The two sects were evangelical and assiduous in a way that no Protestants had ever been before.

The Methodists devised one of the truly effective adaptations to frontier conditions of life, the circuit rider. A minister, instead of being tied to a single church, rode hundreds of miles each month to visit pioneers on their remote farms. If there were neighbors, he would preach; in any case, he could perform all the services of a pastor to a scattered flock, comforting, counseling, marrying young couples, burying the dead. The devotion and indefatigability of these circuit riders became proverbial: Kentuckians remarked of a day of foul weather that no one would be abroad in it "but crows and Methodist ministers."

* The Methodist Church was not founded in America by the Wesleys. As is well known, these brothers had no intention of founding a new denomination, but simply of revivifying the Anglican Church and of recovering for men a deep personal faith to which the Church should minister. It seemed to them that many ministers in all the Established Churches of the time—Anglican, Presbyterian, Puritan, and Roman—had the attitude of Jewish priests in the Temple: that providing the place, means, and ministers of worship was all that was required of the clergy. Thereafter, initiative should rest with the layman, whose duty it was to avail himself of the means provided by the Church.

Though at least two-thirds of the people in the United States of 1789 were of English origin, and though the Anglican Church had been Established in many of the colonies, it soon lost its hold on the average English-American. The new Methodist Church followed the Baptist example of plain talk, direct evangelism, adaptability to circumstance. The Anglicans (after 1789 the Protestant Episcopal Church in the United States) lost proportionately more to the two evangelical denominations than did the Presbyterians.

Despite its losses, the Presbyterian Church of 1789 had become Americanized. It no longer looked to Scotland or England for leadership, nor did it try to follow the pattern of Presbyterianism laid down in those countries. The very fact that it had developed its own church court as early as 1706 gave it an American tone, and made simpler its adaptation to the local situation.* Moreover, forces within and without the Church fused together the divergent elements into an American body, dealing with American problems in pragmatic fashion. The Great Awakening quickened the evangelical spirit until Presbyterian churches flourished in every colony from Maine to Georgia. It can be maintained, with considerable evidence, that the Presbyterian Church more than any other at the time transcended social, geographical, and ethnic lines. It was not, like the Episcopal Church, confined to Englishmen, generally of the privileged class; it was not a sectional church, like the Congregational; it was not a church of one group of recent immigrants, like the Lutheran or Moravian; it did not, like the Baptist, speak primarily to simple folk.

Still further, its form of organization gave a new sense of unity extending far beyond the boundaries of any one province. Trinterud points out that members of a Long Island congregation were united in one church with those in South Carolina. A New Jersey minister might announce that he would, on order from the Synod, spend the next two months preaching in North Carolina and that his place would be filled by a minister from Maine. At the annual meeting of Synod the Scotch-Irish elder of a church in Virginia might meet a brother elder of mixed Dutch and English stock from New York City. Missionaries from the Middle Colonies, by their active work in piedmont Virginia, whose people had no background of Presbyterianism, had made this region a bulwark of that faith.[6]

The College of New Jersey at Princeton was likewise a unifying and Americanizing force. No college in the colonies drew its students from such wide areas. Harvard, Yale, and the Col-

---

* During the colonial period, all other important religious bodies except that in New England were controlled from abroad. The Bishop of London was over American Anglicans. The Dutch Reformed churches were governed by the Classis of Amsterdam. Roman Catholics received orders from Rome.

lege of William and Mary were essentially local institutions; but when James Madison of Virginia entered Princeton, of the eighty-four students in attendance only nineteen were from New Jersey, and every colony was represented in the student body.[7]   Of the 250 Presbyterian ministers who received ordination between 1758 and 1789, 120 were graduates of the College of New Jersey; twenty came from Yale; and the remainder were furnished by Newark Academy, the College of Philadelphia, Hampden-Sydney College, and the academy that eventually became Washington and Lee.[8]

The Presbyterian Church, like the United States of 1789, was federal in its governmental structure, though neither institution was democratic in the modern sense of the word; yet, by an interesting parallelism, each developed a measure of democracy —the church before the state.   In the representative form of Presbyterian government, each congregation is governed by its elders.   In modern practice, these are elected by members of the congregation, but at the beginning of the eighteenth century, it was the usual practice for a minister to nominate the elders or even to manage local affairs with a committee named by himself.*   As the century progressed, more and more congregations demanded a larger part in the choice of their ruling elders.

Another democratic influence within the church was its succession of courts, ranging from the local Session, through the regional Presbytery, to the Synod (composed of at least three Presbyteries), and after 1789 the General Assembly of the entire church.   Any individual who, in a lower court, contended for a cause or was found guilty of an offense, might appeal his case to a higher judicature.   By trials in the Session and debates in church courts, the Scotch-Irish received a training in legal procedure that stood them in good stead when they began to take an active part in legal and judicial affairs of state and nation. Almost from their arrival the Scotch-Irish in many colonies became interested in politics and law.   In all of their places of

---

* Again, in modern practice, elders not only attend the meetings of all church courts, but may be elected to highest offices in them.   Trinterud says that during the entire colonial era there is no record of an elder's having been made Moderator or even Clerk of a Presbytery or Synod.   (Trinterud, *The Forming of an American Tradition*, pp. 205, 211)

larger settlement, and first of all in Pennsylvania, the influence of these frontiersmen began to be felt in colonial assemblies.

It had been Calvin's idea that elders (presbyters) should work in close co-operation with magistrates in upholding public order. This arrangement worked well in theocratic Geneva and likewise in Scotland where the Kirk was the Established Church of the country. Even in America the Secretary of the Province of Pennsylvania at first asked the co-operation of the elders in various Scotch-Irish communities to see that settlers took land only after the proper legal preliminaries. Since the Presbyterian Church, however, was nowhere officially Established in the colonies, but was everywhere one of several competing denominations, complete separation of church and state became the rule. No official pronouncement was made to define the spheres of the two institutions, but in practice the Presbyterian Church, as such, took no part in politics. Regional Presbyteries, each in effect autonomous, were conspicuously adaptable to the American environment, since each region was developing its special characteristics and problems.

Before the arrival of the Scotch-Irish, Presbyterianism in America had naturally reflected the usages of its predominantly English congregations. By 1789, however, a majority of people in the church had a background of Ulster and Scottish Presbyterianism. As the Baptist and Methodist churches increasingly drew away those who set little store by tradition, the Presbyterian Church came to reflect the strict practices of true-blue Calvinism.*

Training of the young in the fundamentals of the faith had been arduous and conscientious from the time of John Knox. The Shorter Catechism must be memorized by every member of the family; the Larger Catechism, with its scriptural "proofs," was sometimes memorized and was generally studied; many families owned copies of the Confession of Faith and knew it thoroughly.

* An Anglican minister in 1760 divertingly sums up his impression of the qualities characteristic of the major denominations in the colony: "The Baptists are obstinate, illiterate, and grossly ignorant, the Methodists, ignorant, censorious and uncharitable, the Quakers, Rigid, but the Presbyterians are pretty moderate except here and there a Bigot or rigid Calvinist." (Letter of James Reed, an S.P.G. minister, to the Secretary of the Colony, June 26, 1760. *Colonial Records of N.C.*, VI, 265)

It was the duty of a good minister to visit the homes under his care and examine its members upon their knowledge and understanding of the faith. Schoolmasters were eagerly sought after in all Scotch-Irish communities, because of the zeal for education brought with them from Reformation days in Scotland. (Many of the indentured servants were engaged as tutors or schoolmasters until their time was up.) The Reverend David McClure, traveling in the frontier region of Pennsylvania in 1792-93, noted that the Presbyterians were "well instructed in the principles of religion" and well indoctrinated by their parents and schoolmasters.[9]

Sunday was a day of strict observance. All work ceased, and the whole day was given over to the public and private exercises of religion. If a minister was at hand, everyone in the neighborhood went to church, remaining most of the day for two long sermons and for worship. As far as possible, all preparations for the Sabbath had been made beforehand; not even baking or needless cooking was allowed on Sunday. Family worship was commonly engaged in, with the reading of a chapter from the Bible, the singing of a psalm or hymn clear through, and a comprehensive prayer, all kneeling; on Sunday the private worship was likely to be extended, especially if there were no preaching on that day.[10] Morton says that Sunday services in the Valley of Virginia continued from ten o'clock until sunset, with an interval of one hour for dinner.[11]

The Lord's Supper, usually celebrated only twice a year, was an especially solemn occasion. It sometimes extended over a four-day period, as was the general practice in Ulster, with earnest sermons of preparation on the three days preceding the Sabbath, and with examination of members by the minister and the Session of elders. Where congregations were without a pastor, Presbyterians frequently traveled many miles to participate; these visitations, though they strained the hospitality of the settlers, were generally welcome since they brought news from afar and renewed old acquaintance. When the congregation was too large to be accommodated in the church building, the preaching might take place in the open air. The bread and wine were placed upon long tables, which sometimes extended down the aisle from pulpit to door. To these tables were admitted none who had not previously received tokens from the Session, as evidence of their right to commune. These tokens, usually small pieces of lead or spelter, with the initial letter of the church or some other symbol upon them, signified the sobriety and piety of the holder or his successful examination by the pastor and Session.[12] Dinsmore's account of the communion service in a Presbyterian church is vivid. After noting the sermons from Thursday through Saturday, with one day of "fasting, humiliation, and prayer," he describes the communion service on Sunday:

Tables were placed across the entire width of the building, and often down the wide centre aisle. These tables were simply made of poplar boards, unpainted, about the height of the ordinary dining table, and fifteen inches wide. They were covered with spotless linen. Along each side were placed lower benches for the people to sit upon. In front of the pulpit stood a small table on which were placed the holy vessels with their contents of unleavened bread and port wine. . . . The morning sermon was called the "action sermon," and was always an earnest and elaborate setting-forth of the vicarious sacrifice of Christ, and usually took a full hour. This, with the accompanying services, required at least two full hours before the celebration proper began. Then, after a hymn, and the reading from scripture of the warrant for the service, came what was called the "fencing of the tables." This was a lengthy address stating with great minuteness, the tests by which people must decide whether they were entitled to come to the Lord's Table, and barring those who were not entitled to come.*[13]

Church services were, by modern standards, unconscionably long and tedious. To understand the persistence of this custom, one must remember the long-standing Scottish tradition of a Hebraic Sabbath, with no work or amusement permitted; and also it is useful to recall the comforting experience of being in close contact with other people after a week's isolation on a remote farm at hard work.

In the Presbyterian tradition, the sermon—the expounding

---

* It is Dinsmore's opinion that the tokens given to communicants originated in the times of persecution "when only those certainly known to be trustworthy could be informed of the time and place of such a service. Informers and spies were abroad, and only such as were known to elders to be faithful were advised of the time and place of these gatherings which must be in secret places." (Dinsmore, *The Scotch-Irish in America*, pp. 157-58)

of the Word—was the central part of the service.   The customary sermon lasted for an hour and a half, and was by no means a simple discourse.   From long practice, the congregation knew what to expect of a preacher: if he did not develop his points logically and in order, with a firstly and secondly, and so on until "Finally, my brethren," he could hardly maintain respect.   The Bible was read; prayers, sometimes as long as three-quarters of an hour, with the whole congregation standing,* were offered extempore; and hymns were sung.   In the stricter congregations only Rouse's metrical version of the Psalms was used, and the number of tunes was very limited; the more liberal congregations used not only the Psalms but also Watts's Hymns and Psalms.   There was no musical instrument of any kind.   In the absence of psalm- and hymn-books, a clerk, from a raised platform, read out a line or two and then led the congregation in singing it; thereupon, he recited other lines, and the singing was continued through all the verses.   It is an evidence of the conservatism of the people that when it was proposed, in later and more affluent days, to have hymn-books for the congregation, and so eliminate the "lining out" of the hymns, a tempest was raised in many churches.   The introduction of a musical instrument was an even more radical innovation, hotly resisted until the nineteenth century.[14]

After the three-hour morning service there was recess, during which the people ate the lunch they had brought with them. Here was an opportunity for sociability and for discussion of community events, crops, illnesses, weather; for quiet courtships; and for decorous diversion among the children.   The strictness of Sabbath observance forbade games or noise or any suggestion of a picnic atmosphere.   After the recess the congregation gathered once more for an afternoon service, with another sermon as long as the first, and more Bible reading, hymns, and prayer. When the hard, backless log benches grew unendurable, the people were permitted to stand and even to move about.†

---

* Scott suggests in his *Rob Roy* that the practice of standing for prayers was begun in Scotland as the posture farthest removed from Roman Catholicism. It has also been suggested that the Scot believed his God preferred a man with self-respect enough to stand in His presence.

† As Dunaway (*Scotch-Irish of Colonial Pennsylvania*, p. 209) remarks,

Presbyterian observances of the Scotch-Irish reveal many aspects of the character of this people, as of their ancestors. At the Reformation there had been a break from Rome and a "return to Scriptural authority." It might have been possible, as in the Episcopal and Lutheran churches, to keep whatever the Roman Church had developed in the service that was not specifically forbidden by Scripture. The Scots, like other Puritans, went to the other extreme: they discarded whatever was not specifically required by the New Testament. The model was the first-century Christian Church therein described. If one is to break with Rome, the break should be complete, according to Scots logic. Nevertheless, in Scotland the Genevan gown was adopted for the minister, the pulpit was opened for him by a lay official, and he was escorted from the pulpit at the end of the sermon. These were formalities, though not Catholic. Knox had prepared a Book of Common Order which contained prayers and a modicum of ritual. In the New World even these remnants of ecclesiasticism disappeared. In a rough log church there was no separate pulpit; the Genevan gown was no longer used; the service was simple and unadorned from necessity—and thus became the right way of doing things.

The Scottish Reformation had developed and cultivated a "Presbyterian conscience" that consorted well with the Scottish temperament. When one knows what is right and wrong, he must stand firm on his principles, without any variation or shadow of turning, for the individual is entirely responsible for his own actions.* Compromise is evil; yielding a point, whether for the sake of politeness or to attain a larger end, is base.† If the Scot was hard on other people, he was first hard on himself. The experience in Ulster had proved the usefulness of such

---

"There was never any hurry about anything; they had come to make a day of it and there was plenty of time."

* Such ideas as attributing personal failure to an unfortunate environment, defective social institutions, or traumatic experiences in childhood were unknown. Marx and Freud, who place the blame for individual woe anywhere but upon the individual, were still in the remote future.

† The Scotch-Irish firmness (stubbornness) of character is revealed in the probably apocryphal prayer of the elder who besought the Lord that he might always be right, adding, "for Thou knowest, Lord, that I am unco' hard to turn." (Futhey, in Lancaster County Historical Society *Papers*, Vol. XI, no. 6, p. 231)

qualities of character, so that, by the time of the migration to America, it was expected of all members of the community. The American Indian, like the Quaker hierarchy in Pennsylvania and the Tidewater politicians of the southern colonies, was to feel the effects of the Presbyterian character.

John Knox had stood up to a queen. His theology, like his character, was four-square and intellectually impregnable, granted his premises. Those who followed him were trained to have reason for the faith that was in them, and having done all, to stand. The inflexible logic of Calvin's *Institutes* could hardly have found a more congenial field than Scotland, Ulster, and the American frontier. Calvin's massive, rock-like stand on religious issues contributed to the making of moral fiber.* Community control over wrong-doing began at any early age, when the child accompanied his parents to church, sat through the long services, learned the catechism and recited it to the minister, and witnessed the disciplining of church members. Thus implanted in his very being before he could effectively resist, his moral standards, like his stern conscience, was ingrained. Episcopal children of the Tidewater, by contrast, had a much less rigorous indoctrination in the home and on the plantation.

The sternness, even severity, of Scotch-Irish religion is seen at its most characteristic in the control over the personal lives of church members. This trait, already observed in Ulster, was carried to the New World, where the Scotch-Irish became, in effect, the Puritans of the Middle and Southern colonies. It was still conceived to be the duty of each Session to be vigilant in the enforcement of high standards of moral discipline. People might be haled before the Session for offenses that strike a modern reader as trivial and ridiculous, just as the Puritan colonists of New England were disciplined for small offenses. For example, the fast-day before the communion service was observed with all the punctilio of the Sabbath itself. When a farmer spread his grain out to dry on such a day—one day of sun in a rainy season—he was duly and solemnly admonished by the

* English Presbyterianism, though stern enough, was of a milder sort. In Maryland and around Philadelphia the first Presbyterian churches were of this persuasion, radically different in effect from that of the Scotch-Irish.

Session. Or again, young people might be "sessioned" for "promiscuous dancing," by which the elders meant the good-humored athleticism of a square dance.[15] All cases of violation of the Lord's Day, fighting, swearing, family disagreements, unmanageability of an indentured servant, came before the Session.*

In the days before increased settlement of different nationalities side by side made the community a varied one, the Session usually dealt with cases that now would come before a civil court. False accusation, disregard of property rights, sexual immorality of all kinds, questionable business dealings, were brought to the Session, with witnesses appearing to testify for and against the accused. If the person tried was found guilty, he was deprived of church membership—and this meant not only that he might not receive his token for the Lord's Supper, but that his children might not be baptized. Restoration to the privilege of membership in full standing was granted only after confession of guilt and expressions of sorrow, sometimes before the whole congregation if the case involved the interests of the whole group.†[16]

The Presbyterian Church was, then, for many Scotch-Irish pioneers the one effective social institution in the community, a real focus and center of community life. If the Scotch-Irish were the vanguard of the "typical" pioneers who were to sweep across the continent during the eighteenth and nineteenth centuries, they were different in this one respect, that they brought with them, when they could, a functioning institution which kept life communal in essence, so that the individual was not an atom, dependent entirely upon himself for inward self-discipline, moral decision, and integrity. The minister, and to a less extent, the elder, was the voice of the community conscience. Where the church could not follow the pioneer and draw him into a community, the result was likely to produce not only strong individualism and adventuresome courage but also a reckless law-

* It might be contended that Presbyterianism and Puritanism represent an apparently strong human leaning toward asceticism, somewhat similar to the monastic and ascetic movements in Roman Catholicism. See Weber, *The Protestant Ethic and the Spirit of Capitalism*, pp. 113-140.

† Ministers usually afforded vivid examples of the Presbyterian conscience at work, in outspokenness both in the community and in the church courts. In the latter, the minister who felt "led by the Spirit" to speak his mind, did so even before his respected "fathers and brothers."

lessness and an insensitiveness to the social values men had so precariously gained through the years.

Whatever objections may be brought against the minute surveillance of private life and morals by the church, it had social advantages: it maintained high moral standards in the community, by asserting the right of the community to judge these. The Presbyterian conscience had already imbued the people with a clear-cut distinction between right and wrong; but moral distinctions always need the support of social institutions, of public pressure on the wrongdoer. When pioneers moved beyond the influence of both church and courts, morality suffered because there was no true community to require an individual to live up to high standards. Violence, sexuality, crudity, and lynch-law were, to judge from contemporary evidence, marks of pioneers without a church. The church brought discipline; and however uncongenial this is to the person upon whom it is exerted, to the Presbyterian the right of the church to exact that discipline was as much a matter of course as that of courts and police is to modern Americans.[17]

Some early Presbyteries kept active watch over ministers and congregations, appointing committees to visit localities to question the pastor upon his full and conscientious discharge of duties, the elders upon their faithful attention to responsibility, the members upon their attendance at worship and sacraments and the discharge of their pecuniary obligations to the minister. All complaints and causes of dissatisfaction were investigated and, if possible, amicably settled. The church was never laissez-faire.

The success of the Baptists and Methodists with people of Scotch-Irish background may be said to have completed the transformation of the Presbyterian Church in the eighteenth century. In the main, those who had been drawn away from the church of their fathers were those who set little store by tradition, theology, and religious "propriety" in comparison with a simple faith that spoke directly to the heart.* With these now

---

* It may be suggested that religious toleration in America hastened the defection of Scotch-Irishmen to other denominations. So long as there is "persecution" by an Established Church, dissenters are likely to maintain a stubborn loyalty to theological positions which distinguish them. To Presbyterians in Ulster, for example, the doctrine of election had been vitally important: it

gone, the prevailing element remaining in the church consisted of the socially conservative. The Presbyterian Church had gradually and imperceptibly become what it was to remain for more than a century—a denomination of the staid, sober, settled people of steady character, of that element generally known as middle class. The church continued to found schools and colleges, to eschew emotionalism and revivals, to esteem both self-discipline and social discipline.

As the nineteenth century dawned, the Presbyterian Church seemed to represent, on both sides of the Appalachians, and from north to south, a special section of the American population. It had lost those who were to form the backbone of Jacksonian democracy. It had never had those who represented high society in America and who took religion as merely a proper adjunct of life to which due form should be paid. Just as it had not succumbed to the Deism of such men as Jefferson, Adams, and Franklin, so it would not succumb to Unitarianism. Presbyterianism remained orthodox and earnest, just as it remained seriously theological; it kept much that had come with it from Scotland by way of northern Ireland; but by 1810 it had fallen in membership far below the Baptists and Methodists, who were sweeping all before them.

---

gave assurance, consolation, and incentive to members of a "persecuted" body. For many Scotch-Irish settlers in America, however, the sense of election grew dim. It certainly interposed no barrier to stop a hitherto elect Presbyterian from becoming a Baptist if the latter denomination provided him with a minister whose sincerity was patent, while his own former church gave him no minister at all. Presbyterian fervor declined among those who, in fair and open competition among denominations, felt their deepest needs met by other faiths.

16

The Scotch-Irish in Politics

NEAR THE BEGINNING OF THE PRESENT CENTURY patriotic descendants of the Scotch-Irish made and listened to many addresses
extolling their ancestors. In orations and articles sweeping
claims were made, insistently attributing much of the best in
American political tradition to Scotch-Irish pioneers. According
to these eulogists, the original democratic influence in the
country came from the Scotch-Irish; they contributed the deciding forces in the Revolutionary War; they helped shape the
Constitution, giving the nation its republican form of government; and after 1789 they provided presidents, justices, legislators, and governors far in excess of their proportional numbers.
All of these contributions (and others) were claimed to be the
natural and inevitable results of the inherent fine qualities of
Scotch-Irish character and of Presbyterianism.*

On the other and less laudatory side, the Scotch-Irish have
been called the first political radicals in America. The streak of
lawlessness Americans have often shown and the attempts to
enforce summary justice outside of the law have been blamed on
them. Rank individualism, the competitive spirit determined to
win at whatever price, ruthlessness in action toward a goal—these
traits, too, have been called Scotch-Irish.

* Dozens of examples could be given of such claims—for example, almost
every volume of the *Proceedings* of the Scotch-Irish Congress; Peter Ross's *The
Scot in America;* Whitelaw Reid's *The Scot in America and the Ulster Scot.*
A characteristic claim reads thus: "After the conflict was over, and the sages of
America came to settle the forms of our government, they did but copy into
every constitution the simple elements of representative republicanism, as found
in the Presbyterian system. It is matter of history that cannot be denied, that
Presbyterianism, as found in the Bible, and in the standards of the several
Presbyterian churches, gave character to our free institutions." (Cited by
Parker, *History of Londonderry,* p. 102)

All such claims, in whatever spirit made, are part of what may be called the "mythology" of the Scotch-Irish. None of them is wholly accurate; some are clearly false; all attest to the impression the Scotch-Irish made upon those who have tried to interpret American political history. It is hardly surprising that the second largest nationality group in colonial America should have had some influence upon political life; yet these people came to the colonies with little political experience. In Ulster, following the Test Act, no Presbyterian for a generation could participate in active politics. Nor is there any record of the emigration from Ulster of any barrister, solicitor, jurist, or politician. By the close of the eighteenth century, however, politics and law absorbed many of the Scotch-Irish in America.

Political opinion and activity among the Scotch-Irish varied enormously from place to place. The whole mythology concerning this people rests upon a false assumption: that all Scotch-Irish thought alike. Why should they? They had come from different social classes back home; they entered America during six decades of remarkable fluctuation in ideas; they lived in colonies whose policies, attitudes, Indian problems, and progress toward stable institutions diverged widely. There was certainly no magic ichor flowing through Scotch-Irish veins to force all minds to share one variety of political opinion.

The engagement of the Scotch-Irish in politics can be examined only in those colonies where their concentration was heavy. In nine of the original colonies settlers from Ulster were too scattered, too few, or too little a "community" to make a unique impression upon politics; but in Pennsylvania, Virginia, and the two Carolinas, where settlement was densest, the Scotch-Irish took an active role in political life. In none of these four provinces was that participation identical; circumstances made it now radical, now conservative, now extra-legal, now orderly.

Events in Pennsylvania proved that the foreboding of the Secretary of the Province in 1729 had been prophetic. His fear lest, "if some speedy Method be not taken" to curb the inrush of Ulstermen, they might take over the province, came near realization by 1756. Circumstances provided a crisis among the Scotch-Irish, and the generous political institutions of the province gave them the opportunity to take action. Just as nothing in their Ulster background had prepared them to become, as they did, adept in Indian methods of fighting, hunting, and forest-craft, so nothing had foreshadowed the skill, and later the delight, they would exhibit in politics.

The occasion of their first entrance ("irruption" may be an apter word) into governmental affairs came in 1754, at the outbreak of the French and Indian wars. The pacific Quakers who ruled the province had, alone among colonial officials, made no preparation for defense against possible Indian attack. When depredations began, they took no steps to meet the emergency, but rather tried to conciliate the aroused Indians. General Braddock's impatience at Quaker inaction was as nothing compared to the anger of settlers who saw their homes burned, men scalped, women and children brutally murdered. The Quakers, their own persons and property safe in the eastern counties, showed themselves apparently indifferent to the fate of the frontier settlements.[1]

Scotch-Irish leaders immediately began an agitation whose upshot led the governor and council to declare war upon the Indians and to prosecute the fight with vigor. The conscientious Quakers in 1756 withdrew, at least momentarily, from the Assembly, leaving control in the hands of the belligerent. This initial foray into provincial affairs showed the Scotch-Irish their potential strength; it also revealed to them a considerable English (non-Quaker) and German support in challenging the oligarchy in Philadelphia.

Immediately upon the official end of the war, with the treaty barely signed, a second occasion arose for political action—and after 1763 the Scotch-Irish never relaxed their interest in political affairs. Pontiac's War in 1763 brought death to hundreds of settlers in the western part of the province and again terrorized their communities. In the tension that followed, the "Paxton Boys," as already noted, slaughtered twenty Conestoga Indians on suspicion of their having aided the Indians from the West, whereupon the Assembly, once more in control of the Quakers, took the rest of the Indians of the province under its protection. Indignant Scotch-Irishmen now drew up a Remonstrance and sent a delegation of more than five hundred men to Philadelphia to present it. This march had the semblance of mob attack and was roundly condemned (and defended) in a war of pamphlets. The men from the West did not achieve their immediate ends, but from now on they exerted steady political pressure, aware that they were not alone in opposing Quaker dominance in provincial government.

The final results of Scotch-Irish activity in Pennsylvania colonial affairs are less important than the fact of participation, the beginning of party lines, and the extension of demands beyond the immediate ones of frontier defense. In the "Declaration and Remonstrance" of 1764 there was also a protest against the inequalities of representation between east and west. Pennsylvania by that time had eight counties; but of the thirty-six members of the Assembly, all but ten were drawn from the three eastern counties around Philadelphia, in which Quaker influence was strongest.[2] This seemed patently unfair: "We apprehend that as freemen and English subjects, we have an indisputable title to the same privileges and immunities with his majesty's other subjects, who reside in the interior counties of Philadelphia, Chester, and Bucks, and therefore ought not to be excluded from an equal share with them in the very important privilege of legislation."[3] This issue, like questions of defense and Quaker dominance, won allies for the Scotch-Irish among other elements of the population.

By contrast with Pennsylvania's heated political atmosphere, the Valley of Virginia saw no movements of political indignation and protest by the Scotch-Irish during the entire colonial period. Officials at Williamsburg from the beginning showed intelligent concern with Valley people and their problems. Two counties had been organized for the pioneers within a decade of their settlement, and other counties were created as population swelled.[*] When Indian troubles arose, no colonial authorities anywhere were more active in facing and conquering the Indian menace: they organized defense and led the attack.

Paradoxically, the greatest political satisfaction of the Valley

[*] The first counties, 1738, were Frederick and Augusta; to these were added, between 1770 and 1772, Berkeley and Dunmore in the north, Botetourt and Fincastle in the south.

settlers came from the unlikeliest source: the Established Church. As in England, local affairs in Virginia were controlled by a parish organization, set up as soon as counties were created. One might suppose that both Scotch-Irish and Germans would resent this Anglican institution; yet with admirable pragmatism these dissenters made use of the device for local self-government, while not abating one whit their dislike of the Established Church and its pretensions. The parish was a division of the county. Vestrymen of the Anglican Church laid down the parish levy (taxes for local purposes) and constituted the local justices; churchwardens were overseers of the poor and executors for orphans; all elections for local posts were conducted by these officials of the Church. In the Valley settlements, however, there were almost no Anglicans. Scotch-Irish communities, like German ones, found the parish useful for their needs, elected members of their own faith as vestrymen and churchwardens, and thus had ready-made for them the vital local institutions.*

Sectional animosities, so obvious a feature of Virginia politics in the next century, did not involve the Scotch-Irish of the 1700's. Nineteenth-century issues have been mistakenly read back into eighteenth-century politics: small farmers *versus* planters, free labor *versus* slavery, Dissenters *versus* Anglicans, deprivation *versus* privilege, individualism *versus* tradition. There were certainly inequities in colonial times; for example Berkeley County in the Valley, with a population of 16,781, had the same representation as Elizabeth City County in the Tidewater, with a population of only 1,574. Yet such disparities did not seem to rankle. Zachariah Johnston, who represented the Scotch-Irish of Augusta County, found himself at times voting on the side of the Federalists and against Patrick Henry, leader of the "liberal" forces.[4]

Leadership against the traditionalists in Virginia came from Piedmont and Tidewater gentry, from Jefferson, Mason, and Henry, for example, not from Scotch-Irishmen in the Valley. It

---

* It has already been noted (above, pp. 208-9) that religious toleration was to be allowed the Scotch-Irish settlers. Peter J. Hamilton, in discussing the paradox of the parish organization among these Presbyterians, wittily remarks, "They were to be tolerated, to be sure, but in their part of Virginia, there was no one to tolerate them, for they practically made up the community themselves." (Hamilton, *The History of North America*, III, 354)

was these leaders who led the fight against primogeniture, entail, quit-rents, and the slave trade, and who pushed through a generous Constitution for the Commonwealth. They had firm allies in the Scotch-Irish and Germans of the Valley, who opposed a society of privilege; but the fight was not yet sectional, still less on the basis of national origin. It is true that many Tidewater planters disdained the "foreigners" in the Valley; Charles Lee, for example, spoke scornfully of the "Mac-ocracy" that prevailed in Augusta County. But the Scotch-Irish sent gentlemen to represent them in Williamsburg—men who, in education, manners, and support of stable institutions, moved comfortably among the coastal gentry.*

North Carolina politics differed from both Pennsylvania and Virginia. New counties were soon organized for the up-country settlers, but parish institutions were either nonexistent or ineffectual. Politics, dominated wholly by eastern planters, revealed the usual inequities. For example, coastal counties had five members each in the legislature while inland counties had but two, thus giving the planters four-fifths of the representation. The crucial fact in North Carolina, however, was that between the plantation region of the coast and the inland settlement was a wide belt of almost unoccupied country. If trade was carried on between Piedmont and Tidewater, the intermediaries were Scots around Fayetteville, not merchants from Eastern towns. Because of this virtual no man's land, Orange County and its western neighbors developed independently for many years, with little in common to bind them to the east.

Sectional differences in North Carolina were palpable. Easterners were not reticent in expressing their low opinion of up-country people, who were not English nor Anglican nor "gentlemen." A governor called them "outcasts and fugitives of other colonies.† This riff-raff of adventurers should, it was generally

---

* With this background of political moderation, it is hardly surprising to discover that many Valley Presbyterians a generation later became confirmed Whigs of a conservative bent, constitutionally averse to Jacksonian Democrats.

† This opinion, expressed by Governor Martin in 1774, reflected his ire at the Regulation movement which had only recently been put down. His attitude was widely shared around New Bern, though certainly not by the governors from 1734 to 1765, who favored the new settlers. (See *Colonial Records of N.C.*, IX, 358.)

felt, be satisfied with whatever they received from the government of the province, even (apparently) if it were second-best and not scrupulously fair.

The back-country, in which the Scotch-Irish element predominated, was not satisfied for long. Trouble began in 1759, when settlers in Orange County seized a tax agent and forced him to give bond for the return of "extortionate fees." Complaints increased during succeeding years, with emphasis upon maladministration of justice, extortion by officials, and the scarcity of money.* By 1768 tension had reached the point of producing a "movement," the Regulation, whose members agreed to combine to take action, outside of the law, against exorbitant taxes and illegal fees.

Regulators caused numerous local tumults, such as that at Hillsborough, when Fanning, a "favorite" of the Governor, was attacked. After months of threats, violence, and disorder, during which it seemed that government by law had collapsed, Governor Tryon in 1771 determined to crush the movement. Sending sufficient troops to the region, he administered a thorough defeat to the Regulators in the "battle" of Alamance (May 16, 1771). Five leaders were hanged. Hundreds of those who had participated moved westward across the mountains into the new Watauga settlement in eastern Tennessee. Governor Martin, who succeeded Tryon, pardoned most of the rest of the Regulators, requiring only that they take the oath of allegiance to the Crown.

The meaning and significance of the Regulation Movement has been much debated. Since it occurred in territory where the Scotch-Irish outnumbered others (though both German and English farmers also participated), it has been called one of the opening struggles for freedom against tyrannical government.

---

* A petition for redress enumerated these causes of discontent: disproportionate taxes, venal lawyers and judges, lack of paper money, quit-rents, abuse of land laws, and religious intolerance. A real problem for the colonial government may have been the ambiguous status of Lord Granville's proprietary. He had not yielded this to the Crown in 1729, when the other proprietors made their cession. He sold and rented lands, but had no right to govern his vast holdings. It seems clear that his proprietary was neglected in the 1760's. See Morison and Commager, *Growth of the American Republic*, I, 53; *Colonial Records of N.C.*, Vol. VII, Introduction, p. 90; Boyd, *Some Eighteenth Century Tracts*, p. 177; DeMond, *The Loyalists in North Carolina*, p. 35.

On the other hand, it can be cited as an egregious display of men taking law into their own hands, in the pattern of later Vigilantes, lynchers, and the Ku Klux Klan. An Anson County petition of 1768 said that "we have too long yielded ourselves slaves to re-morseless oppression"; yet four Presbyterian ministers sent an Address to Governor Tryon, as well as a letter to Presbyterian inhabitants, denouncing the Regulation as "rebellion."[5] It has even been contended that the whole movement was a protest against any "bridling of hitherto unrestricted freedom" in the up-country.†

However one may decide the significance of the Regulation, the Scotch-Irish and the back-country had been thrown into the maelstrom of politics. Sectional animosities were soon to be compounded by bitterness in the War for Independence.

South Carolina's experience paralleled her northern neigh-bor's in the complete control of government by Tidewater plant-ers, their contempt for the character of settlers in the back-country, and their unwillingness to give them the kind of local institutions they needed.* This southern colony likewise had its Regulators; but their movement arose for reasons exactly opposite to those of North Carolina. It was not that government was too much present and too exigent, but that there was no government at all. Ever since the end of Cherokee troubles in 1761 Scotch-Irish and others had been flocking into the back-country by thou-sands, yet the gentlemen of Charleston organized no new coun-ties. Parish lines had been surveyed only a short distance inland, so that few Piedmont settlers knew what parish they were in. This meant no local government whatever, for even to vote, a man would have to take a long trip to parish churches near the coast. The most pressing problem, however, was security for persons and property. With the only court of law in the entire province at Charleston, there was a vacuum into which poured

---

* This curious position is that of Bridenbaugh's. Though he professes sym-pathy with the state of mind of the Regulators, he says that "nowhere in the thirteen colonies was so complete a measure of individual liberty enjoyed by the common people as in Piedmont North Carolina." Their objection, he thinks, was to taxation itself. (Bridenbaugh, *Myths and Realities*, pp. 160-61)

† The general attitude of the elite of Charleston can be seen from the remark of one of them that these up-country people "are strangers to our interests, customs, and concerns." (Douglass, *Rebels and Democrats*, p. 33)

a horde of ruffians, lawless and disorderly men and women who preyed upon decent settlers. Gangs terrorized the countryside.[6]

Repeated petitions for redress in 1766-67 brought no results from the Commons House of Assembly. The settlers thereupon struck back, taking the law into their own hands by forming associations to resist the outlaws. They burnt the cabins of several suspects, killed a few of the leaders, and threatened others. They even refused to pay taxes and planned a march on Charleston to make their governmental needs known. Late in 1772 the Assembly grudgingly provided courts for the region, having already replaced the coastal county system with six new districts, four of them in the up-country.[*]

From the diverse political activities in which they engaged in the colonies, can any generalizations be made about the whole Scotch-Irish people? Hardly. They everywhere exhibited a very human desire for security of life and property. They were willing to take direct action to gain this security, whether it meant physically fighting Indians or verbally contending with officials. Some of their efforts were clearly outside the law; others were scrupulously legal. Not as Scotch-Irishmen, but as human beings, they made a stand for protection against Indians, for proper civil institutions, for recognition as citizens. As human beings, they resented the contemptuous offhandedness of coastal politicians and gentry. If the Regulators and the Paxton Boys were radical, the Presbyterian ministers and the Valley farmers were conservative. If some Scotch-Irish gained a reputation for litigiousness, others were recognized as pillars of community life. While it is certainly true that numerous characteristics of the later American political scene first made their appearance in regions heavily settled by Scotch-Irish, it was no social or ethnic inheritance of this people that called them forth. They wanted a good life and were willing to improvise, if necessary, to achieve it.

A favorite part of the "mythology" of the Scotch-Irish is that "to a man" they favored the break with Britain in 1775 and sup-

---

* It can be seen that the aims of the Regulation in North and South Carolina were quite different. In the former, the aim was to "regulate" local sheriffs, registrars, clerks, and lawyers who exacted "illegal and exorbitant" taxes, fees, and rents. In the latter, it was to secure the benefits of law and order. The regulation activities in South Carolina consisted largely of punishing and driving away bandits who infested the settlements.

ported the War of Independence. There were, indeed, communities in which this was true. As far as is known, few Scotch-Irish sold their property and departed for Canada or the West Indies rather than support rebellion against the Crown, while this was true of many Englishmen and Scots in the colonies. But were there also Scotch-Irish Tories and loyalists?

Much contemporary evidence supports the thesis of Scotch-Irish unanimity of patriotic opinion. An Episcopalian of Philadelphia said that "a Presbyterian loyalist was a thing unheard of."[7] A Hessian captain wrote in 1778, "Call this war by whatever name you may, only call it not an American rebellion; it is nothing more or less than a Scotch Irish Presbyterian rebellion."[8] It was reported that King George III characterized the Revolution as "a Presbyterian war," and that Horace Walpole remarked in Parliament, "There is no use crying about it. Cousin America has run off with a Presbyterian parson, and that is the end of it."[9] A representative of Lord Dartmouth wrote from New York in November 1776 that "Presbyterianism is really at the Bottom of this whole Conspiracy, has supplied it with Vigour, and will never rest, till something is decided upon it."[10] Jonathan D. Sergeant, member of the Continental Congress from New Jersey, said that the Scotch-Irish were the main pillar supporting the Revolution in Pennsylvania.[11] A New Englander who opposed the rupture with England declared the Scotch-Irish to be, with few exceptions, "the most God-provoking democrats on this side of Hell."[12] An English official in America said that the war "is at the Bottom very much a religious War," and that Calvinists had "a pretty strong inclination to every sort of Democracy."[13]

If political opinion were founded upon logic, Scotch-Irishmen should all have been ardent American patriots. When had England ever been friendly to this people from the earliest days in Scotland to the latest days in Ulster? Now that once more she was displaying her tyranny, the Scotch-Irish had a splendid chance not only to strike a blow for freedom but to pay off old scores.* Moreover, it could be shown that Calvin had taught

* This is Froude's interpretation, for example. He writes: "Throughout the revolted colonies, and, therefore, probably in the first to begin the struggle, all evidence shows that the foremost, the most irreconcilable, the most determined in pushing the quarrel to the last extremity, were the Scotch-Irish whom the bishops

the right of rebellion against unjust rulers; that the Kirk in Scotland had stood firm against kings in defense of principle; that the practice of choosing ministers and elders by the people made logical a fight for the same practice in civil rule.* It has also been argued that the frontier experience made Scotch-Irish acutely aware of their rights and the need to fight for them. If a legislature sitting in Philadelphia proved too far away to perceive the needs of western settlers and to defend their rights, what could be expected of a King and Parliament in London?

Scotch-Irish support of independence and of the war was, indeed, ardent and practically unanimous in Pennsylvania, Virginia, and one section of the Carolinas.

No evidence of Scotch-Irish Toryism has come to light in Pennsylvania. In a western district during May 1775 the Scotch-Irish in the log-cabin community of Hanna's Town met to adopt the Westmoreland Declaration, protesting the oppressive acts of Britain and declaring readiness to oppose these with life and fortune.[14] On July 4, 1776, Scotch-Irishmen at Pine Creek (now in Clinton County), unaware of what was happening in Philadelphia on that day, drew up a declaration of their independence from Great Britain.

Scotch-Irish in the Valley of Virginia were enthusiastically patriotic. The people of Augusta sent 137 barrels of flour to relieve the poor of Boston after the famous Tea Party.[15] The new county seat of Rockbridge County, formed in 1777, chose the name of Lexington in honor of the opening battle two years before in Massachusetts, while the classical academy located nearby changed its name to Liberty Hall. Resolutions in support of American rights were frequent.†[16]

In North Carolina, the militia companies of Mecklenburg County, predominantly Scotch-Irish, sent representatives to

and Lord Donegal and Company had been pleased to drive out of Ulster." (*The English in Ireland*, II, 141)

* The logic of this "argument from Presbyterianism" clearly breaks down among the Scots in America, thousands of whom were Tories and loyalists. (See Graham, *Colonists from Scotland*, pp. 150-61, 168-77)

† The epitaph of John Lewis, pioneer settler in Augusta County, is testimony to the fighting spirit of the Scotch-Irish of the Valley: "Here lies the remains of John Lewis, who slew the Irish lord, settled Augusta county, located the town of Staunton, and furnished five sons to fight the battles of the American Revolution."

Charlotte on May 20, 1775, and at midnight on this date, more than a year before the Declaration of Independence at Philadelphia, the convention agreed on resolutions declaring that the people of Mecklenburg were free and independent of the British Crown.*

In contrast to this overwhelmingly patriotic opinion of most Scotch-Irish people in the colonies, there was considerable Toryism and loyalism in the Carolina Piedmont. In North Carolina the men who had been Regulators in 1771 were at best, after 1775, tepid patriots. Urged by their Presbyterian ministers, they had secured forgiveness by taking the oath of loyalty to the Crown; why should they now forswear that oath because the same ministers, not to mention the eastern gentry who had forcibly suppressed their movement, had declared for independence? One minister was even dubbed popish priest because he "absolved" members of his congregation from their oath of allegiance.[17] The hostilities might even give ex-Regulators a good chance of paying off old scores.† So also with participants in the Regulation movement in South Carolina. Wherever these people looked they found their old enemies in control of governmental affairs. They preferred to remain under British rule rather than change to a government entirely in the hands of easterners who had never shown sympathy for them.[18] Toryism was strong wherever the Regulation movement had flourished.‡

* The general tenor of the Resolutions is that of the Declaration of July 4, 1776; what is more curious is that the two documents contain several identical phrases. It is said that the minutes of the midnight meeting were destroyed by fire in 1800 and that in replacing from memory the Mecklenburg documents an inevitable borrowing occurred from the then familiar national Declaration. The whole question is much disputed. See Cooke, *Revolutionary History of North Carolina;* Draper, *The Mecklenburg Declaration of Independence;* Hoyt, *The Mecklenburg Declaration of Independence;* Moore, *Defense of the Mecklenburg Declaration of Independence.* A second "Declaration," the Mecklenburg Resolves of May 31, 1775, asserts that the British government made the colonies free by declaring them outside its protection.

† The issue of loyalism among the ex-Regulators is canvassed in detail in Douglass, *Rebels and Democrats,* pp. 111 ff. John Adams was among those who attributed the loyalism to the desire to pay off old scores. (Adams, *Works,* VII, 284)

‡ A study has been made of the later political opinion of Regulators in Orange County, North Carolina. It indicates that although open Tory opinion was rarely affirmed, and many people were finally won to the patriot cause, the majority maintained an attitude of indifference and detachment. "Of 883 known Regulators" in Orange, "289 were Whigs, 34 Tories, and 560 . . . unknown"

The Continental Congress recognized the bitterness of ex-Regulators and the lukewarmness of other Scotch-Irish in the Piedmont regions. In November, 1775, Congress sent two Presbyterian ministers to North Carolina, at a salary of forty dollars a month, to try to win support for the patriot cause.[19]   Hewes and Hooper, North Carolina delegates to the Congress, persuaded Presbyterian ministers in Philadelphia to write to their fellow-Presbyterians in Carolina, appealing for the Revolution.   Many reluctantly and slowly came over to the patriot side, but with little of the zeal for the cause shown by the Scotch-Irish around Mecklenburg.[20]

Except for defections in the Carolinas, therefore, Scotch-Irish support for independence was generally ardent.   It showed itself in the actual fighting.   There is wide agreement on the excellence of the soldiers who were Scotch-Irish.   Wertenbaker says that they "constituted the very back-bone of Washington's army.   At Valley Forge, when many deserted him, they remained despite cold and hunger, to keep alive the waning cause."[21]   Joseph Galloway claimed, surely with exaggeration, that half the army was Scotch-Irish.[22]   Ralph Barton Perry is more moderate in asserting that "when account is taken of the Scotch-Irish Presbyterians, the Germans of the middle and southern colonies, and the New England congregationalists, it is safe to say that the bulk of the revolutionary armies came from dissenters of the reformed or Calvinistic sects.   From the clergy of these sects came also the religious leadership."[23]   A British major-general is reported to have testified before a committee of the House of Commons that "half the rebel Continental Army were from Ireland"—that is, Scotch-Irish.*[24]   General Howe indirectly paid tribute to the excellent marksmanship of the Scotch-Irish, learned as hunters and Indian fighters, and to their rifles "perfected with little knowledge of ballistics."[25]

Even in the Carolina Piedmont, Scotch-Irish fighting was

---

in their attitude toward independence and the war. (Lefler and Wager, *Orange County, 1752-1952*, p. 39)

* An example of the more fulsome praise of the Scotch-Irish as soldiers is this: "When the alarm of the American Revolution echoed along the rocky walls of the Blue Mountain, it awakened a congenial thrill of blood of that race which years before, in Ireland and Scotland, had resisted the arbitrary powers of England." (Rupp, *History and Topography of Dauphin*, p. 486)

significant. In the latter stages of the war, Cornwallis, having received the surrender of Charleston, marched up through the Carolinas in 1780. His strategy was to link his forces with those of the loyalists of the back-country and the Scottish contingents of North Carolina. Colonel Ferguson, dispatched by Cornwallis toward the west, was met by an American army at King's Mountain, where he and his redcoats were disastrously defeated. The American forces were said to have been predominantly Scotch-Irish; they were led by William Campbell, five of whose colonels were Presbyterian elders.*

Most local historical societies from Maine to Georgia have preserved in their annals both records and eulogies of leaders in the War of Independence. Hundreds of these officers were Scotch-Irish—for example, two of three colonels appointed by New Hampshire in 1775; Stark at Bunker Hill; the Virginian who raised a body of militia to march the six hundred miles to Cambridge to reinforce Washington's army; and so on. These men deserve their meed of praise; but it must be candidly admitted that no Scotch-Irish officer in the Revolutionary War made a name that rings resoundingly through American history.†

The Scotch-Irish "mythology" claims that, following independence, the part played by Scotch-Irish leaders was crucial in establishing liberal principles in the new states. This claim seems valid only in Pennsylvania. There, in 1776, conservatives of the East suffered resounding political defeat: a reapportionment of representation gave western counties a smashing victory. To the convention called to adopt a new constitution and take over the government of the state, delegates were chosen by popular vote, without property qualifications. The constitution provided for representation proportional to the number of tax-

* Tarleton admitted that it was "the vigilance and animosity" of these up-country settlers which spoiled Cornwallis' strategy. (Tarleton, *A History of the Campaigns of 1780 and 1781*, p. 160) The five elders at King's Mountain were Colonels Campbell, Cleveland, Shelby, Sevier, and Williams. In the Carolinas more than elsewhere, the war assumed all the aspects of a civil conflict. Scottish Carolinians fought against Scotch-Irish, Presbyterians against Presbyterians.

† An example of the Scotch-Irish contribution to military leadership is seen in North Carolina: Major-General Robert Howe; Brigadier-Generals William Lee Davidson, Griffith Rutherford, James Hogan; Colonels Benjamin Cleveland, Isaac Shelby, and John Sevier.

ables in each county; there should be no qualifications for voting or office-holding except payment of a state tax. The Scotch-Irish element in the west, with English and German allies, had gained control of Pennsylvania politics.

Virginia likewise adopted a generous constitution, abolishing quit-rents, primogeniture, entails, and the slave trade; church and state were separated; the Anglican Church was disestablished, and religious liberty was guaranteed. Although the Scotch-Irish strongly supported the adoption of this constitution, leadership for all these measures came from east of the Valley. Neither of the Carolinas made great concessions toward democracy or equality. South Carolina's constitution of 1778, for example, retained property qualifications for voting and office-holding, with gross over-representation of the Tidewater; but the Church was disestablished, and Protestants were guaranteed civil rights. Quit-rents and entails had already been abolished, and primogeniture was eliminated in 1791.

The years of the Confederation were ones of economic depression. Thousands of Scotch-Irish who might have exerted political pressure for greater liberties moved away to Kentucky, Tennessee, and Ohio.

One of the proudest political myths of the Scotch-Irish is that Presbyterian influence at the Constitutional Convention of 1787 gave the United States its representative form of government. This claim is wholly fallacious. It rests upon the supposed similarities between the Presbyterian and American structures of government. In the former, there is a federation of largely independent regional Presbyteries; in the latter, a federation of states similarly independent. The local congregation, like the town or county, elects by free vote of those qualified its governing officials and its representatives in the legislative body. Until the present century, there was a further similarity: each Presbytery named the men who should represent it in the highest body of the church, the General Assembly; so likewise each state legislature chose its senators and its members in the Electoral College.

Such similarities, however, seem superficial in contrast with fundamental differences. The government devised for the United

States was a series of practical compromises between those who desired a strong central government and those who cherished states' rights, between large states and small, between proponents and opponents of a strong executive. The new Constitution established, as unique and distinctive features of government, principles and bodies quite unknown to Presbyterianism: executive, legislative, and judicial branches of the Federal government; separation of powers; a complex system of checks and balances; two houses in the legislature, whose members were selected by a different process. More than this, the American President is head of an executive branch, with executive powers in his official capacity, while the Moderator of the General Assembly of the Church is precisely a moderator, with no such powers. These divergences are crucial.

Beyond all this, Presbyterians in the Convention were few and Scotch-Irish even fewer. Only New Jersey and Pennsylvania were represented by Presbyterians. There is no record that any member of the Convention ever mentioned the Presbyterian Church or its structure of government. The roster of delegates from the states shows, not frontiersmen, but quite generally men of wealth, property, and prestige—among whom in 1787 there were numbered but few Scotch-Irish in the United States.[26]

Whether the Scotch-Irish contributed to the American conception of democracy is a question that requires an antecedent one—whether America in 1787 was democratic. Without entangling the discussion in subsequent meanings given to the word "democracy," we may consider the contemporary French definition of liberty, equality, and fraternity.

Liberty had been firmly supported in some aspects by the Scotch-Irish for generations, but at least at the time of their coming to America it had been as firmly denied in others. A man should have freedom of conscience, though not the right to decide for himself whether he should pay tithes in support of an Established Church. He should be free to express his opinion, to worship as he pleased, to present petitions to government for the redress of grievances. But European as he was, he believed in a State Church, established and official. The Scots of 1561 had not hesitated to make their Kirk the Church of Scotland. In the American colonies the Scotch-Irish learned the practicality of religious freedom. Whereas in Ulster they had had to endure life under an Established Church not their own, they now cherished the liberty to worship as they pleased, to choose their own ministers, and (except in the Carolinas) to be free of taxation to support another church. It is idle to speculate whether, if they had formed the majority in any colony, they would have tried to establish the Presbyterian Church as official. The simple fact was that, with Episcopalians, Puritans, Germans of various denominations, Quakers, Baptists, and Methodists living in the same jurisdiction, it would have been foolhardy to seek more than they had.

Liberty was the keynote of the American Revolution. The word in 1776 did not carry all the connotations of the present day: it was much more likely to be limited to political liberty than to extend to personal freedom. The Scotch-Irish without doubt supported American conceptions of liberty, but they seem to have learned as much of its meaning from other Americans as they taught their new fellow-countrymen.

Equality, as a principle of democracy, was hardly a moving force in American politics until the nineteenth century. Neither the Scotch-Irish at the time of their first settlement nor the leaders of the new Republic believed in it. Hamilton and Madison, in the *Federalist Papers*, show equal suspicion of equality.

As has been seen, the distinction between social orders was accepted in Scotland and Ulster as part of the very scheme of nature. Undeniably the experiences of frontier life broke down many of the distinctions, requiring, at least at the moment of pioneering, a measure of practical equality among settlers. Both the achievement of settled community life and the organization of churches, however, tended to revive all those distinctions given by property, education, background, and manners. The Calvinist doctrine of predestination was far from equalitarian; on the contrary, it presupposed an elite. (Among the elect, it is true, there are many from the lowest walks of life.) It has been shown that the Presbyterian Church during the later colonial period tended decidedly to become a church of the respectable and responsible citizens, and to lose to other denominations those to whom equality appealed as a principle. The sedate Presbyterian of 1787 in America was not one to hobnob with everybody.

The real equalitarians in the colonial era were Methodists and Baptists. Corwin notes that Whitefield's doctrine was "distinctly and disturbingly equalitarian," since it fostered criticism of superiors by inferiors, of elders by juniors, and since popular exhorters menaced the intellectual superiority of the clergy.[27] Methodism was Arminian, stressing God's mercy to all, not merely to an elect few. Baptists were equalitarian chiefly for social rather than doctrinal reasons: they included large numbers of the underprivileged classes. To the extent that Scotch-Irish had been won to these denominations or had pushed on to new frontiers beyond the reach of any church, they were certainly equalitarian.

If fraternity means social intermingling without distinction of position, race, or background, few Scotch-Irishmen would have professed fraternity. Only the perennial backwoodsman, going ever farther from settled life in a community, could subscribe to such an idea. Fraternity would imply making little of refinement, of prestige, of the struggles men had made to live a better life than Ulster had provided. Moreover, it would imply a toleration of contrary opinion, and absence of prejudice against people of different background and custom that would have been rare among any people of the eighteenth century. Fraternity also suggests a free expression of emotions, and the Scotch-Irishman was often said to be chary of such expression.

If, rather than taking the French triad as the measure of democracy, the word be equated with American usage of the time, the Scotch-Irish were thorough democrats. They believed in government by the consent of the governed, in representative and republican institutions. Their church had accustomed them to these, and they had been too long removed from personal attachment to a king to feel any affection for monarchy of any sort. But if democracy means law-abiding submission to orderly procedures, even when these are uncongenial, the record is spotty. Needless to say, thousands of Scotch-Irish were as scrupulously law abiding as any other element of the population; ministers always exerted their influence on the side of law; educated people could see the logical consequences of summary action; the respectable and responsible classes were leaders in the establishment of civil institutions.

Yet some of the most egregious cases in colonial times of taking extra-legal action were offered by the Scotch-Irish. They were, if not the first, certainly the most conspicuous squatters in American history. Pioneers over and over again flouted the law when it ran counter to their immediate wishes: the Paxton Boys in 1763 massacred Conestoga Indians because of an unproved rumor; the Regulation Movement in the two Carolinas banded men together to punish those who offended them; the Whisky Rebellion was an open defiance of government. In all of these cases, the people felt they had sound moral justification for their actions. The fact remains that they had taken law into their own hands. What Henderson says of the Regulators applies to all these cases: "The choleric backwoodsmen . . . considered revenge as a sort of wild justice."[28]

Assuming the trans-Allegheny frontier as an extension of the Scotch-Irish movement, one observes there the frequent appearance of lynch law. This phenomenon is again understandable in a region that had outstripped courts and jails; and it was certainly engaged in by pioneers other than the Scotch-Irish. If one were trying to justify the frontiersmen he might cite their rough and ready, but effective, means of establishing justice before courts arrived: hating a man out of a community when he had offended against decent standards, simply by refusing to speak to him or deal with him; improvising a system of determining how much land a squatter might claim; and so on. The point is that, by comparison with certain other groups, notably the Germans, the Scotch-Irish were not models of adherence to the principle of government by laws and not by men.

Self-discipline seems to have been the hardest lesson the Scotch-Irish had to learn, from the time of their barbaric ancestors in Scotland to the end of their frontier days in America. With the establishment of the Kirk a great stride was made toward discipline, and when it was taken the Scot often went to the other extreme of rigid puritanism. Impetuosity remained a characteristic of Scotch-Irish temperament, however, and not even the church could control all pioneers. Rupp cites, for example, the case of certain Scotch-Irish backwoodsmen along the southern borders of Pennsylvania who, during the Revolution, bade defiance to all laws, driving a brisk trade by stealing horses and cattle and then selling them.[29] On occasion, there was fear of actual anarchy in some outlying regions because men took the law into their own hands.[30] There was a criminal element among the Scotch-Irish Americans as there was among the English Americans.

The claim that Scotch-Irish stock contributed many notable political leaders to the American nation after 1789 is defensible, for descendants of Scotch-Irish pioneers from Andrew Jackson to Woodrow Wilson sat in the White House, with many others in the Congress, high courts, and gubernatorial mansions. It is misleading, however, to assume that their achievement resulted from some mysterious genetic quality transmitted from generation to generation by the Scotch-Irish heredity or even that Scotch-Irish culture was so uniform and integrated that it necessarily resulted in political leadership. Some of the officials catalogued in the eulogies have actually been more notable for their deficiencies than for their laudable qualities; moreover, other ancestral strains had long since intermixed with the Scotch-Irish and might easily be claimed as causative; and, finally, it is not evident that other stocks might not name an even more impressive list of political leaders to emphasize the superiority of their heritage.*

* The roster of famous names claimed by Scotch-Irish Americans varies with the eulogist. Davie cites a moderate set of claims. He says: "They have contributed to America few writers and artists, but many generals, politicians, and captains of industry. In literature they claim two eminent names, Washington Irving and Edgar Allan Poe; but in the army, navy, politics, and business they claim Thomas Benton, James G. Blaine, John C. Calhoun, John G. Carlisle, Andrew Carnegie, George Rogers Clark, Jefferson Davis, Ulysses S. Grant, Horace Greeley, Alexander Hamilton, Mark Hanna, Samuel Houston, Andrew Jackson, Stonewall Jackson, John Paul Jones, George B. McClellan, William McKinley, Oliver Perry, John D. Rockefeller, Edward Rutledge, Winfield Scott, Zachary Taylor, Matthew Thornton, Anthony Wayne, Woodrow Wilson, and hundreds alike famous in the more strenuous movements of American life." (World Immigration, p. 22)

Contributions of the Scotch-Irish to American political life, while solid enough, seem to have been more in the nature of support of general tendencies than innovations of significance. It was not the Ulstermen but the English settlers, especially the New Englanders, who introduced to this country the ideas of freehold tenure without entail, of reasonable bail, of the right of appeal, freedom to travel, the rule against double jeopardy, and town meetings with freedom of speech to all citizens. Democracy seems to have been further advanced and more thoroughly understood in the England from which the Puritans came than in the Ulster from which the Scotch-Irish migrated. More than this, the New England town, organized from the first, offered an environment more suitable for the appearance of political leaders than the occasional village and the scattered farms of the Scotch-Irish.

More than the national origin of Americans, their way of life seems to have influenced their political characteristics. Where life was settled, with tendencies toward class distinctions, specialization, and community opinion, political life moved toward both orderliness and conservatism. Where, on the contrary, pioneers were on the move, and must necessarily be jacks-of-all-trades and individualists, equalitarian tendencies prevailed. Great stress upon the rights, interests, and personal fulfillment of each individual meant a centrifugal pull. As De Tocqueville said of men who live in ages of equality: "Their life is so practical, so confused, so excited, so active, that but little time remains to them for thought." Scotch-Irish life in the eighteenth century marked the division between the two political paths, one leading toward individualism, the other toward social order.

17

Final Estimate

THE STORY OF THE SHAPING of the Scotch-Irish people and of the part they played in American life ends, in a very real sense, with the Revolutionary War and the establishment of the United States of America. There can be no doubt that the qualities of character indoctrinated in their children by Scotch-Irish parents, and so passed on through generations in the same family, exerted a continuing influence on the communities in which the people lived and possibly on the nation as a whole. It is also true that the Presbyterian Church they supported left its mark wherever it flourished. The essence of the matter is this, however: that after independence the Scotch-Irish were integral parts of the American nation, making no distinction between themselves and any other Americans, nor having them made, either for praise or blame. If a man left his impress on American life he did it as the individual he was; if the Presbyterian Church exerted influence it did so as the independent national church it had long been, with members drawn from many stocks.

Migration from Ulster, interrupted by the Revolution, began again thereafter. For example, a report of 1796 says that "the emigration from Ireland has this year been very great; I left a large vessel full of passengers from thence at Baltimore. I found three at Newcastle. . . . The number of passengers cannot be averaged at less than 250 each vessel."[1] Again no accurate records exist, but except for the period of the Napoleonic Wars, migrations continued to be made from Ulster to America. These later comers, however, did not seek out Scotch-Irish communities in their country of adoption; they went instead to whatever places economic opportunity offered the best chance for making a home, as did the steady migration of Scots direct from Scotland. No doubt they, too, made their contribution to American life, but they did so as individuals, not as members of a Scotch-Irish community.

Many American historians carry the Scotch-Irish story well through the generation following the formation of the United States, when the great rush of settlers to Kentucky, Tennessee, and the Ohio Valley began. Theodore Roosevelt, in his *The Winning of the West,* considers the Scotch-Irish as the leaders of the push to the west, the vanguard of a pioneer army, the common denominator into which all other stocks might be merged as true Americans; and he attributes their contribution as much to their "race" as to their experiences before the Revolutionary War. Thus, he says:

That these Irish Presbyterians were a bold and hardy race is proved by their at once pushing past the settled regions, and plunging into the wilderness as the leaders of the white advance. They were the first and last set of immigrants to do this; all others have merely followed in the wake of their predecessors. But, indeed, they were fitted to be Americans from the very start; they were kinsfolk of the Covenanters; they deemed it a religious duty to interpret their own Bible, and held for a divine right the election of their own clergy. For generations their whole ecclesiastic and scholastic systems had been fundamentally democratic. In the hard life of the frontier they had lost much of their religion, and they had but scant opportunity to give their children the schooling in which they believed; but what few meeting-houses and school-houses there were on the border were theirs.[2]

There is little doubt that children of the Scotch-Irish were among the vanguard of pioneers in the newly opened region west of the mountains: their own homes, from Pennsylvania to Georgia, were everywhere nearest the frontier; their parents had often had the experience of pioneering, of Indian fighting, of enduring a rough life in the wilderness; soldiers in the Revolution had often been paid in grants of land in the Ohio country; opportunity beckoned there; and thousands of Americans seemed to be on the move. This generation of pioneers, however, was a generation of Americans, not of Englishmen or Germans or Scotch-Irish. If many were Presbyterians, that was likely to be considered an accident of birth—which, in fact, did not prevent them from becoming Baptists or Methodists if these denominations were active in the communities to which they moved.

Emphasis upon Scotch-Irish origin—or upon any other national origin—was never a characteristic of the people who moved west; neither did the annalists of the time call attention to it. On the contrary, and for good reason, identification was more likely to be upon place of recent origin, upon whether a family came from Virginia or Connecticut or Pennsylvania. At the outset these eastern states claimed western lands; it was to the government of the original states that the pioneers must look for the establishment of civil institutions and for defense. If the frank questioning of a newcomer asked who a man was, his answer was almost sure to be, "A Virginian" or "A North Carolinian"; under no circumstances would it be "A German" or "A Scotch-Irishman." Only near the end of the nineteenth century did Americans, with a growing consciousness of their history, develop the research into the distinctiveness of contribution by national groups that many times led to adulation of ancestors and exaggerated claims for a particular stock. For most of the century that intervened between the migration from Ulster and the period after the Civil War the very term "Scotch-Irish" does not appear.*

In assessing the contribution of the Scotch-Irish to American life and culture, three fields stand high on the list: their influence in education, religion, and politics. In only the last of these can they be considered unique in their effect.

Wherever the Scotch-Irish went, schools were almost certain to follow churches among the first institutions to be formed. The Reformation in Scotland was without parallel in implanting in a people, contrary to all their previous ideas, a conviction that education was the mark of a man. Not only must the minister be a university graduate: Knox's desire to have schools in every parish for the general education of the people was wholeheartedly accepted as an ideal that must be achieved. The prestige of the minister and schoolmaster opened a new avenue for the ambitious youth—almost his sole alternative to farming. Families

* See further on this matter, Appendix I, "The Name 'Scotch-Irish.'"

sacrificed to see their sons through university. If ambition were not so soaring, it was still necessary to read the Bible and the catechisms, so that Scotland came closest to having universal education of any country of the time.

This long tradition was engrained in the Ulstermen who came to America, so that it was to be expected that schools would be established in every community that could possibly support them. The practical difficulty, however, was the limited supply of ministers, for the school was a church school. If no minister could be found for the new church, it was useless to build a log cabin for a school; and as has been seen, the Scotch-Irish never during the whole colonial period succeeded in filling all their pulpits. The school was, of course, elementary, in every sense of the word, with a curriculum of reading, writing, arithmetic, the Bible, and the catechisms. A practical substitute was devised in many communities where an indentured servant could be found for teaching; the entire neighborhood contributed to his support, and the curriculum resembled that of the regular school. Lacking any kind of teachers for their children, mothers taught their own children within the home.

Tennent's Log College, as has been seen, was the first of the schools to approximate higher levels of learning, although many later academies came to have more than a local reputation. From some of these eventually grew true colleges. Princeton was the only true institution of higher education the Presbyterians had in colonial times—and this College of New Jersey had been founded by Scots rather than by Scotch-Irish.

Zeal for education remained unabated, despite the practical difficulties. It could be expected of a Scotch-Irish community that, if it had a minister, it also had a school for its children. Of all the religious groups in the colonies, only the Puritans of New England exerted such an influence as the Scotch-Irish on making America literate and on the founding of schools and colleges. Until the time of the Civil War, the great majority of the institutions of higher learning in the United States had been founded by religious denominations and still remained under their control. The state's responsibility for higher education had not yet been widely recognized. Presbyterians were notable for their work in establishing colleges. Of the 207 permanent colleges founded in this country before the Civil War, 49 were begun by Presbyterians, 34 by Methodists, 25 by Baptists, and 21 by Congregationalists; to the extent that Methodist and Baptist strength came from descendants of the Scotch-Irish, the educational record of this people is remarkable.° More than this, the older Presbyterian colleges, like Princeton, Hampden-Sydney, and Dickinson, achieved a notable reputation as "mothers" of new colleges, their alumni taking the lead either in founding new institutions or in providing the first presidents who gave them their character.

The religious contribution of the Scotch-Irish, aside from establishing Presbyterian churches wherever they went, lay in their identification of religion with character. It was as unthinkable to a Presbyterian as it would have been to a New England puritan that a man's religious duty consisted only in occasional attendance at service or in the participation in certain set forms of ritual. Religion was of course a set of beliefs intellectually subscribed to and understood in logical detail; but it was also a quality of character that taught a person a clear distinction between right and wrong, with no compromise permitted. As the medieval knight knew his code of chivalry, as the later English schoolboy knew his code of what a gentleman might do, so the Scotch-Irish Presbyterian early and firmly learned his moral precepts. The result was a definite rigidity of character; it was often a stern severity that was as hard upon others as upon oneself. It was uncompromising; it could be bigoted and even merciless, for it might be quite unsoftened by human kindliness and grace. It tended to hold some individual responsible when things went wrong in general. For all that, it was character—and character was expected of a member of the church.

With the Puritans exerting almost exactly the same kind of influence in New England and the Scotch-Irish spreading the idea from the Middle Colonies southward, it is not surprising that the American people, to a greater degree than many others

° States had founded 21 of the permanent colleges. The remainder had the following origin: Roman Catholic 14, Episcopalian 11, Lutheran 5, Disciples 5, German Reformed 4, Universalist 4, Friends 2, Unitarian 2, Christian 1, Dutch Reformed 1, United Brethren 1, semi-state 3, municipal 3. (Tewkesbury, *The Founding of American Colleges and Universities before the Civil War*, pp. 90 ff.)

in the modern world, still associate moral uprightness with religion. Here is the root of the tension that can be perceived in much of American life throughout the decades. The rigorous standards of Presbyterians and Puritans, shared by Methodists and Baptists (and possibly even derived by them from the older denominations), long taught that it was sinful to dance, to play cards, to attend the theater, to break the Sabbath by any diversion, and to engage in frivolous pastimes. By contrast, the English tradition of the Episcopal Church was much more tolerant; and when later immigrants came, with their "continental laxity" in most of these matters, young Americans faced a dilemma of conscience when their reason convinced them that the puritanical rigidities were senseless.

The political influence of the Scotch-Irish upon America was in many ways determinative. Their prompt alignment with the American cause in the Revolution was in some regions probably decisive. This is not by any means to underestimate the enormous contribution of New Englanders and thousands of other patriots. The point may be made, however, that the Scotch-Irish attachment, more than any other, was likely to be a patriotism for the cause of America as a whole, not a vindication of the rights of Massachusetts or New Jersey or any other state. The communications of a Scotch-Irish family in the Piedmont of North Carolina were much more certain to be northward and southward through the whole area of Scotch-Irish settlement than eastward, where lay the center of provincial government and the capital town of the province. The minister of a church (and it should be once more noted how important an institution the church was for the pioneer) came to Virginia and the Carolinas from Philadelphia or New York. Thus the Scotch-Irish spread through, and formed a connection between, the various colonies.

Again, the Scotch-Irish were not identified with one characteristic form of economic life that might lead to sectional interest. In New England there had already begun the extensive commerce and trade that were soon to lead to the business civilization of the North; in the Tidewater region of the Southern states the plantation economy had taken firm root, with slavery as the South's peculiar institution. The Scotch-Irish (not alone, by any means) stood between. Many of them had already begun to be small businessmen, who could be at home in any town or village of the new Republic, representative of neither North nor South, neither East nor West. The large majority of them were farmers, or derived their livelihood from the family farm—the firm basis for a national life, as Jefferson insisted. Their way of life, in short, was the typical and normal way of life for the majority of Americans throughout the entire next century.

Weber's idea of the Protestant ethic and Tawney's of the connection between Protestantism and the rise of capitalism do not find their most convincing example in the Scotch-Irish; nevertheless, like other Calvinists, they believed in self-reliance, improving their own condition in life, thrift and hard work, the taking of calculated risks. They believed that God would prosper His elect if they, in turn, deserved this material reward by their conscientious effort. Farmers though they generally were, neither they nor their ancestors had been peasants in the sense of blind traditionalism of outlook. Their optimistic self-reliance, with a conviction that God helps those who help themselves,* was to become the congenial American folk philosophy of the next century, not far removed from materialism and a faith in progress.

The Scotch-Irish were no more the originators of these American convictions than they had been the originators of the idea of freedom and individualism. What is significant is that, holding the attitude they did, and being present in such large numbers throughout most of the United States, they afforded the middle ground that could become typical of the American as he was to become. The Scotch-Irish element could be the common denominator into which Americanism might be resolved.

It may be suggested that people in different ages attain to different degrees of comprehension and maturity in various aspects of life. Among the most significant of these aspects are religion, politics, economics, and aesthetics. Of these, the religious comprehension of many Scotch-Irishmen was already,

* It used to be said that "a Scotch-Irishman is one who keeps the commandments of God and every other thing he can get his hands on."

by the time of their arrival in America, highly developed. They soon began the struggle in their new homes toward political maturity and participation. In the nineteenth century they, like most other Americans, became absorbed in economic activities and began to develop mastery in this field. In the realm of aesthetics, however, the Scotch-Irish were, and remained, practically deaf, dumb, and blind.

The deficiencies of this people in aesthetics were, as critics of the young Republic saw them, representative of American deficiencies in general. As has been seen, nothing in the background of the Scotch-Irish, whether in Scotland or in Ulster, had drawn their attention to painting, sculpture, architecture, and music, and nothing in their way of life during the eighteenth century in America provided an incentive to develop interest in the fine arts. In the earliest days of settlement there was no time for the artistic, even if the motive had been present. A home was a house to be lived in; a church was a building in which one might hear the Word; a school was a place for teaching and learning. It is rare, in the recent enthusiasm for the preservation of American antiquities, that a Scotch-Irish edifice is found that can be restored on the grounds of its beauty, originality, or charm, as so often happens in Calvinist New England, the Episcopal Tidewater, and the German farmlands. As for painting, busy people regarded it as a waste of time, and practical people saw no usefulness in it. Education was zealously sought, but in the scholastic tradition of the Middle Ages rather than in the liberal tradition of the Renaissance: belles-lettres were absent; the Bible sufficed for literature. Not only were there no Scotch-Irish artists; there was little even that could be called folk art, if the term implies work that has the extra touch of originality and verve that transforms a useful object into a pleasant bit of handicraft. Museums of colonial household goods rarely display Scotch-Irish manufactures as *objets d'art.*

This artistic deficiency, according to European travelers and critics, was common to America of the nineteenth century. The Scotch-Irish were not the cause of it, but they were certainly representative of it. One never looked to a Presbyterian church for inspiring music, stained glass, religious painting and sculpture, or poetry, nor did one look to the Scotch-Irish for mastery in any of these fields; but similarly, neither these fine arts nor appreciation of them could be expected of the growing American middle class from the Atlantic to the farthest reach of the frontier in the West.*

Even the Scotch-Irish attitude toward humor was prophetic of the shape of things to come. Practical jokes, the charivari on the wedding night, pranks that put another person in an embarrassing situation—these seem to have been from the first the Scotch-Irish staples of humor. This people can hardly be given credit for the invention of the tall tale, though as America went west, the descendant of the Ulsterman became adept as a spinner of wild yarns. Wit and understatement were rarely cultivated, nor did the dry and laconic epigram, considered to be the mark of the Scot, seem to appeal to his remote cousins in America.

Once more the distinction between the perennial pioneer and the settled Scotch-Irish is useful, for each became representative of an American "type." The restless frontiersman, too occupied with elementary affairs of clearing the wilderness and making a home to have time for refinements, is a stock figure in American annals. So also is the rising middle-class person, whose numbers always included many of the Scotch-Irish who had not gone west in pioneer days, but had stayed to improve their farms, increase their businesses, add comfort to their homes, and accumulate things. If one wanted a representative American of the early nineteenth century, whether east of the mountains or in the great river valleys to the west, such a representative could be found very generally among the descendants of the Scotch-Irish.

* Not even in the names of their towns, churches, and districts did the Scotch-Irish show much imagination or awareness of euphony. It might seem invidious to single out such unfortunate and unmusical names as Hogback Mountain, Calfpasture River, Peach Bottom, Bullskin Church, Fourth Creek. Yet they are but a sample; and though other people of colonial times could sometimes match them for insensitivity, one cannot help making a contrast with hundreds of New England place-names. More than this, the drab stolidity of a Scotch-Irish settlement makes a poor contrast with the grace of a New England town with its green.

APPENDIX I

The Name "Scotch-Irish"

One of the most amusing controversies in American annals concerns the name "Scotch-Irish." The American Irish Historical Society, organized in 1897, in its early days devoted a considerable amount of time to an effort to deflate the "Scotch-Irish myth," claiming that the people who came to America from Ulster were Irish, not only in the geographical sense but also in patriotism for Ireland and in biological and in culture. To try to make a distinction between the Irish and the Scotch-Irish is, they say, "a new-fangled notion, first promulgated in America," one that is "born of sheer ignorance and pharisaical, Calvinistic pride."

Much is to be said for several of these contentions. The name "Scotch-Irish" is unknown in Ulster, the northern province of Ireland from which the Scotch-Irish came. Although Presbyterians of this region had not the long history of humiliation at the hands of the English that the Irish Catholics of the south had endured, nothing in the Scottish background of the Ulstermen gave them any love for the long-time enemy of Scotland; and in Ulster itself, the Church of England laid exactions, while the English Parliament crippled industry. By the time of the first migration to America, many of the people from the Scottish Lowlands had lived in Ireland for four generations or more. They had become quite a different people from their Scottish forebears, and every year separated them the more from the country across the Channel. Surrounded by native Irish, they inevitably took on certain aspects of Irish culture. The great distinction between Ulstermen and other Irishmen was religion: Presbyterianism and Catholicism were never congenial. Despite this very important disagreement, the Presbyterian Ulstermen, subordinate as they were in church and state to the English, were in no position to domineer, in any official capacity, over the southern Catholics and thus exacerbate feelings. In their own minds, the Ulstermen were, by 1717 and thereafter, Irish of the North.

When they began to come to America, most colonial officials and others who had occasion to mention them referred to them as Irish, sometimes varying this term with "Ulster Irish" or "Northern Irish" or "Irish Presbyterians." Since the ships bearing them had sailed from Irish ports, and since the people had come from a province of Ireland where their homes had been for generations, what else should the newcomers be called but Irish? Most of the evidence shows that they accepted the designation naturally.

Massachusetts Puritans were opposed to all "Irish immigrants." Cotton Mather in 1700 denounced proposals to bring "Irish" to the colony as "formidable attempts of Satan and his Sons to Unsettle us." Moravian missionaries in 1749 recorded in their diaries that they had "passed confidently and safely through the Irish settlement" on their way to North Carolina—a reference to the Scotch-Irish region of the Valley of Virginia. Cazenove notes in his journal in 1794 that an area around Bethlehem, Pennsylvania, is "the Irish settlement, where the Irish came in 1740."[1] Such instances are characteristic uses of the Irish designation.

In 1737 the Ulstermen who had settled in Boston met with other Irishmen to celebrate St. Patrick's Day, organizing themselves into a benevolent association known as the Irish Society. During the Revolutionary War in Philadelphia the Friendly Sons of St. Patrick, consisting of recent immigrants from Ulster as well as some from other parts of Ireland, subscribed $103,500 in Pennsylvania currency for the relief of the starving patriots at Valley Forge. The Ulstermen in that group might easily have joined the existing Thistle Society if they had regarded themselves as Scots. The first president of the Friendly Sons was the brother of a Catholic bishop, while the second was an Ulster Presbyterian. The second Masonic Lodge formed in New Hampshire, consisting chiefly of Presbyterians from Ulster, called itself St. Patrick's Lodge.[*]

Strong evidence of the feeling for Ireland rather than for Scotland came from the names given by the pioneers to their settlements in the New World. Had they regarded themselves as Scots one would expect the frontier to be dotted with Scottish geographical names. These, however, are few in comparison with Ulster place-names— Derry, Tyrone, Armagh, Donegal, Coleraine, Londonderry, Antrim, and various Irish creeks.

The history of the coinage of the term "Scotch-Irish" is obscure. The extent to which it was used in colonial America can be only guessed at. The first actual use of the term seems to have been in a document of Queen Elizabeth in 1573, although the people she designates by it were not Lowland Scots who lived in Ireland, but rather Highlanders. From an early period Scottish Highlanders from

[*] It should be recalled that St. Patrick is claimed by Protestants as well as Catholics. The Anglican cathedral in Dublin, of which Jonathan Swift was Dean, is St. Patrick's.

the islands and mainland had often gone into Ulster, and had there intermarried with their fellow-Celts and fellow-Catholics among the Irish natives. Many had succeeded in establishing themselves permanently, especially in the county of Antrim. Since Scotland and England were different countries, English rulers objected to having Scots settle in English dominions. Queen Mary in 1556 secured the passage of an Act that would prohibit "bringing in the Scots, retaining them, and marrying with them." (This Act was repealed by the Irish Parliament in 1615.) Queen Elizabeth in 1573 fruitlessly tried to drive out the interloping Scots. Failing in this, she then endeavored, by a pacific policy, to allure them into allegiance. To this end she issued a manifesto setting forth her gracious intentions. It is in this document of April 14, 1573, that she uses the term "Scotch-Irish." She says, in part:

"We are given to understand that a nobleman named 'Sorley Boy' (Macdonnel) and others, who be of the Scotch-Irish race, and some of the wild Irish, at this time are content to acknowledge our true and mere right to the countrie of Ulster and the crowne of Ireland . . ."; and therefore she offers the right of ownership and inheritance of land, upon the taking of an oath of allegiance to "any meer Irish, or Scotch-Irish, or other strangers."[2]

The Queen's use of the term was biologically correct, for it referred to people from Scotland and Ireland who had intermarried.

The next use of the term, however, is a mixture of biological and geographical terminology, and it occurs in a Latin form. In 1675 the register of the University of Glasgow records the enrollment of a youth from Ramelton (in Ulster), Francis Makemie by name, with the explanation that he was "Scoto-Hibernicus," that is, Scotch-Irish.[*] Since Ulster for long had no institution of higher learning, Presbyterian youths continued to go to Scottish institutions throughout the eighteenth century.

The first known use of the term in America is in a report, June, 1695, from Sir Thomas Laurence, Secretary of Maryland, who says: "In the two counties of Dorchester and Somerset, where the Scotch-

---

[*] Reid, *Presbyterian Church in Ireland*, II, 342n. That Makemie should be connected with the first appearance of the name "Scotch-Irish" is particularly appropriate, for he later came to America, established the Presbyterian Church on the continent, and was instrumental in organizing the first Presbytery in Philadelphia in 1706. Reid says that the entry read "Franciscus Makemius, Scoto Hybernicus."

Graham (*Social Life of Scotland*, p. 455) says that a Professor Reid wrote from Glasgow in 1760: "Near a third of our students are Irish. Thirty came over lately in one vessel. . . . Many of the Irish as well as Scotch are poor, and come up late to save money." Professor Reid had a low opinion of these "stupid Irish teagues" from Ulster. Graham adds that during the century "half of the students who took their degrees in Glasgow are entered 'Scoto-Hibernicus.'"

Irish are numerous, they clothe themselves by their linen and woolen manufactures."* The next reference to them is far from complimentary. An Anglican minister, George Ross, missionary of the Society for the Propagation of the Gospel in Foreign Parts, wrote from New Castle, Delaware, in September, 1723: "They call themselves Scotch-Irish,—*ignavus pecus*,—and the bitterest railers against the church [meaning, of course, the Church of England] that ever trod upon American ground."† Another Church of England clergyman, at Lewes, Delaware, wrote in 1723 with reference to the settlers in Sussex County of that province: "The first settlers of this county were for the far greatest part originally English, but of late years great numbers of Irish (who usually call themselves Scotch-Irish) have transplanted themselves and their families from the north of Ireland."³

The official who had most frequent dealings with the first real wave of immigrants from Ulster was James Logan, secretary to the Penn family. Himself a Quaker from Ireland, he at first welcomed the newcomers, but soon came to have a low opinion of them. They had a way of taking up lands in the province of Pennsylvania without proper authorization; and worse still, they were not, like the German settlers, amenable to official direction. "The settlement of five families from Ireland," he laments, "gives me more trouble than fifty of any other people." He usually speaks of them as Irish, and sometimes as "people from the North of Ireland"; but in a letter of 1730 to Thomas Penn he writes, "This is the most audacious attack that has ever yet been offered. They are of the Scotch-Irish (so called here) of whom J. Steel tells me you seem'd to have a pretty good opinion but it is more than I can have tho' their countryman."‡ In the next decade a Marylander was accused of having murdered the sheriff of Lancaster County in Pennsylvania, after having called that officer and his assistants "damned Scotch-Irish sons of b——s."⁴

These few references—and they practically complete the colonial list—seem insignificant by comparison with the constantly appearing name of "Irish," but they indicate at least that the hyphenated title had been coined, was generally known, and was even used by some of the Scotch-Irish. Dunaway, the historian of the Scotch-Irish in Pennsylvania, suggests that "it is probable that the name was first applied to them by the Episcopalians and Quakers, who by no means

---

* It was to these Ulster, English, and other Presbyterians in the Eastern Shore counties that Makemie came to minister.

† As can be seen in the chapters on the Ulster background of the Scotch-Irish, the Presbyterians had good reason to dislike the Established Church, since its bishops had taken severely punitive measures against all nonconformists, treating the Presbyterians as if they were indistinguishable from Catholics.

‡ Penn MSS, *Official Correspondence, 1683-1727*, II, 145. What makes Logan's comment especially informative is that he, a Protestant, but a native Irishman, calls the Scotch-Irish his countrymen.

intended it to be complimentary."[5]   There is no way of ascertaining how readily the name was accepted or applied in each of the colonies.

Only one real protest seems to have been entered by the newcomers against the simple designation of "Irish."   A group of Presbyterians from Ulster, having received permission from the Governor of Massachusetts in 1718 to settle in that colony, finally established their settlement in southern New Hampshire and called it Londonderry.   Their minister, a native of Scotland, wrote to the governor: "We are surprised to hear ourselves termed *Irish* people, when we so frequently ventured our all, for the British crown and liberties, against the Irish Papists, and gave all tests of our loyalty which the government of Ireland required, and are always ready to do the same when required."[6]   His objection was made after the Massachusetts Puritans had several times made it clear that they supposed the new arrivals to be Catholic, like the Irish indentured servants with whom they were already familiar.   It was against this identification with the "Papists" that the Reverend Mr. McGregor protested.

From the time of the Revolutionary War onward for a good part of a century the appellation "Scotch-Irish" simply disappears from the record.   It is one of the principal contentions of the American Irish that the term was revived and then enthusiastically adopted after 1850 solely because of prejudice.   The point seems well taken.

In the history of immigration to this country, it is commonplace to observe that each new group of arrivals, if in numbers great enough to be "visible," has had to endure a period of dislike by older Americans.   In the very nature of things prejudice of this sort would appear.   The advent of numerous "foreigners," with strange manners, ignorant of American ways and ideas, wearing curious clothes and speaking a gibberish, has repeatedly caused dislike, ridicule, and even hostility.   Germans, Scandinavians, Italians, Poles, Jews have all felt it.   The Scotch-Irish also occasionally experienced this prejudice, although, fortunately for themselves, they had to endure it for a very brief time.   Upon their arrival in America they did not, as did the later Irish, linger long in the seaboard region but went on immediately beyond the western fringe of settlement and took up frontier lands. By the time of the American Revolution, which they ardently supported, they had proved themselves good fighters against the Indians and therefore good Americans.   As they moved still farther west to the Ohio Valley frontier, they intermarried with pioneers of other stocks and so completely lost their identity as a separate people.

Prejudice against the Irish was another matter.   Following the potato famines of 1845 and 1846, the Irish began to pour into the United States in numbers far greater than the country had ever known.   The first arrivals were followed by a flood of others: in each year between 1847 and 1854 two hundred thousand arrived—as many within each year, that is, as there had been Scotch-Irish immigrants altogether. Between four and a half and five million came altogether within a century.* The majority of these prevailingly raw immigrants stopped in the big cities of the East, where their presence and their concentration in certain sections of the cities would be most conspicuous.

The Irish arrivals were, in the main, desperately poor, illiterate, and (to American eyes) uncouth; they were Roman Catholics descending upon a Protestant country; they hired themselves out for the most menial labor at wages lower than American workmen received and thus aroused the particular hostility of American laborers. Prejudice against them ranged from the haughty disdain of the pillars of seaboard society, who felt sure that the country was going to the dogs, to the violence of laborers. Mob scenes and murders became frequent. The Know-Nothing Party conducted political campaigns against foreigners, Catholics, and especially Irishmen; and the excesses of the Molly Maguires, a patriotic Irish society, added fuel to the flame of dislike.†

In this atmosphere of prejudice, say the Irish Americans, the Scotch-Irish who up to now had not objected to being known as Irish, looked for a way to dissociate themselves from the newcomers, who were called shanty Irish or bog Irish or worse names. The compound name, already known, thereupon came into general use, first by the descendants of the Ulstermen and then by the public. Its very acceptance contributed to the "myth," as Irish Americans conceived it, that the Scotch-Irish had never been Irish but wholly Scottish. What made the double appellation all the more appealing was that the novels of Sir Walter Scott had so beguiled the American people during the Romantic Era that everything Scottish came to be considered glamorous. The Waverley novels had a tremendous vogue in this country. To claim Scottish ancestry was to have a

* Davie (*World Immigration*, pp. 61-65) says that the Irish immigration totaled 4,500,000 by 1930, and Schrier (*Ireland and the American Emigration, 1850-1900*) claims that Ireland lost 5,000,000 people between 1846 and 1900. The effect of this emigration on Ireland was tremendous. Its population of 8,175,000 in 1841 (including Ulster) had dropped to 6,552,000 a decade later and to 4,459,000 by 1901. It is now less than 3,000,000 although the population of Northern Ireland is not included in this last figure as it was in the earlier censuses.

† A writer about 1860 stated: "More incongruous elements it would be difficult to bring together than the jolly, reckless, good-natured, passionate, priest-ridden, whiskey-loving, thriftless Paddy, and the cold, shrewd, frugal, correct, meeting-going Yankee." (Quoted from a journalist's letter in *Life and Letters of Edwin Lawrence Godkin*, ed. Rollon Ogden [New York, 1907], I, 181)

romantic past when the national mood delighted in the picturesque; to be Scotch-Irish was to claim that past for one's own.*

It appears to be quite true that prejudice played its part in popularizing the Scotch-Irish appellation.† The fact remains, however, that it is a useful term. Despite its hybrid nature, with one term biological and cultural and the other geographical, it expresses a historical reality: the Scots who lived in Ulster before they came to America simply were not, in background, religion, and many other aspects of culture, identical with the Irish of the southern provinces of Leinster, Munster, and Connaught; neither were they, after many decades, any longer identical with the people of Scotland.

A century of use has established the double name, and no substitute is accurate. "Irish Presbyterians" might have done in the eighteenth century, for it was accurate enough; but the conversion of thousands of the pioneers to the Baptist and Methodist denominations soon made that designation completely inapplicable. "Ulster Irish" would not suffice, since it would make no distinction among the Scots, English, and Irish who lived in the northern province. "Ulster Scots" is more satisfactory, except for the unfamiliarity to most Americans of the qualifying geographical adjective—and moreover, this term is, in effect, simply a reversal of the more usual "Scotch-Irish." It is best, therefore, to retain the hyphenated term and make its meaning clear.‡

* It is somewhat ironic to note the manner in which Scott influenced the American mind in establishing its image of Scotland. The careful reader of Scott knows how often he excoriates the lawlessness of the Highlanders, reveals the abject backwardness of most of the country until well in the eighteenth century, and ridicules the benighted zeal of the Covenanters, the pedantry of some of Scotland's learned men, and the partisan spirit that constantly embroiled the country. Yet the romantic reader forgets these matters and remembers the noble lords, the picturesque scenery of the Highlands (made all the more attractive by the image of men in tartans and the skirling of pipes in the glens), and the admirable qualities of his Scottish heroes and heroines.

† It cannot, however, be maintained that the adoption of the term, "Scotch-Irish," was wholly the result of prejudice, nor that it came into wide use only after 1846. The Reverend William Henry Foote, in his exhaustive study of Presbyterianism in Virginia and North Carolina, uses the term regularly and almost exclusively in 1845, for example. The historian James Anthony Froude, an Englishman, also uses the hyphenated term (see, for example, his *The English in Ireland*, II, 141), thus proving that it was known across the Atlantic.

‡ The passion with which certain American Irish authors have stated their objection to the name "Scotch-Irish" reveals the deep wound to native pride. It is called a cant phrase, a shibboleth, a mongrel absurdity, a delusion; the Scotch-Irish Society of America is described as "an organized humbug"; and so on.

Nevertheless, Irish wit enlivens even the diatribes. One Calvin K. Brannigan writes a "Lament of the Scotch-Irish Exile," in which the professional Scotch-Irishman wants "to win me hame to my ain countree," which isn't exactly Tipperary-on-the-Clyde nor yet Glasgow Town in Dublin Bay. More diverting still is his waggish poem entitled, "The Gathering of the Scotch-Irish Clans" (at the Scotch-Irish Society meetings, of course), which begins:

> Are ye gangin' to the meetin', to the meetin' o' the clans,
> With your tartans and your pibrochs and your bonnets and brogans?
> There are Neeleys from New Hampshire and Mulligans from Maine,
> McCarthys from Missouri and a Tennessee McShane.

There follows a succession of straight Irish names, of people all claiming to be Scotch-Irish; and the satire ends:

> We'll sit upon the pint-stoup and we'll talk of auld lang syne
> As we quaff the flowing haggis to our lasses' bonnie eyne.
> And we'll join in jubilation for the thing that we are not;
> For we say we aren't Irish, and God knows we aren't Scot!

Probably some member of the Scotch-Irish Society could have informed Mr. Brannigan that one does not "quaff" haggis; indeed, the ingredients of that dish would repel most American Scotch-Irishmen, no matter how patriotic. (These verses are cited in Smith, *The "Scotch-Irish" Shibboleth*, pp. 28-29. For other examples of the Irish American attitude, see O'Connell, *The "Scotch-Irish" Delusion in America;* Bagenal, *The American Irish;* and Linehan, *The Irish Scots and the "Scotch-Irish,"* among many others.)

APPENDIX II

Important Events in Scottish History

EARLY HISTORY

80. Invasion of North Britain (i.e., Scotland) by the Roman, Agricola
208. Invasion by Severus
412. Departure of Romans from Britain
563. St. Columba lands in Iona; introduces Christianity
565. Irish Christianity established in Pict-land
664. Roman Christianity adopted in Northumbria at Synod of Whitby
710. Roman Christianity accepted in Pict-land
802. Norsemen plunder Iona and western coast
844. Kenneth MacAlpin becomes king of the Picts and Scots
1018. Annexation of Strathclyde (southwest) by King of Scots
1040. Duncan I defeated and slain by Macbeth

MAKING OF THE NATION

1069. Marriage of Malcolm Canmore and the Saxon Margaret
1102. Magnus Barefoot acquires the Western Islands
1124. David I introduces feudalism to Scotland
1174. William the Lion surrenders the independence of Scotland to the English king, Henry II
1189. English king, Richard I (Lion-hearted), acknowledges independence of Scotland
1222. Alexander II conquers Argyle, in west
1266. Western Islands acquired by Scotland

THE WAR OF INDEPENDENCE FROM ENGLAND

1292. English king, Edward I, awards disputed Scottish crown to John Balliol
1296. Balliol dethroned by Edward. Revolt led by William Wallace against English
1305. Execution by English of William Wallace
1306. Coronation of Robert Bruce

1314. Bruce defeats Edward II at Bannockburn, gains independence of Scotland
1326. Meeting of first Scottish Parliament
1329. Death of Robert Bruce. Accession of David II (David Bruce)
1332. Edward Balliol invades Scotland
1333. Scots defeated at Halidon Hill; Balliol restored to Scottish throne; he cedes Scotland south of the Forth to England. Alliance of patriotic party in Scotland with France
1346. Scots defeated at Neville's Cross; David II captured
1350. Black Death (also 1361, 1369, and many times thereafter)

THE STUARTS

1371. Accession of Robert II, first of the Stuart kings
1388. English defeated at Chevy Chase (Otterburn)
1407. Burning of the Lollard, James Resby
1433. Burning of Paul Craw for heresy
1437. Assassination of James I at Perth
1452. James II murders William, Earl of Douglas; defection of Douglases to England
1455-85. Wars of the Roses in England
1460. Accidental death of James II
1468. Orkney and Shetland Islands acquired by Scotland
1472. St. Andrews made an archbishopric
1503. Marriage of James IV and Margaret Tudor
1513. Defeat of James IV at battle of Flodden; death of James
1528. Burning of Patrick Hamilton as a heretic
1542. Defeat of James V at Solway Moss; death of James

MARY STUART, QUEEN OF SCOTS (1542-1567)

1542. Mary born at time of her father's death
1545. Burning of George Wishart as a heretic; murder of Cardinal Beaton
1547. Defeat of Scots and French at Pinkie
1557. First Covenant
1559. Return of John Knox from the Continent
1560. Establishment of Protestantism
1561. Return of Mary, then 19, from France
1565. Marriage of Mary and Darnley
1566. Murder of Riccio. Birth of James (VI)
1567. Murder of Darnley. Marriage of Mary and Bothwell
1568. Flight of Mary to England

JAMES VI OF SCOTLAND (1567-1625), I OF ENGLAND (1603-1625)

1570. Murder of Moray, the Regent
1571. Murder of Lennox, the Regent

1572. Death of John Knox; death of Mar, the Regent
1587. Execution of Mary in England
1603. Union of the crowns of Scotland and England
1606. Episcopacy established in Scotland
1610. Plantation of Ulster
1618. The Five Articles of Perth
1625. Death of James VI

CHARLES I (1625-1649)

1633. Charles visits Scotland
1637. Laud's Liturgy, and riot in St. Giles's
1638. The National Covenant
1638. Episcopacy abolished by General Assembly
1639. First Bishops' War
1640. Second Bishops' War
1643. Solemn League and Covenant
1648. Cromwell annihilates the Scottish army at Preston Pans
1649. Execution of Charles I

CHARLES II (1660-1685)

1661. Restoration of Episcopacy
1666. Battle of Pentland Hills, defeat of Covenanters
1669. First letter of Indulgence
1679. Murder of Archbishop Sharp. Suppression of Covenanters by Lauderdale and Claverhouse
1679. Defeat of Covenanters by the Duke of Monmouth
1681. Passage of a Test Act against Presbyterians

WILLIAM AND MARY

1689. Episcopacy abolished. Battle of Killiecrankie; Highlanders defeated at Dunkeld
1690. Presbyterianism re-established

Notes

PART I: THE SCOT IN 1600

1. POVERTY AND INSECURITY

1. John Warrack, *Domestic Life in Scotland, 1488-1688* (London, 1920), p. 2.

2. John Cleveland, cited in Henry Grey Graham, *The Social Life of Scotland in the Eighteenth Century* (4th ed.; London, 1937), p. 2.

3. *Comedy of Errors*, Act III, sc. ii.

4. Sir William Brereton, *Travels in Holland, the United Provinces, England, Scotland, and Ireland, 1634-35* (Manchester, 1844), p. 118.

5. Wallace Notestein, *The Scot in History* (New Haven, 1946), p. 58.

6. The illiteracy of the nobility is affirmed by Patrick Fraser Tytler, *History of Scotland* (Edinburgh, 1828-43), II, 239, 240; Robert Wodrow, *Collections upon the Lives of the Reformers* (Glasgow, 1834), I, 5, 6; Robert Chambers, *Domestic Annals of Scotland from the Reformation to the Revolution* (Edinburgh and London, 1858), I, 46; George Crawfurd, *The History of the Shire of Renfrew* (Paisley, 1782), pt. III, p. 313; Robert Pitcairn, *Criminal Trials in Scotland from 1488 to 1624* (Edinburgh, 1833), III, 394; and elsewhere.

7. See P. Hume Brown, "Scottish Nobility and Their Part in the Nation's History," *Scottish Historical Review*, III, 161; Chambers, *Domestic Annals of Scotland*, I, 311.

8. See, for example, *Acts of the Parliament of Scotland* (Edinburgh, 1844-75), II, 5, 34, 51, 208, 210, 247, *et passim*.

9. John M. Robertson, in his edition of *Buckle's Introduction to the History of Civilization in England* (London, n.d.), p. 660n.

10. Cited in I. F. Grant, *Social and Economic Development of Scotland before 1603* (Edinburgh, 1930), p. 197.

11. *Complaynt of Scotlande*, p. 139.

12. William Robertson, *Ayrshire: Its History and Historic Families* (Kilmarnock and Ayr, 1908), Vol. I, ch. 7, entitled, "The Ayrshire Vendetta."

13. Chambers, *Domestic Annals of Scotland*, I, 292, writing of the year 1597, mentions the Armstrongs, Johnstones, Bells, Batisons, Carlyles, and Irvings.

14. *Ibid.*, I, 414, Chambers writing of 1608.

15. John Major, *Historia Majoris Britanniae tam Angliae q. Scotiae* (1521), trans. in P. Hume Brown, *Scotland before 1700 from Contemporary Documents* (Edinburgh, 1893), pp. 54-56.

16. *Register of the Privy Council of Scotland*, I, ed. J. H. Burton, D. Masson, Hume Brown, and H. Patton (Edinburgh, 1877-1924), 66, 660; II, 74, 176, 365-67; Pitcairn, *Criminal Trials in Scotland*, I, 48, 74-75, 154-57, 217. The quotation is from John Mackintosh, *The History of Civilisation in Scotland* (Paisley and London, 1893), II, 229. For making officers eat and swallow their letters, see Chambers, *Domestic Annals of Scotland*, I, 258.

17. Grant, *Social and Economic Development of Scotland*, p. 172.

18. Chambers, *Domestic Annals of Scotland*, I, 72.

19. William Mackenzie, *The History of Galloway, from the Earliest Period to the Present Time* (Kirkcudbright, 1841), I, 236.

20. See the poems of Sir David Lyndsay of the Mount, Maitland of Lethington, and the anonymous author of the *Complaynt of Scotlande*.

21. See, for example, *Register of the Privy Council*, I, 277.

22. *Acts of the Parliament of Scotland*, II, 254; III, 139, 217.

23. Sir Herbert Maxwell, *A History of Dumfries and Galloway* (Edinburgh, 1896), p. 167. See also Chambers, *Domestic Annals of Scotland*, I, 100; *Register of the Privy Council*, III, lxxvii, 109; V, 6-8 (for 1592-93); VI, 283, 318, 501 (for 1601-2).

24. Henry Jones Ford, *The Scotch-Irish in America* (Princeton, 1915), p. 89.

25. Dr. Johnson, *Journey to the Western Islands of Scotland*, ed. R. W. Chapman (Oxford, 1924), 31, 79, 108. See also Sir Walter Scott, *Rob Roy* (Boston, 1923), throughout, but especially p. 290.

2. DOMESTIC LIFE OF THE LOWLAND SCOT

1. Sir Walter Scott, *The Heart of Midlothian* (Boston, 1923), II, 194-95.

2. The standard account of the feudal system is I. F. Grant, *The Social and Economic Development of Scotland before 1603* (Edinburgh, 1930).

3. Henry Grey Graham, *The Social Life of Scotland in the Eighteenth Century* (4th ed.; London, 1937), p. 185; John S. Jackson and Jean McI. Dixon, "The Plague," in *The Royal Burgh of Ayr: 750 Years of History*, ed. Annie I. Dunlop (Edinburgh and London, 1953), p. 268.

4. John Major, *Historia Majoris Britanniae tam Angliae q. Scotiae* (1521), trans. in P. Hume Brown, *Scotland before 1700 from Contemporary Documents* (Edinburgh, 1893), pp. 44-45.

5. Graham, *Social Life of Scotland*, p. 155.

6. *Acts of the Parliament of Scotland* (Edinburgh, 1844-75), II, 13.

7. Graham, *Social Life of Scotland*, p. 155.

8. William Mackenzie, *The History of Galloway from the Earliest Period to the Present Time* (Kirkcudbright, 1841), I, 230; Graham, *Social Life of Scotland*, p. 156; Grant, *Every-Day Life on an Old Highland Farm, 1769-1782* (London, 1924), p. 45.

9. Graham, *Social Life of Scotland*, p. 159.

10. Bishop Leslie (1578), in Brown, *Scotland before 1700*, pp. 166 ff.; Aeneas Sylvius (1437), in *Early Travellers in Scotland*, ed. P. Hume Brown (Edinburgh, 1891), pp. 24 ff.; Mackenzie, *History of Galloway*, I, 230 ff.; *Regiam Majestatem. The Auld Lawes and Constitutions of Scotland*, ed. Sir J. Skene (Edinburgh, 1609), p. 243; George Wallace, *Nature and Descent of Ancient Peerages, connected with the State of Scotland* (Edinburgh, 1785), p. 39.

11. Scott, *The Antiquary*, I, 346.

12. Graham, *Social Life of Scotland*, pp. 179-80.

13. Mackenzie, *History of Galloway*, I, 230-33; Wallace, *Nature and . . . State of Scotland*, p. 60.

14. Mackenzie, *History of Galloway*, II, 5-7.

15. Graham, *Social Life of Scotland*, p. 2.

16. See Jackson and Dickson, "The Plague," in *Royal Burgh of Ayr*, ed. Dunlop, pp. 266 ff.

17. I. M. M. MacPhail, "Review of *A Source Book of Scottish History*," *Scottish Historical Review*, XXXIII (1954), 144.

18. See W. Croft Dickinson, Gordon Donaldson, and Isabel A. Milne, *A Source Book of Scottish History* (London, 1952-54), I, 70 ff.

19. On the prevalence of barter and the lack of specie, see *Spalding Club Miscellany* (Aberdeen, 1841-52), IV, lvii-lx. Fynes Moryson, who was in Scotland around 1598, says that "the gentlemen reckon their revenues not by rents of money, but by chauldrons of victuals." Moryson, *Itinerary* (1598), pt. III, in *Early Travellers in Scotland,* ed. Brown, p. 85.

20. J. William Dillon, "Fairs and Markets," in *Royal Burgh of Ayr,* ed. Dunlop, p. 185.

21. Mackenzie, *History of Galloway,* II, 8-9.

22. Estienne Perlin (1551), in *Early Travellers in Scotland,* ed. Brown, pp. 71-80.

23. Brown, in his Introduction to *Early Travellers in Scotland.*

24. Robert Chambers, *Domestic Annals of Scotland from the Reformation to the Revolution* (Edinburgh and London, 1858), I, 337.

25. John Mackintosh, *The History of Civilisation in Scotland* (Paisley and London, 1893), II, 261.

26. Chambers, *Domestic Annals of Scotland,* I, 335-37; *Booke of the Universall Kirk of Scotland: Acts and Proceedings of the General Assemblies of the Kirk of Scotland, from the Year 1560* (Edinburgh, 1839), Vol. I, *passim.*

27. *Acts of the Parliament of Scotland,* II, 298, 377, 486; Robert Pitcairn, *Criminal Trials in Scotland from 1488 to 1624* (Edinburgh, 1833), I, 28, 406; Mackintosh, *History of Civilisation in Scotland,* II, 255; *Statuta Ecclesiae Scoticanae,* ed. Joseph Robertson (Edinburgh, 1866), Vol. II, *passim.*

28. Mackintosh, *History of Civilisation in Scotland,* II, 235.

29. *Ibid.,* pp. 268 ff.

30. See J. William Dillon, "Witchcraft," in *Royal Burgh of Ayr,* ed. Dunlop.

31. Chambers, *Domestic Annals of Scotland,* I, 5.

32. Hector Boece, "The Boundis of Albioun" (1527) in *Scotland before 1700,* ed. Brown, p. 98.

33. William Robertson, *The History of Scotland during the Reigns of Queen Mary and of King James VI* (London, 1759), 2 vols.; II, 89.

34. Mackenzie, *History of Galloway,* I, 236.

35. Chambers, *Domestic Annals of Scotland,* I, 223.

36. Mackenzie, *History of Galloway,* I, 236.

37. Jean Froissart, *Les Chroniques de Froissart,* trans. in *Early Travellers in Scotland,* ed. Brown, pp. 7 ff.

38. See Wallace Notestein, *The Scot in History* (New Haven, 1946), p. 60.

39. Sir Walter Scott, Introduction to *The Legend of Montrose* (Boston, 1923).

40. For the Leslie comment, see Notestein, *The Scot in History,* p. 95; Lithgow is cited in Charles Sanford Terry, *A History of Scotland from the Roman Evacuation to the Disruption, 1843* (Cambridge, 1920), p. 309; Fuchs is cited in *Scottish Historical Review,* XXVII (1948), 187. The number of Scots reported by Lithgow certainly sounds excessive, but it indicates the considerable number of Scots in Poland.

41. John Harrison, *The Scot in Ulster: Sketch of the History of the Scottish Population of Ulster* (Edinburgh and London, 1888), p. 2.

3. SCOTTISH SOCIAL INSTITUTIONS IN 1600

1. John Gibson, *History of Glasgow from the Earliest Accounts to the Present Time* (Glasgow, 1777), p. 203.

2. See I. F. Grant, *The Social and Economic Development of Scotland before 1603* (Edinburgh, 1930), pp. 110, 350; Maude V. Clarke, *Mediaeval City States* (London, 1926), 35; *Early Travellers in Scotland,* ed. P. Hume Brown (Edinburgh, 1891), pp. 10, 75.

3. Patrick Fraser Tytler, *History of Scotland* (Edinburgh, 1828-43), IV, 225, 131; John Pinkerton, *An Enquiry into the History of Scotland* (London, 1789),

II, 179; Raphael Holinshead, *The Scottish Chronicle; or a Complete History and Description of Scotland* (Arbroath, 1805), II, 230; Andrew Brown, *History of Glasgow* (Glasgow and Edinburgh, 1795-97), II, 154.

4. "The Anglican Settlement and the Scottish Reformation," in *Cambridge Modern History*, II, 550.

5. *Ibid.*, p. 559.

6. *Ibid.*, p. 550.

7. See J. D. Mackie, "Notestein's *The Scot in History*," *Scottish Historical Review*, XXVII (1948), 98.

8. Neilson cites the *Acta Dominorum Concilii* (*Acts of the Lords of Council in Secret Causes*), II, lix.

9. Andrew Lang, "Scotland," in *Encyclopaedia Britannica* (11th ed.), XXIV, 440.

10. A good brief account of this period is found in the article by David Daiches, "Scottish Language and Literature," in *Encyclopaedia Americana* (Canadian ed., 1958), XXIV, 436-38.

11. Michael Grant, *Roman Literature* ("Pelican Series" [Baltimore, 1958]), p. 255.

12. Lang, "Scotland," in *Encyclopaedia Britannica* (11th ed.), XXIV, 441.

13. See Annie I. Dunlop, "Scottish Student Life in the Fifteenth Century," *Scottish Historical Review*, XXVI (1947), 47-63; "Notestein's *The Scot in History*," *Scot. Hist. Rev.*, XXVII, 98.

14. P. Hume Brown, *History of Scotland to the Present Time* (Cambridge, 1911), II, 221.

15. John Mackintosh, *History of Civilisation in Scotland* (Paisley and London, 1893), II, 398.

16. "Scottish Student Life in the Fifteenth Century," *Scot. Hist. Rev.*, XXVI, 47-63.

17. John Major, *Historia Majoris Britanniae tam Angliae q. Scotiae* (1521), trans. in P. Hume Brown, *Scotland before 1700 from Contemporary Documents* (Edinburgh, 1893), p. 59.

18. Robert Chambers, *Domestic Annals of Scotland from the Reformation to the Revolution* (Edinburgh and London, 1858), I, 5; *Acts of the Parliament of Scotland* (Edinburgh, 1844-75), II, 238.

19. James McClelland, "Schools," in *The Royal Burgh of Ayr: 750 Years of History*, ed. Annie I. Dunlop (Edinburgh and London, 1953), p. 214.

20. I. F. Grant, *The Social and Economic Development of Scotland before 1603* (Edinburgh, 1877-1924), pp. 191-92.

4. RELIGION IN SCOTLAND

1. See J. William Dillon, "The Pre-Reformation Church," in *The Royal Burgh of Ayr: 750 Years of History*, ed. Annie I. Dunlop (Edinburgh and London, 1953), ch. 7.

2. Noted in I. M. M. Macphail's review of "Source Book of Scottish History," *Scottish Historical Review*, XXXIII (1954), 33, 166.

3. F. W. Maitland, "The Anglican Settlement and the Scottish Reformation," in *Cambridge Modern History*, II, 554.

4. W. Croft Dickinson, Gordon Donaldson, and Isabel A. Milne, *A Source Book of Scottish History* (London, 1952-54), II, 142-43.

5. *Ibid.*, pp. 143-44.

6. John Major, *Historia Majoris Britanniae tam Angliae q. Scotiae* (1521), trans. in P. Hume Brown, *Scotland before 1700 from Contemporary Documents* (Edinburgh, 1893), pp. 136-37.

7. *Statuta Ecclesiae Scoticanae*, ed. Joseph Robertson (Edinburgh, 1866), II, 82-84.

8. *Acts of the Parliament of Scotland* (Edinburgh, 1844-75), II, 370, c.4.

9. Sir James Balfour Paul, "Clerical Life in Scotland in the Sixteenth Century," in *Scottish Historical Review*, XVII (1920), 179, 180. Paul also notes, p. 185, that many of the priests had children.

10. See Dickinson, Donaldson, and Milne, *A Source Book of Scottish History*, II, 136-38, for an account of "Archbishop Hamilton's Catechism," as it was called.

11. *Statuta Ecclesiae*, ed. Robertson, II, 137-38.

12. William Robertson, *Ayrshire: Its History and Historic Families* (Kilmarnock and Ayr, 1908), I, 196.

13. Macnab, "The beginnings of Lollardy in Scotland," in *Records* of the Scottish Church History Society, Vol. XI, pt. iii, pp. 254-60.

14. *Statuta Ecclesiae*, ed. Robertson, II, 148, 149.

15. Andrew Lang, *History of Scotland from the Roman Occupation* (Edinburgh and New York, 1900-1907), II, 31.

16. John Knox, *The Works of John Knox*, ed. David Laing (Edinburgh, 1846), II, 222.

17. D. Calderwood, *History of the Kirk of Scotland* (Edinburgh, 1842-49), I, 423-24; see also Knox, *Works*, I, 320.

18. According to Robert Chambers, *Domestic Annals of Scotland from the Reformation to the Revolution* (Edinburgh and London, 1858), I, 133.

19. John Mackintosh, *The History of Civilisation in Scotland* (Paisley and London, 1893), II, 257.

20. Archibald Mackenzie, "The Church from the Reformation till the End of the Eighteenth Century," in *Royal Burgh of Ayr*, ed. Dunlop, p. 107.

21. Brown, *Scotland before 1700*, pp. 291 ff.

22. See J. D. Mackie, "Notestein's *The Scot in History*," *Scottish Historical Review*, XXVII (1948), 100. Wallace Notestein, who in his book on *The Scot in History* (New Haven, 1946) studies the character of the Scots, devotes a whole chapter to the subject of "An Undisciplined People" (pp. 22-30).

23. Notestein, *The Scot in History*, p. 169.

24. See George Fraser Black, *A Calendar of Cases of Witchcraft in Scotland* (New York, 1936), p. 12.

25. Sir Herbert Maxwell, *A History of Dumfries and Galloway* (Edinburgh 1896), p. 193; Chambers, *Domestic Annals of Scotland*, I, 6.

26. *Buckle's Introduction to the History of Civilization in England*, ed. John M. Robertson (London, n.d.), p. 748.

27. *History of Civilisation in Scotland*, II, 443.

5. THE MIND AND CHARACTER OF THE LOWLANDER

1. W. I. Thomas and F. Znaniecki, *The Polish Peasant in Europe and America* (Chicago, 1918), II, 1859, 1882.

2. John Barbour, *The Brus* (modernized in language), ed. C. Innes (Aberdeen, 1856).

3. John Major, *Historia Majoris Britanniae tam Angliae q. Scotiae* (1521), trans. in P. Hume Brown, *Scotland before 1700 from Contemporary Documents* (Edinburgh, 1893), p. 54.

4. John Pinkerton, *An Enquiry into the History of Scotland* (London, 1789), I, 149.

5. J. D. Mackie, "Notestein's *The Scot in History*," *Scottish Historical Review*, XXVII (1948), 100.

PART II: THE SCOTS IN IRELAND

6. THE PLANTATION OF ULSTER, 1610 AND AFTER

1. "Ireland, to the Settlement of Ulster," in *Cambridge Modern History*, III, 587.

2. "View of the State of Ireland" (1890 ed.), pp. 123, 125.

3. Dunlop, "Ireland, to the Settlement of Ulster," in *Cambridge Modern History*, III, 593.

4. James B. Woodburn, *The Ulster Scot* (London, 1914), pp. 43-44.

5. William E. H. Lecky, *Ireland in the Eighteenth Century* (London and New York, 1883), I, 22.

6. The whole account of this "plantation" is contained in the fascinating *Montgomery Manuscripts*, ed. George Hill (Belfast, 1869). See I, 27 ff., 94, 97.

7. *Ibid.*, p. 62.

8. *Ibid.*, p. 66. See also Woodburn, *The Ulster Scot*, p. 57.

9. *Montgomery MSS*, p. 32.

10. *Calendar of State Papers for Ireland, 1603-1625* [Carew] (London, 1872-80), pp. 154, 269; *Register of the Privy Council of Scotland*, IX, 693.

11. David Stewart, in a series of pamphlets entitled *The Scots in Ulster* (Belfast, 1952, 1955, 1957), gives the names of hundreds of the colonists and their place of settlement. The sources for the names include the *Hamilton MSS*, ed. T. K. Lowrey (Belfast, 1867) and the *Montgomery MSS*; George Hill, *An Historical Account of the Plantation of Ulster at the Commencement of the Seventeenth Century, 1608-1620* (Belfast, 1877), pp. 283-309; State Calendars; the Commissioner's Report in the *Carew MSS*; the Survey made by Pynnar. See also Henry Cairnes Lawlor, *Ulster: Its Archaeology and Antiquities* (Belfast, 1928), pp. 158 ff.

12. "Ireland to the Settlement of Ulster," in *Cambridge Modern History*, III, 616.

13. *Montgomery MSS*, p. 58.

7. CAUSES OF THE SCOTTISH MIGRATION

1. The figures are those of S. R. Gardiner, *History of England, from the Accession of James I. to the Outbreak of the Civil War, 1603-1642* (London, 1883-84), IX, 213.

2. See P. Hume Brown, *Scotland before 1700 from Contemporary Documents* (Edinburgh, 1893), pp. 285-90; Thomas Hamilton, "How the Burgh helped the Poor," in *The Royal Burgh of Ayr: 750 Years of History*, ed. Annie I. Dunlop (Edinburgh and London, 1953), ch. 15; Pryde, *Ayr Burgh Accounts*, lxxx-lxxxiii; and many other sources.

3. I. F. Grant, *The Social and Economic Development of Scotland before 1603* (Edinburgh, 1930), p. 278.

4. Lyndsay, *Satire on the Three Estates* (Laing's ed.), lines 2575-2695. See also Johnston, *History of the Working Classes in Scotland;* Mathieson, *Politics and Religion: A Study in Scottish History from the Reformation to the Revolution;* and the anonymous *Complaynt of Scotlande* (date circa 1549).

5. Grant, *Social and Economic Development of Scotland*, p. 282.

6. Dramatic contemporary accounts appear in John Nicoll, *A Diary of Public Transactions and other Documents Chiefly in Scotland, 1650-67* (Edinburgh, 1836), pp. 110 ff; in *The Diary of Mr. John Lamont of Newton*, pp. 56-57; Robert Baillie, *Letters and Journals; containing an Account of Public Transactions, Civil, Ecclesiastical, and Military in England and Scotland, 1637-1662* (Edinburgh, 1775), III, 225, 226.

7. William Henry Foote, *Sketches of Virginia, Historical and Biographical* (Philadelphia, 1850), p. 62, has some interesting comment on this point.

8. THE PIONEER SCOTS IN ULSTER (1606-34)

1. *Life of Mr. Robert Blair, containing his Autobiography, from 1593 to 1636* ed. William Row (Edinburgh, 1848), p. 55.

2. Stewart, "Short Account of the Church of Christ as it was amongst the Irish," (also called, in the Wodrow MSS, *History of the Church of Ireland*) in

Patrick Adair, *A True Narrative of the Rise and Progress of the Presbyterian Church in the North of Ireland* (Belfast and Edinburgh, 1866), p. 2.

3. Sir William Brereton, *Travels in Holland, the United Provinces, England, Scotland and Ireland, 1634-35* (Manchester, 1844), pp. 118, 119, 129-30.

4. *Ibid.*

5. John Harrison, *The Scot in Ulster: Sketch of the History of the Scottish Population of Ulster* (Edinburgh and London, 1888), pp. 45-46.

6. Stewart, *History of the Church of Ireland*, p. 6. An estimate cited by Guy S. Klett, *The Scotch-Irish in Pennsylvania* (Gettysburg, 1948), p. 3, that in 1641 there were one hundred thousand Scots and only twenty thousand English, is clearly exaggerated in favor of the Scots.

7. Cited in Charles A. Hanna, *The Scotch-Irish or the Scot in North Britain, North Ireland, and North America* (New York and London, 1902), I, 525-26; see also Ford, *The Scotch-Irish in America*, p. 117.

8. Henry Jones Ford, *The Scotch-Irish in America* (Princeton, 1915), p. 119.

9. George Hill, *An Historical Account of the Plantation of Ulster at the Commencement of the Seventeenth Century, 1608-1620* (Belfast, 1877), pp. 348-50.

10. Ford, *The Scotch-Irish in America*, p. 116.

11. Hanna, *The Scotch-Irish*, I, 545.

12. Robert Dunlop, "Ireland, to the Settlement of Ulster," in *Cambridge Modern History*, III, 616.

13. Reported by Ford, *The Scotch-Irish in America*, pp. 107-8.

14. *Ibid.*, pp. 108-9.

15. *Ibid.*, pp. 109-10.

16. Daniel Neal, *The History of the Puritans* (New York, 1844), p. 98.

17. James Seaton Reid, *History of the Presbyterian Church in Ireland* (London, 1853), I, 98.

18. John Livingstone and Robert Blair, quoted in Reid, *History of the Presbyterian Church in Ireland*, I, 125.

19. Adair, *A True Narrative of the . . . Presbyterian Church in the North of Ireland*, p. 317.

20. Blair, *Autobiography*, p. 70.

21. Peter Heylin, *History of the Presbyterians from 1536 to 1647* (Oxford, 1670), p. 343.

9. THE HARD YEARS, 1634-1690

1. George Pratt Insh, *Scottish Colonial Schemes, 1620-1686* (Glasgow, 1922), p. 57.

2. Cited in Henry Jones Ford, *The Scotch-Irish in America* (Princeton, 1915), p. 126.

3. *Life of Mr. Robert Blair, containing his Autobiography from 1593-1636* ed. William Row (Edinburgh, 1848), p. 156.

4. James B. Woodburn, *The Ulster Scot* (London, 1914), p. 96.

5. William E. H. Lecky, *Ireland in the Eighteenth Century* (London and New York, 1883), I, 40-41.

6. S. R. Gardiner, *History of England, 1603-1659* (London, n.d.), p. 69.

7. Cited in Ford, *The Scotch-Irish in America*, pp. 152-53.

8. James Seaton Reid, *History of the Presbyterian Church in Ireland* (London, 1853), II, 187, 552; J. D. Prendergast, *The Cromwellian Settlement in Ireland* (2d ed.; Dublin, 1875), p. 90.

9. John Harrison, *The Scot in Ulster: Sketch of the History of the Scottish Population of Ulster* (Edinburgh and London, 1888), p. 79.

10. Cited in Ford, *The Scotch-Irish in America*, pp. 153-54.

11. See Harrison, *The Scot in Ulster*, p. 84.

12. Reid, *History of the Presbyterian Church in Ireland*, II, 341. Laggan is

a region in the northwestern part of Ulster, in eastern Donegal, between the Foyle and Swilly rivers.

13. Macaulay, *History of England from the Accession of James the Second* (Philadelphia, 1857), I, 80.

14. *Ibid.*, III, 55.

15. Lecky, *Ireland in the Eighteenth Century*, II, 400-1; Arthur L. Perry, *Scotch-Irish in New England* (Boston, 1891), p. 7.

16. Woodburn, *The Ulster Scot*, p. 172.

10. INTERMARRIAGE WITH THE IRISH

1. James Seaton Reid, *History of the Presbyterian Church in Ireland* (London, 1853), I, 91.

2. Many instances are noted in a paper by T. H. Murray, "Certain Scottish Names derived from Irish ones," cited in John C. Linehan, *The Irish Scots and the 'Scotch-Irish'* (Concord, N.H., 1902), p. 94.

3. William E. H. Lecky, *Ireland in the Eighteenth Century* (London and New York, 1883), II, 405.

11. THE CHARACTER OF THE ULSTER SCOT

1. It may be suggested that the Ulster Scot was in the transitional stage between the *Gemeinschaft* and the *Gesellschaft* analyzed by Tönnies.

2. See James Seaton Reid, *History of the Presbyterian Church in Ireland* (London, 1853), throughout. The example of the rules at Templepatrick (1646) is reported by Henry Jones Ford, *The Scotch-Irish in America* (Princeton, 1915), pp. 158-59.

3. Calvin, *Institutes*, trans. John Allen (7th American ed.; Philadelphia, 1936), Book IV, ch. xx, pp. 802, 805.

4. *The Protestant Ethic and the Spirit of Capitalism*, trans. Talcott Parsons (London, 1930), p. 234.

5. Arthur L. Perry, *Scotch-Irish in New England* (Boston, 1891), pp. 5-6.

6. Richard H. Lee, *Life of Arthur Lee* (Boston, 1829), 2 vols.; II, 385.

7. John Gamble, *Sketches of History, Politics and Manners in Dublin and the North of Ireland* (London, 1826), p. 348.

8. Perry, *Scotch-Irish in New England*, p. 41.

9. Gamble, *Sketches of History, Politics and Manners*, p. 262.

PART III: THE SCOTCH-IRISH IN AMERICA

12. THE MIGRATION

1. Guy S. Klett, *The Scotch-Irish in Pennsylvania* (Gettysburg, 1948), p. 4.

2. J. R. Green, *A Short History of the English People* (New York, 1876), p. 458.

3. G. L. Beer, *The Old Colonial System* (New York, 1912), I, 91-92.

4. Several American historians seem to assume that this law was aimed primarily at the American colonies. R. D. W. Connor (*Race Elements in the Population of North Carolina* [Raleigh, 1920]), p. 80) disputes this view.

5. By 1741 they had risen to £480,000, and by 1771 to £1,691,000. David Macpherson, *Annals of Commerce, Manufactures, Fisheries and Navigation* (London, 1805), III, 228.

6. Arthur Young, *A Tour in Ireland, 1776, 1777 1778* (London, 1780), I, 124.

7. Hugh Boulter, *Letters Written by Hugh Boulter, D.D., Lord Primate of Ireland*, ed. M. Wall (Oxford, 1769-70), I, 292.

8. Philip H. Bagenal, *The American Irish and Their Influence on Irish Politics* (London, 1882), p. 7.

9. William King, *A Great Archbishop of Dublin, William King, D.D., 1650-1729. His Autobiography, Family, and a Selection from his Correspondence,* ed. Sir Charles Simeon King (London and New York, 1906), p. 301.

10. Swift, *Proposal for a Universal Use of Manufactures.*

11. J. G. Craighead, *Scotch and Irish Seeds in American Soil* (Philadelphia, 1878), p. 273.

12. Charles Knowles Bolton, *Scotch-Irish Pioneers in Ulster and America* (Boston, 1910), p. 43.

13. Craighead, *Scotch and Irish Seeds in American Soil,* pp. 257-59.

14. James Anthony Froude, *The English in Ireland in the Eighteenth Century* (New York, 1878), I, 392.

15. King, *Autobiography,* p. 301.

16. *Ibid.;* Jonathan Dickinson, *Copy Book of Letters* (MS, Historical Society of Pennsylvania), 163, 288, and *Letter Book* (MS, Ridgway Branch, Library Company of Philadelphia), 294, cited in Wayland F. Dunaway, *The Scotch-Irish of Colonial Pennsylvania* (Chapel Hill, 1944), p. 34; Bolton, *Scotch-Irish Pioneers in Ulster and America,* pp. 319-23.

17. Wodrow MSS, *Letters,* XX, no. 129.

18. James Logan, *The Logan Papers,* III, 303.

19. Boulter, *Letters,* I, 226-32.

20. Oscar Theodore Barck and Hugh Talmage Lefler, *Colonial America* (New York, 1958), p. 286.

21. Young, *A Tour in Ireland,* I, 125.

22. Connor, *Race Elements,* p. 83.

23. Young, *A Tour in Ireland,* I, 146.

24. J. Smith Futhey, "The Scotch-Irish," Lancaster County Historical Society *Papers* (1907), XI, 227.

25. *The English in Ireland,* II, 125.

26. T. A. Spencer, *History of the United States,* quoted by Bagenal, *The American Irish,* p. 6.

27. Abbot Emerson Smith, *Colonists in Bondage: White Servitude and Convict Labor in America, 1607-1776* (Chapel Hill, 1947), p. 325.

28. Young, *A Tour in Ireland,* I, 146.

29. Froude, *The English in Ireland,* II, 140, 146-48.

30. Boulter, *Letters,* I, 226.

31. Smith, *Colonists in Bondage,* p. 336.

32. See T. J. Wertenbaker, *Patrician and Plebeian in Virginia* (Charlottesville, 1910), pt. II.

33. For an analysis of the indentured servant, see Smith, *Colonists in Bondage,* chs. 1-3; Herbert L. Osgood, *The American Colonies in the Seventeenth Century* (New York, 1904), I, 82 ff; Wertenbaker, *Patrician and Plebeian in Virginia,* pt. II; Cheesman Abiah Herrick, *White Servitude in Pennsylvania* (Philadelphia, 1926), throughout.

34. Herrick, *White Servitude in Pennsylvania,* p. 143n.

35. See Smith, *Colonists in Bondage,* ch. 4, on kidnaping and spiriting.

36. An analysis of laws regulating the treatment of indentured servants in the provinces is made by Smith, *Colonists in Bondage,* ch. 11.

37. E. C. Kirkland, *History of American Economic Life* (New York, 1933), p. 64.

38. Herrick, *White Servitude in Pennsylvania,* p. 57.

39. Maurice R. Davie, *World Immigration* (New York, 1936), p. 24; Marcus L. Hansen, *The Atlantic Migration, 1607-1860* (Cambridge, Mass., 1940), p. 41; Dunaway, *The Scotch-Irish of Colonial Pennsylvania,* p. 41; Barck and Lefler, *Colonial America,* p. 285.

40. King, *Autobiography,* p. 301.

41. Dickinson, *Copy Book of Letters,* pp. 163, 288.
42. Bolton, *Scotch-Irish Pioneers,* pp. 319-23.
43. W. H. G. Flood, in *Journal of the Irish American Historical Society,* XXVI (1927), 204.
44. Boulter, *Letters,* I, 232.
45. Logan, *The Logan Papers,* III, 303.
46. Cited in John F. Watson, *Annals of Philadelphia and of Pennsylvania in the Olden Time* (Philadelphia, 1854), II, 261.
47. New Jersey *Archives,* 1st Ser., XI, 185, citing *The New-England Weekly Journal* of August 25, 1729.
48. Smith, *Colonists in Bondage,* p. 318.
49. Young, *A Tour in Ireland,* I, 146.
50. Cited in Charles A. Hanna, *The Scotch-Irish, or the Scot in North Britain, North Ireland, and North America* (New York and London, 1902), I, 622.
51. Stella H. Sutherland, *Population Distribution in Colonial America* (New York, 1936), p. 141.
52. Sir Thomas Newenham, *A Statistical and Historical Inquiry into the Progress and Magnitude of the Population of Ireland* (London, 1805), 59-60.
53. *Gentleman's Magazine,* XLIV (1774), 332.
54. Futhey, "The Scotch-Irish," p. 227.
55. Froude, *The English in Ireland,* II, 125.
56. Smith, *Colonists in Bondage,* pp. 325, 329.
57. John Fiske, *The Dutch and Quaker Colonies in America* (Boston and New York, 1889), II, 254.
58. Bureau of the Census, "A Century of Population Growth" (1909), 57, 117.
59. *Annual Report* of the American Historical Association (1931), I, 124.

13. SCOTCH-IRISH SETTLEMENTS

1. William H. Egle, *History of the Commonwealth of Pennsylvania* (3rd ed.; Philadelphia, 1883), p. 820.
2. I. Daniel Rupp, *History and Topography of Dauphin, Cumberland, Franklin, Bedford, Adams, and Perry Counties* (Lancaster, 1846), pp. 55-56; Egle, *History of the Commonwealth of Pennsylvania,* p. 615.
3. J. Smith Futhey and Gilbert Cope, in Egle, *History of the Commonwealth of Pennsylvania,* p. 526.
4. Cited in John H. Finley, *The Coming of the Scot* (New York, 1940), pp. 58-59.
5. George Chambers, *A Tribute to the Principles, Virtues, Habits and Public Usefulness of the Irish and Scotch Early Settlers of Pennsylvania* (Chambersburg, 1856), p. 10.
6. *Official Correspondence, 1683-1727* (Penn MSS, Historical Society of Pennsylvania), I, 185.
7. *Colonial Records of Pennsylvania, 1683-1790* (Harrisburg, 1851-53), IX, 380.
8. *Pennsylvania Archives,* 1st Ser. (Philadelphia and Harrisburg, 1852-1931), I, 40-46.
9. Rupp, *History and Topography of Dauphin,* pp. 514-15; Hubertis Cummings, *Richard Peters, Provincial Secretary and Cleric, 1704-1776* (Philadelphia, 1944), pp. 106-7.
10. I. Daniel Rupp, *History and Topography of Northumberland, Huntington, Mifflin, Centre, Union, Columbia, Juniata, and Clinton Counties, Pa.* (Lancaster, 1847), p. 17.

11. *William Allen's Letter Book*, p. 25, cited in Theodore Thayer, *Pennsylvania Politics and the Growth of Democracy, 1740-1776* (Harrisburg, 1953), p. 47.

12. H. M. J. Klein, *Lancaster County, Pennsylvania: A History* (New York and Chicago, 1924), I, 101.

13. Carl Bridenbaugh, *Cities in Revolt: Urban Life in America, 1743-1776* (New York, 1955), pp. 50-51.

14. I. Daniel Rupp and others, in Egle, *History of the Commonwealth of Pennsylvania*, p. 615.

15. Wayland F. Dunaway, *The Scotch-Irish of Colonial Pennsylvania* (Chapel Hill, 1944), p. 59.

16. M. O. Smith, in Egle, *History of the Commonwealth of Pennsylvania*, p. 1170. The Scotch-Irish farms in York were chiefly in the present townships of Chanceford, Fawn, Peach Bottom, Hopewell, and Windsor.

17. Carl Bridenbaugh, *Myths and Realities: Societies of the Colonial South* (Baton Rouge, 1952), p. 132.

18. Egle, *History of the Commonwealth of Pennsylvania*, p. 615.

19. William Henry Foote, *Sketches of Virginia, Historical and Biographical* (Philadelphia, 1850), pp. 100-1.

20. Charles A. Hanna, *The Scotch-Irish, or the Scot in North Britain, North Ireland, and North America* (New York and London, 1902), II, 45-46.

21. When the Augusta County Court was established in 1745 the price to new settlers was almost doubled. Howard McKnight Wilson, *The Tinkling Spring, Headwater of Freedom* (Fishersville, Va., 1954), p. 19.

22. See William Couper, *History of the Shenandoah Valley* (New York, 1952), I, 269; F. B. Kegley, *Kegley's Virginia Frontier* (Roanoke, 1938), p. 58.

23. Called the "Irish Track" in the 1775 map of Fry and Jefferson. See John W. Wayland, *Twenty-five Chapters on the Shenandoah Valley* (Strasburg, Va., 1957), p. 81.

24. Cited in Bridenbaugh, *Myths and Realities*, p. 123.

25. Testimony of E. E. Keister, editor in 1925 of the fourth edition of Samuel Kercheval, *History of the Valley of Virginia* (Strasburg, Va., 1925), p. 52n.

26. *The Official Records of Robert Dinwiddie*, ed. R. A. Brock (Richmond, 1883-84), I, 8.

27. W. W. Hening, *Statutes-at-Large, being a Collection of All the Laws of Virginia, 1619-1792* (Philadelphia and New York, 1823), V, 78; Couper, *History of the Shenandoah Valley*, I, 286.

28. *Records of the Presbyterian Church in the U.S.A.*, ed. William M. Engles (Philadelphia, 1841), p. 18.

29. Quoted in Hanna, *The Scotch-Irish*, II, 48.

30. For an account of the Scotch-Irish in this region, see Lewis Preston Summers, *History of Southwest Virginia, 1748-1786, Washington County, 1777-1870* (Richmond, 1903).

31. Bridenbaugh, *Myths and Realities*, p. 121.

32. Marshall, quoted in *Records of the Moravians in North Carolina*, ed. Adelaide Fries (Raleigh, 1922-54), I, 294.

33. S. A. Ashe, *History of North Carolina* (Greensboro, N.C., 1925), I, 276-77.

34. Archibald Henderson, "The Origin of the Regulation in North Carolina," *American Historical Review*, XXI (1916), 321.

35. William L. Saunders, Prefatory Notes to *Colonial Records of North Carolina* (Raleigh, 1886-90), V, xi.

36. *Colonial Records of N.C.*, IV, xxi.

37. *Ibid.*, IV, 1073.

38. R. D. W. Connor, *Race Elements in the White Population of North Carolina* (Raleigh, 1920), p. 85.

39. *Ibid.*, p. 83.

40. *Orange County, 1752-1952*, ed. Hugh T. Lefler and Paul Wager (Chapel Hill, 1953), p. 15.

41. *Records of the Moravians*, ed. Fries, I, 59.

42. Bridenbaugh, *Myths and Realities*, p. 125.

43. William Francis Guess, *South Carolina: Annals of Pride and Protest* (New York, 1957), p. 65.

44. Frank Nash, "The Scotch-Irish in Orange County," Program for North Carolina Day (Raleigh, 1908), p. 10.

45. A good account of the Cherokee War is found in Chapman J. Milling, *Red Carolinians* (Chapel Hill, 1940), XV, 286-306, and R. S. Cotterill, *The Southern Indians: The Story of the Civilized Tribes before Removal* (Norman, Okla., 1954), pp. 32 ff.

46. R. L. Meriwether, *The Expansion of South Carolina, 1729-1765* (Kingsport, Tenn., 1940), XV, 213-40.

47. William Gilmore Simms, *The History of South Carolina* (New York, 1860), p. 120.

48. Bridenbaugh, *Cities in Revolt*, p. 261.

49. This Great Road is shown on the 1775 maps of Virginia, by Joshua Fry and Peter Jefferson, and of North and South Carolina, by Henry Mouzon.

50. Connor, *Race Elements*, p. 83.

51. Meriwether, *The Expansion of South Carolina*, p. 163.

52. *Orange County*, ed. Lefler and Wager, p. 16.

53. Bridenbaugh, *Myths and Realities*, p. 139.

54. David Ramsey, *The History of South Carolina* (Charleston, 1809), I, 16.

55. Guess, *South Carolina*, p. 67.

56. Bridenbaugh, *Cities in Revolt*, p. 262.

57. Nash, "The Scotch-Irish in Orange County," pp. 11-12.

58. Guess, *South Carolina*, pp. 69-70.

59. Bridenbaugh, *Myths and Realities*, p. 132.

60. See Couper, *History of the Shenandoah Valley*, I, 99-109, on the southern Indians and their relations with settlers.

61. See above, p. 217.

62. Kercheval, *Valley of Virginia*, p. 53.

63. Homer C. Hockett, *Political and Social Growth of the American People, 1492-1865* (3d ed.; New York, 1940), I, 142.

64. B. J. Witherow, *The Insurrection of the Paxton Boys* (n.p., 1860), p. 645.

65. *Official Correspondence, 1683-1727* (Penn MSS, Historical Society of Pennsylvania), VII, 9.

66. Winthrop Sargent, Introductory Memoir to the Journal of *Braddock's Expedition*, cited in Philip H. Bagenal, *The American Irish and Their Influence on Irish Politics* (London, 1882), p. 11.

67. Francis Parkman, *The Conspiracy of Pontiac* (Boston, 1898), II, 219.

68. Thomas Barton, *The Conduct of the Paxton Men, Impartially Represented* (Philadelphia, 1764), throughout.

69. An excellent account of the distinctive qualities of the Scots in America and of their various settlements is given by Ian Charles Cargill Graham, *Colonists from Scotland: Emigration to North America, 1707-1783* (Ithaca, 1956).

70. *Magnalia Christi Americana* (Hartford, 1820), Vol. I.

71. *Suffolk Deed Records*, Book, I, pp. 5-6.

72. Abbot Emerson Smith, *Colonists in Bondage: White Servitude and Convict Labor in America, 1607-1776* (Chapel Hill, 1947), p. 38.

73. Arthur L. Perry, "The Scotch-Irish in New England," in *Proceedings and Addresses* (Nashville, 1890-1900) of the Scotch-Irish Society of America, II, 119.

74. Carl Bridenbaugh, *Cities in the Wilderness: The First Century of Urban Life in America* (New York, 1938), p. 250, where sources are cited.

75. *Report of the Record Commissioners of the City of Boston,* XI, 50, 134, 182.

76. Bridenbaugh, *Cities in the Wilderness,* pp. 391-92, 410.

77. *Ibid.,* p. 410, where sources are cited.

78. *Gentleman's Magazine,* XLIV (1774), 332.

79. *Documents Relating to the Colonial History of the State of New York* (Albany, 1856-87), III, 399.

80. *Ibid.,* VII, 629-31; Ruth Higgins, *Expansion in New York with Especial Reference to the Eighteenth Century* (Columbus, 1931), p. 73; William W. Campbell, *Annals of Tryon County* (New York, 1831), p. 19.

81. See Bridenbaugh, *Cities in the Wilderness,* pp. 201, 357-58; and *Cities in Revolt,* pp. 87, 334.

82. On the climate, see Stella H. Sutherland, *Population Distribution in Colonial America* (New York, 1936), p. 150.

83. The Scot mentioned was Colonel Ninian Beall. J. William McIlwaine, "Early Presbyterianism in Maryland."

84. Margaret S. Morriss, *Colonial Trade in Maryland, 1689-1715,* p. 71.

85. Sutherland, *Population Distribution,* p. 197, where reference is made to "Report of a Traveller," *London Magazine,* XV, 327.

86. *Maryland State Papers,* June 25, 1695.

87. Smith, *Colonists in Bondage,* pp. 325, 329, 337.

88. George Howe, *History of the Presbyterian Church in South Carolina* (Columbia, 1870), I, 201.

89. Meriwether, *Expansion of South Carolina,* pp. 79 ff.

90. Frederick Lewis Weis, *The Colonial Churches and the Colonial Clergy of the Middle and Southern Colonies, 1607-1776* (Lancaster, Mass., 1938), throughout.

91. Guess, *South Carolina,* p. 20.

92. Edward McCrady, *History of South Carolina under the Royal Government, 1719-1776* (New York, 1899), p. 318n.

93. *Colonial Records of N.C.,* IV, 489-90.

94. The estimate is Connor's, in *Race Elements,* p. 57.

95. See Graham, *Colonists from Scotland,* pp. 118 ff.

14. FRONTIER SOCIETY

1. Frederick Jackson Turner, *The Frontier in American History* (New York, 1920), especially the influential essay on "The Significance of the Frontier in American History," appearing as the first chapter in this book of Turner's essays.

2. See, for example, Frederic L. Paxson's *History of the American Frontier* (Boston and New York, 1924); E. D. Branch's *Westward: The Romance of the American Frontier* (New York, 1930); Robert E. Riegel's *America Moves West* (New York, 1930); and many others.

3. Jeremy Belknap, *The History of New-Hampshire* (Boston, 1792), III, 257-59.

4. See Allan Nevins, *American Social History as Recorded by British Travellers* (New York, 1923), especially chapters 4 and 6.

5. *Le Suicide* (Paris, 1897), ch. 1. (Translated by George Simpson, *Suicide* [Glencoe, 1951].)

6. Max Weber, *The Protestant Ethic and the Spirit of Capitalism,* trans. Talcott Parsons (London, 1930), pp. 111 ff.

7. For a discussion of the mental problems of later immigrants, see Everett V. Stonequist, *The Marginal Man* (New York, 1937), throughout.

15. THE PRESBYTERIAN CHURCH

1. Ernest Trice Thompson, *Presbyterian Missions in the Southern United States* (Richmond, 1934), pp. 17, 20.

2. A. Alexander, *Biographical Sketches of the Founder and Principal Alumni of the Log College* (Princeton, 1845), throughout; Elias Boudinot, *The Life of the Reverend William Tennent* (Hartford, 1845); E. R. Craven, "The Log College of Neshaminy and Princeton University," in *Journal* of the Presbyterian Historical Society, I, 314.

3. William Henry Foote, *Sketches of Virginia, Historical and Biographical* (Philadelphia, 1850), p. 107.

4. John Walker Dinsmore, *The Scotch-Irish in America* (Chicago, 1906), p. 80.

5. Leonard J. Trinterud, *The Forming of an American Tradition. A Re-Examination of Colonial Presbyterianism* (Philadelphia, 1949), p. 201.

6. *Ibid.*, p. 197.

7. William Sweet, *The Presbyterians*, Vol. II of *Religion on the American Frontier, 1783-1840* (Chicago, 1936), pp. 7-8.

8. E. F. Humphrey, *Nationalism and Religion in America, 1774-1789* (Boston, 1924), p. 267.

9. *Diary of David McClure, 1748-1820*, ed. F. B. Dexter (New York, 1899), p. 112.

10. Dinsmore, *The Scotch-Irish in America*, pp. 123-34.

11. Oren F. Morton, *A History of Rockbridge County, Virginia* (Staunton, Va., 1920) p. 39.

12. J. G. Craighead, *Scotch and Irish Seeds in American Soil* (Philadelphia, 1878), pp. 283-84.

13. Dinsmore, *The Scotch-Irish in America*, pp. 159-61.

14. *Ibid.*, pp. 83, 129; Roy H. Johnson, "Frontier Religion in Western Pennsylvania," *Western Pennsylvania Historical Magazine*, XVI, 30; S. M. J. Eaton, *History of the Presbytery of Erie* (New York, 1848), pp. 20-22.

15. The first example is from New England, in the Londonderry colony of New Hampshire—Arthur L. Perry, *Scotch-Irish in New England* (Boston, 1891), p. 49. The second is from Pennsylvania, although it also occurred elsewhere: Dinsmore, *The Scotch-Irish in America*, p. 181.

16. Guy S. Klett, *The Scotch-Irish in Pennsylvania* (Gettysburg, 1948), p. 35.

17. See on this point, William Henry Foote, *Sketches of North Carolina, Historical and Biographical* (New York, 1846), p. 122.

16. THE SCOTCH-IRISH IN POLITICS

1. George A. Cribbs, *The Frontier Policy of Pennsylvania* (Pittsburgh, 1919), pp. 42 ff.

2. William Smith, *A Brief Review of the Conduct of Pennsylvania for the Year 1755*, p. 52; cited in Wayland F. Dunaway, *The Scotch-Irish of Colonial Pennsylvania* (Chapel Hill, 1944), p. 130.

3. "A Declaration and Remonstrance of the distressed and bleeding Inhabitants of the Province of Pennsylvania," in *Colonial Records of Pennsylvania, 1683-1790* (Harrisburg, 1851-53), IX, 141.

4. Howard McKnight Wilson, *The Tinkling Spring, Headwater of Freedom* (Fishersville, Va., 1954), pp. 222-36.

5. *Colonial Records of North Carolina* (Raleigh, 1886-90), VII, 813-15.

6. For details, see Charles Woodmason, *The Carolina Backcountry on the Eve of the Revolution, The Journals and Other Writings of Charles Woodmason, Anglican Itinerant*, ed. Richard J. Hooker (Chapel Hill, 1953), pp. 190 ff.

7. Quoted by Edward L. Parker, *The History of Londonderry* [New Hampshire] (Boston, 1851), p. 102.

8. Jonathan Smith, "The Scotch Presbyterians in the American Revolution," *Granite Monthly*, p. 41.

9. H. M. J. Klein, *Lancaster County, Pennsylvania: A History* (New York and Chicago, 1924), I, 86.

10. *Facsimiles of Manuscripts in European Archives relating to America*, ed. B. F. Stevens (London, 1889-98), Vol. XXIV, no. 2045.

11. John Adams, *Works*, ed. Charles Francis Adams (Boston, 1850-56), II, 426; Theodore Thayer, *Pennsylvania Politics and the Growth of Democracy, 1740-1776* (Harrisburg, 1953), pp. 184-85.

12. Cited by Vernon L. Parrington, *Main Currents in American Thought* (New York, 1927-30), 3 vols.; I, 359.

13. Stevens, ed., *Facsimiles of Manuscripts . . . Relating to America*, Vol. XXIV, no. 2057.

14. Dunaway, *The Scotch-Irish of Colonial Pennsylvania*, p. 157 ff.

15. George Bancroft, *A History of the United States from the Discovery of the American Continent* (Boston, 1846-75), VII, 74.

16. See Wilson, *The Tinkling Spring*, ch. 13.

17. E. W. Caruthers, *Life of David Caldwell* (Greensboro, 1842), pp. 172-73. Governor Martin also regarded the sanctity of oath as the dominant reason for loyalism; see *Colonial Records of North Carolina*, IX, 1228.

18. Robert O. DeMond, *The Loyalists in North Carolina during the Revolution* (Durham, 1944), pp. 48 ff.

19. *Colonial Records of N.C.*, X, 331.

20. See Edward R. R. Green, "The Scotch-Irish and the Coming of the Revolution in North Carolina," *Irish Historical Studies*, VII (1950), 82-84.

21. Wertenbaker, "Early Scotch Contributions to the United States," p. 24.

22. Guy S. Klett, *The Scotch-Irish in Pennsylvania* (Gettysburg, 1948), p. 16.

23. Ralph Barton Perry, *Puritanism and Democracy* (New York, 1944), p. 211.

24. Reported, with citation, in Philip H. Bagenal, *The American Irish and Their Influence on Irish Politics* (London, 1882), pp. 12-13.

25. R. Bennett Bean, *The Peopling of Virginia* (Boston, 1938), p. 37.

26. See Max Farrand, *The Framing of the Constitution of the United States* (New Haven, 1913), ch. II. This is the major point of Charles A. Beard's *An Economic Interpretation of the Constitution of the United States* (New York, 1914).

27. Edward S. Corwin, "The 'Higher Law' Background of American Constitutional Law," *Harvard Law Review*, XLII (1929), 397.

28. Archibald Henderson, *The Conquest of the Old Southwest* (New York, 1920), p. 172.

29. I. Daniel Rupp, *History and Topography of Dauphin, Cumberland, Franklin, Bedford, Adams, and Perry Counties* (Lancaster, 1846), p. 486.

30. See Thayer, *Pennsylvania Politics*, pp. 90-91. The McCoys, in their famous feud with the Hatfields in later days, are a further example of Scotch-Irish "folk" independence in taking crude reprisal on their enemies.

17. FINAL ESTIMATE

1. William Priest, *Travels in the United States of America, 1793-1797*, p. 146, cited in Wayland F. Dunaway, *The Scotch-Irish of Colonial Pennsylvania* (Chapel Hill, 1944), p. 42.

2. Theodore Roosevelt, *The Winning of the West* (New York, 1904), I, 168n.

APPENDIX I: THE NAME "SCOTCH-IRISH"

1. Carl Wittke, *The Irish in America* (Baton Rouge, 1956), p. vii.

2. *Calendar of Patent and Close Rolls of Chancery*, cited in David Stewart,

The Scots in Ulster: Their Denization and Naturalisation (Belfast, 1954), pt. I, pp. 2-3.

3. "The Rev. William Becket's Notices and Letters Concerning Incidents at Lewes Town, 1721-1742" (MS, Historical Society of Pennsylvania), p. 21.

4. Hubertis Cummings, *Richard Peters, Provincial Secretary and Cleric, 1704-1776* (Philadelphia, 1944), p. 142.

5. Wayland F. Dunaway, *The Scotch-Irish of Colonial Pennsylvania* (Chapel Hill, 1944), p. 8.

6. Edward L. Parker, *History of Londonderry* (Boston, 1851), p. 68.

Bibliography

PART I: THE SCOT IN 1600

Acta Dominorum Concilii (*Acts of the Lords of Council in Secret Causes*). Edinburgh, 1811.

Acts of the Parliament of Scotland, 1593-1707. 12 vols. Edinburgh, 1814-75.

Adair, Patrick. *A True Narrative of the Rise and Progress of the Presbyterian Church in the North of Ireland.* Belfast and Edinburgh, 1866.

Adams, George Burton. "Feudalism," *Encyclopaedia Britannica* (11th ed.), X, 297-302.

Aeneas Sylvius. "Account of Scotland" (c. 1430). Reprinted in Brown, *Early Travellers in Scotland*, q.v.

Ayala, Pedro de. "Letter to Ferdinand and Isabella." Reprinted in Brown, *Early Travellers in Scotland*, q.v.

Baillie, Robert. *Letters and Journals; containing an Account of Public Transactions, Civil, Ecclesiastical, and Military in England and Scotland, 1637-1662.* Edinburgh, 1775.

Balfour, Sir James. *Annales* (*The Historical Works of Sir James Balfour*). Edinburgh, 1824-25.

Black, George Fraser. *A Calendar of Cases of Witchcraft in Scotland.* New York, 1936.

Boece, Hector. "The Boundis of Albioun" (1527). Reprinted in Brown, *Scotland before 1700*, q.v.

Booke of the Universall Kirk of Scotland: Acts and Proceedings of the General Assemblies of the Kirk of Scotland, from the Year 1560. 3 vols. Edinburgh, 1839.

Brereton, Sir William. *Travels in Holland, the United Provinces, England, Scotland, and Ireland, 1634-35.* Manchester, 1844.

Brown, Andrew. *History of Glasgow.* 2 vols. Glasgow and Edinburgh, 1795-97.

Brown, P. Hume. *History of Scotland to the Present Time.* 3 vols. Cambridge, 1911.

——. *Scotland before 1700 from Contemporary Documents.* Edinburgh, 1893.

——. *A Short History of Scotland.* New ed. rev. and enlarged. Edinburgh, 1951.

——. "Scottish Nobility and Their Part in the Nation's History," *Scottish Historical Review* (1906), III, 161 ff.

——. (ed.). *Early Travellers in Scotland.* Edinburgh, 1891.

Buckle, Henry Thomas. *Introduction to the History of Civilization in England,* ed. John M. Robertson. London, n.d.

Burton, John Hill. *History of Scotland from Agricola's Invasion to the Extinction of the Last Jacobite Insurrection.* 8 vols. Edinburgh, 1905-1906.

——. *Narratives from Criminal Trials in Scotland.* London, 1852.

Calderwood, D. *History of the Kirk of Scotland.* 8 vols. Edinburgh, 1842-49.

Cameron, John. "Clan," *Chambers's Encyclopaedia* (Oxford, 1950), III, 614 ff.

Chalmers, George. *Caledonia: or, A Historical and Topographical Account of North Britain from the Most Ancient to the Present Times.* 8 vols. Paisley, 1887.

Chambers, Robert. *Domestic Annals of Scotland from the Reformation to the Revolution.* 3 vols. Edinburgh and London, 1858.

The Complaynt of Scotlande. In *Satirical Poems of the Time of the Reformation,* ed. James Cranstoun. 2 vols. Vol. I, pp. 95-99. Edinburgh and London, 1891.

Crawfurd, George. *The History of the Shire of Renfrew.* Paisley, 1782.

Daiches, David. "Scottish Language and Literature," *Encyclopaedia Americana* (Canadian ed.), XXIV, 436 ff.

Dickinson, W. Croft. "Scotland: History," *Chambers's Encyclopaedia* (Oxford, 1950), XII, 301-6.

——, Donaldson, Gordon and Isabel A. Milne. *A Source Book of Scottish History.* 3 vols. London, 1952-54.

Dillon, William J. "Fairs and Markets." Ch. 12 in Dunlop, *The Royal Burgh of Ayr,* q.v.

——. "The Pre-Reformation Church." Ch. 7 in Dunlop, *The Royal Burgh of Ayr,* q.v.

——. "Witchcraft." Ch. 10 in Dunlop, *The Royal Burgh of Ayr,* q.v.

Dunlop, Annie I. "Scotland: Church History," *Chambers's Encyclopaedia,* XII, 306 ff.

——. "Scottish Student Life in the Fifteenth Century," *Scottish Historical Review* (1947), XXVI, 47-63.

————. (ed.). *The Royal Burgh of Ayr: 750 Years of History*. Edinburgh and London, 1953.

Dunlop, Robert. "Sixteenth Century Schemes for the Plantation of Ulster," *Scottish Historical Review*, XXII, 51-60, 115-26, 199-212.

Eglinton Manuscripts. (Historical Manuscripts Commission.) London, 1885.

Exchequer Rolls of Scotland. (Ed. J. Stuart and G. Burnett.) Edinburgh, 1867——.

Fergusson, Sir James. *Lowland Lairds*. London, 1949.

Finlay, Ian. *Scotland*. Oxford, 1944.

Franck, J. *Northern Memoirs*. Edinburgh, 1821.

Fraser, James. *Chronicles of the Frasers* (Wardlaw MS, 916-1674). Edinburgh, 1905.

Froissart, Jean. *Les Chroniques de Froissart*, ed. J. A. C. Buchon. 3 vols. Paris, 1835. (Also selections in Brown, *Early Travellers in Scotland*, q.v.)

Gardiner, S. R. *History of England, from the Accession of James I. to the Outbreak of the Civil War, 1603-1642*. 10 vols. London, 1883-84.

Gibson, John. *History of Glasgow from the Earliest Accounts to the Present Time*. Glasgow, 1777.

Gilbert, John Thomas. *History of the Viceroys of Ireland*. Dublin and London, 1865.

Graham, Henry Grey. *The Social Life of Scotland in the Eighteenth Century*. (First ed., 2 vols., 1899). 4th ed.; London, 1937.

Grant, I. F. *Every-Day Life on an Old Highland Farm, 1769-1782*. London, 1924.

————. *The Social and Economic Development of Scotland before 1603*. Edinburgh, 1930.

Hamilton, Henry. "Scotland: Economic History: The Middle Ages," *Chambers's Encyclopaedia*, (Oxford, 1950), XII, 309-10.

Hamilton, Thomas. "How the Burgh Helped the Poor." Ch. 15 in Dunlop, *The Royal Burgh of Ayr*, q.v.

Harleian Miscellany. Eds. W. Oldys and T. Park. 10 vols. London, 1808-13.

Holinshead, Raphael. *The Scottish Chronicle; or A Complete History and Description of Scotland*. 2 vols. Arbroath, 1805.

Hume, David. *Commentaries on the Law of Scotland, respecting Trial for Crimes*. Edinburgh, 1800.

Innes, Cosmo. *Scotch Legal Antiquities*. Edinburgh, 1878.

————. *Sketches of Scottish History and Social Progress*. Edinburgh, 1861.

Insh, George P. *Scottish Colonial Schemes, 1620-1686*. Glasgow, 1922.

Jackson, John S., and Jean McI. Dixon. "The Plague." Ch. 16 in Dunlop, *The Royal Burgh of Ayr*, q.v.

Johnston, Thomas. *History of the Working Classes in Scotland.* Glasgow, n.d. (1923?)

Johnston, W., and A. K. Johnston. *Gazetteer of Scotland.* Edinburgh and London, 1937.

Knox, John. *The Works of John Knox*, ed. David Laing. 7 vols. Edinburgh, 1846.

Lamont, John. *The Diary of Mr. John Lamont of Newton.* Glasgow, 1830.

Lang, Andrew. *History of Scotland from the Roman Occupation.* 4 vols. Edinburgh and New York, 1900-1907.

———. "Scotland," *Encyclopaedia Britannica* (11th ed.), XXIV, 429-57.

Leslie, Bishop. "De origine, moribus, et rebus Scotorum" (1578). Three parts translated in Brown, *Scotland before 1700*, q.v.

Lithgow, William. *Nineteen Years' Travels in Scotland* (1628). Reprinted in Brown, *Scotland before 1700*, q.v.

McClelland, James. "Schools." Ch. 14 in Dunlop, *The Royal Burgh of Ayr*, q.v.

Mackenzie, Archibald. "The Church from the Reformation till the End of the Eighteenth Century." Ch. 8 in Dunlop, *The Royal Burgh of Ayr*, q.v.

Mackenzie, William. *The History of Galloway, from the Earliest Period to the Present Time.* 2 vols. Kirkcudbright, 1841.

Mackie, J. D. "Notestein's *The Scot in History*," *Scottish Historical Review*, XXVII, 94-100.

Mackinnon, James. *Social and Industrial History of Scotland from the Earliest Times to the Union.* Edinburgh, 1920.

Mackintosh, John. *The History of Civilisation in Scotland.* 4 vols. Paisley and London, 1893.

Macnab, T. M. A. "The Beginnings of Lollardy in Scotland," *Records of the Scottish Church Society*, Vol. XI, pt. iii, pp. 254-60.

MacPhail, I. M. M. "Review of *A Source Book of Scottish History*," *Scottish Historical Review*, XXXIII (1954), 144-48.

Macpherson, David. *Annals of Commerce, Manufactures, Fisheries and Navigation.* London, 1805.

Maitland, F. W. "The Anglican Settlement and the Scottish Reformation," in *Cambridge Modern History*, II, 550-98.

Major, John. *Historia Majoris Britanniae tam Angliae q. Scotiae* (1521). Published as *The History of Greater Britain*, by the Scottish Historical Society, Edinburgh, 1892; selections reprinted in Brown, *Scotland before 1700*, q.v.

Mathieson, William Law. *Politics and Religion: A Study in Scottish History from the Reformation to the Revolution.* 2 vols. Glasgow and New York, 1902.

Maxwell, Sir Herbert. *A History of Dumfries and Galloway.* Edinburgh, 1896.

Moryson, Fynes. "Itinerary" (1598). Reprinted in Brown, *Early Travellers in Scotland*, q.v.

Nicoll, John. *A Diary of Public Transactions and other Documents Chiefly in Scotland, 1650-67.* Edinburgh, 1836.

Notestein, Wallace. *The Scot in History.* New Haven, 1946.

Paterson, James. *History of the Counties of Ayr and Wigton.* 3 vols. Edinburgh, 1863.

Paul, Sir James Balfour. "Clerical Life in Scotland in the Sixteenth Century," *Scottish Historical Review* (1920), XVII, 177-89.

——. "Social Life in Scotland in the Sixteenth Century," *Scottish Historical Review* (1920), XVII, 296-309.

Pinkerton, John. *An Enquiry into the History of Scotland.* 2 vols. London, 1789.

Pitcairn, Robert. *Criminal Trials in Scotland from 1488 to 1624.* 3 vols. Edinburgh, 1833.

Pryde, George S. "Development of the Burgh." Ch. 2 in Dunlop, *The Royal Burgh of Ayr*, q.v.

—— (ed.). *Ayr Burgh Accounts, 1534-1624.* Edinburgh, 1937.

Rait, Sir Robert S. *The Making of Scotland.* London, 1929.

——., and George S. Pryde. *Scotland.* 2d ed. rev.; New York, 1954.

Ray, John. *Itineraries* (1661). (Ed. Edwin Lankester) London, 1846.

Regiam Majestatem. The Auld Lawes and Constitutions of Scotland, ed. Sir J. Skene. Edinburgh, 1609.

Register of the Privy Council of Scotland, ed. J. H. Burton, D. Masson, P. Hume Brown, and H. Paton. 8 vols. Edinburgh, 1877-1924.

Robertson, John M. (ed.). *Buckle's Introduction to the History of Civilization in England.* London, n.d.

——. *Statuta Ecclesiae Scoticanae.* 2 vols. Edinburgh, 1866.

Robertson, William. *Ayrshire: Its History and Historic Families.* 2 vols. Kilmarnock and Ayr, 1908.

Rogers, Charles. *Social Life in Scotland from Early to Recent Times.* 3 vols. Edinburgh, 1884-86.

Scott, Sir Walter. *Novels.* (Houghton Mifflin edition) Boston, 1923.

Sinclair, John. *Statistical Account of Scotland.* Edinburgh, 1793.

Skene, William F. *Highlanders of Scotland.* London, 1837.

Spalding Club Miscellany. 5 vols. Aberdeen, 1841-52.

Terry, Charles Sanford. *A History of Scotland from the Roman Evacuation to the Disruption, 1843.* Cambridge, 1920.

Tytler, Patrick Fraser. *History of Scotland.* 9 vols. Edinburgh, 1828-43.

Wallace, George. *The Nature and Descent of Ancient Peerages, connected with the State of Scotland.* Edinburgh, 1785.

Warrack, John. *Domestic Life in Scotland, 1488-1688.* London, 1920.

———. *History of Old Cumnock.* London, 1899.

Weldon, Sir Anthony. "A Perfect Description of the People and Country of Scotland" (1649). Reprinted in Brown, *Early Travellers in Scotland,* q.v.

Wodrow, Robert. *Collections upon the Lives of the Reformers.* 2 vols. Glasgow, 1834-48.

PART II: THE SCOTS IN IRELAND

Abstracts of the Irish Patent Rolls of James I. Dublin, n.d.

Adair, Patrick. *A True Narrative of the Rise and Progress of the Presbyterian Church in the North of Ireland.* Belfast and Edinburgh, 1866.

Baillie, Robert. *Letters and Journals; containing an Account of Public Transactions, Civil, Ecclesiatsical, and Military in England and Scotland, 1637-1662.* Edinburgh, 1775.

Benn, George. *History of Belfast.* Belfast, 1877.

Blair, Robert. *Life of Mr. Robert Blair, containing his Autobiography, from 1593 to 1636.* Ed. William Row. Edinburgh, 1848.

Boulter, Hugh. *Letters written by Hugh Boulter, D.D., Lord Primate of Ireland.* 2 vols. Oxford, 1749.

Brereton, Sir William. *Travels in Holland, the United Provinces, England, Scotland, and Ireland, 1634-35.* Manchester, 1844.

Calendar of State Papers for Ireland, 1603-1625 [Carew]. London, 1872-80.

Croskery, Thomas. *Irish Presbyterianism.* Dublin, 1884.

Davies, Godfrey. *The Early Stuarts, 1603-1660.* Oxford, 1937.

Dobbs, Arthur. *Essay on the Trade of Ireland.* London, 1729-31.

Dunlop, Robert. "Ireland to the Settlement of Ulster," in *Cambridge Modern History,* III, 579-616.

Falls, Cyril. *The Birth of Ulster.* London, 1936.

Fasti of the Irish Presbyterian Church, 1613-1840, ed. James and Samuel G. McConnell. Belfast, 1951.

Ford, Henry Jones. *The Scotch-Irish in America.* Princeton, 1915.

Forde, Hugh. *Sketches of Olden Days in Northern Ireland.* Belfast, 1927.

Froude, James Anthony. *The English in Ireland in the Eighteenth Century.* 3 vols. New York, 1878.

Gamble, John. *Sketches of History, Politics and Manners in Dublin and the North of Ireland.* (First ed., 1811) New ed., London, 1826.

Gardiner, S. R. *History of England, 1603-1659.* London, n.d.

Gilbert, John Thomas. *History of the Viceroys of Ireland.* Dublin and London, 1865.

Green, J. R. *A Short History of the English People.* New York, 1876.

Hamilton, Ernest. *The Irish Rebellion of 1641.* London, 1920.

Hamilton Manuscripts, T. K. Lowrey. Belfast, 1867.

Hamilton, Thomas. *History of the Irish Presbyterian Church.* Edinburgh, 1886.

Hanna, C. A. *The Scotch-Irish, or the Scot in North Britain, North Ireland, and North America.* 2 vols. New York and London, 1902.

Harris, Walter. *Hibernica, or Ancient Tracts relating to Ireland.* Dublin, 1770.

Harrison, John. *The Scot in Ulster: Sketch of the History of the Scottish Population of Ulster.* Edinburgh and London, 1888.

Heylin, Peter. *History of the Presbyterians from 1536 to 1647.* Oxford, 1670.

Hickson, Mary. *Ireland in the Seventeenth Century.* 2 vols. London, 1884.

Hill, George. *An Historical Account of the Plantation of Ulster at the Commencement of the Seventeenth Century, 1608-1620.* Belfast, 1877.

———. *Plantation Papers: containing a Summary Sketch of the Great Ulster Plantation in the Year 1610.* Belfast, 1889.

——— (ed.). *The Montgomery Manuscripts.* Belfast, 1869.

Insh, George Pratt. *Scottish Colonial Schemes, 1620-1686.* Glasgow. 1922.

James VI., State Papers of. (Abbotsford Club) Edinburgh, 1838.

Latimer, W. T. *History of the Irish Presbyterians.* Belfast, 1893.

Lawlor, Henry Cairnes. *Ulster: its Archaeology and Antiquities.* Belfast, 1928.

Lecky, William E. H. *Ireland in the Eighteenth Century.* 8 vols. London and New York, 1883.

McCarthy, Justin. *The Reign of Queen Anne.* 2 vols. New York and London, 1903.

Macaulay, Thomas B. *History of England,* ed. Butler. 4 vols. Philadelphia, 1857.

McDonnell, John. *The Ulster Civil War of 1641 and its Consequences.* Dublin, 1879.

Montague, F. C. *The History of England from the Accession of James I. to the Restoration.* London, 1907.

Neal, Daniel. *The History of the Puritans.* (First ed., 2 vols., 1754) New York, 1844.

O'Brien, George. *The Economic History of Ireland in the Eighteenth Century.* Dublin and London, 1918.

Petty, William. *Political Anatomy of Ireland.* London, 1719.

Plowden, Francis. *Historical View of the State of Ireland.* 3 vols. London, 1803.

Prendergast, J. D. *The Cromwellian Settlement in Ireland.* 2d ed.; Dublin, 1875.

Pynnar, Captain Nicholas. *Census,* in Carew MSS, *Calendar of State Papers,* q.v.

Reid, James Seaton. *History of the Presbyterian Church in Ireland.* 3 vols. London, 1853.

Royal Irish Academy, Proceedings. Dublin, 1841-62.

Shearman, Hugh. "Irish Church History," *Chambers's Encyclopaedia* (Oxford, 1950), VII, 730-32.

Stewart, Andrew. *Short Account of the Church of Christ as It Was Amongst the Irish,* appendix to Adair, *A True Narrative,* q.v.

Stewart, David. *The Scots in Ulster.* Pamphlets, subtitled: "Their Denization and Naturalization, 1605 to 1634" (1954); "The Years Between, 1636 to 1642" (1955); "Their Campaign in the County of Antrim" (1956); "Early Scots Settlers in the County of Down" (1957). Belfast, 1954-57.

Transactions of the Royal Irish Academy. Dublin, 1787-1862.

"Ulster and its People," in *Fraser's Magazine,* August, 1876.

Ulster Journal of Archaeology. Belfast (First series), 1853-62; (Second series), 1894 *et seq.*

Witherow, Thomas. *Derry and Enniskillen in 1688-1689.* Belfast, 1885.

Wodrow, Robert. *History of the Sufferings of the Church of Scotland from the Restoration to the Revolution.* 4 vols. Glasgow, 1828.

Woodburn, James B. *The Ulster Scot.* London, 1914.

Young, Arthur. *A Tour in Ireland, 1776, 1777, 1778.* 2 vols. London, 1780.

PART III: THE SCOTCH-IRISH IN AMERICA

(Primary sources for Scotch-Irish settlement and social life in America are almost inexhaustible. There are county records, with their details of wills, purchase of land, and the like; court records, such as Chalkley's compilations for Augusta County; tax rolls—these make dull reading, yet afford such raw material as specific dates of settlement in an area, size of farms, movement of families, marriages, and offenses against order. County and state historical societies have preserved memoirs, letters, and thousands of other documents of the past; the records of the Pennsylvania Historical Society and of the historical societies especially of the eastern counties of Pennsylvania, and likewise the collections at the University of North Carolina, must be especially mentioned. States have assembled from their colonial past hundreds of volumes in whose pages are indispensable materials and insights. I have found the Pennsylvania collections and the *Colonial Records* of North Carolina the most useful of all; but much material has come from the *Archives* of Maryland, *Votes and Proceedings* of the House of Representatives of the Province of Pennsylvania, Virginia's *Statutes-at-Large*, and other state papers.

For religious aspects, the Presbyterian Historical Society in Philadelphia contains a mine of material, both primary and secondary. There are manuscript records of the early Presbyteries, minutes of the original Synod and its offshoots, records of local churches, and illuminating studies in the *Journal* of the Society about most phases of church affairs in the eighteenth century.)

Abernethy, T. P. *Three Virginia Frontiers.* Baton Rouge, 1940.

Adams, James Truslow. *The Epic of America.* Boston, 1931.

Adams, John. *Works,* ed. Charles Francis Adams. 10 vols. Boston, 1850-56.

Alexander, A. *Biographical Sketches of the Founder and the Principal Alumni of Log College.* Princeton, 1845.

Ambler, C. H. *History of West Virginia.* New York, 1933.

American Council of Learned Societies: "Report of Committee on Linguistic and National Stocks in the Population of the United States." *Annual Report* of the American Historical Association, 1931, Vol. I. Washington, 1932.

Andrews, Matthew Page. *The Founding of Maryland.* New York, 1933.

Archives of Maryland. Baltimore, 1883 ff.

Arthur, J. P. *Western North Carolina.* Raleigh, 1914.

Ashe, S. A. *History of North Carolina.* 2 vols. Greensboro, 1925.

Bagenal, Philip H. *The American Irish and their Influence on Irish Politics.* London, 1882.

Baldwin, Leland D. *Whiskey Rebels: The Story of a Frontier Uprising.* Pittsburgh, 1939.

Bancroft, George. *A History of the United States from the Discovery of the American Continent.* 10 vols. Boston, 1846-75.

Barck, Oscar Theodore, and Hugh Talmage Lefler. *Colonial America.* New York, 1958.

Barton, Thomas. *The Conduct of the Paxton Men, Impartially Considered.* Philadelphia, 1764.

Bassett, J. S. *The Regulators of North Carolina.* Washington, 1895.

Bean, R. Bennett. *The Peopling of Virginia.* Boston, 1938.

Beard, Charles A. *An Economic Interpretation of the Constitution of the United States.* New York, 1914.

Becket, Rev. William. Notices and Letters Concerning Incidents at Lewes Town, 1717-1742 (MS, Historical Society of Pennsylvania).

Beer, G. L. *The Old Colonial System.* 2 vols. New York, 1912.

Belknap, Jeremy. *The History of New-Hampshire.* 3 vols. Boston, 1792.

Billington, Ray Allen. "The West in American History," *Encyclopedia Americana* (1961), XXIX, 201-4.

Black, George Fraser. *Scotland's Mark on America.* New York, 1921.

Bolton, Charles Knowles. *Scotch-Irish Pioneers in Ulster and America.* Boston, 1910.

Boulter, Hugh. *Letters Written by Hugh Boulter, D.D., Lord Primate of Ireland.* Ed. M. Wall. 2 vols. Oxford, 1769-70.

Boudinot, Elias. *The Life of the Reverend William Tennent.* Hartford, 1845.

Boyd, W. K. *Some Eighteenth Century Tracts concerning North Carolina.* Raleigh, 1927.

Branch, E. D. *Westward: The Romance of the American Frontier.* New York, 1930.

Breed, W. P. *Presbyterians and the Revolution.* Philadelphia, 1876.

Bridenbaugh, Carl. *Cities in Revolt: Urban Life in America, 1743-1776.* New York, 1955.

————. *Cities in the Wilderness: The First Century of Urban Life in America.* New York, 1938.

————. *Myths and Realities. Societies of the Colonial South.* Baton Rouge, 1952.

Briggs, C. A. *American Presbyterianism: Its Origin and History.* New York, 1885.

Brock, R. A. (ed.). *The Official Records of Robert Dinwiddie.* 2 vols. *The Dinwiddie Papers.* Richmond, 1883-84.

Brunhouse, Robert Levere. *The Counter-Revolution in Pennsylvania.* Harrisburg, 1942.

Bureau of the Census. *A Century of Population Growth in the United States, 1790-1900.* Washington, 1909.

———. *Historical Statistics of the United States: Colonial Times to 1957.* Washington, 1960.

Campbell, Douglas. *The Puritans in Holland, England, and America.* New York, 1892.

Campbell, John C. *The Southern Highlander and His Homeland.* New York, 1921.

Cartmell, T. K. *Shenandoah Valley Pioneers and Their Descendants.* Winchester, 1909.

Caruthers, E. W. *Life of David Caldwell.* Greensboro, 1842.

Chalkley, Lyman. *Chronicles of the Scotch-Irish Settlement in Virginia, extracted from the original Court Records of Augusta County, 1745-1800.* 3 vols. Rosslyn, Va., 1912.

Chambers, George. *A Tribute to the Principles, Virtues, Habits and Public Usefulness of the Irish and Scotch Early Settlers of Pennsylvania.* Chambersburg, 1856.

Christian, Bolivar. *The Scotch-Irish in the Valley of Virginia.* Richmond, 1860.

———. "The Scotch-Irish Settlers in the Valley of Virginia," Washington and Lee University Historical Papers, No. 3 (1892), 3-43.

Colonial Records of North Carolina. 10 vols. Raleigh, 1886-90.

Colonial Records of Pennsylvania, 1683-1790. 16 vols. Harrisburg, 1851-53.

Connor, R. D. W. *Race Elements in the White Population of North Carolina.* Raleigh, 1920.

Cooke, William D. *Revolutionary History of North Carolina.* New York, 1853.

Corwin, Edward S. "The 'Higher Law' Background of American Constitutional Law," *Harvard Law Review,* XLII (1929), 365-409.

Cotterill, R. S. *The Southern Indians: The Story of the Civilized Tribes before Removal.* Norman, Okla., 1954.

Couper, William. *History of the Shenandoah Valley.* 3 vols. New York, 1952.

Craighead, J. G. *Scotch and Irish Seeds in American Soil.* Philadelphia, 1878.

Craven, E. R. "The Log Cabin of Neshaminy and Princeton University," *Journal* of the Presbyterian Historical Society (1902), I, 314-25.

Cribbs, George A. *The Frontier Policy of Pennsylvania.* Pittsburgh, 1919.

Cummings, Hubertis. *Richard Peters, Provincial Secretary and Cleric, 1704-1776.* Philadelphia, 1944.

Davie, Maurice R. *World Immigration.* New York, 1936.

Day, Sherman, *Historical Collections of the State of Pennsylvania.* Philadelphia, 1848.

DeMond, Robert O. *The Loyalists in North Carolina during the Revolution.* Durham, 1944.

Dinsmore, John Walker. *The Scotch-Irish in America.* Chicago, 1906.

Doddridge, Joseph. *Notes on the Settlement and Indian Wars of the Western Parts of Virginia and Pennsylvania.* (First ed., 1824) 2d ed.; Albany, 1876.

Douglass, Elisha P. *Rebels and Democrats: the Struggle for Equal Political Rights and Majority Rule during the American Revolution.* Chapel Hill, 1955.

Draper, Lyman C. *The Mecklenburg Declaration of Independence.* New York, 1874.

Dunaway, Wayland F. *A History of Pennsylvania.* New York, 1935.
——. "Pennsylvania as an early distributing center of population," *Pennsylvania Magazine of History and Biography,* LV (1931), 134-56.
——. *The Scotch-Irish of Colonial Pennsylvania.* Chapel Hill, 1944.

Eaton, S. J. M. *History of the Presbytery of Erie.* New York, 1848.

Egle, William H. *History of the Commonwealth of Pennsylvania.* 3d ed.; Philadelphia, 1883.

Farrand, Max. *The Framing of the Constitution of the United States.* New Haven, 1913.

Faust, A. B. *The German Element in the United States.* New York, 1927.

Ferguson, Russell J. *Early Western Pennsylvania Politics.* Pittsburgh, 1938.

Finley, John H. *The Coming of the Scot.* New York, 1940.

Fisher, S. G. *The Making of Pennsylvania.* Philadelphia, 1896.

Fiske, John. *The Dutch and Quaker Colonies in America.* 2 vols. Boston and New York, 1889.

Foote, William Henry. *Sketches of North Carolina, Historical and Biographical.* New York, 1846.
——. *Sketches of Virginia, Historical and Biographical.* Philadelphia, 1850.

Ford, Henry Jones. *The Scotch-Irish in America.* Princeton, 1915.

Fries, Adelaide (ed.). *Records of the Moravians in North Carolina.* 8 vols. Raleigh, 1922-54.

Fry, Joshua, and Peter Jefferson. "A Map of the Most Inhabited Parts of Virginia, containing the whole province of Maryland, with part of Pensilvania, New Jersey and North Carolina." London, 1775.

Futhey, J. Smith. "The Scotch-Irish," Lancaster County Historical Society *Papers* (1907), Vol. XI, no. 6, 220 ff.

Garland, Robert. *The Scotch-Irish in Western Pennsylvania.* Pittsburgh, 1923.

Garrard, L. H. *Chambersburg in the Colony and in the Revolution.* Philadelphia, 1856.

Geiser, K. F. *Redemptioners and Indentured Servants in the Colony and Commonwealth of Pennsylvania.* New Haven, 1901.

Gewehr, W. M. *The Great Awakening in Virginia, 1740-1790.* Durham, 1930.

Gillett, E. H. *History of the Presbyterian Church in the United States of America.* 2 vols. Philadelphia, 1864.

Gipson, L. H. *The Southern Plantations.* Caldwell, Idaho, 1939.

Glasgow, Maude. *The Scotch-Irish in Northern Ireland and in the American Colonies.* New York, 1936.

Graham, Ian Charles Cargill. *Colonists from Scotland: Emigration to North America, 1707-1783.* Ithaca, 1956.

Green, Edward R. R. "The Scotch-Irish and the Coming of the Revolution in North Carolina." *Irish Historical Studies,* VII (Sept. 1950), 77-86.

Green, Samuel Swett. *The Scotch-Irish in America.* Worcester, 1895.

Gregg, Alexander. *History of the Old Cheraws.* Columbia, S.C., 1867.

Guess, William Francis. *South Carolina: Annals of Pride and Protest.* New York, 1957.

Hamilton, Peter Joseph. *The Colonization of the South.* (*The History of North America,* Vol. III.) Philadelphia, 1904.

Hanna, Charles A. *The Scotch-Irish, or the Scot in North Britain, North Ireland, and North America.* 2 vols. New York and London, 1902.

Hansen, Marcus L. *The Atlantic Migration, 1607-1860.* Cambridge, Mass., 1940.

Hart, Freeman H. *The Valley of Virginia in the American Revolution, 1763-1789.* Chapel Hill, 1942.

Henderson, Archibald. *The Conquest of the Old Southwest.* New York, 1920.

———. "The Origin of the Regulation in North Carolina," *American Historical Review* (1916), XXI, 320-32.

Hening, W. W. *The Statutes-at-Large, being a Collection of All the Laws of Virginia (1619-1792).* 13 vols. Philadelphia and New York, 1823.

Herrick, Cheesman Abiah. *White Servitude in Pennsylvania.* Philadelphia, 1926.

Higgins, Ruth. *Expansion in New York with Especial Reference to the Eighteenth Century.* (Ohio State University Studies, Vol. XIV.) Columbus, 1931.

Hockett, Homer C. *Political and Social Growth of the American People, 1492-1865.* 3d ed.; New York, 1940.

Howe, George. *History of the Presbyterian Church in South Carolina.* 2 vols. Columbia, 1870.

Hoyt, W. M. *The Mecklenburg Declaration of Independence.* New York, 1907.

Humphrey, E. F. *Nationalism and Religion in America, 1774-1789.* Boston, 1924.

Hunter, C. L. *Sketches of Western North Carolina, Historical and Biographical.* Raleigh, 1877.

Johnson, Roy H. "Frontier Religion in Western Pennsylvania," *Western Pennsylvania Historical Magazine,* XVI, 30 ff.

Journal of the Presbyterian Historical Society. Philadelphia, 1902——.

Kegley, F. B. *Kegley's Virginia Frontier.* Roanoke, 1938.

Kercheval, Samuel. *A History of the Valley of Virginia.* (First ed., 1833) 4th ed.; Strasburg, Va., 1925.

King, William. *A Great Archbishop of Dublin, William King, D.D., 1650-1729. His Autobiography, Family, and a Selection from his Correspondence,* ed. Sir Charles Simeon King. London and New York, 1906.

Kirkland, E. C. *History of American Economic Life.* New York, 1933.

Kittochtinny Historical Society. *Papers Read before the Kittochtinny Historical Society.* Chambersburg, 1900.

Klein, H. M. J. *Lancaster County, Pennsylvania: A History.* 3 vols. New York and Chicago, 1924.

Klett, Guy S. *Presbyterians in Colonial Pennsylvania.* Philadelphia, 1937.

——. *The Scotch-Irish in Pennsylvania.* Gettysburg, 1948.

Koontz, L. K. *The Virginia Frontier, 1754-1763.* (Johns Hopkins University Studies) Baltimore, 1925.

Lancaster County Historical Society. *Historical Papers and Addresses.* Lancaster, 1896——.

Lefler, Hugh T. *History of North Carolina.* 4 vols. New York, 1956.

—— (ed.). *North Carolina History Told by Contemporaries.* 2d ed.; Chapel Hill, 1948.

——, and Paul Wager (eds.). *Orange County, 1752-1952.* Chapel Hill, 1953.

Lewis, Virgil A. *History of West Virginia.* Philadelphia, 1889.

Linehan, John C. *The Irish Scots and the "Scotch-Irish."* Concord, N.H., 1902.

Logan, James. The Logan Papers (MS, Historical Society of Pennsylvania).

Lundin, Leonard. *Cockpit of the Revolution: The War for Independence in New Jersey.* Princeton, 1940.

McCrady, Edward. *The History of South Carolina under the Royal Government, 1719-1776.* New York, 1899.

McGee, Thomas D'Arcy. *A History of the Irish Settlers in North America, from the Earliest Period to the Census of 1850.* Boston, 1852.

McIlwain, J. William. "Early Presbyterianism in Maryland." (Johns Hopkins University Studies) Baltimore, 1890.

McKelway, A. J. "The Scotch-Irish of North Carolina." (North Carolina Booklet, Vol. IV, no. 11, March 1905.) Raleigh, 1905.

Mather, Cotton. *Magnalia Christi Americana.* 2 vols. Hartford, 1820.

Maxon, Charles H. *The Great Awakening in the Middle Colonies.* Chicago, 1920.

Mebane, C. H. (ed.). "The Scotch-Irish Settlements." (Program for North Carolina Day.) Raleigh, 1908.

Memoirs of the Historical Society of Pennsylvania, ed. Edward Armstrong. Philadelphia, 1864——.

Meriwether, R. L. *The Expansion of South Carolina, 1729-1765.* Kingsport, Tenn., 1940.

Milling, Chapman J. *Red Carolinians.* Chapel Hill, 1940.

Minutes of the Provincial Council of Pennsylvania. Philadelphia, 1852-53.

Moore, Arthur K. *The Frontier Mind.* Lexington, Ky., 1957.

Moore, J. H. *Defense of the Mecklenburg Declaration of Independence.* Raleigh, 1908.

Morison, Samuel Eliot, and Henry Steele Commager. *The Growth of the American Republic.* 2 vols. New York, 1937.

Morriss, Margaret S. *Colonial Trade of Maryland, 1689-1715.* (Johns Hopkins University Studies) Baltimore, 1914.

Morton, Oren F. *A History of Rockbridge County, Virginia.* Staunton, Va., 1920.

Mouzon, Henry. *An Accurate Map of North and South Carolina.* London, 1775.

Nash, Frank. "The Scotch-Irish in Orange County." (Program for North Carolina Day.) Raleigh, 1908.

Newenham, Sir Thomas. *A Statistical and Historical Inquiry into the Progress and Magnitude of the Population of Ireland.* London, 1805.

New Hampshire Records. 27 vols. Concord, 1867-96.

New York: *Documents Relative to the Colonial History of the State of New York.* 15 vols. Albany, 1856-87.

Nevin, Alfred. *Churches of the Valley.* Philadelphia, 1852.

Nevins, Allan. *American Social History as Recorded by British Travellers.* New York, 1923.

O'Brien, J. F. "Irish Pioneers in New England," *Journal* of the American Irish Historical Society, XVIII, 127-35.

O'Connell, J. D. *The "Scotch-Irish" Delusion in America.* Washington, 1897.

Orange Presbytery: *Manual of the Presbytery of Orange.* n.p., 1953.

Osgood, Herbert L. *The American Colonies in the Seventeenth Century.* 3 vols. New York, 1904.

Parker, Edward L. *The History of Londonderry* (New Hampshire). Boston, 1851.

Parkman, Francis. *History of the Conspiracy of Pontiac.* 3 vols. Boston, 1898.

Paxson, Frederic L. *History of the American Frontier.* Boston and New York, 1924.

Pendleton, W. C. *History of Tazewell County and Southwest Virginia.* Richmond, 1920.

Penn, William. *Collection of the Works of William Penn,* ed. J. Sowle. 2 vols. London, 1726.

Penn MSS. *Official Correspondence, 1683-1727* (Historical Society of Pennsylvania).

Pennsylvania Archives. 9 series. Philadelphia and Harrisburg, 1852-1931.

Pennsylvania Magazine of History and Biography. Philadelphia, 1877——.

Perry, Arthur L. "The Scotch-Irish in New England, in Volume II of *Proceedings and Addresses* of the Scotch-Irish Society of America (Nashville, 1890-1900), 107-14.

Perry, Ralph Barton. *Puritanism and Democracy.* New York, 1944.

Peyton, J. Lewis. *History of Augusta County, Virginia, from 1726 to 1871.* 2d ed., revised and enlarged; Staunton, Va., 1902.

Posey, Walter Brownloe. *The Presbyterian Church in the Old Southwest, 1778-1838.* Richmond, 1952.

Presbyterian Church in the U.S.A. *Minutes of the General Assembly.* Philadelphia, 1789 ff.

——. *Records of the Presbyterian Church in the U.S.A.* (ed. William M. Engles). Philadelphia, 1841.

——. *Records of the Presbyterian Church in the U.S.A.* (ed. W. H. Roberts). Philadelphia, 1904.

——. *Records of the Presbytery of New Castle upon Delaware* (MSS, Presbyterian Historical Society).

Presbyterian Historical Society *Journal.* Philadelphia, 1902——.

Ramsay, David. *History of South Carolina.* 2 vols. Charleston, 1809.

Ray, Worth Stickley. *The Lost Tribes of North Carolina.* Austin, Tex., 1947.

Reid, Whitelaw. *The Scot in America and the Ulster Scot.* London, 1912.

Riegel, Robert E. *America Moves West.* New York, 1930.

Rights, Douglas L. *The American Indian in North Carolina.* Durham, 1947.

Roosevelt, Theodore. *The Winning of the West.* 4 vols. New York, 1904.

Ross, Peter. *The Scot in America.* New York, 1896.

Rossiter, W. S. *A Century of Population Growth in the United States, 1790 to 1890.* Washington, 1890.

Royce, Charles C. *Indian Land Cessions in the United States* (Bureau of American Ethnology, 18th Annual Report, Part 2, 1896-97). Washington, 1899.

Rupp, I. Daniel. *Early History of Western Pennsylvania and of the West, and of Western Expeditions and Campaigns, from 1744 to 1833.* Pittsburgh and Harrisburg, 1846.

——. *History and Topography of Dauphin, Cumberland, Franklin, Bedford, Adams, and Perry Counties.* Lancaster, 1846.

——. *History and Topography of Northumberland, Huntington, Mifflin, Centre, Union, Columbia, Juniata and Clinton Counties, Pa.* Lancaster, 1847.

——. *History of Lancaster and York Counties.* Lancaster, 1847.

Scharf, J. T. *History of Western Maryland.* Philadelphia, 1882.

Schrier, Arnold. *Ireland and the American Emigration, 1850-1900.* Minneapolis, 1958.

Scotch-Irish Society of America, *Proceedings and Addresses.* 10 vols. Nashville, 1890-1900.

Shaw, James. *The Scotch-Irish in History.* Springfield, Mass., 1899.

Simms, William Gilmore. *The History of South Carolina.* New York, 1860.

Smith, Abbot Emerson. *Colonists in Bondage: White Servitude and Convict Labor in America, 1607-1776.* Chapel Hill, 1947.

Smith, Jonathan. "The Scotch Presbyterian in the American Revolution," *Granite Monthly* (1918), 37-47.

Smith, Joseph. *The "Scotch-Irish" Shibboleth Analyzed and Rejected.* Washington, 1898.

Stacy, James. *A History of the Presbyterian Church in Georgia.* n.p., 1912.

Steen, James. *New Aberdeen, or the Scotch Settlement of Monmouth County, New Jersey.* Matawan, N.J., 1899.

Stevens, B. F. (ed.). *Facsimiles of Manuscripts in European Archives relating to America, 1773-1783.* 25 vols. London, 1889-98.

Summers, Lewis Preston. *History of Southwest Virginia, 1748-1786, Washington County, 1777-1870.* Richmond, 1903.

Sutherland, Stella H. *Population Distribution in Colonial America.* New York, 1936.

Sweet, William Warren. *The Presbyterians (Religion on the American Frontier, 1783-1840,* Vol. II). Chicago, 1936.

Tarleton, Banastre. *A History of the Campaigns of 1780 and 1781, in the Southern Provinces of North America.* London, 1787.

Taylor, R. H. *Ante-Bellum South Carolina.* Chapel Hill, 1942.

Tewkesbury, D. G. *The Founding of American Colleges and Universities before the Civil War.* New York, 1932.

Thayer, Theodore. *Pennsylvania Politics and the Growth of Democracy, 1740-1776.* Harrisburg, 1953.

Thompson, Ernest Trice. *Presbyterian Missions in the Southern United States.* Richmond, 1934.

Trinterud, Leonard J. *The Forming of an American Tradition. A Re-Examination of Colonial Presbyterianism.* Philadelphia, 1949.

Turner, Frederick Jackson. *The Frontier in American History.* New York, 1920.

Tuttle, J. F. *Presbyterianism on the Frontiers.* Philadelphia, 1877.

Waddell, Joseph A. *Annals of Augusta County, Virginia, from 1726 to 1871.* 2d ed. revised and enlarged; Staunton, Va., 1902.

Watson, John F. *Annals of Philadelphia and of Pennsylvania in the Olden Time.* 2 vols. Philadelphia, 1854.

Wayland, John W. *The German Element of the Shenandoah Valley of Virginia.* Charlottesville, 1907.

———. *Twenty-five Chapters on the Shenandoah Valley.* Strasburg, Va., 1957.

Weatherford, W. D. *Pioneers of Destiny: The Romance of the Appalachian People.* Birmingham, 1955.

Weeks, S. B. "Church and State in North Carolina." (Johns Hopkins University Studies, series XI) Baltimore, 1911.

Weis, Frederick Lewis. *The Colonial Churches and the Colonial Clergy of the Middle and Southern Colonies, 1607-1776.* Lancaster, Mass., 1938.

Wertenbaker, T. J. "Early Scotch Contributions to the United States." Glasgow, 1945.

———. *Patrician and Plebeian in Virginia.* Charlottesville, 1910.

———. *The Old South: the Founding of American Civilization.* New York. 1942.

Williamson, Hugh. *History of North Carolina.* Philadelphia, 1812.

Wilson, Howard McKnight. *The Tinkling Spring, Headwater of Freedom.* Fishersville, Va., 1954.

Winsor, Justin. *Narrative and Critical History of America.* 8 vols. Boston, 1884-89.

——. *The Westward Movement.* Boston and New York, 1897.

Witherow, B. J. *The Insurrection of the Paxton Boys.* n.p., 1860.

Wittke, Carl. *The Irish in America.* Baton Rouge, 1956.

——. *We Who Built America: the Saga of the Immigrant.* New York, 1939.

Woodmason, Charles. *The Carolina Backcountry on the Eve of the Revolution. The Journals and other Writings of Charles Woodmason, Anglican Itinerant,* ed. Richard J. Hooker. Chapel Hill, 1953.

Wright, J. E., and Doris Wright. *Pioneer Life in Western Pennsylvania.* Pittsburgh, 1940.

Index